The Odyssey of Political Theory
The Politics of Departure and Return

Patrick J. Deneen

ROWMAN & LITTLEFIELD PUBLISHERS, INC.
Lanham • Boulder • New York • Oxford

ROWMAN & LITTLEFIELD PUBLISHERS, INC.

Published in the United States of America
by Rowman & Littlefield Publishers, Inc.
4720 Boston Way, Lanham, Maryland 20706
http://www.rowmanlittlefield.com

12 Hid's Copse Road
Cumnor Hill, Oxford OX2 9JJ, England

British Library Cataloguing in Publication Information Available

Library of Congress Cataloging-in-Publication Data

Deneen, Patrick J., 1964–
    The odyssey of political theory : the politics of departure and return / Patrick J. Deneen.
        p.   cm.
    Includes bibliographical references and index.
    ISBN 0-8476-9622-7 (alk. paper)
    1. Political science—History.   2. Homer. Odyssey.   I. Title.

    JA81.D43   2000
    320'.01'1—dc21

                                                            00-024133

Printed in the United States of America

∞™ The paper used in this publication meets the minimum requirements of American National Standard for Information Sciences—Permanence of Paper for Printed Library Materials, ANSI/NISO Z39.48—1992.

To the memory of my grandmother

Wilma L. Dionne

1917–2000

storyteller, reader, and Muse

Contents

~

Acknowledgments   viii

Preface   ix

Introduction   Between Oikos and Cosmos   1

Chapter 1   The Odyssey as Political Theory   27

Chapter 2   Resolving the Ancient Quarrel between Poetry and Philosophy: Plato's Odyssey   81

Chapter 3   The Harrowing of Rousseau's Emile   131

Chapter 4   Escaping the Dialectic: Vico, the Frankfurt School, and the Dialectic of Enlightenment   169

Chapter 5   Against Cosmopolitanism: Resisting the Sirens' Song   211

Appendix   Illustrations   243

Bibliography   251

Index   267

About the Author   275

Acknowledgments

⁓

The publisher and author gratefully acknowledge permission to reprint excerpts from the following sources:

Excerpt from *The Odyssey of Homer* by Richmond Lattimore. Copyright © 1965, 1967 by Richmond Lattimore. Copyright Renewed. Reprinted by permission of HarperCollins Publishers, Inc.

Excerpt from *The Republic of Plato* (2nd ed.), translated by Allan Bloom. Copyright © 1968 by Allan Bloom. Preface to the paperback edition, copyright © 1991 by Allan Bloom. Reprinted by permission of Basic Books, a member of Perseus Books, L.L.C.

Excerpt from *Emile or On Education* by Jean-Jacques Rousseau, translated by Allan Bloom. Copyright © 1979 by Basic Books, Inc. Reprinted by permission of Basic Books, a member of Perseus Books, L.L.C.

Excerpt from *The New Science of Giambattista Vico* by Giambattista Vico (revised and abridged translation of the 3rd ed.), translated by Thomas Goddard Bergin and Max Harold Fisch. Copyright © 1948 by Cornell University.

Excerpt from *Dialectic of Enlightenment*, translated by John Cumming. Copyright © 1972 by Herder and Herder, Inc. Copyright © 1991 by The Continuum Publishing Company.

Illustrations in the appendix are from Rousseau's *Emile*, 1762, and Vico's *Principi di Scienza Nuova*, 1744. Reprinted with permission from Princeton University Library, Department of Rare Books and Special Collections.

Preface

~

Only with utmost difficulty will I resist again resorting to the inviting resonance of the word *odyssey* to describe the long and halting path of this book. I suspect that all authors must travel a trying and circuitous route, so the subject of my study—the *Odyssey* of Homer as a work of political theory and the ways that the work has been understood, interpreted, or even misinterpreted in the history of political thought—gives me little right to its exclusive use. Yet, along the way, although I have encountered many obstacles that to me have been as daunting, if not as dangerous, as those faced by Odysseus, unlike Odysseus—who only found true friendship at the end of his journey—I have had the help of friends, old and new, from the outset.

This book began, as many first books do, as a dissertation and, perhaps not unlike many dissertations, had its origins amid the many conversations with my friends from graduate school. I can recall the first time I floated the idea of pursuing Homer's *Odyssey* as a subject of political inquiry. My friends Joseph Romance, Clifford Fox, and Deirdre Condit supported the idea, I would like to think, on its merits; however, their enthusiasm was perhaps magnified by the libations that we liberally shared at Tumulty's pub, where, half joking, we imagined that the bar stools might eventually be inscribed with our names in honor of our long patronage.

I am deeply grateful to my teachers at Rutgers University, especially to Benjamin R. Barber, whose early support of this idea convinced me that it was worth pursuing and whose continued friendship has, at several points, made a difference in my life path for the better. P. Dennis Bathory taught the first undergraduate course I attended—a fact that he acknowledges with a grimace—which, I still recall, was devoted to an exploration of the meaning of Plato's "Allegory of the Cave." He posed a conundrum that continued to fascinate me for many years, and my furtive attempts to add to the vast literature on Plato in the pages that follow are a testament to our attempts to come to terms with Plato's meaning on that warm afternoon almost two decades ago. Arlene Saxonhouse served as an outside reader on my dissertation and asked questions that I still ponder and have tried to answer, I'm sure in ways that would provoke more searching and thoughtful questions.

At Princeton I have gained valuably from the insights of my colleagues, especially George Kateb, who continues to insist, perhaps rightly, that I am too hard on Achilles; and Maurizio Viroli, whose prowess at soccer is the closest analogue I have witnessed to a kind of Homeric athletic virtue in today's academia. Parts of the manuscript were read by "students"—I use the term loosely because I guiltily realize that often I learn more from them than I suspect they do from me—and among them I am especially grateful to Lynn Robinson and Jonathan Allen for their generous comments.

The manuscript was also read by Norma Thompson and Michael Davis for Rowman & Littlefield, both of whom "revealed" themselves to me after encouraging the project. Each provided a wealth of suggestions on how I might improve the manuscript, and I have attempted to address many of their points. Jacob Howland subsequently read the manuscript, in a gesture of extraordinary kindness. I am deeply grateful to Jacob for his extensive comments and for sharing his ranging knowledge of Greek thought. Steve Wrinn at Rowman & Littlefield lent this project his enthusiastic support; and aside from his good taste in manuscripts, he is a good fellow to boot.

I have also benefited from material support from several sources. The Earhart Foundation generously provided assistance during the summer before the project's completion, and the Pew Foundation's Pew Evangelical Fellows Award allowed me to take a leave in the following semester as I completed the manuscript. Princeton University provided additional research assistance for preparation of the manuscript. Susan McWilliams and James Mastrangelo quite miraculously transformed the rough collection of citations into a consistent whole.

Special thanks are owed to my mentor and friend, Wilson Carey McWilliams, who showed me that literature, politics, and philosophy are rightly pursued together. More importantly, I thank him for showing me that one's academic life does not exist at a remove from how one can live one's life generally. Generosity, laughter, and beauty of expression deserve an honored place within the university.

If this book wouldn't have been started without Carey, it never would have been finished without the care and support of my family—my wife, Inge, and our sons, Francis and Adrian. Sometimes I suspect that my praise of *nostos*—homecoming—to which Odysseus dedicates himself is not wholly derived from my understanding of the *Odyssey* but, rather, reflects the warmth of the home to which I gladly return daily and from which I never really leave.

INTRODUCTION

$\sim$

Between Oikos and Cosmos

Until then I had thought each book spoke of things, human or divine, that lie outside books. Now I realized that not infrequently books speak of books: it is as if they spoke among themselves. In the light of this reflection, the library seemed all the more disturbing to me. It was then the place of a long, centuries-old murmuring, an imperceptible dialogue between one parchment and another, a living thing, a receptacle of powers not to be ruled by a human mind, a treasure of secrets emanated by many minds, surviving the deaths of those who had produced them or had been their conveyors.

—Umberto Eco, The Name of the Rose

Contested Origins

Origins are contested objects, the battleground of self-definition on all fronts of today's culture wars.[1] How we define ourselves as human beings is deeply intertwined with commonly held stories about our respective beginnings as a person, a culture, or a polity. Among the first questions children formulate is "Where did I come from?" and among the first lessons they will have in school is the story of the founding of the United States. A family, a society, and a nation use origins as maintaining myths, precious to the continuance of an organization's spirit and serving as both reminders of past glory and, at times, correctives to contemporary shortcomings. These myths create order out of chaos by organizing our self-perception and our relationships to others—friends, acquaintances, and enemies. Mythic stories of origins are thus limiting tales, placing borders around the self and the self's understanding of others—perhaps out of necessity, given the ultimate limitations of human perception, but limitations nonetheless that can be contested at some level as arbitrary.

1

As a fabled unanimity about those origins attenuates over time, battles that seem out of proportion to the contested objects themselves can arise between various camps seeking to preserve, to amend, or even to overthrow stories about one's origins. The recent observance of the bicentennial of the U.S. Constitution and of the Bill of Rights was a source of simultaneous celebration of and contestation over origins, depending on one's understanding of the relative benefits or disadvantages brought about by the ratification of those documents. Some—such as former Chief Justice Warren Burger, who resigned his chair to head the Committee on the Bicentennial of the Constitution—sought to use the opportunity to renew America's common claim to the principles enunciated in the document. Others viewed it as a chance to point out the Constitution's inherent weaknesses, even its dubious claim to represent any population in its entirety.[2]

Similarly, the infamous "Battle of the Books" at Stanford University was also provoked by a series of sallies about contested origins, this time more broadly concerning the foundations of the West.[3] The many-sided question of whether a select group of books can be defined as core to the Western tradition, or whether the Western tradition is in itself admirable and worthwhile, or even whether such a Western tradition could be said to exist was eagerly displayed by a variety of political spectrums in the 1980s and continues unabated into the present.[4] The core curriculum, or canon, of Western thought at Stanford was swept aside in a wave of reformist fury against sexism, racism, and finally Westernism. By the time the debate ended, formerly required readings by such authors as Plato, Dante, Machiavelli, Marx, and Freud and books such as the Bible, the *Odyssey*, and the *Aeneid* were no longer required reading for Stanford's students; they were replaced by whatever was chosen by individual professors. Even any concept of shared origins was rejected, suggesting that the students' lack of common origin was in itself a defining feature of American identity—multiculturalism as a simultaneously shared and separating norm. The pluralism set into play by the U.S. Constitution was apparently applicable to the university as well, now better defined as a "multiversity" because it was no longer in any sense unified.

The two debates at roughly the same time—one concerning the U.S. Constitution and one regarding the Western canon—share some striking resemblances and, indeed, emanate out of the same intellectual divisions. The American polity was founded uniquely on the basis of documents; as Alexander Hamilton wrote at the outset of the *Federalist*, the American founding was one that provoked the question of "whether societies of men are really capable or not of establishing good government from reflection and choice, or whether they are forever destined to depend for their political constitutions on accident and force."[5] Partaking of the unique *writtenness* of the Western tradition, the Constitution is in some senses the culmination of Enlightenment theories that *ideas* rather than custom and accident should be the ruling principle of polities. Even this apparent Enlightenment view is suffused with traditions dating from the Middle Ages, from church documents and edicts of nobility, and even from the antiquity of Greece and Rome, where written philosophy sought to convince that reason and persuasion should rule over opinion and arbitrary force. The debate over the Constitution was effectively based on the same arguments used in the debate over the Western canon.

On the one side, traditionalists sought to defend the written text or texts against the claims of reformers who argued, on the more moderate side, that other texts were relevant and deserved inclusion and, in the more extreme case, that the written classics were instruments of repression and should be criticized or excised altogether rather than revered. In the debate over the Constitution's meaning, this ground had been well-prepared by the confirmation hearings of Judge Robert Bork in 1986, who claimed that the Constitution's exact words alone, informed by the intentions of the Framers, should be the guiding text for judges seeking to apply constitutional standards to state and federal laws. Critics of this view contended that the Constitution was fundamentally undefinable in the manner Judge Bork claimed, or that the Constitution should be subject to considerations of "evolving standards," or even that the Framers had intended that future generations should not be held captive to any literal reading of the Constitution.[6] Similarly, in the debate about the canon, reformers argued that works other than those select few by "dead white males" should be included in the required reading lists of college freshmen.[7]

The critique of the canon is surprising and ironic, coming as it does almost without exception from intellectuals on the Left who don the postmodernist mantle. Their attack on the monolithic, repressive canon in fact contradicts the postmodernist creed that signifiers are protean, that the written word is finally resistant to final interpretive definition, and that even authorial intentions are irrelevant to determining meaning.[8] Critics of the canon have created a straw man—an extraordinarily stationary one—whose existence otherwise contradicts postmodernist literary theory; for contained within the "authoritative" list of books that defined, for example, the Stanford "Great Books" courses, are countless contradictions, dichotomies, and intellectual disagreements. Taken as a whole, those works that compose what is recognized as the canon—as much as what books should be included—represent an ongoing battlefield, from Aristotle's critique of Plato's *Republic* to Rousseau's rejection of Locke and Hobbes's state of nature, from Luther's demolishing of Aquinas to Marx's re-vision of Hegel. Such a canon of books, then, is not a source of undying and unchanging norms as its critics suggest but is, in fact, a storehouse of unsolved and even ongoing debates, including the very debate over the validity of canons: in addition to Luther's attack on the Catholic doctrine of received tradition, recall the *Querelle des Anciens et des Modernes*.[9]

Those who seek to defend the canon largely play into the hands of its critics, adopting this monolith as in some sense worthy of defense. Typical of such attempts is that of William J. Bennett, former secretary of education in the Reagan administration. He severely criticized the reform of the Western civilization core at Stanford, lamenting that "American colleges and Universities [have] given up on what was once a central task: the study of a core curriculum, a set of fundamental courses, ordered, purposive, and coherent, that should constitute the central, foundational part of the liberal education."[10] Core curricula on Western culture are consistently defended by Bennett because they are "important": why they are important is "self-evident."[11] If critics of the canon joust at an immobile straw man, conservatives such as Bennett prop him up nicely for the kill. Although Bennett noted that Western culture is "the most self-critical of cultures," the validity of such self-criticism evidently does not extend to current critics of the West.[12] If the canon according to the Left is an invariable repository of repression and inequality, the canon according to the Right is an invariable repository of virtue and high culture. In the creation of this contested monolith, the Left and the Right come out well defined, but any reasoned discussion of the canon's internal dynamics—including the dynamic of internal contradiction and constant re-creation—is lost.[13]

Typical to many of the debates comprising the "Culture Wars," both the Left and the Right seized the ground at the extremes, leaving the middle undefended and even unnoticed. Both the Left and the Right created and fostered the straw man called the canon for rhetorical purposes. Despite the Left's seeming dedication to postmodernist literary theories, many of those on the Left refused to turn such theories introspectively on the "repressive" literature they sought to reject. And in spite of the apparent dedication of those on the Right to the works of the canon, they ignored that the individual works that comprise their beloved canon are contradictory, subversive, and even, at times, leftist. If it can be said that there is a canon—and laying aside all cant, thinkers on both the Left and the Right would have to admit that what is canonical can and has changed throughout space and time—then it is not entirely "self-evident" that such works that comprise this canon, when actually *read* and interpreted, always and everywhere transmit the same enduring message (whether repressive or virtuous).

In a sense, both the Left and the Right were correct to see the specter or the vision of authority in the canon, even if they both overlook its internally subversive dynamic. In the Greek, *kanōn* means "a straight rod," a "ruler," and hence "standard" or "norm." A canon is "established" in order to afford such standards;

yet, inasmuch as a literary canon, and even a religious one, is subject to interpretation and even to fundamental change, its constancy as a standard-bearer is dubious. At issue are two different but not unrelated definitions of *canon*. The first definition consists of a list, like that famous list of books that was the subject of Stanford's Battle of the Books. This contested list is like a photo negative of the Catholic Church's *Index Librorum Prohibitorum*. Conservatives sought to stake out and to defend a specific list of accepted titles, whereas more radical critics attempted either to modify the list (for example, to include nondead, nonwhite, nonmales) or to eliminate the list, and hence its authoritative claim, altogether.

Although this first definition of *canon* claims much of the attention paid by the media and the general public to this debate—inevitably due to the very nature of lists, which simplifies complicated matters—the second definition is much more fluid and changing than either its defenders or critics suggest. Given that such a shifting set of books is not a singular work of museum art but a temporal accumulation of contested and contesting words, the entire configuration of this supposed monolith is subject to constant change as new works are added to it and as new interpretations of existing works surface through the dense secondary literature that invariably seeks to accord or to rescind canonical status. Jorge Luis Borges (a canonical or anticanonical author?) made precisely this point in a provocative essay entitled "Kafka and His Precursors," in which he relates how once Kafka had written his haunting stories and novels, one could never again read his precursors in the same light. Had Kafka never written a line, Borges writes, one would not read the poems of Browning, for example, in quite the same light they are now read. "The fact is that every writer *creates* his own precursors."[14] Borges's observation is profound: rather than suggesting a fixed canon of unchanging works, he posits that with the addition of each new canonical work, the seemingly fixed words that preceded it (while not changing in its black-and-white form) change ever so imperceptibly in *meaning*. Stated less radically than Borges, T. S. Eliot wrote that "what happens when a new work of art is created is something that happens simultaneously to all the works of art which preceded it . . . ; the whole existing order must be, if ever so slightly, altered."[15] The past influences the creation of the present; but like the ripples of a stone thrown in water, the ripples emanate back to shore. So, too, the present influences the perception of the past.

If the canon can be defined in any way, it is perhaps by the inclusion of those works that have perpetually challenged human beings in their attempts at self-understanding, works that have remained relevant to human concerns and aspirations despite changes in politics and technology, works that have adamantly resisted interpretive closure and, hence, have ever beckoned new generations to sharpen their wits against the pages of those works. As such, the very meaning of the word *canon* at some level contradicts the defining features that constitute the canon: such works do not represent a "rule" per se as much as, in one guise, an ongoing inquiry into how such ruling principles are arrived at. They are works that do not necessarily provide answers to the many questions they pose but rather pose those questions in endlessly provocative ways. If such works do provide answers, those answers can be no more than, in the words of Benjamin Barber, "a provisional resting point for knowledge and conduct."[16] Together they compose what Sheldon Wolin, referring to interpretations of the Constitution, has called a "public hermeneutic" in which no one voice dictates its final answer to the rest.[17] The canon is itself a dialogue, one of profound depth and disagreement, one that does not permit easy conclusions.

Philosophy versus Poetry

A profound irony lies at the heart of this contemporary debate. Those on the Left defend the values of multiculturalism against the conforming magic that the canon proposes; those on the Right defend the universal truths that the canon affords its students. The Left assumes a stance of particularism against intrusive universalism; the Right succors universalism against the devolving ferocities of particularism. Such posturing was not always the case. Traditionally, the Left, as defined by the thought deriving from the Enlightenment, has sought the overthrow of cultural, political, and religious particularism by appealing to such universal values as liberty, equality, and human rights as derived solely from the dictates of reason. In response, the Right attempted to preserve—to *conserve*—the particular customs and practices that constitute a given society against the radically univeralizing tendencies of liberal thought, expressed most cogently in the work of Edmund Burke and recently in the work of Michael Oakeshott.

The Left, especially those branches represented by liberalism and Marxism, has historically aligned itself with appeals to universal truths that cut across national and ethnic lines. Developed most fully in the Enlightenment, this universalist project is captured in such works as the *Encyclopedia*, or, as it was fully titled, *Encyclopédie, ou Dictionnaire universel des arts et des sciences*. The attempt at *universality* was explicitly set forth in the editorial plan of the *Encyclopédie* by Diderot, who, although claiming to respect national differences, revealed his true regard for such prejudices:

> In all cases where a national prejudice would seem to deserve respect, the particular article ought to set it respectfully forth, with its whole procession of attractions and probabilities. But the edifice of mud ought to be overthrown and an unprofitable heap of dust scattered to the wind, by references to articles in which solid principles serve as a base for the opposite truths. This way of undeceiving men operates promptly on

minds of the right stamp, and it operates infallibly and without any troublesome consequences, secretly and without disturbance, on minds of every description.[18]

Such sentiments, abhorring local and particularist sentiments, culminated in the French "Declaration of the Rights of Man and Citizen" of 1789, declaring the inviolability of "the natural, inalienable, and sacred rights of man." These rights, notably, applied first and foremost to "*hommes*," not "*citoyens*"; where regimes did not recognize such rights, they nevertheless derived from each person's inherent humanity. Thus could Condorcet write that he sought the improvement not merely of the French, but "that the perfection of man is truly indefinite."[19]

In explicit reaction to these universalizing doctrines of the Enlightenment and to the attempt to put them into practice in the French Revolution, conservatives (or, according to some, reactionaries) such as Edmund Burke and Joseph de Maistre appealed to the dignity of existing custom, the practicality of prejudice, and the steadiness of tradition. Burke scoffed:

Whilst they [the Revolutionaries] are possessed by these notions, it is vain to talk to them of the practice of their ancestors, the fundamental laws of their country, the fixed form of a constitution, whose merits are confirmed by the solid test of long experience. . . . They have "the rights of men." Against these there can be no prescription; against these no agreement is binding: these admit no temperament and no compromise: anything withheld from their full demand is so much fraud and injustice. Against these rights of men let no government look for security in the length of its continuance, or in the justice and lenity of its administration.[20]

This condemnation of the universalizing, uncompromising, and leveling philosophy of the Enlightenment was trenchantly echoed by Maistre, who similarly attacked the Declaration of the Rights of Man: "There is no such thing as a *man* in the world. I have seen, during my life, Frenchmen, Italians, Russians, etc. . . . But as far as *man* is concerned, I declare that I have never in my life met him; if he exists, he is unknown to me."[21] Beyond the empirical *falsehood* of wholly rationalist claims to universal humanity are the *dangers* that accrue when applying such rational theories to the unruly reality of particularist politics, attempting to fit particular customs and circumstances into the Procrustean straightjacket of reason.[22]

Until recently, this gaping division between the traditional Left and the traditional Right has been the defining feature of modern political philosophy. Even of late an astute political observer such as Leo Strauss could define *liberal* theory as "homogeneity grasped by reason" and *conservative* theory as "heterogeneity unfolded through tradition."[23] Recently, however, the reversal that has taken place has been noted by perceptive critics, notably Todd Gitlin, who has lamented the Left's embrace of the particularistic doctrine formerly claimed by the Right.

The right, traditionally the custodian of the privileges of the few, now speaks in an apparently general language of merit, reason, individual rights, and virtue that transcends politics, whereas much of the left is so preoccupied with debunking generalizations and affirming the differences among groups—real as they often are—that it has ceded the very language of universality that is its birthright. . . . The left and the right have traded places, at least with respect to the sort of universalist rhetoric that can still stir the general public. Unable to go beyond the logic of identity politics, the left has ceded much political high ground to the right.[24]

Gitlin dates this shift to the student movement of the 1960s, when civil rights for blacks and equal rights for women began to move the Left to identify reform with group-based politics and into identity politics in which not rights but self-definition and group identity became the goals of reform. In response, the Right ironically called on the Left to cease politicizing debates by appeals to group identity—"ironically" because for centuries the Right had claimed that a form of traditional group identity centered around the nation was the only *legitimate* form of politics.

Recent developments, however, suggest that some thinkers on the Left and the Right are seeking to return to their more traditional positions vis-à-vis their sympathy or condemnation of the Enlightenment. Critics of the multiculturalist position have arisen in order to recover a form of universalism and rationality that accords with the cosmopolitan outlook of the Enlightenment. Not willing to cede to the Right the mantle of universalism (which they have rightly suspected was never a comfortable fit) thinkers like Martha Nussbaum, Russell Jacoby, David Hollinger, Todd Gitlin, and Stephen Eric Bronner, among others, have sought to reclaim for the Left a vision of transcendence beyond clan, region, or nation that regards suspiciously what they view as an overly deterministic assignment of identity according to ethnicity, race, gender, or any number of inescapable factors.[25] Ranging from arguments about the need for a "postethnic" understanding that recognizes that "most individuals live in many circles simultaneously" to the lament that the embrace of multiculturalism has led to the "end of utopia" because "with few ideas of how a future is to be shaped, they embrace all ideas," like-minded thinkers on the Left have pointed out many of the excesses of the multicultural position.[26]

Homer's Canon

Winnowing through the many books and articles that were written in roughly the decade from the mid-1980s to the mid-1990s, when the Cold War was ending and the culture wars heated up, one is struck by the great anger, accusation, recrimination, denial, and defensiveness in those writings. Reading the almost countless pages that were written in that ten-year period, one can see the same stories being told over and over again. Bogeymen of various ideological stripes were brought onstage to terrify the packed house of like-minded observers. Conservatives would hiss at Paul de Man, at Jesse Jackson at Stanford, at "the masturbating girl" in Jane Austen; others on the opposite side would drag out "the killer 'B's'"—William Bennett, Allan Bloom, and Saul Bellow—for resounding disapproval. Name-calling abounded: *The Closing of the American Mind* was called "Hitleresque" by one scholar, according to Roger Kimball;[27] whereas one of the more grotesque epithets on the Right remained Rush Limbaugh's use of the cobbled word "feminazis." Everywhere scowls were evident.

Curiously, it is the canon itself that may tell the most, or may tell most deeply, about these contemporary debates. One figure among many cropped up more often, perhaps, than any other, a name dropped often alongside Plato, Shakespeare, Dante, and Cervantes, a figure consciously invoked for his ancient authority and sometimes reputed wisdom—Homer. For many, more than any other figure, Homer represented the West because he represented Greece, and Greece prefigured and determined the West. Homer became either *the* standard around which conservatives would circle their wagons or one of the primary objects of criticism among the multicultural Left.

The very title of a recent book lamenting the decline of classical studies in the university by Victor Davis Hanson and John Heath insists on this identification. To the question posed by their title, *Who Killed Homer?*, Hanson and Heath answer, those classicists who no longer either teach Homer seriously or attend to the virtues of antiquity. By contrast, they hope to revive "the meaning and significance of this ancient Greek vision of life—what we mean in our title by Homer—and the consequences for the modern world for its complete abandonment. Homer is the first and best creative dividend of the *polis*, and so serves as a primer for the entire, subsequent world of the Greeks."[28] For Hanson and Heath, as for Werner Jaeger before them, Homer represents "Greek Wisdom": he is the "Educator of Greece," the authority whose "ideas and values . . . have shaped and defined all of Western civilization."[29]

For proponents of multiculturalism, if Homer were to remain at all, he was not to be revered as a source of authority nor imbibed as a font of timeless wisdom, but presented as an example of cultural particularity, an exemplar of early, Greek, Western, male thought. All cultures and traditions were to be viewed as equal, not allowing one to make judgments between and among them. If conservatives looked to a tradition that appealed at some level to commonality, for example, a tradition that might unite all people of the West or bind Americans by means of a documentary heritage, others saw only difference as defining humans across time and place. Barbara Herrnstein Smith, a multiculturalist, related that "there is no knowledge, no standard, no choice that is objective. Even Homer is a product of a specific culture, and it is possible to imagine cultures in which Homer would not be very interesting."[30] Similarly, Stanley Fish has contended that "*it is difference all the way down*; difference cannot be managed by measuring it against the common because the shape of the common is itself differential."[31] Ironically, in the debate in which one side declared that all cultures were distinct and at some level incomparable and the other insisted on the superiority of Western culture for its universalist claims, the universalists often became cultural nationalists and the multiculturalists, through their critique of conservatives, at times slipped into a stronger denunciation of that Western tradition than their relativist position otherwise should have allowed them.[32]

Homer, then, appeared on stage either as, according to Hanson and Heath, a source of all wisdom about not only the West but also humankind, or as an irrelevant cipher that might draw us away from relevant social concerns. Leaving aside these extreme and, in my view, misleading views of antiquity, what I would like to suggest in the subsequent chapters is that Homer, especially through the *Odyssey*, is neither of these two things, neither savior nor bogeyman, but rather that he was among the first authors to raise the questions that animate this current debate without himself ultimately succumbing too easily and securely to any one position. Stating this of course, I argue that Homer is closer to the first position—a source of some wisdom—than to the second—an irrelevant cipher—but for reasons different from those often argued by traditionalists. What is particularly fascinating about the *Odyssey* in particular is the extent to which it seems to be in part animated by some of the same fundamental causes that underlie this current debate. In traveling the world of the known and the unknown, the world of beasts, gods, and even the dead, Odysseus is confronted by the question of whether one can escape one's culture, in a sense one's apparent destiny. Of course, Odysseus insists on his return and secures it after awesome effort and travail. Nevertheless, we sense that he is not the same for it. Although the *Odyssey* can at one level be seen as asserting the primacy and undeniability of the claims of culture—indicated by Odysseus's homecoming—at the same time it seems to indicate the possibility of at least limited transcendence reflected in Odysseus's constant if dangerous willingness to partake of divine or beastly qualities that are most often forbidden to humanity.

The Political Theory of the *Odyssey* and the Odyssey of Political Theory

Thus, Odysseus is the consummate wayfarer, the man of the sea, the sky, and the underworld; but he is also a man dedicated to *nostos*, return to hearth and home.

He can be, as in the *Iliad*, as great a warrior as any of the leading soldiers, yet also a trickster as crafty as Hermes. He can be a tender lover and father figure, as seen in the touching departure scene from Nausicaa, a scene that inspired Goethe to begin a play on the theme. And yet Odysseus can be a vicious and unforgiving bringer of vengeance, exhibited most gruesomely through the savage execution he arranges for the suitors and their helpers. The breadth of his character was the central inspiration for James Joyce in writing his modern retelling of the *Odyssey*, *Ulysses*: only one so simultaneously homely yet weighty as Odysseus could be transformed into the wandering Irish Jew, Leopold Bloom; it is difficult to imagine Achilles or Hector assuming that role. Homer was clearly aware of Odysseus's chameleon—or better, protean—character: as described in the opening line of the *Odyssey*, he is *polutropos*, an almost untranslatable word meaning "man of many devices or ways."[33] He is a hero almost defined by his indefiniteness; a mirror whose reflection allows his interpreters to give him whatever form they want to see him take. Thus, throughout the centuries, Odysseus has been a receptacle for every age's hopes and aspirations, a conduit for every poet's imaginative flights, and a parodic figure for every detractor's condemnation.[34]

As Pietro Boitani relates in *The Shadow of Ulysses*, much subsequent interpretation of Odysseus has hinged on one's understanding of the key episode in Book 11 of the *Odyssey*, in which Odysseus travels to Hades to hear from Teiresias the prediction of his future.[35] As Teiresias cryptically relates to Odysseus in the kingdom of the dead:

> After you have killed these suitors in your palace,
> either by treachery, or openly with the sharp bronze,
> you must take up your well-shaped oar and go on a journey
> until you come where there are men living who know nothing
> of the sea, and who eat food that is not mixed with salt, who never
> have known well-shaped oars. . . .
> When, as you walk, some other wayfarer happens to meet you,
> and says you carry a winnow-fan on your bright shoulder,
> then you must plant your well-shaped oar in the ground, and render
> ceremonious sacrifice to the lord Poseidon. . . .
> Death will come to you from the sea (*thanatos de toi ex halos*), in
> some altogether unwarlike way, and it will end you
> in the ebbing time of sleek old age. Your people
> about you will be prosperous. All this is true that I tell you.
> (11.119–137)[36]

There are two elements to Teiresias's prediction: (1) the description of the journey Odysseus must take far inland in the near future once he has secured justice at home; and (2) a description of the manner of his death in the more distant future. In the first instance, the fact that Odysseus is destined to travel again proves significant in future portrayals of Odysseus's life subsequent to the end of the *Odyssey*: does he travel unwillingly, longing as ever to return to Penelope and his son Telemachus; or does Odysseus *polutropos* rapidly tire of the staid life of his island-kingdom, longing again for the open seas and the fabulous adventures they supply?[37] How one interpreted Odysseus's attitude toward the necessity of future travels—with glee or resignation—could be determined from one's perspective on Odysseus's character and indeed on how that character served as a model for human nature.

In the second instance, Teiresias's prediction of Odysseus's eventual death would perhaps prove even more central in determining the extent of Odysseus's commitment to humanity and his *polis*. There is uncertainty how best to interpret Teiresias's prediction that *thanatos de toi ex halos*, which can be rendered either "death shall come to you at sea" or "death shall come to you from out of the sea."[38] The Greek can imply either, as it seems to mean death shall come "by agency of the sea." According to the former interpretation of this passage, one can conclude that Odysseus will again be wandering when he meets his death— if he is at sea, then he will not be on Ithaca, an island. It was this interpretation that served as the basis for Dante's portrayal of Odysseus's end in the *Inferno*. The latter interpretation suggests he will be at home when someone or something lands on Ithaca from the sea and causes his death. A later epic arrived at the latter possibility, telling of a child by Odysseus and Circe seeking revenge on his father.[39]

Less noticeable than literary renditions of Odysseus's wanderings, but no less frequent, have been the appeals to Odysseus as an exemplary figure by political theorists over the course of centuries, and for much the same reason as he has served as a *typos* in literature. As the redeemer who institutes Justice in his homeland or as the immoral originator of *raison d'état*, Odysseus has served often as both a positive and a negative example in the pages of political theory. Yet, beyond this relatively narrow definition of *politics* as the institution of political order, the story of the *Odyssey* has provided an understanding of politics that might be called typically Greek: a broader conception of relations between human beings that includes more than, as Hannah Arendt puts it, "counting noses," but rather attempts to form among individuals in a *polis* "the capacity for an 'enlarged mentality,'" a vision of commonality and association that bridges the loneliness of the single soul to the incomprehensible otherness of strangers.[40] It is this aspect of the *Odyssey*—the theme of human interconnectedness and yet the sometimes insurmountable gap that separates people from one another, either through physical or psychological barriers—to which political philosophers have returned repeatedly in attempting to describe (and to change) the prevailing understanding of human nature. Depending on how the *Odyssey* was individually or collectively understood, one's answer to the possibility of real political community was arrived at through a rendering of Odysseus as either relentless traveler abroad or dedicated pursuer of *nostos*, homecoming.

What follows, then, is an exploration of the *Odyssey* as it might be understood politically and as it might be seen both as a work within the "canon" of political theory and as a work that, like most "canonical" works, finally resists easy inclusion or co-optation by any party or camp. From Odysseus's appearances in post-Homeric epic cycles to his frequent sightings in the plays and the philosophy of democratic Athens, from his transformation into the stoic Ulysses of imperial Rome to his punishment in Hell for *hubris* recorded by Dante, from his political portrayals by the bard of Stratford-on-Avon to Tennyson's scientific and colonial depiction, one realizes that Odysseus's odyssey merely began with the *Odyssey*'s conclusion.[41]

Subsequent chapters in this book present an unfamiliar journey into the known: a revisitation of several "canonical" texts of political philosophy, viewing them through the character of Odysseus who appears in their pages so often and to such great effect. The choice of Homer's *Odyssey* for examining the vagaries of the canon of political theory is obvious for reasons other than its simple antiquity: the Homeric epics are among the oldest known Western texts; but, more important, they have served for centuries as a foundation in Western education. Yet, beyond the antiquity of the texts themselves, there is a less obvious but perhaps more compelling reason for exploring the *Odyssey* in particular. Odysseus for the first time embodies the dilemma of Western political philosophy and perhaps the human paradox more generally. He is, in one guise, the *universal man*, wandering the world and encountering the varieties of gods, beasts, and mankind above and below the earth. He constantly tempts the limits imposed on mortals, threatening his extinction as a mortal, either through death or immortality. His temptation by the Sirens best exemplifies his craving for universal knowledge: they sing that "over all the generous earth we know everything that happens" and offer to share that knowledge with Odysseus. Of course, such knowledge is deadly, but it is tempting nonetheless. The similar offer of immortality by Calypso represents the philosophic wish to escape the bonds of the mortal condition, to attain godlike wisdom. Although again a deadly wish, it is one often grasped by desperate mortals, as demonstrated by numerous humans in mythology who accepted the offer and were struck down for it.

In his other guise, Odysseus is the *particular man*: he is king, father, husband, son; his longing to return to the tiny kingdom of Ithaca, his home, is the paramount goal that fuels the action of the *Odyssey*. If he is tempted by the Sirens' offer, he makes sure beforehand that he is bound to the mast—perhaps the image of such bonds were later to inspire Plato in devising his description of the Cave. Those bonds effectively tie him to the imperfect mortal community, in essence to Ithaca, toward which his ship sails. Similarly, he refuses Calypso's offer of immortality, tenderly describing the imperfections of Penelope in comparison to the godlike perfection of Calypso and claiming to love his mortal wife and home more than Calypso. The only moment in the epic when Odysseus forgets home is in his dalliance with Circe: while seeming to have mastered her, he has done so only with the assistance of the gods. He masters her through a mastery of nature: his subsequent obliviousness of home is a direct result of that mastery. Partaking, if only at second hand, of that project that would define the Enlightenment—the mastery of nature—Odysseus momentarily loses his way and must be pointed back by his men, who succumbed to the more bestial aspect of Circe's magic. Even if Odysseus did not seek the mastery of nature, Homer suggests that even at a remove it is nevertheless a dangerous enterprise for mortals.

In a certain respect, these twin perspectives on the *Odyssey*—the one, a description of the explorer, the cosmopolitan, the expansive "Ulysses"; the other a tender rendition of Odysseus the Ithacan, the lover of Penelope and Telemachus, the just king of a modest island far from Troy—capture a vital aspect of what could justifiably be regarded as *the* debate animating political theory both in recent history and most certainly in contemporary America: the seemingly eternal clash between the autonomy of individuals and the high place accorded to community, public things, or more broadly "the common good." Odysseus *polutropos* captures both of these qualities and offers to proponents on each side of what has come to be known as the "liberal-communitarian debate" an appealing, if partial, literary embodiment of each respective ideal.

Although it would be incorrect to attribute to Homer any kind of protoliberalism on the one hand nor, on the other hand, a foretaste of Tocqueville's citizen for whom political participation was as vital as life itself, to a significant extent the *Odyssey* captures an elemental quality of this divide. In the profound tension between Odysseus the consummate homeseeker and Odysseus the grand explorer who is finally dissatisfied with the provincial and insular life on Ithaca, one perceives the central tension that animates contemporary debates. Among the many arguments that one finds within this overarching debate are ones that pit proponents of cosmopolitanism, like Martha Nussbaum, against defenders of more local allegiances, like Charles Taylor and Michael Walzer; that find formidable proponents of neutrality in politics, like John Rawls, criticized by philosophers, like Michael Sandel, who remind of the "situatedness" of selves; and that pit critics of "private" family life, ranging from Susan Okin to Catharine MacKinnon, against defenders of valuable "attachments," like Jean Bethke Elshtain and Christopher Lasch.

Underlying each aspect of these similar debates, it seems, is the extent to which relationships and even commitments can be said to be finally freely chosen and embraced. At one extreme would be the multiculturalists, who, in attempting to defend and to promote what have been minority or repressed cultures, in fact, often assume an ethnic or biological determinism that horrifies proponents of choice in one's identity. David A. Hollinger, for example, questions how Alex Haley determined that his roots belonged in Africa and not in Ireland, why he assumed his ethnicity—while mixed—was wholly African rather than at least partially Gaelic.

In a different context, responding to the seemingly unlimited recommendation of choice posed by the Enlightenment position, thinkers like Sandel, Elshtain, and Lasch have argued for the "situatedness" of individuals and on behalf of boundaries in politics and restraint on the seemingly limitless capacity for optimism in progress.[42] Each of these thinkers is cautious about the possibility of fundamentally altering or even eliminating the family as the basis of human relationships.[43] For such thinkers, the assertion of infinite choice governing the fashioning of our identities and of our relationships represents both a fiction, inasmuch as such unlimited choice is impossible, and a dangerous suggestion, inasmuch as to act on this fiction is to undermine the basis of a decent and stable polity without actually achieving the debatably desirable goal of autonomy and unbridled individualism.

Proponents of a liberal view—hearkening back to the very origins of liberal contractarian theory, which posits an original State of Nature in which human beings *freely* agree to live under shared social and political conditions and reserve the right just as freely to alter or to abolish those commitments—see all human and social relations as fundamentally fungible. Humans are individually autonomous, and the relations we share with others define us, if at all, only provisionally and at our pleasure. Thus, for Nussbaum, we may be born involuntarily as a citizen of a particular place, but our more fundamental commonality demands that we devote our primary commitments to humanity at large—to cosmos, not to *oikos* or *polis*.[44] Although various critics of Nussbaum's position may differ as to the desirability of cosmopolitanism as an ideal—some are more sympathetic than others—most critics agree that there can be no real "choice" involved because cosmopolitanism is not a real possibility for limited human beings. Instead, respondents to Nussbaum's original defense of cosmopolitanism generally point to "the limits of affection" or "the difficulty of imagining other people."[45]

These positions mirror some long-standing debates about how we should understand the actions of Odysseus during the course of his wanderings. Can he be said to actually *choose* the various courses he sets on that eventually bring him *nostos*, return to Ithaca? Or is he devoid of agency, simply a product of culture then as much as we are products of cultures now, in the view of some multiculturalists? The latter position was once dominant in Homeric scholarship, inaugurated in some respects by Bruno Snell in his masterpiece *The Discovery of the Mind*. Snell recognized that Homer's characters are faced with choices all of the time. However, he argued, "Homeric man does not yet regard himself as the source of his own decisions; that development is reserved for tragedy. When the Homeric hero, after duly weighing his alternatives, comes to a final conclusion, he feels that his course is shaped by the gods."[46] In a different vein, Hermann Fränkel held the widely influential view that Homeric man had no inner capacity by which to make judgments that could put him potentially at odds with his culture: rather, "[Homeric] man is completely part of his world."[47]

Several recent interpretations criticize this deterministic view of the Homeric corpus and instead locate in the text a number of key moments when it can be said that characters act with foresight, freedom, and agency. Prominent among these recent revisions is Bernard Williams's Sather Lectures, published as *Shame and Necessity*.[48] Williams recognizes many of the same instances in which agency is seemingly avoided as those noted by Snell and Fränkel; however, Williams goes on to note a number of instances that can only be understood as demonstrating human choice and agency. One apparently insignificant moment receives special attention: a scene in Book 22 of the *Odyssey* in which Telemachus berates himself for leaving a door open. Telemachus states that "no one else is to blame" for the mistake that allows the suitors to enter the storehouse and arm themselves. This small instance for Williams proves a larger point: throughout the epics the characters understand themselves as acting on their own volition, as choosing incorrectly or inadvertently in some instances. The greater significance goes to the core of the contemporary debate about choice and identity: if Odysseus can indeed choose from a variety of possible outcomes in his larger journey home, why does he choose the seemingly most mundane—the return to the unattractive Ithaca with his aging wife and unpleasant home circumstance? The possibility that his homecoming might in fact be a choice he makes in opposition to several more or less attractive options during the course of his return might prove instructive in our contemporary debate. Odysseus's actions seem to confirm the view of neither of the prevailing opponents but instead appear to offer a third option: neither embracing infinite choice nor denying its attractiveness, but rather "choosing" limitation. The extent and the reasons for his choices will be of particular focus in the following chapters.

Chapter 1 offers an interpretation of the *Odyssey* as a work of political theory, in particular by exploring the "middle course" that Odysseus adopts in his confrontations with nature, the gods, immortality, and humanity. Odysseus is notable for his simultaneously refusing to overstep the bounds of nature and pushing the limits that nature imposes. The revelatory moment is Odysseus's refusal of immortality: that refusal affirms his connectedness to humanity, his acceptance of the limits of mortality. His choice is worth contrasting to that of Achilles, who also seemingly chose "the short, glorious life" by fighting on the plains of Troy, but only after much hesitation and in a fit of passion. Odysseus's careful and conscious decision to embrace mortality—even if it entails the descent to Hades, the horrific land he has already seen—stands in opposition to Achilles' choice. In the subsequent interpretations of the *Odyssey* by Plato and Rousseau, this more reflective quality of Odysseus is explicitly adopted, whereas Achilles as a model of excellence is rejected. However, the poet stops short of fully endorsing Odysseus as a successful citizen or a leader of a polis. Despite his moderation, he is also too defined by the heroic world from which he comes. A person of Odysseus's many ambiguous qualities is necessary for the *founding*, in this case the refounding, of a polity; the more staid and patient qualities of citizenship are to be found in the swineherd, Eumaeus. The extent to which even the gods honor such a citizen's craving for justice suggests a democratic kernel in the *Odyssey*: the strong and powerful, ever conscious of the claims of honor, must in turn secure justice for the law-abiding populace lest they withhold that honor. A regulative democratic principle is thus suggested with the closing of the *Odyssey*.

Chapter 2 turns to a consideration of Plato, for whom the attractions of the *Odyssey* prove to be the opposite of the then-current popularity of the *Iliad* and the *Iliad*'s great hero, Achilles. Odysseus offers for Plato the example of a protophilosopher, one who is cognizant of the attractions of life both inside and outside the cave and who, like Odysseus, chooses finally to return to mortal life inside the cave, if informed throughout by his journey above and by prudence once below. Chapter 2, then, attempts to grapple with two apparent contradictions in Plato's *Republic*. Although Socrates explicitly banishes the poets and poetry—particularly Homer and his epics—from his ideal city in speech, there is nevertheless contradictory evidence throughout that poetry is to be permitted, indeed is required, for the institution of Justice, culminating in the elevation of Odysseus to philosophic status in the Myth of Er. The second contradiction concerns the philosopher's relationship to the city: although the philosopher is apparently warned to avoid redescent into the Cave once having escaped it, the example of Socrates in fact belies this admonition. Such a portrait is compounded by the alignment of the reluctant philosopher with the example of Achilles, whereas Socrates is aligned with Odysseus, who embraces his death inasmuch as his mortality entails his embeddedness in his community. The two contradictions are connected: through a "philosophic" understanding of poetry, Socrates hopes to teach the young men in Piraeus that philosophy, rather than hanging back like Achilles in his tent, must engage however imperfectly with the city from which it arises. However, because philosophy can pose a danger to the existence of the "Cave"—philosophy is offensive to tradition and custom—the example of Odysseus is again appealed to, particularly to the hero who returns to his home in disguise. Thus philosophy is moderated by politics, whereas politics is challenged by philosophy.

Alternatively, Jean-Jacques Rousseau could reasonably find an opposite lesson in the *Odyssey*, the image of Odysseus as the consummate wanderer, one who loves his home and family only to the point where that love does not encroach on his own independence of spirit and mind. Like Odysseus, who is fated to leave Ithaca even after his long-awaited return and whose death is foretold as taking place quite possibly "far out at sea," Rousseau models his own heroic and even epic character "Emile" on that basis.

Chapter 3 moves to a consideration of Rousseau's *Emile*, a work that at once addresses Homer's *Odyssey* and Plato's *Republic*. Emile is to be educated not as a "citizen" but as a "man": therefore, the tutor avoids all particularity, building a fence around his young pupil to protect him from the vagaries of place and custom. Although the example of Achilles is initially recommended—especially concerning Emile's physical upbringing—ultimately Achilles must be rejected because his passions are not controlled; rather, Odysseus is adopted as Emile's model. This is particularly true in regard to his relationship with Sophie, whom he will marry. However, instead of building with her the relationship shared by Odysseus and Penelope, Emile is to look to Odysseus because of his qualities as wanderer. Odysseus's commitment to home and family, to polity and community, is ignored by Rousseau, who ultimately seeks to preserve Emile's universal quality as "man" against the encroachments of citizenship. Political life is finally rejected as too encumbering: Emile escapes his family and city and becomes a "solitary wanderer," man of no country but of all. Universalism triumphs over particularism, but at the cost of disfiguring the Odyssean model.

Chapters 2 and 3 set up something of a "dialectic": both Plato and Rousseau find in the *Odyssey* an attractive model for human cultivation, but on different grounds: if, for Plato, Odysseus appeals for his dedication to homecoming—a commitment tantamount to the decision of the philosopher to redescend from above the Cave—for Rousseau, Odysseus represents the ideal model for Emile when it becomes necessary for him to assume the role of wanderer, a figure able to live *among* humans without fostering excessively strong bonds between them. This dialectic might still be identifiable in the text of the *Odyssey*—and the text itself might instruct further between these two poles—but for another dialectic that intervenes. Chapter 4 confronts one of the greatest critiques ever leveled at the *Odyssey*—the extraordinary treatment of the *Odyssey* rendered by Horkheimer and Adorno in *Dialectic of Enlightenment*. Horkheimer and Adorno locate the *Odyssey* in the universality of the Enlightenment: Odysseus represents both all that is rational, hence destructive, and all that is irrational, hence vicious, about the dialectic of myth and enlightenment. Their interpretation raises some significantly different issues than those of Plato and of Rousseau and hence must be judged more extensively against the text of the *Odyssey* itself.

The interpretation by Horkheimer and Adorno is driven foremost by a revised theory of history that departs significantly from that of Hegel or Marx. Their argument that "myth" and "enlightenment" are inextricably intertwined is reminiscent more of the theories of the eighteenth-century writer Giambattista Vico, with whose work Max Horkheimer in particular was well acquainted. Therefore, to promote a better understanding of the more "historicist" understanding of the *Odyssey* proffered by Horkheimer and Adorno, first an analysis of the historical theory of Giambattista Vico is undertaken, especially to the extent that Vico begins a tradition of regarding the Homeric epics as broadly representational of the sweep of historical development, an analytical approach that the Frankfurt School would accept even as they substantially altered it. Critical Theory's departures from Vico prove as telling as its similarities: whereas Vico values the existing relationships formed from mythic or poetic substructures in political communities, the Frankfurt School looks at such "particularist" relationships as fundamentally repressive. On the other hand, if they attack "particularism," their critique also encompasses "enlightenment" as well, particularly its universalizing tendencies in economics and mass culture. Horkheimer and Adorno locate the origins of "enlightenment" with the *Odyssey*, claiming that Odysseus's drive toward self-preservation indicates the drive toward mastery of nature. Although their interpretation is in many ways fascinating, the extent to which they discount the importance or even note the existence of Odysseus's embrace of mortality suggests the final weakness of their argument. If the *Odyssey* and its subsequent interpretations in Plato and in Rousseau offer constructive if competing visions of political philosophy, the simultaneous rejection of both *politics* and *philosophy* by the Frankfurt School reveals quite how negative their dialectic finally is. For the Frankfurt School, there can be no redeeming quality in either "particularism" or "universality," in either "community" or "autonomy," in either "liberalism" or "communitarianism," because for them these are finally false divisions that merely obscure the overarching power relationships that underlie and make fundamentally similar all attempts to seek human improvement in the political realm.

Chapter 5 concludes the study with a broader examination of current debates on what is alternatively held to be "cosmopolitanism" versus "patriotism," or "universalism" versus "particularism," as I described it earlier. I turn to this issue in an attempt to reengage the many themes that the *Odyssey* subtly addresses with recent concerns of political theory. Many of these contemporary debates arise first as a response to multiculturalism, with various thinkers on the Left aiming their criticism against others on the Left for their multiculturalist stance. However, the cosmopolitan Left also increasingly engages with the traditional Right—once fierce critics of multiculturalism and defenders of a form of universalism who now, in response to cosmopolitan arguments, revisit the arguments of Burke and Maistre in defense of locality and tradition. Underlying most of these contemporary debates are current concerns about the fate of the nation-state, the threat of ethnic and nationalist fervor, and the prospects of Enlightenment dreams of cosmopolitanism against the likelihood of a market-driven homogenization of popular culture and branded products.

The *Odyssey*, of course, has little or nothing to say directly about these pressing contemporary concerns. However, what the analyses by Plato and Rousseau will suggest, and the resistance demonstrated by the *Odyssey* to claims of the Enlightenment leveled by Horkheimer and Adorno will reveal, is the recurrent attractiveness of the *Odyssey* in giving dimension and depth to this most ancient debate between those of a particularist and a universalist perspective. Although the insufficiency of Horkheimer and Adorno's critique of the Enlightenment would appear to help the prospects of those seeking to reclaim the Enlightenment's embrace of cosmopolitanism, at the same time the force of the *Odyssey*'s manifold lessons about the simultaneity of human longing for and limits on transcendence presents a powerful middle ground between today's two competing positions. If, as I suggest in the following chapters, the *Odyssey* offers us a story that helps us get beyond recent debates in the culture wars, so, too, I would like to conclude, the *Odyssey* and subsequent attentive readers of the *Odyssey* help us to formulate a conception of "limited transcendence" that would seem the most possible and most attractive option for a human perspective on and relation with the world.

In the chapters that follow, I attempt to tell the story of political philosophy by demonstrating the storytelling quality of some of its preeminent philosophers. At the same time, I demonstrate how a work of poetry—the *Odyssey* of Homer— can be interpreted *politically* and how its political elements come to be adopted or transformed as the story of political philosophy unfolds. Political philosophy will thus be revealed in both its particularist and universal guises: as poetic in quality, but philosophic in ambition; as rooted in political communities and temporal circumstances, but tapping both its past traditions and engaging in more timeless speculations. I offer one possible interpretation of the *Odyssey*, but subsequent chapters on Plato, Rousseau, and Vico and the Frankfurt School will provide alternative and competing interpretations. My interpretation of the

Odyssey attempts to prepare the way for these latter interpretations by making a case for the *Odyssey's* political aspect; however, unavoidably, my own interpretation is undeniably formed and influenced by those philosophers who follow. The works "whisper" to one another, and the eavesdropper is ever uncertain which words are uttered by the voices and which are the echoes.

Notes

1. The phrase, as well as its broader definition, is found in James D. Hunter's *Culture Wars* (New York: Basic, 1991).

2. See, for example, Sanford Levinson's discussion of the Constitution's inherent "undefinability" in *Constitutional Faith* (Princeton, NJ: Princeton University Press, 1988).

3. The most notorious moment in the debate over the core curriculum at Stanford came during a march led by the Reverend Jesse Jackson when the students chanted, "Hey, hey, ho, ho, Western Culture's got to go!"

4. For a summary of the Stanford debate and the outcome from a reformer's perspective, see Marie Louise Pratt, "Humanities for the Future: Reflections on the Western Culture Debate at Stanford," in *The Politics of Liberal Education*, ed. Darryl J. Gless and Barbara Herrnstein Smith (Durham, NC: Duke University Press, 1992), 13–31. Critical summaries of the debate can be found in Dinesh D'Souza, *Illiberal Education: The Politics of Race and Sex on Campus* (New York: Free Press, 1991), chap. 3, and in William J. Bennett, *The De-valuing of America: The Fight for Our Culture and for Our Children* (New York: Simon & Schuster, 1992), chap. 5.

5. Alexander Hamilton, John Jay, and James Madison, *The Federalist* (New York: Modern Library, n.d.), 3.

6. See John Hart Ely, *Democracy and Distrust: A Theory of Judicial Review* (Cambridge, MA: Harvard University Press, 1980), on the view that the Constitution is an expansive document. Justice William Brennan's 1985 speech is an excellent example of a "changing standards" argument. A conservative response to this view of a "living Constitution" is afforded by then Justice (now Chief Justice) William Rehnquist ("The Notion of a Living Constitution," *Texas Law Review* 54 [1976]: 693–706).

7. See Pratt, "Humanities for the Future." 1992.

8. See Roland Barthes's "The Death of the Author" in *Image, Music, Text*, trans. and ed. by Stephen Heath (New York: Hill and Wang, 1977), for postmodernist background to the indefinability of texts.

9. Even would-be critics of the canon have had their minds changed by delving into the canon's contents: John Evan Seery discovered after teaching the Stanford "Great Books" course (despite misgivings) that "the 'Western tradition' consists not of a protracted pack of high-minded cultural elites (or those in effect promoting elitism) but rather encompasses an extraordinary series of cultural subversives, one right after the other, with Socrates and Jesus as the most famous." Cited in Benjamin R. Barber, *An Aristocracy of Everyone: The Politics of Education and the Future of America* (New York: Ballantine, 1992), 105.

10. Bennett, *The De-valuing of America*, 162.

11. Bennett, *The De-valuing of America*, 173.

12. Bennett, *The De-valuing of America*, 174.

13. Despite his reputation as *the* preeminent conservative defender of the canon, Allan Bloom has recognized the danger in conservatives' attempts to defend the "canon" by accepting the use of that specific word and the concept of unchanging uniformity that underlies it. "'The canon' is the newly valued, demagogically intended, expression for the books taught and read by students at the core of their formal education. But as soon as one adopts the term, as both sides have—foolishly so for those who defend Dante, Shakespeare, and Kant—the nature of the debate has thereby been determined. For *canon* means what is established by authority, by powers, hence not by criteria that are rationally defensible" (in "Western Civ," *Giants and Dwarfs: Essays 1960–1990* [New York: Simon & Schuster, 1990]). Bloom's own arguments in *The Closing of the American Mind* indicate his awareness that "canonical" works are not an organized conspiracy of repression, inasmuch as he poses the thought of Plato and Aristotle against that of Nietzsche and Heidegger. Critics of Bloom—few who have probably read, much less understood, his book—take him to be simply a defender of "the Great Books" in the likeness of Mortimer Adler or E. D. Hirsch. Pratt, for example, contends that Bloom and his followers "simply have trouble seeing how good books could possibly do any harm" (Pratt, "Humanities for the Future," 16). One who has read Bloom's arguments about the dangers of nihilistic German political theory for the United States simply could not make such a baldly mistaken assertion.

14. Jorge Luis Borges, "Kafka and His Precursors," trans. James E. Irby, in *Labyrinths: Selected Stories and Other Writings*, ed. Donald A. Yates and James E. Irby (New York: New Directions, 1962), 201.

15. Eliot's argument is less radical than Borges's because Eliot attempts to fit this subversive theory into an otherwise orderly conception of tradition. He writes: "The existing monuments form an ideal order among themselves, which is modified by the introduction of a new (a really new) work of art among them.... The relations, proportions, values of each work of art toward the whole are readjusted; and this is conformity between the old and the new" (T. S. Eliot, "Tradition and the Individual Talent," in *Selected Essays* [New York: Harcourt, Brace & World, 1932], 5). It is almost amusing to observe Eliot attempting to escape from the implications of his theory: by using such words as "monument" and "work of art," he attempts to give literary works more solidity than they otherwise might actually possess. For an appreciative critique of Eliot's position, see George Steiner, *In Bluebeard's Castle: Some Notes towards the Redefinition of Culture* (New Haven, CT: Yale University Press, 1971), chap. 3.

16. Barber, *An Aristocracy for Everyone*, 123.

17. Sheldon S. Wolin, *The Presence of the Past: Essays on the State and the Constitution* (Baltimore: Johns Hopkins University Press, 1989), 84.

18. Denis Diderot, *Encyclopedia: Selections by Diderot, D'Alembert, and a Society of Men of Letters*, trans. Nelly S. Hoyt and Thomas Cassirer (Indianapolis, IN: Bobbs-Merrill, 1965). Cited in George H. Sabine, *A History of Political Theory*, 4th ed. (Hinsdale, IL: Dryden Press), 516–17.

19. Condorcet, (Marie-Jean-Antoine-Nicolas Cavitat) Marquis de, "Sketch for a Historical Picture of the Progress of the Human Mind" (1793), in *Condorcet—Selected Writings*, ed. Keith Michael Baker (Indianapolis, IN: Bobbs-Merrill, 1976).

20. Edmund Burke, *Reflections on the Revolution in France* (1790; reprint, New York: Dutton, Everyman's Library, 1964), 55–56.

21. Cited in Stephen Holmes, *The Anatomy of Antiliberalism* (Cambridge, MA: Harvard University Press, 1993), 14.

22. Michael Oakeshott, *Rationalism in Politics and Other Essays* (London: Methuen, 1962), 1–36.

23. Leo Strauss, *Liberalism Ancient and Modern* (Ithaca, NY: Cornell University Press, 1989), v–ix.

24. Todd Gitlin, "The Left, Lost in the Politics of Identity," *Harper's* 287 (September 1993): 16–20.

25. Martha Nussbaum, *For Love of Country: Debating the Limits of Patriotism*, ed. Joshua Cohen (Boston: Beacon, 1996) and *Cultivating Humanity* (Cambridge, MA: Harvard University Press, 1997); Conor Cruise O'Brien, *On the Eve of the Millennium* (New York: Free Press, 1994); Russell Jacoby, *The End of Utopia: Politics and Culture in an Age of Apathy* (New York: Basic Books, 1999); Todd Gitlin, *The Twilight of Common Dreams: Why America Is Wracked by Culture Wars* (New York: Metropolitan Books, 1995); S. E. Bronner, *Socialism Unbound* (New York: Routledge, Chapman and Hall, 1990), and *Ideas in Action* (Lanham, MD: Rowman & Littlefield, 1999).

26. David A. Hollinger, *Postethnic America* (New York: Basic, 1995), 106; Jacoby, *End of Utopia*, 33.

27. Roger Kimball, *Tenured Radicals: How Politics Has Corrupted Our Higher Education* (New York: Harper and Row, 1990), 3.

28. Victor Davis Hanson and John Heath, *Who Killed Homer?* (New York: Free Press, 1998), xvi–xvii.

29. Hanson and Heath, *Who Killed Homer?* 7, xvii. Werner Jaeger summarized his own thoughts in *Paideia* in a chapter entitled "Homer the Educator" as follows: "We must not underestimate the immeasurable effect on later Greece of Homer's creation of a complete human world. That world was the first work of the Panhellenic spirit: it made the Greeks conscious for the first time that they were a nation and thereby set an ineffaceable stamp on all later Greek culture" (*Paideia: The Ideals of Greek Culture*, 3 vols., trans. Gilbert Highet [New York: Oxford University Press, 1945], 1:56). See also Jaeger's early critique of cultural "leveling" in *Humanistische Reden und Vorträge*, 2d ed. (Berlin: Walter de Gruyter, 1960), 117–24.

30. Cited in D'Souza, *Illiberal Education*, 157.

31. Stanley Fish, "The Common Touch," in Gless and Herrnstein Smith, *Politics of Liberal Education*, 247.

32. A good example of this latter inconsistency is afforded by the example of a self-declared "tenured radical," Cary Nelson, who, in discussing how he went about designing his model course on modern poetry, stressed the importance of including "many important perspectives about race, class, and gender." The poems comprising this "progressive pedagogy" were assigned because they had something to *teach*: one reads them for their content and for the ability of the words to present new perspectives and information to students. Nelson also stressed the need to present aspects of the traditional canon as well. However, it was not assumed that the poems included in the *Norton Anthology of Modern Poetry* could instruct; rather, it was the *circumstances* surrounding the very *inclusion* of those poems within the "canon" that instructed more than their content did. Thus, rather than simply assigning those poems, Nelson instead assigned the *table of contents* from several editions of the *Norton Anthology* so that the students could learn "how little progress it had made in expanding the canon" (Cary Nelson, *Manifesto of a Tenured Radical* [New York: New York University Press, 1997], 91). One of the poems Nelson approvingly assigned revealed his assumption that "canonical" works not only offered no instructive content but, in fact, undermined justice and decency. A 1929 poem by Lucia Trent ("Pa-

rade the Narrow Turrets") reads, "What do you care if blacks are lynched beneath a withering sky? / What do you care if two men burn to death in a great steel chair"—"Thumb over your well-worn classics with clammy and accurate eyes, / Teach freshman [sic] to scan Homer and Horace and look wise" (Cited in Nelson, *Manifesto of a Tenured Radical*, 88). The choice is clear: be committed to justice and compassion for humanity, inspired by "noncanonical" poets, or read Homer and become an irrelevant pedant.

33. Henry George Liddel and Robert Scott (A *Greek-English Lexicon* [Oxford, U.K.: Clarendon Press], 1968) offer the following translations for *polutropos*: "much-turned," "travelling," "wandering," "turning many ways," "versatile," "ingenious," "changeful," even "shifting and shifty." Richmond Lattimore's translation, "man of many ways," is perhaps the best compromise because it reflects both aspects of traveling and ingeniousness. For a discussion of the term, see Pietro Pucci's *Odysseus Polutropos* (Ithaca, NY: Cornell University Press, 1987).

34. See W. B. Stanford, *The Ulysses Theme* (Oxford, U.K.: Basil Blackwell, 1963). Stanford remains the most exhaustive account of Odysseus's various reappearances in ancient and modern literature. See also Pietro Boitani, *The Shadow of Ulysses: Figures of a Myth*, trans. Anita Weston (Oxford, U.K.: Clarendon Press, 1994). Although less exhaustive, Boitani nevertheless provides a more subtle and evocative analysis of the "exploration" theme most famously rendered by Dante in the *Inferno*.

35. Boitani, *The Shadow of Odysseus*, chap. 1.

36. Throughout my analysis, I will use Richmond Lattimore's translations of the *Iliad* and the *Odyssey* (*The Iliad of Homer*, trans. Richmond Lattimore [Chicago: University of Chicago Press, 1951]; *The Odyssey of Homer*, trans. Richmond Lattimore [New York: HarperCollins, 1965, 1967]). Occasionally, particularly regarding technical terms or words that will have later resonance in political theory, I indicate the word in transliterated Greek following the English translation. Greek versions of selected passages are provided from the Loeb editions of the epics. Additionally, I have adopted the customary manner of citing the Homeric epics. Citations to the *Iliad* utilize a Roman numeral for the Book number and arabic numerals for the line numbers (e.g., VI.11–12), whereas citations to the *Odyssey* will adopt both arabic numerals for the Book and line numbers (e.g., 6.11–12).

37. See Boitani, *The Shadow of Odysseus*, chap. 1. In his fascinating account, Boitani relates how Dante's version of Odysseus's later voyages would be taken up in the Renaissance to apply to the journey of Christopher Columbus to the New World. In this manner, Odysseus can be said to have figuratively "discovered" America. According to Boitani (*The Shadow of Odysseus*, 68–92), given the characteristic American trait of forlorn rootlessness, it should come as no surprise that in American literature Odysseus would often serve as a typological figure of wayfaring adventure, for example, in the works of Poe and Melville.

38. See *The Odyssey*, trans. A. T. Murray (Cambridge, MA: Harvard University Press, Loeb Classical Library, 1919), 1:394–95, n. 1.

39. See Stanford, *The Ulysses Theme*, 87–89.

40. Hannah Arendt, *Between Past and Future* (New York: Viking, 1968), 241.

41. Stanford's *The Ulysses Theme*.

42. Michael J. Sandel, *Liberalism and Limits of Politics* (New York: Cambridge University Press, 1982); Jean Bethke Elshtain, *Real Politics* (Baltimore: Johns Hopkins University Press, 1997), and *Augustine and the Limits of Politics* (South Bend, IN: University of Notre Dame Press, 1995); Christopher Lasch, *The True and Only Heaven* (New York: Norton, 1991) and *The Revolt of the Elites* (New York: Norton, 1995).

43. Michael J. Sandel, *Democracy's Discontent* (Cambridge, MA: Harvard University Press, 1996), chap. 4; Jean Bethke Elshtain, *Public Man, Private Woman* (Princeton, NJ: Princeton University Press, 1981) and *Real Politics*; Christopher Lasch, *Haven in a Heartless World* (New York: Basic, 1977).

44. Nussbaum in *For Love of Country* and *Cultivating Humanity*.

45. The phrases come, respectively, from Nathan Glazer and Elaine Scarry in essays of the same title in Nussbaum's *For Love of Country*.

46. Bruno Snell, *The Discovery of the Mind in Greek Philosophy and Literature*, trans. T. G. Rosenmeyer (New York: Dover, 1982), 31. Charles Taylor cites Snell approvingly as a definitive source in his *Sources of the Self* (Cambridge, MA: Harvard University Press, 1989), 117–18.

47. Hermann Fränkel, *Early Greek Poetry and Philosophy: A History of Greek Epic, Lyric, and Prose to the Middle of the Fifth Century*, trans. Moses Hadas and James Willis (New York: Harcourt Brace Jovanovich, 1973), 80.

48. Bernard Williams, *Shame and Necessity* (Berkeley: University of California Press, 1993).

~

CHAPTER ONE

The *Odyssey* as Political Theory

Ithaca gave you the splendid journey.
Without her you would not have set out.
She hasn't anything else to give you.

And if you find her poor, Ithaca has not deceived you.
So wise have you become, of such experience,
That already you will have understood what these Ithacas mean.

—C. P. Cavafy, "Ithaka"

Freeing Homer

If Homeric man possesses no inner depths, no ability to see his situation from outside the social structures that govern his life—his place, according to M. I. Finley, being "predetermined"—finally lacking the ability to *choose* between meaningful alternatives, then, according to this worldview, this lack of true autonomy only reflects a fundamental lack of creative autonomy on the part of the poet Homer.[1] Homer's artistic world is as structured as his characters' heroic world. This view, of course, finds forceful expression in the work of Milman Parry, who demonstrated that Homeric poetry follows a strict repetitive structure that allows only little variation.[2] Yet beyond these metrical limitations, numerous scholars have asserted a more fundamental limitation of vision and imagination that governs Homeric poetry and allows us to appreciate the poetry as cultural iconography, but fundamentally uninstructive and even diverting from more contemporary concerns.

It does not surprise to hear multiculturalist Barbara Herrnstein Smith relate that "there is no knowledge, no standard, no choice that is objective. Even Homer is a product of a specific culture, and it is possible to imagine cultures in which Homer would not be very interesting."[3] It is startling to read Herrnstein Smith's use of "even," as if admitting momentarily that Homer might occupy a unique position that might appeal across cultures; but rapidly she avoids this conclusion, using the *even* instead to note that "even" the singular antiquity and "even" presumably the legitimate claim of Homer to an exalted position in the Western canon holds only limited appeal for anyone outside of that limited cultural context. What is most striking about Herrnstein Smith's formulation, however, is the causal assumption underlying her observation of Homer's limited relevance—not that Homer was the primary *founder* and initiator of Western culture, as was argued by Jaeger and more recently by Hanson and Heath, but rather that he is merely its product. One wonders, in Herrnstein Smith's view, from what source human culture arises, but clearly the source is a force under which even a given culture's most creative and unique artists can only labor in unconscious servitude. Like Homeric man, according to one version, Homer is powerless to write anything that will interest more than a small group of ancient Greeks and, Herrnstein Smith suggests, several contemporary, white, European or American males.

More surprising is how pervasive a version of this view of Homer as the involuntary servant of his culture is, even among sympathetic interpreters of Homer. Notable among these interpreters is Alasdair MacIntyre, who in *After Virtue* expounds a largely admiring view of the ancients, especially Aristotle, for allowing the possibility of ethical choice and agency. This admiration, however, does not extend to Homer, about whom MacIntyre writes largely by paraphrasing the version of Homeric man found in Snell, Fränkel, and Finley. Moreover, MacIntyre goes further by suggesting that Homer, in framing such limited characters, was himself limited by poetic and historical circumstances. MacIntyre makes this point in the larger context of suggesting that we are ourselves governed by circumstances wholly outside our choosing, in an effort to refute the more liberal assertion of infinite choice in self-fashioning. Yet the effect of MacIntyre's argument is simultaneously to constrain our possibilities to some extent by noting the influences such as Homer that have contributed to our identities—arguing that "we are, whether we acknowledge it or not, what the past has made us"—and to constrain Homeric poetry *entirely* because, given that it represents for MacIntyre the West's starting point, there were no other "options" such as those of which we may now avail ourselves.[4] If subsequent history and ethical development, especially Aristotle, allow contemporary humanity some volition and agency given a broader tradition from which to select, Homer had only Homeric society; and like Homeric man, Homer the poet could only write in a specific and predictable way that precludes the possibility of true ethical choice.

MacIntyre proves strikingly receptive to Marx's argument about the development of cultural history as analogous to the development of the human organism. He approvingly quotes Marx's observation about the historical, cultural, and material determinants that allowed for the creation of Homer's epics and that preclude such creation now. Writing in the *Grundrisse*, Marx begins by discussing "Production," observing that "material production" determines not only implements available to human beings, but also the very cultural existence of humanity. Rejecting Rousseau's image of the "naturally independent, autonomous subject" as nothing more than "simple-mindedness," Marx instead argues that "the more deeply we go back into history, the more does the individual, and hence also the producing individual, appear as dependent, as belonging to a greater whole."[5] Humanity is never the wholly autonomous agent imagined by Rousseau or the "Robinsonades" that arose from the imagination of utopians like Defoe; rather humanity is always fundamentally defined by the material conditions of production at a given point in history.

Marx demonstrates the derivative nature of culture, in this case, the arts, from the material conditions that afford its creative materials. Using Homer as his example, Marx argues that the epics of Homer could only be conceived by a culture in which mythology is the manner of fundamental explanation, in which the "real mastery of nature" represented by "the self-acting mule spindles and railways and locomotives and electrical telegraphs" have not yet replaced mythology's ability to dominate nature "in the imagination and by the imagination."[6] If the subject of Homer's epics is dominated by the mythology of a simpler time, so too its form is only possible in an age in which the printing press is still unimagined. "Do not the song and the saga and the muse necessarily come to an end with the printer's bar, hence do not the necessary conditions of epic poetry vanish?"[7] Yet, despite the widely disparate material conditions separating contemporary humanity from Homer's characters, Marx must nevertheless account for the appeal of Homer across the ages, even as the material conditions that permitted the epic form have been surpassed. Marx suggests that the artistic pleasure that Homer provides is akin to the attractiveness that childish art can exercise over adults. The Greeks, he writes, "were normal children. The charm of their art for us is not in contradiction to the undeveloped stage of society on which it grew. . . . [It] is its result, rather, and is inextricably bound up, rather, with the fact that the unripe social conditions under which it arose, and could alone arise, can never return."[8]

MacIntyre finds Marx's analysis finally compelling, explaining why the ancient myths continue to fascinate but fail to instruct properly as do later expressions of moral philosophy. In exploring the origins of virtue in Western society, MacIntyre writes that "any attempt to write this history will necessarily encounter Marx's claim that the reason why Greek epic poetry has the power over us which it still retains derives from the fact that the Greeks stand to civilized modernity as the child to the adult." Although averse to assumptions of contemporary philosophical superiority to antiquity—arguing throughout *After Virtue* that Aristotelian moral philosophy is superior to that of the more modern Nietzsche—MacIntyre nevertheless acknowledges Marx's perspicacity, at least as regards the Homeric epics. For, in considering Homer's poems, we must ask "whether the narrative forms of the heroic age are not mere childlike storytelling, so that moral discourse while it may have use of fables and parables as aids to the halting moral imagination ought in its more serious adult moments to abandon the narrative mode for a more discursive style and genre."[9]

Viewing Homer as "childlike" has an even more ancient pedigree than the observations of Marx and more recently MacIntyre. This sentiment was expressed earlier by Giambattista Vico in his *New Science*, which sought to explicate a historical explanation to the development of civilization in part by turning to Homer. By exploring the distinctions between the *Iliad* and the *Odyssey*, Vico was able to expand on Longinus's observation that the former appeared to be the work of a young man and the latter of an old man.[10] Instead of attributing the distinctions to the aging of a single poet, Vico instead credits the development of the poems to changes within ancient civilization itself. According to this reading, then, Homer is merely an expression of ancient civilization, an idea akin to Herrnstein Smith's suggestion. However, unlike Herrnstein Smith's assumption that Homer exerts little influence outside a limited cultural circumstance, Vico especially argues that the mythic origins of Western humanity inherent in the Homeric epics continue to exercise considerable influence over the subsequent course of human history, an argument similar to the one that Marx and MacIntyre pose, but ultimately more sympathetic to the positive and, indeed, inescapable qualities of those mythic influences.

In particular, Vico argues that Homer is the greatest and most sublime of all the ancient poets, and he concludes that the "true" Homer is, in fact, the ancient civilization of Greece itself. Homer's greatest educational epic is the more advanced and civilized *Odyssey*: by implication, if Greece is the most important "poet" of antiquity and the *Odyssey* its most important poem, then to the lessons of the *Odyssey* we can attribute most of modern humanity's virtues and vices. Inasmuch as ancient myth has constituted modern institutions and determinatively formed human "nature," then by logical extension one must turn to the *Odyssey* for evidence of modern humanity's origins. It is precisely in this spirit that Max Horkheimer and Theodor Adorno take up some of Vico's observations in their original extension of Vico's thesis of the intertwining of myth and enlightenment in their remarkable analysis of the *Odyssey* in the *Dialectic of*

Enlightenment.[11] The connection between Vico and these founders of the Frankfurt School and their respective analyses of the *Odyssey* will be discussed in more detail in chapter 4; for present purposes, however, it is of special interest to note some of Horkheimer and Adorno's most severe conclusions about the *Odyssey* that bear on my analysis in this chapter.

For Horkheimer and Adorno, the *Odyssey* represents the earliest expression of the inescapable condition of human depravity. Departing in this respect from Marx and subsequently from MacIntyre, humanity's "childhood" has never been superseded because humanity has never truly progressed, nor can humanity hope to progress. Instead, the original condition of exploitation both of nature and of other human beings that Horkheimer and Adorno detect in the *Odyssey* remains an inescapable feature of the human condition. The child and the adult are never truly separate: the myth from which human societies arise undergirds our belief in nature's objectivity, in historical progress, and in the demands of self-preservation and aggrandizement that supposedly mark the modern era. The Enlightenment, in its single-minded pursuit to discover nature's secrets, to objectify both humanity and nature under its searching and exploiting gaze, effectively creates a new mythic discourse: the tools of enlightenment claim to afford an all-encompassing explanation to human and natural phenomena. Just as primitive humans turned to Zeus to explain thunder, modern humans turn to science and instrumental reason to explain, among other things, beauty, human emotion, and politics. Horkheimer and Adorno locate this dual embrace of myth and Enlightenment originally in the *Odyssey*, especially in Odysseus's will for self-preservation at all costs, his domination of other human beings, and his view of nature as fundamentally an object for exploitation. In this respect, the *Odyssey* is "the basic text of European civilization."[12]

All of these explanations, perhaps especially this last by Horkheimer and Adorno, view the *Odyssey* as the involuntary expression of certain cultural traits and foundations that Homer only channeled without essentially creating. Like his character Odysseus, Homer had no choice: Odysseus was as much an unwitting prisoner of his own culture as Homer proved to be in writing his "representative" works. The assumptions underlying each of these explanations should be finally tested against the text of the *Odyssey* itself and, by extension, against subsequent understandings of the *Odyssey* arrived at in differing ways by Plato and Rousseau. Then we can return to a lengthier consideration of Vico and of Horkheimer and Adorno to determine the final merit of this understanding of Odysseus of many ways, but no choices. The *Odyssey* will be examined with special attention to the claims of Odysseus as exploiter of nature, as captive without choice, and as political dominator of his society.

The Nature of the *Odyssey*

The human position in the Homeric world is a precarious one. Everywhere and always the gods threaten oblivion: on the sea, by land, on the battlefield, or in one's sleep, the gods function in a natural world that is more dangerous than nurturing. Yet, for all the arbitrary violence that nature visits on humanity, a surprisingly peaceful coexistence is nevertheless wrought by humankind with this seeming nemesis. As Jean-Pierre Vernant has written, "In general, humans don't seek to transform nature, but to conform to nature."[13]

Of all the heroes portrayed in both of the epics, perhaps Odysseus's relationship to nature is the most ambiguous but hence the most revealing of the human condition and finally the place of politics in the human and natural spheres. The whole of the *Odyssey*—particularly inasmuch as the epic is suffused with chthonic locations, primal and powerful female goddesses, and a remarkable emphasis on the development of the human arts and sciences as a means of extracting sustenance from nature—marks a radical departure from the mise-en-scène of the *Iliad*. But of particular notoriety even in the *Odyssey* is an episode in Book 9, when Odysseus, surveying an uninhabited island next to the island of the Cyclopes, remarks in almost a personal aside on the island's inviting natural qualities, even its wealth:

> There is a wooded island that spreads, away from the harbor,
> neither close in to the land of the Cyclopes nor far out
> from it; forested; wild goats beyond number breed there,
> for there is no coming and going of humankind to disturb them,
> nor are they visited by hunters, who in the forest
> suffer hardships as they haunt the peaks of mountains,
> neither again is it held by herded flocks, nor farmers,
> but all its days, never plowed up and never planted,
> it goes without people and supports the bleating wild goats.
> For the Cyclopes have no ships with cheeks of vermilion,
> nor have they builders of ships among them, who could have made them
> strong-benched vessels, and these if made could have run them sailings
> to all the various cities of men, in the way that people
> cross the sea by means of ships and visit each other,
> and they could have made this island a strong settlement for them.
> For it is not a bad place at all, it could bear all crops
> in season, and there are meadowlands near the shores of the grey sea,
> well-watered and soft; and there could be grapes grown there endlessly,
> and there is smooth land for plowing, men could reap a full harvest
> always in season, since there is very rich subsoil. Also
> there is an easy harbor, with no need for a hawser
> nor anchor stones to be thrown ashore nor cables to make fast;

one could just run ashore and wait for the time when the sailors'
desire stirred them to go and the right winds were blowing.
(9.116–139)

At first glance, in accordance with the reading by Horkheimer and Adorno in
Dialectic of Enlightenment, Odysseus appears here as transparently acquisitive,
viewing each natural element of so-called Goat Island through the eyes of human development rather than through an appreciation of its simple natural state.
Yet also present is a remarkably political aspect in his appraisal: what is most
lacking is not economic development in itself, but those useful arts that undergird
and afford the opportunity for political life. Other than the potentials for food—
and Odysseus is ever attentive to the needs of his stomach[14]—the island's other
obvious provision is that of "a strong settlement" comprised of laborers and artisans seeking together mutual protection and companionship. For lacking the useful
arts, in this instance shipbuilding, the Cyclopes cannot travel the "various cities
of men in the way that people / cross the seas by means of ship and visit each
other." The course of normal, even natural human relations drives people to visit
each other, to speak, and to share knowledge, goods, and stories.

The Cyclopes do not lack, strictly speaking, technical knowledge. The catalogue of Polyphemus's activities as he enters his cave after a day's shepherding
gives witness to an accomplished if still primitive *techne* as dairy farmer. The
Cyclopes' shortcoming is one of vision—notably that of inquisitiveness—and of
communicativeness, either among themselves or with others. As Norman Austin suggests, given the absence of social intercourse among the Cyclopes, all
activities live and die with their practitioners: "there is, simply, no tradition: each
Cyclops starts afresh, truly a *tabula rasa*."[15] Political communities preserve memory
as much as they allow the preservation of life: given the Cyclopes' lack of memory
born of their lack of inquisitiveness, Polyphemus's ultimate failure to perceive
the threat from Odysseus as well as the other Cyclopes' misunderstanding of
Polyphemus's pain (being that "Noman" injured him) result quite literally from
their ignorance of human community.[16]

For Odysseus, the absence of people knowledgeable in the practice of such
useful arts is indicative of a wider absence of *political* life, and as such he recognizes the deficiencies of the Cyclopes' social arrangements without having yet
encountered them. Seeing the undeveloped state of this easily reached island,
Odysseus rightly suspects that they might encounter on the populated island

a man who was endowed with great strength,
and wild, with no true knowledge of laws or any good customs.
(9.214–215)

His initial suspicion—one that might obviously have persuaded Odysseus from confronting Cyclops at all but for his combined selfishness for a guest-gift and desire for knowledge of what such creatures could be like (9.229)—is substantiated by his description to the Phaiacians of the Cyclopes' way of life:

> we sailed on further along,
> and reached the country of the lawless outrageous
> Cyclopes who, putting all their trust in the immortal
> gods, neither plow with their hands nor plant anything,
> but all grows for them without seed planting, without cultivation. . . .
> These people have no institutions, no meetings for councils;
> rather they make their habitations in caverns hollowed
> among the peaks of high mountains, and each one is the law
> for his own wives and children, and cares nothing about the others.
> (9.105–115)

Although the Cyclopes live in proximity to one another, they do not meet in order to deliberate, neither to settle conflict (which one imagines is settled through a test of strength) nor to satisfy what Aristotle described as the characteristics of "political animals," to see and to be seen, to speak and to listen, to rule and to be ruled.[17] Odysseus's disdain for the Cyclopes is not, after a fleeting initial impression, provoked by a developer's greedy eye but derives from Odysseus's understanding that humanity's ability to cultivate nature's bounty, to extend the flexible albeit naturally imposed boundaries over land and sea, is necessarily inseparable from the development of political life. Were food all that Odysseus desired, he might well have remained on Calypso's bountiful island, one that combined the plenty of Goat Island with the manicured splendors of the Phaiacian gardens.[18] In a similar vein, were the value of property his paramount interest, the unsettled island beside that of the Cyclopes clearly has more potential value than the already settled yet rocky Ithaca.[19] But Odysseus craves more than merely material satiation—he longs for "sight of the very smoke uprising / from his country," or, short of return, "longs to die" (1.58–59). There are many instances in the *Odyssey* during which Odysseus exhibits what might be deemed a kind of crass materialism, but almost always his interests in material bounty are conditioned by this overarching connection that draws him home. Thus, his appraisal of Goat Island, far from being simply acquisitive, is fundamentally political.

The extent to which Odysseus's vision is political becomes apparent when we compare his assessment of the Cyclopes to another similar political situation in the *Odyssey*. There is indeed another island described in the *Odyssey* that is remarkable for having "no meetings for councils" and where evidently "each one is the law for his own wives and children, and cares nothing about the others." This island, of course, is Ithaca itself, at least in the nineteen years since Odysseus's departure, before Athena prods Telemachus to call for a council meeting. As the aged Aigyptos reminds the assembled Ithacans, "Never has there been an assembly (*agora*) of us or any session / since great Odysseus went away in the hollow vessels" (2.26–27).[20] Telemachus asks the gathering of citizens to assist him in curtailing the behavior of the ravenous suitors; until now, the affairs of the ruling family of Ithaca have been solely the concern of that family, even given the absence of their *basileus*, Odysseus. Indeed, Telemachus has matured under a type of political organization that fundamentally assumes that all conflicts are private by nature and that excuses his summoning the assembly as the indulgence of private concerns in a public setting: "nor have I some . . . public matter to set forth and argue, but my own need, the evil that has befallen my household (*oikos*)" (2.44–45). By calling the assembly through Athena's prompting, Telemachus begins a process of education in which he will begin to see the entanglements of public and private life, and the extent to which a ruling family's seemingly private concerns are never strictly without implications for the polity at large. By extension, Odysseus vigorously pursued an explicitly political role in Ithaca by regularly seeking out the counsel of Ithaca's deliberative agora.[21]

Knowing Nature: Gods, Beasts, and Political Animals

If Odysseus evinces something approaching disdain at the Cyclopes' lack of political life—a disdain of a decidedly inhuman, even animal existence—further evidence suggests that such disdain derives from an understanding that an unmediated relationship between humanity and nature is largely impossible when one properly understands human limitations. Borrowing again from Aristotle's description of what constitutes a truly human life, one can find in the *Odyssey* the implicit acknowledgment that "one who is incapable of participating or who is in need of nothing through being self-sufficient (*autarkein*) is no part of a city, and so is either a beast or a god."[22] *Autarkein* is achieved through two possibilities that are not mutually exclusive: one may be "incapable of participating" or one may be "in need of nothing through being *autarkein*." How are we to understand Aristotle's conditions of those not included in the partnership (*koinōnia*) of the city? Clearly, one must be human or possessing of those qualities that entail full humanity. Those that are literally "beasts or gods" are disqualified from the possibility of political partnership through either their incapacity (the condition of the beasts) or their autarky (the condition of the gods). Yet is there something of these two conditions that draws these two excluded categories into commonality?

In the *Odyssey* the gods and the beasts share one notable quality in common:

the innate ability to apprehend nature in an immediate and unmediated fashion. Whereas humans constantly doubt the evidence of their senses—and rightly so, given the propensity of gods to disguise themselves as humans or beasts—the gods and the beasts of the *Odyssey* are never in doubt of their senses, which afford them a direct conduit to a thing's essence.[23] Jenny Strauss Clay has shown the stark difference between human vision and divine vision through an analysis of the word *eidenai*, which encompasses both the meaning "sight" and the meaning "knowledge," noting that: "The gulf between divine and mortal *eidenai* reveals itself most clearly in men's inability to see or recognize the gods. Hence men cannot have any sure knowledge of them."[24] Alternatively, the gods perceive one another at will regardless of disguise. Moreover, the gods possess a direct knowledge of nature's properties that is hidden to humans except through divine assistance.

Acknowledgment of this divine knowledge of nature is indicated by a god's own admission of that knowledge and its revelation to an unapprehending human. The only use of the word *phusis*, or nature, in the entirety of the Homeric corpus occurs in the *Odyssey* when Hermes reveals to Odysseus the herb that will protect him from the transformative powers of Circe. Significantly, the godly knowledge of a natural property in this case will allow a human to remain unscathed by direct divine power—it is divine knowledge of nature, more than divine powers, that distinguishes the gods from humans.

> So spoke Argeïphontes, and he gave me the medicine,
> which he picked out of the ground, and he explained the nature [*phusis*]
> of it to me. It was black at the root, but with a milky
> flower. The gods call it moly. It is hard for mortal
> men to dig up, but the gods have power to do all things.
> (10.302–306)

Hermes explicitly contrasts the gods with mortal beings by noting the difficulty that humans have extracting the herb from the concealing earth. Yet there is a certain commensurability between mortal and immortal physical ability, if the immortals nevertheless possess a distinct advantage in strength and skill.[25] What is implicitly *incommensurable* is the distinct immortal ability to see and know nature, a nature that is inaccessible to even the normally perceptive and resourceful Odysseus. Physically, human beings share many godlike attributes with the deities; but not that of immortality; yet in matters of apperception, mortal vision is enclosed in a fog that obscures true knowledge.[26]

Human frailty is highlighted by the ultimate ineffectiveness of Hermes' gift—part of the gods' exclusive knowledge of nature is the ability to know humanity as part of that nature, whereas humans are ever unaware of their own proximity

to the animalistic. Although Odysseus is not turned into a pig by Circe, he nevertheless falls prey to her wiles (if not outright spells), remaining with her for a
year until he is reawakened by his men. Though he does not outwardly manifest
the form of an animal, Odysseus falls into a torpor, a form of animal forgetfulness
of his home and his family, and must be reminded of his mission. Despite his
avowed and in most instances evident dedication to Ithaca, Odysseus is ultimately
nearly as susceptible as anyone to the temptations of oblivion.

Just as the immortal gods are capable of seeing and knowing the nature of
divine and earthly things without mediation or effort, so are the beasts endowed
with this ability of unmediated perception. In Book 17 of the *Odyssey*, although
Odysseus is disguised and unrecognizable to his closest friends, his enemies, even
his family, the hound Argos briefly glances at him and immediately recognizes
him:

> There the dog Argos lay in dung, all covered with dog ticks.
> Now, as he perceived that Odysseus had come close to him,
> he wagged his tail, and laid both his ears back; only
> now no longer had the strength to move any closer
> to his master. . . .
> But the doom of dark death now closed over the dog, Argos,
> when, after nineteen years had gone by, he had seen Odysseus.
> (17.300–304, 326–327)

Argos's sight ("he had seen," *idont'*, from *eidenai*) is remarkable: despite, on
the one hand, his physical deterioration (emphasized by tick infestation atop a
dung hill) and, on the other hand, the recitation of nineteen years passing, Argos
is still capable of easily recognizing his master without effort from his physically
weakened body, which cannot even lift itself. Like the gods, the beasts possess
senses that immediately comprehend a thing's nature, overcoming with ease those
obstacles that would make even basic human comprehension impossible. Alternatively, humankind in the *Odyssey* is ever uncertain of a thing's nature: Noemon
is confused whether it is a god or Mentor who has traveled with Telemachus on
his sea-journey (4.653–656), and likewise Odysseus himself expresses the difficulty of recognizing divine or mortal natures when he reproaches the suitors for
their cruelty:

> Antinoös, you did badly to hit the unhappy vagabond: a curse on you,
> if he turns out to be a god from heaven.
> For the gods do take on all sorts of transformations, appearing
> as strangers from elsewhere, and thus they range at large through the cities,
> watching to see which men keep laws and which are violent.
> (17.483–487)

Whether a being might be a beggar or a god remains a constant uncertainty to human beings. Odysseus here acknowledges the limits of human vision and suggests that justice must be pursued among human beings through laws—human contrivances erected to assist mortals living amid uncertainty. The irony in Odysseus's statement is that at that moment he is disguised as a lowly beggar—not the god of whom he warns Antinoös, but decidedly not the form of human that he appears to be either. Not only are mortals incapable of knowing the gods by sight, they cannot even trust their ability to recognize one another. This human uncertainty of their own senses drives them—unlike the gods or beasts—to embrace an admixture of nature and artifice, or politics, as the means to secure justice among each other.

Artifice and Nature

Surveying Goat Island, Odysseus sees the potential that unspoiled nature affords to humans in their quest to form political communities. From twenty-first-century perspective, it is a fearful gaze, one that reminds us of Columbus and Cortez, of native tribes wiped out, and of landscapes razed to provide for ever more luxurious living. Yet Odysseus does not endorse such a relationship with nature; his vision is less about creating wealth and dominion than about allowing human survival in order to pursue life together. As Norman Austin describes the human relationship with nature in the *Odyssey*, humans are not conceived in Homer as fundamentally opposed to nature: "Man, as a part of nature, is already of that order, but it is also his task to contribute to the maintenance of that order by imitation. Whether man structures nature with reproductions of his social forms . . . or whether the situation is reversed and social forms are derived from nature, the important fact is that Homeric man *believes* that the natural order exists independent of man and man is but the copy of that external order."[27]

Evidence of humanity's ambiguous relationship with nature, neither one of pure opposition nor one of pure unmediated identification, is suggested in the description of Odysseus's making of the marriage bed in Book 23:

What man has put my bed in another place? But it would be difficult
for even a very expert one, unless a god, coming
to help in person, were easily to change its position.
But there is no mortal man alive, no strong man, who lightly
could move the weight elsewhere. There is one particular feature
in the bed's construction. I myself, no other man, made it.
There was the bole of an olive tree with long leaves growing
strongly in the courtyard, and it was thick, like a column.

I laid down my chamber around this, and built it, until I
finished it, with close-set stones, and roofed it well over,
and added the compacted doors, fitting closely together.
Then I cut away the foliage of the long-leaved olive,
and trimmed the trunk from the roots up, planing it with a brazen
adze, well and expertly, and tried it straight to a chalkline,
making a bed post of it, and bored all the holes with an auger.
I began with this and built my bed, until it was finished.
(23.183–199)

The outset of this passage bears a striking resemblance to Hermes' words describing the "nature" of moly at 10.302–306, particularly inasmuch as Odysseus explicitly compares a god's physical ability to perform a certain task to a human's significantly less capable mortal endeavors.[28] Both activities suggest the incommensurable abilities of gods and humans, although on both occasions the *possibility* for mortals to accomplish the *physical* task is left open. Again, the difficulty lies in perceiving the *nature* of a thing. In the bed making, Odysseus possesses an advantage in perception that he lacked in the case of the wholly natural entity, moly—for the bed, Odysseus changed, by artifice and design, the nature of a natural object, placing a distinctively human imprint on its original form. Thus, "I myself, no other man, made it" (23.189).[29]

The bed maintains a remarkably dual aspect: it is both natural and artificial, a living organism inseparable from the earth yet an artistic icon. All of Odysseus's "craftiness" does not go toward remaking ordinary raw materials into a piece of unnoticed furniture; rather, his work is the crowning achievement of his *oikos*, a place both private (familial), hence natural, yet also public, inasmuch as the fate of his *oikos* is also intimately bound up with the fate of the *polis* itself.[30] His intensive labor is indicative of the direction Odysseus's activity would likely have taken had he actually decided to settle Goat Island and build there "a fortified town." Not destroying nature nor literally uprooting it, but fashioning from nature a mutual coexistence of necessary human artifice while maintaining nature's portion, Odysseus demonstrates through his craft a form of moderation and restraint in the ambivalent and undemarcated relationship between humanity and nature.[31]

Penelope's test, by means of which Odysseus is asked to identify himself through a knowledge of their shared existence, is achieved through this knowledge of nature and artifice, in this case the alteration of a natural object into a practical and symbolic object of wedded life. Like the bed itself, marriage represents in human life a profound mixture of the natural and the artificial: marriage contains the natural phenomena but augments it through human artifice. Such an understanding of this admixture is indicated in an earlier mention of the bed by

Penelope, expressed to Odysseus while still believing him to be a nameless beggar:

> It is in no way possible for people forever
> to go without sleep; and the immortals have given to mortals
> each his own due share [moira] all over the grain-giving corn land.
> So I shall go back again to my upper chamber,
> and lie on my bed, which is made a sorrowful thing now.
> (19.591–595)

Sleep is part of a human's nature ordained by the gods; it comes upon a human as naturally as plants grow from the earth. Yet, plants can be cultivated to form "grain-giving corn land"—as Odysseus assesses on Goat Island—and so can sleep be accomplished upon a crafted bed. Nature, too, demands reproduction, but humanity constructs around nature the frame of marriage: confined to nature's demands, human beings nevertheless manipulate its expression.

Marriage occupies that curiously central position between nature and artifice, combining natural imperatives of eros with the social forms that contain and direct it. Thus, marriage shares many common features with politics, and the two are viewed as intimately connected by Homer, inasmuch as both reflect the necessary and even admirable combination of the natural and the conventional. On Achilles' shield crafted by the god Hephaestus, there are two scenes pictured for the city at peace: one a marriage celebration, the other an agora dispensing justice (XVIII.489–508). On the shield, marriage and politics are equated: both are artifices that are built by humans to contain natural phenomena. Like Plato and then Aristotle, Homer endorses a natural source to political life but also suggests that its form is ordered by human invention. Jenny Strauss Clay notes this connection, writing:

> Marriage and justice, the continuity and legitimacy of the family, on the one hand, and the establishment of social order, on the other—both are essential to the city at peace, and both are central to the Odyssey. Marriage and justice are affairs of anthropoi, men like us; and while gods may legitimate both, neither demands constant divine intervention. The gods are not visible in the peaceful city; presumably they have retired to the lofty isolation of Olympus and allow the world to run itself for the most part.[32]

Politics, then, maintains the dual aspect that comprises the bed and marriage: it, too, is both natural and artificial, an artifice in some sense "crafted" by human skill from natural foundations, different from its natural antecedent but qualitatively superior, having been in some senses perfected beyond what nature could alone engender. This view is reflected in Odysseus's famous benediction on Nausicaa in praise of *homophrosyne* between man and wife and, by extension, to the relations between citizens in a *polis*:

> May the gods give you everything your heart longs for;
> may they grant you a husband and a house and sweet agreement [*homophrosyne*]
> in all things, for nothing is better than this, more steadfast
> than when two people, a man and his wife, keep a harmonious [*homophroneonte*]
> household; a thing that brings much distress to the people who hate them
> and pleasure to their well-wishers, and for them the best reputation.
> (6.180–185)

Marriage, and politics it is suggested, may begin at least by being nothing more than help to one's friends and harm to one's enemies. Yet, through human attempts at excellence, there are hints of nobler possibilities as well.

Odysseus and Human Community: Choosing Death

Marriage and politics both involve the attempt to extend one's influence and one's legacy beyond the span of one's lifetime, to bear children or to create institutions that outlive any individual. For all the promise of these endeavors, nevertheless the temptation of true immortality remains constant for the Homeric hero. Odysseus understands the true and only possibility for human immortality: not as a being that is literally undying, as is the case for the undying gods, but again through human artifice, now aided and ennobled by the goddess, through words and art. Like Tom Sawyer hearing his own eulogy, Odysseus is honored to hear his own future in the songs of Demodocus (8.72–83, 499–520). Odysseus's singular forbearance in sparing Phemios the bard indicates his esteem for poets. Phemios, in begging to be spared, perhaps unknowingly but rightly implores Odysseus in terms that appeal to Odysseus's sense of poetic destiny:

> You will be sorry in time to come if you kill the singer
> of songs. I sing to gods and to human people, and I am
> taught by myself, but the god has inspired in me songways
> of every kind. I am such a one as can sing before you
> as to a god.
> (22.345–349)

The link forged here between the gods and poetry is not infelicitous: for the Homeric society, poetry necessarily partakes of the immortal world. The poet is inspired by the Muse, figuratively becoming the outlet for the immortal perspective and hence capable of knowing what humans cannot know. The difference between the narrative of Homer and that of Odysseus is striking in this regard; whereas Homer is ever confident of which god inspired a human to act in some fashion, Odysseus must admit to ignorance of the source of motivation.[33]

Odysseus is supremely conscious of the immortal yet wholly human possibilities of poetry because of his firsthand knowledge of the immortality he did not accept—life everlasting with Calypso. As suggested earlier, thinkers such as Alasdair MacIntyre do not credit the Homeric heroes with the ability to even contemplate much less *make* a choice. For MacIntyre,

> the self of the heroic age lacks precisely that characteristic which . . . some modern moral philosophers take to be an essential characteristic of human self-hood: the capacity to detach oneself from any particular standpoint or point of view, to step backwards, as it were, and view and judge that standpoint or point of view from the outside. In heroic society there is no "outside" except that of a stranger. A man who tried to withdraw himself from his given position in heroic society would be engaged in the enterprise of trying to make himself disappear.[34]

MacIntyre's conclusion about the impossibility of achieving a standpoint of pure objectivity attracts and persuades; yet in considering Homer's heroes as incapable of *achieving* such removal from society at large, or objectivity, he similarly denies the *temptation* for objectivity, which was no less powerful for the Homeric heroes than it continues to be for modern humanity. The desire to (effectively or actually) become a god is precisely that selfsame desire for unmediated objectivity or for the direct and unmediated knowledge of nature.

Elsewhere Odysseus is explicitly offered such "detached" knowledge of the world, that clear unmediated vision only permitted to the gods. His hunger for this wisdom is manifest: he strains against the self-imposed and twice-fastened bonds that keep him from the Sirens' offer:

> Come this way, honored Odysseus, great glory of the Achaeans,
> and stay your ship, so that you can listen here to our singing;
> for no one else has ever sailed past this place in his black ship
> until he has listened to the honey-sweet voice that issues
> from our lips; then goes on well pleased knowing more than ever
> he did; for we know everything that the Argives and Trojans
> did and suffered in wide Troy through the gods' despite.
> Over all the generous earth we know everything that happens.
> (12.184–191)

Odysseus's *physical* temptation to fling himself off the ship to *possess* the Sirens' knowledge reveals the power of this offer over Odysseus; the rotting corpses of other humans who lay about the water's edge further indicate this power over all humans (12.45–46).[35] Yet, having experienced the magnitude of this temptation for immortal vision, and having been told of its likely result, Odysseus is well-prepared for Calypso's offer; while still holding forth a temptation to the mortal who faces death, Odysseus's decision is an informed one.[36]

The reality of the temptation that Calypso's offer entails should not be underestimated: at stake is Odysseus's eternal existence, either on the paradisic island with the beautiful and unaging goddess Calypso or among the immaterial shades in the cold necropolis, Hades. Within the epic itself we learn of Odysseus's existence on Calypso's island Ogygia at the outset (as related by Athena to Zeus, 1.48–59) and again return to his existence there after the *Telemachia* in Book 5. Yet, chronologically Odysseus's journey to Hades occurs *before* his exile on Ogygia, to be related later to the Phaiacians upon escaping Calypso in Book 11. Odysseus decides to refuse Calypso's offer of immortality, already having descended to the underworld and already having learned there his fate both in the near term, regarding his return to Ithaca, and in the longer term, concerning his mortal fate.

The classical analytical scholar Denys Page has suggested that the Hades episode is interpolated, given its ostensible dislocation from the rest of the work.[37] The episode is only dubiously connected to the epic by utilizing Circe in order to explain the purpose of the journey to the underworld. Odysseus must consult Teiresias, Circe informs him, who

will tell you the way [*hodon*] to go, the stages of your journey,
and tell you how to make your way home on the sea where the fish swarm.
(10.539–540)

Page has asserted that two requirements must be fulfilled for Circe to make this demand of Odysseus: "First, that Circe is unable herself to supply this information, secondly, that Teiresias will in fact do what she says he will do."[38] Page is further correct to note that neither of these conditions is fulfilled to the letter: for while Teiresias does give Odysseus certain directions concerning the island of Thrinicia and advises him on the state of affairs in Ithaca, it is nevertheless clear that Circe also knows the steps of Odysseus's immediate path, and far more precisely than does Teiresias (12.37–141). Nevertheless, Teiresias *does* afford Odysseus some information that Circe does not and such knowledge that would not contradict the spirit of Circe's instructions. From Teiresias Odysseus learns the subsequent course of his life, including a prediction of his manner of death. While *hodon* does not yet clearly indicate a metaphorical sense of "way" or "path" that the word later accrues in Greek philosophy and Christian thought, such a possibility is not forestalled by its absence and is in fact suggested by the type of information that is provided by Teiresias. Thus, in a larger sense Teiresias does explain to Odysseus his "way," not only in terms of his life-course, but also insofar as the implications that this knowledge has for his immediate journey home.

Teiresias's words are not Fate: they are predictions based on what has preceded and on knowledge of Odysseus's character, but they do not entail an external force that prevents all other possibilities. Thus Teiresias tells Odysseus that he has a "chance" of surviving to reach Ithaca, if "you can contain your own desire, and contain your companions" (11.103–104). Certain conditions must be met before certain outcomes can be achieved, but at all points Odysseus has a choice (within the limits imposed by previous choices, of course) until a decision is reached and the certain consequences are set in motion.[39] Thus one suspects that if Odysseus had eaten of the cattle of Helios, he would have died along with his men, just as he could have chosen to remain or to die at any point on his journey, temptations often contemplated by Odysseus. It is this knowledge that Odysseus to some extent controls his own fate that indicates how Teiresias's advice will assist Odysseus's journey home as much as Circe's subsequent advice helps him to get safely past some immediate dangers.

Odysseus's choice, made with the knowledge of Teiresias's prediction of his eventual death, is stressed indirectly at the outset of Book 5, in which for the final time Odysseus refuses Calypso's offer of immortality. The first line of the book departs from Homer's usual description of Dawn's "rosy fingers" and instead reads:

Now Dawn rose from her bed, where she lay by haughty Tithonus . . .
(5.1)

Homer calls attention to Eos's companion at this particular moment implicitly in order to contrast Tithonus with Odysseus—both men are mortals with whom goddesses fall in love and offer immortality. Tithonus accepts, and Eos begs Zeus to grant him immortal life, to which Zeus assents—literally. Tithonus lives, but ages, decays, and withers, eventually to be hidden from sight: he has been granted immortality without endless youth.[40] "Haughty" Tithonus accepts what is unacceptable for mortals to attain, but which is nevertheless clearly tempting to normal mortal desires.[41]

The poet notes that the desire of heroic mortal men to share the beds of goddesses is almost commonplace and that the offer of immortality is thus all the more attractive. However, Calypso reveals the dangers of such a course in her complaints to Hermes, who informs her of Zeus's decision to free Odysseus.

You are hard-hearted, you gods, and jealous beyond all creatures
beside, when you are resentful toward the goddesses for sleeping

openly with such men as each has made her true husband.
So when Dawn of the rosy fingers chose out Orion,
all you gods who live at your ease were full of resentment,
until chaste Artemis of the golden throne in Ortygia
came with a visitation of painless arrows and killed him;
and so it was when Demeter of the lovely hair, yielding
to her desire, lay with Iasion and loved him
in a thrice-turned field, it was not long before this was made known
to Zeus, who struck him down with a cast of shining thunderbolt.
(5.118–128)

Along with Tithonus, other evidence is given of mankind's propensity to accept the favor of immortal *eros* when offered. Also indicated is the propensity of the gods to prevent such liaisons, either through subterfuge (in the case of Tithonus) or through force (as with Orion and Iasion). Odysseus's decision not to accept Calypso's offer of immortality may be made with the knowledge of its likely consequences as well as out of his desire to be reunited with Penelope and his community. The causes are fundamentally connected: both indicate an acknowledgment of the proper scope of activity for humans, not as ersatz gods, but as mortals whose very limitations sometimes cause them to crave more than their measure. Odysseus knows from Teiresias that he will die *if* he chooses to return home and reenter the flow of time. The choice is not foreordained, although Odysseus's eventual death is if he decides to leave Calypso. His choice is made through his acceptance of his mortal position, as Odysseus begins his tale to the Phaiacians, thus framing his denial of Calypso's offer of immortality:

But [she] did not at all persuade the *thymos* in my chest as
nothing is more sweet in the end than country and parents
ever, even when far away one lives in a fertile
place, when it is an alien country, far from his parents.
(9.33–36)

Another Kind of Hero I: Menelaus

At nearly every point in the tale of his return, the homecoming of Odysseus is hindered; but the fact remains that he was only one of few of the many warriors of Troy who successfully returned. The story of *nostos*, the return of the victorious warriors from Troy, constituted a significant portion of the Trojan cycle: the immortal deeds of the ancient heroes were not limited to their battlefield prowess and to the tragedies of Hector and Achilles, but included as well the travails of those who did and did not return to tell those tales.[42] Achilles met his fate on the plains of Troy, but Agamemnon's *nostos* was an equally compelling tale. Agamemnon was not fated the glorious death of a hero amid the cries of war, but the ignominious treachery of his wife Clytemnaestra and her lover in his own bathtub. The *Odyssey* opens with Zeus recalling this most glaringly unsuccessful of the *nostoi* and so forms the frame in which Odysseus's own homecoming to an equally dangerous home will unfold (1.32–43).

As celebrated as Odysseus's long-awaited and trying *nostos* rightly is in the text of the *Odyssey*, often overlooked is another homecoming retold in those same pages, one almost equally dangerous and almost as long in coming—that of Menelaus, husband of Helen. Regaling the history of his own journey to Telemachus, who has come in search of news of his father, Menelaus imparts that his own journey required eight years and passage through locales nearly as exotic as those traversed by Odysseus (3.130–209; 4.81–85, 351–587). The two men, both returning late and after much sorrow and hardship, are meant to be compared. Homer composes their stories too similarly for us not to notice the resemblances and, more tellingly, their differences.

Nestor relates the outset of the journey home by the Achaeans following the sack of Troy. The gods are angry at the Greeks after the victory, but Menelaus and Odysseus along with a portion of the Achaeans decide to risk the journey. They have argued with Agamemnon, who chooses to stay behind with the rest of the army at Troy and there to seek to appease the gods' anger through sacrifice (3.130–146). For some reason not given, Menelaus and Odysseus argue after having gone some distance together; as a result, Odysseus returns to join Agamemnon at Troy. The subject of their argument provokes curiosity, as initially at least they mutually decided not to remain with Agamemnon; no further reason is stated that would have changed the situation. At least hinted at, however, is the nature of the offense against the gods, which was committed against none other than the Achaeans' benefactor and Odysseus's special protector, Athena.

> But after we had sacked the sheer citadel of Priam,
> and were going away in our ship, and the god scattered the Achaeans,
> then Zeus in his mind devised a sorry homecoming
> for the Argives, since not all were thoughtful or just [*noēmones oude dikaioi*]
> therefore many of them found a bad way home, because of
> the ruinous anger of the Grey-eyed One, whose father is mighty.
> (3.130–135)

Because "not all were thoughtful and just"—meaning that some were—some of the Achaeans returned home with ease, while others encountered considerable difficulties and even death, notably Menelaus, Odysseus, and Agamemnon. These three are the protagonists in the argument of how to appease Athena, while the others mentioned by Nestor—the Myrmidons, Philoctetes, Ideomeneus, and Nestor himself—return home with relative alacrity and ease (3.183–192).[43] We may deduce, then, that the actions of Agamemnon, Menelaus, and Odysseus during the sacking of Troy were considered by Athena not to be "thoughtful or just."

If Athena's anger can at least be understood to include these three prominent Achaeans, the fact that it is *Athena's* anger indicates a possible ground for the quarrel between Odysseus and Menelaus. Odysseus provides the cause of his grievance with Athena upon meeting her face-to-face for the first time after ten years, complaining bitterly:

> But I know this well: there was a time when you were kind to me
> in the days when we sons of the Achaeans were fighting in Troy land.
> But after we had sacked the sheer city of Priam,
> and went away in our ships, and the god scattered the Achaeans,
> I never saw you, daughter of Troy, after that.
> (13.312–318)

It is quite possible, given this admission and his awareness that he was no longer under the protection of Athena, even that it was *she* who was angry at him, that Odysseus realized his precarious position on the sea and rushed back to Troy in order to devote hecatombs to the goddess.[44]

The disagreement between Odysseus and Menelaus is thus significant, for whereas Odysseus suddenly realizes that he has no protection among the gods— that his patron goddess has turned against him in response to uncharacteristic lack of *noēmenes* if not *dikaios*—Menelaus alternatively proceeds with disregard for the possible consequences, thinking foremost "upon going home over the seas wide ridges" (3.141).

Each protagonist in this debate, then, acts according to his typical characteristics: Agamemnon is cautious, even cowardly;[45] Odysseus, while tempting the gods with *hubris*, ever pushing the border between moderation and excess, nevertheless heeds the goddess's anger and turns back; Menelaus is moved by desire for comfort, bravado, and disregard for the consequences of his action. Ironically, each is ultimately brought to an end that follows from their characteristics rather than from the original act against the goddess: Agamemnon is slain in a cowardly fashion; Odysseus makes a difficult way home through cleverness although his difficulties are exacerbated by his *hubris*;[46] and Menelaus finally arrives home with difficulty but finally in comfort, wealth, and self-satisfaction.

Norman Austin revels in the description of the Lacedaimonian residence and Telemachus's reception by Menelaus and Helen, "the poem's first exemplars of family *homophrosyne*. . . . As hosts they are impeccable—solicitous and discreet. Menelaus and Helen are ideal hosts in all practical ways . . . [and they have] an intuitive understanding of the hidden meanings behind spoken words, an understanding even of unspoken thoughts. Homer has endowed Menelaus, and more especially Helen, with such gifts in ample measure."[47]

In his attempt to capture what he describes as the "sympathetic magic" between Telemachus's experience in Lacedaimon with Menelaus and Helen and Odysseus's in Phaiacia, Austin's usual acuity is perhaps influenced too extensively by what might very well be *Telemachus's* perception of the interplay between Menelaus and Helen. A consideration of Menelaus without reference to Telemachus's concerns, however, may provide a considerably different portrait.

From the outset of his meeting with Telemachus, Menelaus evinces a certain breezy contentment and a disregard of the consequences of his actions through a seeming hyperbole regarding his affection for Odysseus:

> I would have settled a city in Argos for him, and made him
> a home, bringing him from Ithaca with all his possessions,
> his son, all his people. I would have emptied one city for him
> out of those that are settled round about under my lordship.
> (4.174–177)

Perhaps clearly impossible, an imaginary offer to a still-absent friend exaggerated to his bereaved son, nevertheless the import of Menelaus's vision and his consideration of politics stands revealed. Not only is he willing to uproot the island community of Ithaca to be resettled in Lacedaimon, but he recommends resettling an existing community whose inhabitants will be turned out.[48] Compared to Odysseus's vision on Goat Island—where he contemplates the *presence* of political community by confronting its absence—Menelaus contemplates the displacement of existing communities, the Ithacans and those of the nameless town that will be uprooted to accommodate them. Local traditions and webs of fellowship are incomprehensible to Menelaus from his standpoint of detachment, a standpoint exacerbated by his enormous wealth and self-contentment.

A key difference from Odysseus's homecoming is subsequently revealed when Menelaus relates the tale of his own *nostos*, including his own pale encounter with mortality and the prediction of his death. In a shadow-scene of Odysseus's descent to the underworld and his consultation of Teiresias, Menelaus also confronts a seer, Proteus, to learn how to appease the gods' anger and to make his return (4.389–390, 475–480).[49] Perhaps also to learn his "way" (*hodon*), his end is conveyed to him by Proteus:

> But for you, Menelaus, O fostered of Zeus, it is not the gods' will
> that you should die and go to your end in horse-pasturing Argos,
> but the immortals will convey you to Elysian
> Field, and the limits of the earth, where fair-haired Rhadamanthys
> is, and where there is made the easiest life for mortals. . . .
> This, because Helen is yours, and you are son-in-law
> to Zeus.
> (4.561–570)

If until now the resemblance between Odysseus's and Menelaus's journeys has been striking, the departure of their *hodoi* is startling: whereas Odysseus's conventional mortal end is predicted amid the horrors of cold Hades, Proteus reveals to Menelaus that he will enjoy an idyllic afterlife because of his "possession" of Helen.[50] Nothing Menelaus has done directly contributes to his good fortune—even his marriage to Helen has been less than definitively deserving of such an honor.[51] Menelaus lives now, and forever, like the gods—his actions have no consequence, and he lives in perpetual comfort and without contemplation.[52] Indeed, like the temptations of self-forgetting that have been offered and refused by Odysseus—most particularly the Lotus—Menelaus lives in a drugged stupor provided by his wife (who significantly also provides his immortality) whenever unpleasant thoughts interrupt their comfort (4.220–232).[53]

Given this overall portrait of Menelaus—that of an unperturbed, detached, complacent soul who is destined for immortality through no effort of his own and who is uncaring of the people he rules—one returns to Austin's portrait of the relationship between Helen and Menelaus as "the first example of family *homophrosyne*." A closer examination of the seemingly pleasant storytelling reveals a less than harmonious reconciliation between the protagonists in the Trojan War. Helen, with notable graciousness, relates her encounter with Odysseus within the walls of Troy, during which she assists him and promises not to reveal his identity. She finishes, undoubtedly with a nod to her husband,

> My heart had changed by now and was for going back
> home again, and I grieved for the madness that Aphrodite
> bestowed when she led me there away from my own dear country,
> forsaking my own daughter, my bedchamber, and my husband,
> a man who lacked no endowment in either brains or beauty.
> (4.260–264)

Odysseus's secret journey to Troy obviously occurs before the introduction of the Trojan Horse; indeed, perhaps his mission is to gather information for that very plan. Helen, then, claims to have changed her mind *before* the end of the war. Menelaus, in turn, tells his own reminiscence of Odysseus, relating the evening they spent inside the belly of the Wooden Horse:

> Then you came, dear Helen; you will have been moved by
> some divine spirit who wished to grant glory to the Trojans. . . .
> Three times you walked around the hollow ambush, feeling it,
> and you called out, naming them by name, to the best of the Danaans,
> and made your voice sound like the voice of the wife of each of the Argives.
> (4.274–279)

Menelaus clearly relishes the description of his wife's *subsequent* treachery, relating with detail how she "touched" the horse and circled it precisely three times. Coming as his story does, after Helen's claim to have changed her mind, his reminiscence constitutes a challenge to his wife.[54] Little wonder that Telemachus's next statement is a request to retire.[55]

It seems that Menelaus holds a grudge over Helen's desertion. Even the one relationship that would indicate the possibility of a meaningful human relationship for Menelaus is tainted by mistrust and spite. This subdued spat serves as a final contrast to Odysseus, whose reunion with Penelope, although difficult and tenuous at first, is finally one that joins them in an embrace framed by a simile that truly does seem to partake of "sympathetic magic":

> As when the land appears welcome to men who are swimming,
> after Poseidon has smashed their strong-built ship on the open
> water, pounding it with the weight of wind and the heavy seas,
> and only a few escape the gray water landward
> by swimming, with a thick scurf of salt coated on them,
> and gladly they set foot on the shore escaping all evil;
> so welcome was her husband to her as she looked upon him,
> and she could not let him go from the embrace of her white arms.
> (23.233–240)

Suddenly Penelope *is* Odysseus as he crawled up on the surf, saved from devastation; like him, having weathered the travails of a nineteen-year journey alone, she arrives home for the first time.

Another Kind of Hero II: Achilles

The *Odyssey* tells us of an old argument between Odysseus and Menelaus, the cause of which we can only infer from an examination of their characters. Their disagreement goes to the essence of their differences in vision of how to live and how to approach death: in contrast to Odysseus's vigorous embrace of mortality, Menelaus is comparatively complacent in his detachment from humanity. However, this perspective on Odysseus's character is limited by the presence of another argument in the *Odyssey*, one at the other pole: that between Odysseus and Achilles. We learn of this quarrel from Demodocus:

> The Muse stirred the singer to sing the famous actions
> of men on that venture, whose fame goes up into the wide heavens,
> the quarrel between Odysseus and Peleus' son, Achilles,
> how they once contended at the gods' generous festival,
> with words of violence, so that the lord of men, Agamemnon,
> was happy in his heart that the best of the Achaeans were quarrelling.
> (8.73–78)

Again the teller of the tale leaves us ignorant of the reason for the confrontation. But even more clearly than in the case of the quarrel with Menelaus, the difference in characters between Achilles and Odysseus is obvious: Achilles is the man of force (*biē*), Odysseus the man of mind (*nous*).

These alternative worldviews are set forth early in the *Iliad* as oppositional. Achilles indicates the two styles of thought in reproaching Agamemnon for cowardice:

> Never once have you taken courage in your heart to arm with your people for
> battle [*polemos*]
> or go into ambuscade [*lochos*] with the best of the Achaeans.
> (I.226–227)

The two approaches to battle are set forth here, both of which will be pursued to different ends in the battle for Troy. Fighting by *polemos* requires the skills of Achilles: speed, agility with a spear, and raw physical strength. Planning victory through a *lochos* is Odysseus's domain, requiring reason, cleverness, and foresight, as well as knowledge of human temptation and frailty.[56] These methods of contest are constantly contrasted in the *Iliad* and the *Odyssey* and are embraced by their respective lead characters.[57] Similarly, the *Iliad* is a poem of force, or *biē*; the *Odyssey* is a poem of trickery, or *doloi*.[58]

The differences between Achilles and Odysseus are well established by the time Demodocus sings of their argument nine years after the conclusion of the Trojan War; listeners of the *Iliad* know they meet in some adversity there as well. Most particularly, their dramatic differences in worldview are evident in the most dramatic moment of the epic—the Embassy of Book IX, in which Odysseus, Ajax, and Phoenix attempt to persuade Achilles to return to the battlefield. Typical of their characters, Odysseus's attempt is measured, logical, and elegant. He appeals by turn to self-interest, familial obligation, honor, and the common good. The most powerful moment of Odysseus's argument concerns the common good, which is invoked through the memory of Achilles' mortal father, and hence is an appeal to his human half:

> Dear friend, surely thus your father Peleus advised you
> that day when he sent you to Agamemnon from Phythia:
> "My child, for the matter of strength, Athena and Hera will give it
> if it be their will, but be it yours to hold fast in your bosom
> the anger of your proud heart [*thumos*], for friendly spirit [*philophrosunē*] is better."
> (IX.252–256)

Odysseus's praise of *philophrosunē* through the words of Achilles' father is a pointed warning against the godlike tendency toward a belief that the world is malleable to one's will, a belief that easily turns to an all-consuming form of anger when one is confronted with obstacles. This invocation of Peleus as a reminder of Achilles' own mortal frailness is revisited by Odysseus during a later confrontation with Achilles over whether the Achaean soldiers should be allowed to eat before battle:

> Son of Peleus, Achilles, far greater of the Achaeans,
> you are stronger than I am and greater by not a little
> with a spear, yet I was born before you and have learned more things. . . .
> There is no way the Achaeans can mourn a dead man by denying the belly. . . .
> No, but we must harden our hearts and bury the man who dies,
> when we have wept over him on the day, and all those
> who are left about from the hateful work of war must remember
> food and drink.
> (XIX.216–231)

Breaking into a dramatic moment when Achilles rejects the necessities of the body, Odysseus's reproof again invokes Achilles' human side by his lineage to Peleus. Seemingly prosaic in the face of Achilles' profound passion, sadness, and anger, Odysseus's words again remind Achilles of the need to concern oneself with other human beings in their own plights, in short, of *philophrosunē*. Odysseus, then—here admitting his more extensive mortality, as well as a kind of worldliness that Achilles lacks—attempts on many occasions to balance the detached and godlike aspect of Achilles (the godlike portion inherited from his mother Thetis) with a more humanly embedded appeal to his father's legacy.

Despite these attempts by Odysseus, there is a deep mistrust and even a fundamental divide that separates Achilles from Odysseus. After Odysseus's speech in the "Embassy," Achilles' response is passionate, direct, and powerful. He begins by implicitly repudiating not only Odysseus's words, but also his manner of thought and action:

> For as I detest the doorways of death, I detest that man, who
> hides one thing in the depths of his heart, and speaks forth another.
> (IX.311–312)

Achilles goes on to set forth, in a sense, the premise of the *Iliad*, and defines the basis of his own heroism. He is a mortal man fated to die. Yet, according to the heroic code, he has been dishonored because Agamemnon has taken away the prizes of battle. Rehearsing his grievances to Odysseus, Achilles reveals the extent of his dilemma, the quandary that concerns his fate:

> For my mother Thetis the goddess of silver feet tells me
> I carry two sorts of destiny toward the day of my death. Either,
> if I stay here and fight beside the city of the Trojans,
> my return home [*nostos*] is gone, but my glory [*kleos*] will be everlasting;
> But if I return home to the beloved land of my fathers,
> the excellence of my glory is gone, but there will be a long life
> left for me, and my death will not come to me quickly.
> (IX.410–416)

It is notable that Achilles does not explicitly link the dishonor that Agamemnon's confiscation of Briseis has caused with his two possible destinies. A typical hero might have reasoned, "If I must die in Troy, at least my death should be accompanied by the honor that has now been taken from me." Achilles, however, goes beyond this relatively simple heroic code, refusing the bounty of gifts offered by Agamemnon and suggesting a new ethic: honor and warfare are ultimately not enough if the cost is one's life.[59]

> For not worth the value of my life are all the possessions they fable
> were won for Ilion. . . .
> Of possessions cattle and fat sheep are things for the lifting,
> and tripods can be won, and the tawny high heads of horses,
> but a man's life cannot come back again, it cannot be lifted
> nor captured again by force, once it has crossed the teeth's barrier.
> (IX.401–409)

Faced with a choice if not literally between life and death, then between long life and certain impending death, Achilles appears to choose long life. Odysseus, also faced with the prospect of an inglorious and uninteresting long (even eternal) life with Calypso or certain (but not impending) death if he leaves her, makes the opposite choice—he leaves and he will die.

Yet Achilles does not ultimately live according to this choice: despite his rejection of the heroic code, he rejoins the battle after the death of Patroclus and kills Hector. His fate is sealed by his subsequent choice—he will live a short, glorious life. Yet one wonders about the status of his earlier decision: did he never really mean to leave Troy, merely prolonging the inevitable, or does he simply reject his earlier choice in the blindness of his thirst for revenge?[60] In a discussion with Thetis after Patroclus's death, Achilles at least indicates a full awareness of the consequences of rejoining the battle:

> I must die soon then. . . .
> I will accept my own death, at whatever
> time Zeus wishes to bring it about.
> (XVIII.98, 115–116)

However, unlike Odysseus, who decided on Ogygia to live because of his connections to other human beings, his love of family and home, Achilles chooses death to some extent because of an absence of all human connections embodied in his loss of Patroclus, an absence that reflects a general lack of something or someone to live for:

> my dear companion has perished,
> Patroclus, whom I loved beyond all other companions,
> as well as my own life.
> (XVIII.80–81)

More disconnected even than when he retreated to his tent, Achilles' decision is less the embracing of mortality out of companionship and *philophrosunē* than the cry of one forlorn, without hope of human attachment and meaning, one who no longer perceives any reason to remain alive.

If Odysseus's decision to leave Calypso marks his return to humanity, to time and nature, Achilles' choice increasingly announces his departure from these same. His rage, the anger that moved him initially against the Achaeans, now moves him against the Trojans and Hector. But more, he ends confronting nature itself, in the form of the river Skamandros.[61] The battle now becomes phantasmagoric: Achilles, described as "something more than mortal" (XXI.229), battles the waters of the river, only to be saved by a fire that devours the corpses he has slaughtered and the very plain of battle itself—its trees, the grass, fish, and finally Skamandros. Achilles has left the bounds of the purely mortal. As Thomas Van Nortwick observes:

> In some respects his behavior is like a god's, powerful and impatient in opposition, removed from the worries attendant on mortals—his pitiless treatment of various sup-

pliants who approach him in books 20–22 has about it the cruel indifference of deities. In some unsettling way, he is moving away from the mortal part of his nature toward the divine. But if Achilles approaches godliness, it is an increasingly savage, bestial kind of divinity.[62]

This savagery reaches an apex with the killing of Hector, whom he must not only slay but defile. Perhaps more shocking even than his mistreatment of Hector's body are his earlier threats that border on cannibalism:

No more entreating of me, you dog, by knees or parents.
I only wish that my spirit and fury would drive me
to hack your meat away and eat it raw for the things that
you have done to me.
(XII.345–348)

To eat a victim raw is an act of utmost depravity, and one committed elsewhere in the Homeric corpus, by Polyphemus in the *Odyssey*. Increasingly Achilles resembles the *Odyssey*'s portrayal of this savage beast who lives without reason or regard for humanity and the gods but who is so far from the tenets of propriety that he claims the desire to devour living humans. Like Polyphemus—also a half-child of the immortal gods—Achilles has departed the realm of the human, rather embodying dual aspects of godliness and beastliness; and like that figure described by Aristotle who lives without a city, Achilles has withdrawn with ever increasing isolation from the human community.[63]

In the end, Achilles seems to choose *kaluptein*, the cover of his tent and within the tomb commemorating his short, glorious life. If Achilles leaves the sphere of humanity at the death of Patroclus, however, a redemption of sorts is accomplished by the end as he connects his own human despair with that of his victim's father, Priam. A certain equilibrium is reinstated, and Achilles again embraces the ambiguity inherited from the connection of his immortal mother and mortal father. Nevertheless, Achilles' life and story do not end in the *Iliad*: the *Iliad* points beyond itself to later epics, to the death of Achilles and to his afterlife. Even as the story of Achilles continues, even as the integrity of his character remains, the frame surrounding his words and deeds changes, and indeed changes enough to reinterpret his earlier portrayal.[64]

Although we have lost for the most part those later epics, the *Iliad*'s true counterpart remains: the *Odyssey* represents not only an alternative to the *Iliad*'s vision, but also the first full-length commentary on and critique of the heroism of Achilles. The argument between Achilles and Odysseus that is sung about by Demodocus may have been specifically about how best to conquer Troy—through *polemos* or *lochos*—or even the subject of an alternative version of the *Iliad*, in which Odysseus is the source of Achilles' anger.[65] But the larger argument is, in fact, captured in the very epics about the two respective heroes and the question they pose: which of their lives, as captured and interpreted through song, constitutes the greatest *kleos* and makes one or the other finally *the* best of the Achaeans?[66]

Whether the writer of the *Odyssey* was familiar with the *Iliad* has long been debated: typically, analysts answer in the negative, literally finding no *explicit* evidence;[67] unitarians take the longer view, advocating the general continuity of the *Odyssey* with the *Iliad* as definitive. Again the question is largely unanswerable, although finally the assumptions of the analysts regarding the manner of composition of the epics seem to refute their stance regarding the connection between the two epics: given the fluidity and widespread knowledge among the poetic community of the epic cycle, we can infer that the poet of the *Odyssey* had at the very least knowledge of the *Iliad* tradition; even without full-blown knowledge of the very words of the *Iliad*, the general story line, including the developed characterizations, would have been widely shared.[68]

Indeed, the *Odyssey*'s "explicit" avoidance of the *Iliad*'s theme suggests less an ignorance of the epic story than a purposeful avoidance. From antiquity to the present the two epics have been qualitatively compared, and such, it seems, was intended: the epics, like their heroes, were meant to compete with one another.[69] "Competitive excellences," to use the phrase coined by Adkins, represented the predominant value system for activity and accomplishment available to the Homeric hero, and, this agonistic ethic would appear to extend to the competing songs of bards as well.[70] The competition would not merely decide whose song was most dramatic or whose voice the most lovely, although such factors could be influential. Rather, at stake was the cosmos, a description of human and divine order, even the very existence of such an order. As Edwards posits, such competition "assumes a distinctly ethical dimension. . . . The contest of songs, then, in which each poet asserts the superiority of his song and his hero, must set in opposition competing value systems."[71]

This contest comes to a head in the only meeting between Odysseus and Achilles in the *Odyssey*: the meeting in Hades in Book 11, or the *Nekyia*. There Achilles greets Odysseus with the word *schetliē*, meaning "rash one" or "headstrong man." Generally a term expressing annoyance, disgust, or anger,[72] it is applied to Odysseus only by Achilles, from among those souls that Odysseus meets in Hades, and only after every other speaker has expressed welcome and concern. Achilles' reaction is a singular disapproval of Odysseus's presence in the underworld.[73]

Achilles' annoyance is not surprising: the portrait of the hero of the *Iliad* by the poet of the *Odyssey* is one that is faithful to that earlier portrayal and yet stresses finally that least heroic aspect of Achilles from the *Iliad*. In the *Odyssey* his former ambivalence is now set in bold relief, no longer torn between the short, glorious life or the long, unnoticed one, but now rather firmly in the camp of the latter. After Odysseus praises Achilles for his honor on earth and his power over the dead beneath, Achilles retorts with characteristic sharpness:

> O shining Odysseus, never try to console me for dying.
> I would rather follow the plow as thrall to another
> man, one with no land allotted to him and not much to live on,
> than be a king over all the perished dead.
> (11.488–491)

Through these four lines the entire ambiguity of Achilles' famous "choice" in the *Iliad* is undone: in fact, his words suggest that his true choice was never firmly decided, was never one with which he could live and die. In his numbness and rage he abandoned his earlier decision to leave the plains of Troy for home—to achieve *nostos* at the cost of *kleos*—in order to avenge the death of Patroclus. Claiming to accept the consequences of his fate—*kleos* instead of *nostos*—an ambivalence about which choice was truly in his most innermost heart is left delicately unsettled by the poet of the *Iliad*. Yet now in Hades and in a new poem, Achilles reveals his true inclination: he would prefer slavery to death.[74]

It is notable that Achilles hates death so much—recall, as much as he hates Odysseus (IX.312)—that he would choose the life of the most abused and unlucky human possible, and moreover one who is not part of the life of a *polis*, recalling Aristotle's later formulation. Achilles' soul has all along revealed an aspect of servitude, for all the nobility his godlike birth and talent give him: he is constantly subject to his passions, first his anger at Agamemnon, then his fear of death, thereafter a renewed anger at Hector, which drives him to his own death through nondecision. It is perhaps unrealistic to expect such a character to choose his own fate in a measured and final manner; a person, especially a half-divine person, so subject to fleeting passions may finally be incapable of such a choice.

Only after meeting Achilles in Hades and hearing the curse of the greatest of the Achaeans over death is Odysseus offered his own choice of similar proportions. Yet given not a single evening to make a "rash" decision like Achilles' before rushing into battle (hence the irony of Achilles' epithet, *schetliē*) but seven years on the island Ogygia, Odysseus's choice is long-pondered, considered, and final. Up to the moment he leaves Calypso, he is asked by her to remain and accept immortality, finally giving an impassioned defense of his own lot as mortal through reference to Penelope:

> all you say is true and that circumspect Penelope
> can never match the impression you make for beauty and stature.

She is mortal after all, and you are immortal and ageless.
But even so, what I want and all my days I pine for
is to go back to my house and see my day of homecoming.
And if some god batters me far out on the wine-blue water,
I will endure it, and keep a stubborn spirit within me.
(5.216–222)

Odysseus's choice is apparently simpler than Achilles': *nostos* and *kleos* or an uneventful immortality. Yet, given a longer-term view, Odysseus's decision to decline Calypso's offer of immortality finally and precisely resembles Achilles' "choice" as well—the "short eventful life," the life of *kleos*, which, even if Odysseus's life is to be longer than Achilles', still necessitates his eventual death. Odysseus, born of mortal parents and accepting human limitations, finally values human fellowship and communion over the life of either a god or a slave. So the *Odyssey* closes the book on the *Iliad*.

The Homeric Gods, the Founder, and Justice

If the relationships between the human actors portrayed in the epics are rich and complex, the relationship between human beings and the gods is perhaps almost incomprehensible in comparison. Classicists have long grappled to understand whether the divine powers act in accordance with a moral dimension in their interference in the lives of humanity. The Homeric epics contain no explicit theodicy: Homer rarely removes himself to a contemplative distance in order to justify the gods' ways to men. The gods merely act and rarely explain their motivations. To attempt to construct a theodicy from the often conflicting episodes of the epics is thus an interpretive act that to some extent allows prior notions of godly qualities to dictate how divine episodes will be construed. Even concentrating on the same significant episodes in the *Iliad* and the *Odyssey* have provided generations of classicists with competing interpretations of divinity of which few can be said not to contain an element of plausibility.

Nonetheless, a few points of broad agreement about the nature of the Homeric gods do seem to be shared by a number of prominent Homer scholars. All agree that the Greek gods are not to be confused with the God of Judaism and Christianity and that the gods of the Greek pantheon are less ineffably divine than they are superlatively human. In the words of Erland Ehnmark, the Greek gods are differentiated from human beings by an "intensification of human characteristics [that] at most amounts to a difference in degree, not to a difference in kind."[75] Hermann Fränkel agrees, arguing that the Greek god "enjoys a superhuman abundance of vital existence."[76] Similarly, Arthur W. H. Adkins writes that "Zeus has no perfections: he merely possesses the qualities that he does possess in a super-lative degree."[77] And B. C. Dietrich writes simply that "the main difference [of the gods from humans] lies in their superior strength."[78] To some extent, the gods can be described as exceptional human beings in regard to the things for which they are renowned or in which they excel. No human excels Aphrodite in beauty nor Athena in wisdom. The Homeric gods are not distinguishable in strictly moral terms but in most cases merely exceed humans in aspects physical and mental. They are notoriously lacking in an elevated moral capacity, appearing often in a disgraceful parody of petty combat the likes of which kills humans on earth but merely entertains the immortal gods.

It is also universally agreed that part of this physical differentiation from humanity at large includes the gods' immortality.[79] If in other respects humanity and the gods differ only in degrees of excellence, divine immortality represents a fundamental difference in kind: every action that each being takes is informed by its respective relationship to death. As Snell writes, "The gods alone act in such a manner that they achieve their ends, and even if a god sometimes cannot realize all his designs . . . the supreme frustration of the human race, eventual death, is not for them."[80] The gods, then, act without fear of serious personal danger and consequence and without impatience. If Odysseus is ultimately to be aided by Athena to achieve his return, he is nevertheless allowed to wait seven precious human years on Calypso's island before she takes action.

Yet general agreement about divine qualities ceases at the acknowledgment of immortality and the intensification of mortal characteristics that distinguish the gods from the mortals. Arousing widespread disagreement is the question of the gods' attitude toward morality, particularly justice. Both the Homeric epics are arguably foremost concerned with justice, and the gods' role in effecting the outcome of both stories is decisive. Interpretations of the gods' general devotion to effecting a *just* outcome vary. B. C. Dietrich speaks for many in contending that the gods' intervention in the lives of men "is always arbitrary, and is not motivated by any moral consideration of balance or right, but by their own personal whim and preferences. For this reason they have rightly been called immoral."[81] Nevertheless, most observers are forced to recognize that both epics conclude, however tenuously, with a certain degree of justice. Adkins, generally dismissive of the existence of "ethical values" in the Homeric corpus, writes that "though Right triumphs in the main plots of both the *Iliad* and the *Odyssey*, it does not do so *because* it is right." Indeed, "the gods as portrayed generally in the Homeric poems are far from just."[82] Although excepting several isolated episodes as exhibiting a concern for justice,[83] Adkins's main point remains: notwithstanding occasional glimpses of an undeveloped appeal to justice (and rarely its actual demonstration), Homer's epics are not *about* justice even if they *result* in justice.

One must grant his argument some credence, but Adkins's conclusion is peculiarly uninquisitive about this coincidence.

At the other interpretive pole are critics such as Erland Ehnmark, who contends that "the gods are not immoral."[84] In a society in which one's *timē*, or honor, was one's greatest asset, any impingement on what one "deserved" for one's level of honor—be it mortal or god—called for a response that can be more properly described as vengeance than justice. That such acts of vengeance occasionally resulted in a just outcome—witness Odysseus's slaughter of the suitors, who foremost besmirch his and his family's honor—is merely that coincidence described by Adkins and acknowledged by Ehnmark.[85] It is necessary, however, to distinguish individual acts from the collective judgment of the gods, often embodied in the will of Zeus.[86] Precisely *because* the *Iliad* and the *Odyssey* result in an arguably just conclusion, a divine plan is revealed whereby fate and the gods act contemporaneously, or rather the gods act actively to ensure fate's passive decree.[87] Ehnmark's demonstration of fate is none other than the conclusions of the epics themselves: they could not have ended in any other way, ergo, fate ensures justice. However, an argument as circular as Adkins's is disconnected results; in both cases, the gods' relationship to the just outcome of the epics is circumstantial. Either the epics end justly despite the gods, or the gods are demonstrably just because of the epics' endings; but in both cases the relationships between the epics' endings and the gods' enforcement of justice are tenuous and unpersuasive.

Part of the problem of discovering whether the gods act justly or not arises inevitably from the difficulty of defining precisely what justice *is*. That vexed question, one that has occupied thinkers from Plato to Rawls and beyond, is not one that Homer explicitly seeks to answer; instead, he leaves the reader to winnow through the episodes for an active definition. One possibility is to take Homer at his word, literally, and to tally the usage of the word *dikē* or related words and arrive at a working definition in such a manner. Such is Eric Havelock's method in his book *The Greek Concept of Justice*, in which he arrives at a customarily pragmatic working definition of Justice—largely the one that the poet or the characters use the word *dikē* to mean. Justice, according to Havelock, is portrayed in Homer to be "a procedure, not a principle or any set of principles. It is arrived at by a process of negotiation between contending parties carried out rhetorically. As such, it is particular, not general. . . ."[88] Havelock's interpretation is sufficient as far as he will allow the material to demonstrate, but nowhere does he make the explicit distinction between the literary method and the philosophical. Of course there are no "broad" principles of justice in the *Iliad* and the *Odyssey*, just as such principles are absent in Shakespeare and Tolstoy. Yet, to say that the words do not amount to a "principle" of justice in Homer does not necessarily mean that the sum of its parts does not. The result of Havelock's method is often to arrive at the definition of the *word* at the expense of the *text*.

An opposite approach, and one of considerable persuasiveness, is that of Hugh Lloyd-Jones, who rejects this method as too narrow in its reading and instead seeks to discover a Homeric conception of justice through an examination of select episodes of the epics.[89] Lloyd-Jones approaches Homer's conception of justice through the question of the justness of Achilles' argument against Agamemnon and thus focuses on the root contention that fuels the action of the *Iliad*. Zeus sides with Achilles in his argument with Agamemnon, and with the Greeks over the Trojans, not out of personal preference but because the twin causes are just. Moreover, there is no contradiction between the two positions: Achilles' slight is righted, as eventually is Menelaus's. Lloyd-Jones argues with some force that Agamemnon is not entitled simply to confiscate a warrior's possessions, this in explicit disagreement with Adkins's position.[90] Indeed, as Lloyd-Jones points out, Agamemnon several times admits as much (IX.115–121; IX.158–162); only when Achilles refuses to accept Agamemnon's offer of reconciliation does Achilles lose the moral high ground and call upon himself the wrath of the gods for hubris. "Achilles has had his wish granted, only to have it recoil on him with bitter irony . . . ; according to the terms of Zeus's justice, each has got what he deserved."[91]

Thus, Lloyd-Jones's account implicitly accepts the outcome of the Trojan War to be just; yet earlier he poses "the big question" that often goes unasked by close readers of the *Iliad* who allow the action of Achilles' quarrel with Agamemnon to obfuscate the larger cause of the Trojan War: "Can we really feel certain that the eventual triumph of the Greeks has no connection with the undoubted truth that Paris provoked the quarrel by abducting Helen?"[92] Having opened this Pandora's box, Lloyd-Jones avoids it by concentrating on Achilles' claim to justice against Agamemnon. As Lloyd-Jones concluded, the fact of the Greek victory over the Trojans governs the decision as to whether their cause was just or not: "The Trojans will finally receive rough justice in return for their aggression against Menelaus."[93] If it is easily concluded that Zeus, given his position as protector of oaths and guest-friendship, is guided by the imperatives of these values to decree the victory of the Greeks over the Trojans, is it likewise as simple to conclude that such Justice demands total destruction of the Trojans? Does the affront against Menelaus constitute Trojan "aggression"? Cannot the Trojans' reaction to an invading army be easily interpreted as defensive in nature? Such questions going to the root cause of the Trojan War are not asked by critics, who simply accept the premises of the war and subsequently its results. What Lloyd-Jones calls "rough justice" may rather be so rough as to cease being just at all; for if we are to agree that justice means anything, we must consider not only whether the *cause* is just, but whether the *response* to injustice is just as well.

Of course, one must be cautious of importing contemporary notions of justice back to the Homeric texts; yet, one should be equally cautious attributing to Homer the system of values he attributes to his heroes. Having separated Odysseus's voice from that of Homer, we must be willing to do the opposite and consider whether Homer finally assumes a critical stance regarding the warrior ethic of retribution he describes, even finally distancing himself from the best of the Achaeans, Odysseus. If the *Odyssey* is a critique on the warrior ethic of the *Iliad*, it may be no less true that it contains also a critique of Odysseus himself, inasmuch as he participates in that ethic. And if the gods are as guilty as humans in perpetrating the continuation of the blood vendetta that marks the action of both poems, then it is notable that it is finally they who must stop it.

How insidious the conflict of the Trojan War is, and even how ridiculous its action is, is suggested by Herodotus—a somewhat anachronistic source, but one worth noting. Herodotus notes that the cause of the war with Troy actually precedes the abduction of Helen, that in fact a chain of the theft of women between the two continents is at fault. The venture that finally culminates in the Trojan War is not considered to be universally admirable. Herodotus cites one of the aggrieved parties as saying:

> It is the work of unjust men, we think, to carry off women at all; but once they have been carried off, to take seriously the avenging of them is that part of fools, as it is the part of sensible men to pay no heed to the matter: clearly, the women would not have been carried off had they no mind to be.[94]
>
> The Persians say that they, for their part, made no account of the women carried off from Asia, but that the Greeks, because of a Lacedaemonian woman, gathered a great army, came straight to Asia, and destroyed the power of Priam. (I.4; 34)

Herodotus's apparent scoffing at the cause of the war and the magnitude of the response does not seem wholly absent in Homer either; at the very least, we know that Odysseus initially resisted joining the endeavor, indicating some disagreement with the cause (24.118–119). But more generally, it is finally the outcome of the war—disaster for nearly all the participants, supposed victors or victims—that sows doubt in the listener's mind. The chain of violence does not cease on the shores of Troy but continues unabated to the shores of Agamemnon's palace and to Ithaca. The *Odyssey* suggests the excessiveness of this chain of retribution; its inappropriateness finally in Ithaca—where political solutions should be the norm; and the mutual responsibility of the gods and men both in causing it and finally in ending it.

In some sense, the continuation of violence has as its basis the very disagreement between the gods and men about the root causes of human action in general. Humans are ever accusing the gods, with good reason, of causing their strife and misery; even the argument at the basis of the *Iliad* is blamed on the gods by Agamemnon (XIX.134–139). Yet the gods also seek to avoid their participation in the perpetuation of violence. It is Zeus, in fact, who distances himself from the continuing chain of violence with some impatience at the outset of the *Odyssey*:

> Oh for shame, how the mortals put the blame upon us
> gods, for they say evils come from us, but it is they, rather,
> who by their own recklessness win sorrow beyond what is given,
> as now lately, beyond what was given, Aigisthos married
> the wife of Atreus' son, and murdered him on his homecoming,
> though he knew it was sheer destruction, for we ourselves had told him,
> sending Hermes, the mighty watcher, Argeïphontes,
> not to kill the man, nor court his lady for marriage;
> for vengeance would come on him from Orestes, son of Atreides,
> whenever he came of age and longed for his own country.
> So Hermes told him, but for all his kind intention he could not
> persuade the mind of Aigisthos. And now he has paid for everything.
> (1.32–43)

Zeus's complaint against Aigisthos, one that is long celebrated and debated by critics, is rightly astonishing. Even though it reinforces the existence of humanity's capacity for choice over their individual fates, it seemingly denies the otherwise obvious presence of divine interference in the lives of men evident in both the epics. However, twice Zeus accuses humans of bringing misfortune upon themselves "beyond what is given" (1.34, 35); Zeus at least acknowledges a divine role in human affairs, just or unjust, that can be exacerbated by human choice. Such is in keeping with the general import of Teiresias's prediction: choice is limited by necessity, but within even this sometimes restricted limit humans create their own fates. On the shield of Achilles, the gods are more in evidence in the city of war than in the city of peace; the problem for the *Odyssey* is how to travel from one city to the other.

Despite the gods' constant *claim* to be attentive to justice among humans and their occasional actions that would seem to effect a "rough justice," the gods are fundamentally inconstant in their enforcement of justice among humans. More baldly, the gods are arbitrary; and because of that arbitrariness, they *sometimes* deign to look kindly on humans, and sometimes not, but humanity finally has no way of apprehending from one moment to the next the inclination of the Olympians, just as they cannot apprehend the gods themselves.[95] Justice is then a human endeavor that the gods may alternatively help or hinder. Yet, notwithstanding such arbitrariness, the *Odyssey* *does* end in a just outcome (however rough), and the gods—specifically Athena, with the consent of Zeus—both open and end the poem in pursuit of that outcome. In between, we discover that it is Poseidon who has waged a petty and one-sided war against Odysseus for his eminently justifiable treatment of Polyphemus. Despite Polyphemus's savageness and hubris (9.275–295)—including acts and words that would otherwise have called down the gods' wrath against ordinary humans—Poseidon is moved by his blood kinship with Polyphemus to punish the victim, Odysseus. If it is Athena's anger at Troy that initially endangers Odysseus's *nostos*, it is Poseidon's unconscionable vendetta that prolongs it for years.[96]

The cause of the gods' action finally to pursue justice is obscure. Only after Odysseus has languished on the island of Calypso for seven years does Athena finally broach the topic of Odysseus's homecoming to Zeus (1.45–62). Ostensibly, her reason for waiting so long is her fear of Poseidon, who is now finally out of earshot among the Aithiopians (1.22–23); such forms the excuse she later gives to Odysseus for her long absence (13.341–343). Yet, Athena might have effected his return home long before Odysseus ever landed on the Cyclopes' island or assisted in his escape there without resort to blinding. Rather, her absence *from the time Odysseus left Troy* is noted by Odysseus and serves to belie her excuse of Poseidon's anger as the single reason for her absence (13.316–323).[97] If Athena might have assisted Odysseus at any time before his encounter with Polyphemus— effectively forestalling the need to confront the suitors, who would not have gathered so quickly after the war's end—why then does she choose to act when she does, so long after Odysseus's embarkation and for no apparent reason? Nothing has changed in Ogygia—Odysseus still pines to return as he has since arriving there, and Calypso continues to hold him captive while offering him immortality. As in the case of the arguments between Odysseus and both Menelaus and Achilles, Homer does not explicitly tell us the cause but provides the clues needed to deduce the reason.

The answer lies in Athena's decision to go first to Ithaca, and not, as logic would demand, to free Odysseus. Many analysts have rejected the *Telemachia* as an interpolation by a later poet because it seemingly does not advance the action of Odysseus's renewed voyage from Calypso's island.[98] Yet, such criticisms ignore the basis of Athena's sudden decision to call for Odysseus's release. Her action does not necessarily indicate her concern for Odysseus, as many assume, but perhaps more for the breakdown of morality in Ithaca. The punishment of Odysseus for nine years, effected first by Athena and then unjustly prolonged by Poseidon, has created an intolerable situation among the ordinary people of Ithaca. Even the superficial veneer of decency that would normally attach itself to the nobly born suitors has worn off: they not only gluttonously devour Odysseus's property but also threaten death to Odysseus, attempt to kill his son and heir, and finally disregard pious warnings about their fate (2.246–251; 4.668–674; 1.160; 20.364–383). Athena, on first arriving in Ithaca, is provoked to ask Telemachus:

> Is it a festival or a wedding? Surely no communal dinner.
> How insolently they seem to swagger about in their feasting
> all through the house. A serious man who came in among them
> could well be scandalized, seeing much disgraceful behavior.
> (1.226–229)

Her concern is admittedly for "a serious man's" perception of the suitors' behavior and for the effect such unpunished disgraces would have on persons of decency.

Appropriately, then, upon witnessing the sudden deterioration of morals on Ithaca, Athena proceeds *not* to Ogygia to release Odysseus (rather she sends Hermes) but directly to Ithaca, where she advises Telemachus to call the first *agora* in nineteen years.[99] In the absence of a just leader, the gods must finally attempt to reinstitute justice, not directly but through the auspices of human institutions. As both Zeus and Odysseus recognize, justice is finally a human affair. However, the suitors' disregard of justice is by now so firmly established and they are so confident of acting with impunity that the assembly is unsuccessful; it merely hardens their determination to act lawlessly.[100] The restoration of order requires not only *nous*—symbolized on Ithaca by the aged Mentor—but also *biē*, both possessed in sufficient degree by Odysseus. Telemachus the child notes that the citizens of the *polis* are physically incapable of restoring order—"we ourselves are not the men to do it; we must be / weaklings in such a case, not men well seasoned in battle" (2.60–61)—and as such admits that persuasion, and hence politics, has failed. If Odysseus throughout demonstrates a sympathy for political life, its fellowship, and the means of persuasion, it is ultimately his ability to act *apolitically* and even amorally that will restore justice to Ithaca.

Such a conclusion gives pause: Odysseus has been portrayed throughout as a man of moderation, engaged with political vision and his community and heedful of justice. Yet he is also the consummate liar, a likely desecrator of temples during the sack of Troy, a selfish commander who exposes his men to unnecessary risk, a Homeric soldier equally capable of *polemos* or *lochos*.[101] If the action of the *Odyssey* moves from lawlessness to justice, from a violent world to one of moderation, the development of Odysseus's character moves in the opposite direction, from moderation toward violence, from restraint toward anger. Odysseus by the end of the poem must become more *like* Achilles than his opposite; he must learn not to *control* his anger, a restraint he practices throughout the poem, but to *release* it. As such, he must cease being "No-man," abandon *metis*, and become his own name, which has as its root the word *anger* or *pain*.[102] Odysseus must found anew a political order, which calls forth a different skill than that with which he apparently ruled earlier through frequent assemblies.

It is Odysseus's ability ultimately to act amorally—exhibited in his most re-nowned qualities of endurance and trickery—that makes him the successful hero of the *Odyssey* and of that world in which neither the gods nor man can be counted on to act justly.[103] If Odysseus's character is striking for his sense of both justice and moderation and equally for his ability to disencumber himself of these quali-ties, then it is precisely these attributes that may make Odysseus more effective as a founder of a political community than as its long-term ruler, despite his pre-vious claims to rule justly. The Homeric hero—even Odysseus, who most expands the boundaries of the heroic code—is finally a dubious participant in political life because either violence or trickery is his sine qua non of activity, both of which can serve to found or to destroy a community, but neither of which can serve as a long-term basis for its continuation. An integral part of persuasion, *peitho*, is trust, in Greek it's passive, *peithomai*. As Alcinous does not fully trust Odysseus after his persuasive tale (11.363–369), so Odysseus indicates upon his return to Ithaca that he will not be a fully trustworthy and constant leader.[104]

Like Achilles' anger on the plain of Troy, Odysseus's anger, when it is finally released, also becomes difficult to control. The kinsmen of the suitors prepare to destroy Odysseus and his family, prolonging the long chain of retribution that dates back to before the war with Troy and continues unabated on the shores of the homecoming soldiers. Odysseus, too, prepares for civil war: the violence of destruction and restoration again become indistinguishable. Only by the gods' intervention can the chain be broken; having allowed it to proceed in the de-struction of community after community, the general spread of *anomie* finally brings Zeus to stop it (24.482–486). Yet up to the very last line of the poem, Odysseus pursues retribution—when all the parties scatter at Athena's command to throw down arms, Odysseus leaps up to pursue them farther (24.537–538). He must be stopped by the gods:

But the son of Kronos then threw down a smoky thunderbolt
which fell in front of the grey-eyed daughter of the great father:
"Son of Laertes and seed of Zeus, resourceful Odysseus,
hold hard, stay this quarrel in closing combat [*polemos*], for fear
Zeus of the wide brows, son of Kronos, may be angry with you."
So spoke Athena, and with happy heart [*thumos*] he obeyed her.
And pledges for the days to come, sworn by both sides,
were settled by Pallas Athena, daughter of Zeus of the aegis,
who had likened herself in appearance and voice to Mentor.
(24.529–548)

If Odysseus in these last lines puts down his weapons "with happy heart," it is only after having disobeyed Athena once and receiving an explicit threat from Zeus. Odysseus is finally incapable of stopping the chain of violence himself; he is as much a link in a series as the rest of the heroes.[105] He must be stopped by the gods and brought to the bargaining table, not only now to achieve homecoming, but to recreate a home. The institution of justice among humans, if created and maintained by humanity, is instigated perforce by the gods.[106] Appropriately, following a demonstration of force, *biē*, politics is restored in the form of *metis*, in the person of Mentor.

These final lines of the *Odyssey* mark the end not only of homecoming but also of the entire circuit to Troy and back: it is the peace on Ithaca that ends the Trojan War. With that great invasion, political life had literally ceased, both for Troy and also for Ithaca. Its reinstatement must be effected by a founder who has both Odysseus's profound sympathy for politics and also his ability to act by the traditional amoral, apolitical heroic code when necessary. Yet the founder is not wholly successful without the assistance of the gods or, at the very least, cannot be successful if the gods actively obstruct the institution of justice. Justice is restored, prompted by the gods but organized and maintained through human, and thereby political, means. But if the gods aid in its creation and if Odysseus is its conduit, then, as Teiresias predicts, and as Dante later expands, the founder may not long be able to remain in the community he founds but may have to leave the community he creates to be maintained by the citizens of the *polis*.

The Kernel of Democracy

Even if we are persuaded that the gods are prompted finally to act on the behalf of justice because the resulting *anomie* in Ithaca threatens moral order, the question still remains as to *why* such *anomie* should trouble the immortal gods. Their physical existence is not threatened by Ithaca's unrest; indeed, the gods have hitherto delighted in both fomenting discord and joining mankind in its consequences. The gods' own social structure is notably marked by strife: although Zeus exercises final control over the panoply of the gods (primarily through the threat of physical violence, and not moral excellence [8.5–27, 209–211]), he also avoids open conflict and is even subject to deception by individual gods who by diverting his attention circumvent his preferences (XIV.243–262).

As such, the most burlesque portrayal of the gods in the *Odyssey* is also arguably its most serious—the song of Ares and Aphrodite's adultery (8.266–367). By treating the subject of adultery, Demodocus's song touches on the source of the Trojan War, the tragedy of Agamemnon, and also alludes to the question of Penelope's fidelity that hangs over Odysseus's homecoming. Thus, a portrayal of the gods' own version of this breach of conduct is indicative of the difference between divine and mortal attitudes toward decency and justice.

Hephaestus is in certain respects the god closest to mortal expression because he is an artist and hence a mediator between nature and artifice, reflected in the portrayal of marriage and the city that he forges on the shield of Achilles. Hence, it is not surprising that he takes seriously his discovery of his wife's adulterous relationship with Ares, as a human might do.[107] He therefore devises a trap designed not only to catch the pair but also to humiliate them. The reaction of the other gods is illuminating: they admit sympathy not for Hephaestus's outrage, but for the adultery. Apollo asks Hermes, "Would you, caught tight in these strong fastenings, be willing / to sleep in bed by the side of Aphrodite the golden?" to which Hermes replies:

> Lord who strikes from afar, Apollo, I wish it could only
> be, and there could be thrice this number of endless fastenings,
> and all you gods could be looking on and all the goddesses,
> and still I would sleep by the side of Aphrodite the golden.
> (8.339–342)

Unarguably a mirthful exchange, it serves in addition to reveal the gods' disregard for the forms of decency that must be followed by humankind to maintain order in a precarious world. The price of adultery for the Olympians is but momentary humiliation in their immortal lives—a harsh penalty by divine standards, because for the gods honor (*timē*) is paramount—but a price the gods are willing to pay for playful iniquity. Alternatively, the price for humans who flout such civil standards is steep, often entailing blood feud or war, estrangement, and death.[108]

The gods under normal circumstances are not prompted to act by norms of decency; thus, their personal stake in upholding an order of justice among humankind would appear tenuous. Yet Athena and (through her imploring) Zeus both act to restore order to Ithaca with unwonted intensity. *Why* they act finally is also suggested by the story of Ares and Aphrodite: recall that the adulterers flee from the scene in shame because their honor has been soiled. The gods are jealous of their honor; hence, human beings are continuously punished because they threaten the gods' honor.[109] Thus, in view of Athena's sudden decision to restore justice in Ithaca, the equal possibility arises that the divine protection of their honor may also prompt the gods occasionally to *uphold* human justice rather than to allow or even to perpetuate injustice.

This latter possibility is strongly suggested in Laertes' prayer upon hearing of the slaughter of the suitors and the return of his son. Through his words, we witness the effect of unpunished injustice on common beliefs:

Father Zeus, there are gods indeed upon tall Olympos,
if truly the suitors have had to pay for their reckless violence [*hubris*].
(24.351–352)

Laertes acknowledges the gods' existence because injustice has been punished; however, he also indicates by extension a prior and growing disbelief in the gods' existence that arises from the unpunished *hubris* of the suitors. Such disbelief points to the cause of Athena's sudden action on behalf of justice: the indiscriminate rule of the strong over the weak has eroded any widespread belief in a just order. Jenny Strauss Clay, perceptive as ever in her assessment of hidden motivations in the *Odyssey*'s characters, also notes Laertes' implicit complaint: "to extrapolate from what [Laertes] says, if the gods are never just, act only to protect their interests and according to whim, ultimately their very existence may be called into question. . . . Laertes' words suggest that men exert a kind of pressure on the gods to act justly, at least once in a while. Otherwise, there is a danger that no one will attend them."[110]

The gods' valuation of human honor places restrictions on how disregarding of justice they can finally be. Having observed, in Demodocus's song of Ares and Aphrodite, that the gods are only too willing to exist without governance of civic norms, we find it is the *human* demand for justice in their own lives that entices the gods to enforce these norms that they themselves do not follow. The gods, without human worship, have no *raison d'être*; only their entanglement with humanity serves to ennoble their frivolous and fractious existence.

Noting this influence of human demands for justice on divine governance, Clay uncharacteristically does not pursue its implications. Yet its resonance is unavoidable: the call for justice by ordinary people, prompting rulers to act not in their own interest, but on behalf of the common good, is a *democratic* response— rule by the authority of the *demos*. The new foundation of Ithaca—initially demanded through the *agora*, finally agreed upon by warring parties, and both actions guided by the gods—is motivated and ultimately secured through the people's devices. Odysseus's "army" in the reestablishment of justice does not consist of Homeric warriors seeking to plunder a wealthy city; at his side stand a swineherd and a cowherd, both of whom have been praying continuously for a return of decency and justice. It is the prayers and the actions of these weakest characters that move the most powerful—the gods, and even Homeric heroes—to action.

The influence of the people's bestowal of honor as a control on the actions of the powerful is implicit even in the *Iliad*. There Sarpedon describes the obligation of honor that impels him to fight, even against his impulse to survive:

Glaukos, why is it that you and I are honored before others
with pride of place, the choice meats and the filled wine cups
in Lykia, and all men look on us as if we were immortals . . . ?
It is our duty in the forefront of the Lykians
to take our stand, and bear our part of the blazing battle,
so that a man of the close-armoured Lykians may say of us:
"Indeed, these are no ignoble men who are lords of Lykia,
these kings of ours . . . ,
since they fight in the forefront of the Lykians."
Man, supposing you and I, escaping this battle,
would be able to live on forever, ageless, immortal,
so neither would I myself go on fighting in the foremost.
(XII.310–328)

The mechanism of honor—and goods—in exchange for battle is at base feu-
dal. But remove the military imperative from the people's expectations—as finally the *Odyssey* does with the people's demands for peace—and a kernel of
democratic rule is revealed. Sarpedon's partial vision also mistakes the role of the
immortals in this mechanism: it is instead by the very *fact* of their immortality
that they are prompted to act on the behalf of the people. Their endless existence is given content by humanity's attention; disregard their appeals for justice
and their immortality is rendered meaningless.

Of course, democracy proper is not to be found in the Homeric epics; indeed,
defenders of Divine Right long used Odysseus's rebuke of Thersites as evidence
against the wisdom of popular rule.[111] Nonetheless, the natural human—and, for
Greece, divine—craving for honor would become a source in later political philosophy, justifying at least an initial consideration of rule based on the common
good. Unarticulated perhaps, hidden in the curious motions of gods and men,
this early principle nevertheless functions in the pages of Homer. The main audience of the *Odyssey* were not warriors and kings primarily, but common people
whose continued struggle to survive natural, divine, and human cruelty demanded
standards of civility, decency, and justice. Appropriately, the poet addresses only
Eumaeus, the lowly but pious swineherd, directly as "you" (14.14, 55, 165, 360,
etc.).[112] This simple audience's piety finally forces a response from the gods, and
so marks the beginning of a longer odyssey—the education of both god and human
in the ways of justice.

Notes

1. In keeping with Snell and Fränkel, Finley writes: "The basic values of [Homeric]
society were given, predetermined, and so were a man's place in the society and the privi-

leges and duties that followed from his status" (M. I. Finley, *The World of Odysseus*, rev. ed. [New York: Viking Penguin, 1979], 134).

2. Milman Parry, *The Making of Homeric Verse*, ed. Adam Parry (Oxford, U.K.: Clarendon Press, 1971).

3. Cited in Dinesh D'Souza, *Illiberal Education: The Politics of Race and Sex on Campus* (New York: Free Press, 1991), 157.

4. Alasdair MacIntyre, *After Virtue*, 2d ed. (South Bend, IN: University of Notre Dame Press, 1984), 130. See also Alasdair MacIntyre, *A Short History of Ethics* (New York: Macmillan: 1966), chap. 2.

5. Karl Marx, *Grundrisse*, in *The Marx-Engels Reader*, 2d ed., ed. Robert C. Tucker, trans. Martin Nicollaus (New York: Norton, 1978), 222.

6. Marx, *Grundrisse*, 245–246.

7. Marx, *Grundrisse*, 246.

8. Marx, *Grundrisse*, 246.

9. MacIntyre, *After Virtue*, 130.

10. Longinus, *On the Sublime*, in *Classical Literary Criticism*, trans. T. S. Dorsch (New York: Viking Penguin, 1965), 113. On Giambattista Vico's view of Homer, see *The New Science of Giambattista Vico*, trans. Thomas Goddard Bergin and Max Harold Frish (Ithaca, NY: Cornell University Press, 1948), book 3.

11. Max Horkheimer and Theodor Adorno, *Dialectic of Enlightenment*, trans. John Cummings (New York: Herder and Herder, 1972).

12. Horkheimer and Adorno, *Dialectic of Enlightenment*, 46.

13. Vernant writes, "de façon générale, l'homme n'a pas le sentiment de transformer la nature, mais plûtot de se conformer à elle" (Jean-Pierre Vernant, "Travail et Nature dans la Grace Ancienne," *Journal de Psychologie* 52 [1955]: 18–38).

14. See W. B. Stanford on this feature of Odysseus's character (*The Ulysses Theme* [Oxford, U.K.: Basil Blackwell, 1963]). Mera Flaumenhaft notes that "Odysseus's eating, like his marriage and his city, is not merely for life, but for *good* life. . . . He knows that feasting sustains men, not only because bodies need food, but because breaking bread with other men is a social event, a communion" (Stanford, *The Ulysses Theme*, 31). It is important to note his enormous appetite, particularly inasmuch as one of his severest tests will come on the island of Thrinicia, where *restraint* of his appetite to eat the kine of Helios will become a paramount virtue. See Darrell Dobbs on the wider implications of this particular act of restraint in "Reckless Rationalism and Heroic Reverence in Homer's *Odyssey*," *American Political Science Review* 81 (1987): 491–508.

15. Norman Austin, *Archery at the Dark of the Moon: Poetic Problems in Homer's Odyssey* (Berkeley: University of California Press, 1975), 146.

16. See Hannah Arendt, *The Human Condition* (Chicago: University of Chicago Press, 1958), 177. Arendt's description of political life figures aptly here:

> The organization of the polis, physically secured by the wall around the city and physiognomically guaranteed by its laws—lest the succeeding generations change its identity beyond recognition—is a kind of organized remembrance. It assures the moral actor that his passing existence and fleeting greatness will never lack the reality that comes from being seen, being heard, and, generally, appearing before an audience of fellow men, who outside the polis could attend only the short duration of the performance and therefore needed Homer and "others of his craft" in order to be presented to those who were not there. (176–77)

17. Aristotle, *Politics*, trans. Carnes Lord (Chicago: University of Chicago Press, 1984), (1253a; 3). Aristotle describes the social arrangements of the Cyclopes as a village (*kōmē*), a partnership (*koinōnia*), that has not attained full self-rule and hence is not fully political (1252b; 22–27).

18. The lush description of Ogygia occurs at 5.63–74. The description of idyllic Scheria is found at 7.112–132. See Austin, *Archery at the Dark of the Moon*, 149–58, on the significance of these voluptuous gardens regarding the ordering of the external world through artifice and nature.

19. We learn from Telemachus that he cannot accept the offer of horses from Menelaus because the topography of Ithaca does not allow for either the caring for or the riding of horses. The absence of horses on Ithaca attests to the likely perception by one such as Menelaus that it was a relatively poor, disadvantaged location.

20. See Eric Havelock, *The Greek Concept of Justice: From Its Shadow in Homer to Its Substance in Plato* (Cambridge, MA: Harvard University Press, 1978), 143. Havelock makes much of the *agora* called by Telemachus, serving, as it does in the *Iliad*, a dual public function: "It is to provide a forum which will (1) listen to the terms of a dispute as these are made the subject of harangue by contending parties and (2) attest as listeners statements made on oath by either party, attestations in which the gods are to be included." It is because of the very importance of the *agora* in both epics that Havelock denies the real possibility of its absence on Ithaca during the nineteen years of Odysseus's wanderings, easily dismissed as "part of the fantasy of the story" (146). It seems to me the opposite conclusion is, in fact, demanded by the logic of the *Odyssey's* development: the absence of the *agora* for nineteen years does not lessen its importance but increases our understanding of Odysseus's importance as a ruling presence. Indeed, as Mentor, one of Odysseus's fervent defenders in the *agora* attests, and whose shape will be assumed shortly by Athena because his wisdom is renowned,

> No longer let one who is a sceptered king [*basileus*] be eager
> to be gentle and kind, be one whose thought is schooled in righteousness [*aisa*],
> but let him always rather be harsh, and act severely,
> seeing the way no one of the people he was lord over
> remembers godlike Odysseus, and he was kind, like a father.
> (2.230–234)

The net effect, then, of such testament is to elevate Odysseus's position in the community, his renowned commitment to justice or "righteousness [*aisa*]," and, in the final estimate, to equate the civilizing force of the *agora* with the wise and judicious ruler who encourages justice among the *demos*.

21. The deliberative aspect of the Ithacan council should be contrasted with the only other civilization in the *Odyssey* that also holds an *agora*, the Phaiacians. After summoning the *agora* at the beginning of Book 8, as Havelock writes, "No deliberation follows. The king stands up, harangues and gives orders, and leads his princes in a kind of ceremonial exit to escort the stranger to the palace for a banquet. There is no mention of the termination of the agora; its existence has been forgotten" (*The Greek Concept of Justice*, 93). According to the forms of civilization—and the Phaiacians are supremely civilized— an *agora* must be held. But according to the perfection of the Phaiacian civilization, attested to by their closeness to the gods, no deliberation is necessary: the solution is already embodied by the king.

22. Aristotle, *Politics*, 1253a.

23. See J. H. Lesher, "Perceiving and Knowing in the *Iliad* and *Odyssey*," *Phronesis* 26

(1981): 2–24. Lesher notes the emphasis in the *Odyssey* on human inability to recognize the gods, other humans, and even the meaning of language:

> How different is the *Odyssey*. Not only does it frequently display the failure to comprehend the true identity and meaning of what is seen, it also trades significantly on the possibility of failing to grasp correctly the meaning of what is said. . . . [There is evident] a sense of the subtle and potentially deceptive powers of speech, and the corresponding powers of intelligence and ingenuity that is [sic] needed to master them. (17)

Lesher considers these aspects of the *Odyssey* to indicate a philosophic quality, inasmuch as philosophy too must confront the problems of our senses and their perception of apparent reality.

24. Jenny Strauss Clay, *The Wrath of Athena: Gods and Men in the* Odyssey (Princeton, NJ: Princeton University Press, 1983), 17–18.

25. See Erland Ehnmark, *The Idea of God in Homer: Inaugural Dissertation* (Uppsala, Sweden: Almquist & Boltrycken, 1935), 3–21, on this physical commensurability. Similarly, see Arthur W. H. Adkins, *Merit and Responsibility: A Study in Greek Values* (Chicago: University of Chicago Press, 1960), 26. Adkins writes: "In saying that the gods can do anything, the poet has no more in mind than 'if you think of anything which is very difficult for a man, a god can do it easily.'" The ability of humans to injure the gods in battle should indicate the physical similarity of gods and men (V.318–351, in which Diomedes injures Aphrodite, "a weakling goddess"; and V.855–887, in which Diomedes even injures Ares [with the assistance of Athena], himself hardly a "weakling" god).

26. See *Iliad* V.127–128: The human perception is constantly obscured by "mist before the eyes," which is only occasionally lifted by the gods.

27. Austin, *Archery at the Dark of the Moon*, 104.

28. Compare Odysseus's words, "But it would be difficult for even an expert," with Hermes' language, "It is hard for mortal men to dig."

29. Here, in stating "no other man" (*oude tis*), there seems to be a clear echo of Odysseus's "other" name, "Outis" (9.366), or "No-man," that is provided to Cyclops. Only he and "No-man" know the secret of the bed. In both instances, Odysseus is revealing his identity—respectively, to Cyclops and Penelope.

30. As such, the bed seems to partake of all three types of distinctively human activity—labor, work, and action—described in Arendt, *The Human Condition*.

31. See Mera Flaumenhaft, "The Undercover Hero: Odysseus from Light to Dark," *Interpretation* 10 (1982): 9–41. Flaumenhaft points to Odysseus's characteristic ability to locate the means between the extremes: "[Odysseus] is a middleman, specializing in means, in betweens, in the twilights through which one moves from desires to well-defined ends; he excels at dawn, between night and day, and in the middle of the night. His ships are located exactly in the center of the Achaean line (XI.6, 806–807), and Homer places him and his troops exactly at the center of the catalogue of the Danaan ships" (II.631–637).

32. Clay, *The Wrath of Athena*, 184.

33. See Clay, *The Wrath of Athena*, 10–53. Clay is particularly critical of interpreters who take exception to the awkwardness of Odysseus's occasional reference to a divine source for his own knowledge of events of which he otherwise could not possibly know (especially 12.389–390). She writes in response: "It is precisely the awkwardness of Odysseus's necessary aside that draws our attention to the gulf between ordinary mortal knowledge of the gods and the extraordinary knowledge the poet possesses through his privileged relation to the Muses" (*The Wrath of Athena*, 25).

34. MacIntyre, *After Virtue*, 126.

35. I will have more to say about the simultaneous temptations and dangers of the Sirens' song and its relation to the position of "objectivity" or the cosmopolitan view in chapter 5.

36. See Gabriel Germain, "The Sirens and the Temptation of Knowledge," trans. George Steiner, in *Homer: A Collection of Critical Essays*, ed. George Steiner and Robert Fagles (Englewood Cliffs, NJ: Prentice Hall, 1962), 96. Germain compares the temptation of the Sirens to the great temptations throughout ancient literature, including those of Gilgamesh and of Eve in Eden. Notably, both succumb to their dangerous desire. He writes: "To abstain in the face of divine temptation is the mark either of a primitive mistrust . . . or of a superhuman sage." Odysseus's abstention, however, is neither: his is simple physical restraint, in the case of the Sirens. His resistance to Calypso's offer is more complicated but finally suggests neither primitivism nor "superhuman" wisdom, but simple acceptance of his humanity, located between his animal and his godlike propensities.

37. Denys Page, *The Homeric Odyssey* (Oxford, U.K.: Clarendon Press, 1955), 21–51.

38. Denys Page, *Folktales in Homer's Odyssey* (Cambridge, MA: Harvard University Press, 1973), 27.

39. On the interaction of Fate and human choice, see B. C. Dietrich, *Death, Fate, and the Gods* (London: Athlone Press, 1965), 256, n. 3.

40. This tale is told by the poet of the Homeric hymn, *Hymn to Aphrodite*. On this hymn and the subject of aging and decay in the *Odyssey*, see Clay, *The Wrath of Athena*, 141–48.

41. MacIntyre is unwittingly correct to note that the attempt to achieve an existence of objectivity beyond one's own limitations would resemble for the Homeric hero "the enterprise of trying to make himself disappear," given Tithonus's shrunken demise (*After Virtue*, 126). This suggestion is further reinforced by the meaning of Calypso's name, from the verb *kaluptein*, meaning "to cover" or "to conceal." Such a fate is offered figuratively to Odysseus by "the Concealor," and concealment and disclosure are seen by some as the theme of the *Odyssey*. See Agathe Thornton, *People and Themes in Homer's Odyssey* (London: Methuen, 1970). For a subtle and interesting examination of *kaluptein*, Calypso, and Odysseus, see George E. Dimock, "The Name of Odysseus," in *Homer: A Collection of Critical Essays*, ed. George Steiner and Robert Fagles (Englewood Cliffs, NJ: Prentice Hall, 1962), 106–11.

42. See Hermann Fränkel, *Early Greek Poetry and Philosophy: A History of Greek Epic, Lyric, and Prose to the Middle of the Fifth Century*, trans. Moses Hadas and James Willis (New York: Harcourt Brace Jovanovich, 1973). Fränkel's summary of the Trojan cycle is concise: "The complete cycle consisted of eight epics, which went together without gap or overlap. Five epics, of which the *Iliad* was the second, recounted the Trojan War from its beginning until the capture of the city; the sixth, *Nostoi*, reported the homecomings of those who sailed to Troy, with the exception of Odysseus; the seventh was the *Odyssey*; and the eighth dealt with the further travels of Odysseus and his death" (6).

43. One other tragic *nostos* related is that of Ajax (4.499–511), who despite Athena's anger (perhaps deriving from the same cause as that directed against Agamemnon, Menelaus, and Odysseus) would have been saved by Poseidon had Ajax not suddenly "gone wildly mad and tossed out a word of defiance" (4.503).

44. Clay, *The Wrath of Athena*, 49.

45. On this quality, see especially Agamemnon's response to his dream in the *Iliad* (2.1–

76). Rather than calling for the Achaeans to arm for attack, as the dream instructs, he decides to "make a trial" and call a retreat. Richmond Lattimore characterizes Agamemnon at that moment as "a worried, uncertain man" (Lattimore, "Introduction" to *The Iliad*, trans. Richmond Lattimore [Chicago: University of Chicago Press, 1951], 50).

46. His entire journey is undoubtedly extended by the *hubris* of revealing his name to Polyphemus, enabling Cyclops to curse him by name.

47. Austin, *Archery at the Dark of the Moon*, 188–89.

48. As such, Menelaus's offer reminds us of a later "hero" in the Greek tradition, Pericles—this time an Athenian leader responding to the actions of Menelaus's descendants, the Spartans. Pericles uproots the citizens of Athens from their ancestral homes, thus effectively uprooting the community he at the same time praises. See Thucydides, II.13–17 (97–100) and II.35–46 (108–115). On Socrates' critique of Pericles, see J. Peter Euben, *The Tragedy of Political Theory: The Road Not Taken* (Princeton, NJ: Princeton University Press, 1990), 206.

49. Eidotha's advice to Menelaus is in fact identical to the advice given to Odysseus by Circe:

He could tell you the way to go, the stages of your journey,
and tell you how to make your way home on the sea where the fishes swarm.
(4.389–390; 10.539–540)

50. *"ounek echeis Helenen"* can mean literally "because you hold Helen" in a physical sense. If the result of the presence of Helen is immortality, then it makes the desirability of Helen to men the more comprehensible and perhaps suggests an unstated reason for the Trojan War, at least in the minds of Menelaus and Paris, both of whom were willing to sacrifice a people for her.

51. See Erwin Rohde, *Psyche: The Cult of Souls and Belief in Immortality among the Greeks*, trans. W. B. Hollis (New York: Harcourt Brace Jovanovich, 1975). Rohde writes concerning Menelaus's "ascension": "Nothing of the kind is warranted by these lines. Menelaus was never particularly remarkable for those virtues which the Homeric age rated highest."

52. Beye puts a substantially more positive spin on their lives, arguing that theirs is not "spiritual torpor"; nevertheless, he grants that "basically, however, their mood is comfortable" (Charles Rowan Beye, *The Iliad, the Odyssey, and Epic Tradition* [New York: Doubleday, 1966], 172. His analysis does not reflect on Menelaus's immortality, however, and thereby overlooks the source of his "comfort."

53. This drug will even allow one to remain unperturbed at the death of one's parents and even if one's brother or son was murdered in one's presence. The efficacy of such a drug only extends Menelaus's already considerable detachment from mortal troubles. Compare this with Odysseus's reaction to his mother's death (11.87–89).

54. Beye also notes the disharmony in the exchange (*The Iliad, the Odyssey, and Epic Tradition*, 173–74). Again, however, he seeks to downplay any negative aspects, claiming that the interplay contains both "animosity . . . and reconciliatory attempts." I see no evidence of these latter.

55. Telemachus's impatience with his mother's unwillingness to believe that the killer of the suitors is really Odysseus seems a similar response from a young man who dislikes dissent between parental figures (23.97–104).

56. The only episode containing a *lochos* in the *Iliad* is the *Doloneia* of Book X. Odysseus is chosen to accompany the strongest fighting warrior (Diomedes) because "his mind is best at devices" (X.226).

57. See, for example, 1.296; 9.406; 11.120.

58. See Simone Weil's essay "The *Iliad*, or Poem of Force" in *Revisions* (ed. Stanley Hauerwas and Alasdair MacIntyre [South Bend, IN: University of Notre Dame Press, 1983]) for an enthralling account of the intended effects of the constant description of violence in the *Iliad*. Anthony T. Edwards examines at length the contrasting styles of *polemos* and *lochos* in *Achilles in the Odyssey: Ideologies of Heroism in the Homeric Epic* (Konigstein, Germany: Verlag Anton Hain Meisenhem GmbH, 1985), 15–41. Jenny Strauss Clay similarly analyzes *biē* and *nous* in her own excellent treatment of Achilles and Odysseus (*The Wrath of Athena*, 89–112). Finally, see also Gregory Nagy, *The Best of the Achaeans: Concepts of the Hero in Archaic Greek Poetry* (Baltimore: Johns Hopkins University Press, 1979), 42–58. Nagy bases his examination of Achilles and Odysseus on the contrast of *biē* and *metis*. Each of these accounts was instrumental in the development of my own comparison of Odysseus and Achilles.

59. Beye suggests that Achilles rejects the "heroic code": "He finds that he can define himself only through being alive. Glory, material things do not create him. The meaning of existence is existing. . . . Life is all, no metaphysical superstructure or system makes it more meaningful. He will withdraw" exchange (*The Iliad, the Odyssey, and Epic Tradition*, 134). Redfield extends this portrait of withdrawal by suggesting that Achilles has been pushed to the very edge of culture, that "we see a specific version or transformation of the heroic consciousness" (James M. Redfield, *Nature and Culture in the Iliad: The Tragedy of Hector* [Chicago: University of Chicago Press, 1975], 103).

60. Many critics, for example, Redfield, believe that Achilles could not possibly have meant his earlier rejection of the heroic code (*Nature and Culture in the Iliad*, 17).

61. Redfield writes: "Achilles appears . . . an isolated destroyer—a kind of natural force, like fire or flood" (*Nature and Culture in the Iliad*, 107). Yet, in his rage, Achilles is actually an *anti*-natural force.

62. Thomas Van Nortwick, *Somewhere I Have Never Travelled: The Second Self and the Hero's Journey in Ancient Epic* (New York: Oxford University Press, 1992), 68–73. Van Nortwick is also attentive to Achilles' resistance to nature following Patroclus's death, in particular noting his use of nectar both to stop Patroclus's inevitable decay and to substitute his own refusal of food. It is notable that having previously refused to eat, Achilles will later express his hunger by threatening to devour Hector.

63. Redfield, *Nature and Culture in the Iliad*, 108.

64. As Redfield notes, "The poet of the *Odyssey* is, among other things, the first great critic of the *Iliad*" (*Nature and Culture in the Iliad*, 39).

65. These possibilities are reviewed and weighted by Clay (*The Wrath of Athena*, 96–112). Clay pushes her thesis to suppose a hypothetical earlier epic, although I am not quite persuaded that the poet gives us enough evidence about the content of the argument except in a very general sense (nor, for that matter, is Clay so persuaded in the final estimation).

66. See Klaus Rüter, *Odysseeinterpretationen: Untersuchungen zum ersten Buch und zur Phaiakis* (Göttingen, Germany: Vandenhoek & Ruprecht, 1969), 253. Rüter writes: "Indem der Dichter der Odyssee . . . den Helden seines Epos dem größten Helden der Ilias ebenbürtig sein läst, meldet er, wie wir meinen, zugleich für sein Gedicht den Anspruch an, ebenbürtig neben die Ilias zu treten."

Regarding *kleos*, Nagy's discussion is authoritative: "'That which is heard,' *kleos*, comes to mean 'glory' because it is the poet himself who uses the word to designate what he hears from the Muses and what he tells the audience. Poetry confers glory" (*The Best of the Achaeans*, 16). See also Nagy, *Comparative Studies in Greek and Indic Meter* (Cambridge,

MA: Harvard University Press, 1974), 231–55; and Redfield, *Nature and Culture in the Iliad*, 32–38.

67. Page writes with characteristic dispatch:

It is as if the Odyssean poet were wholly ignorant of that particular story which is told in the *Iliad*. Nowhere is there any allusion to the wrath of Achilles or to the death of Hector, or indeed to any other incident, large or small, described in the *Iliad*. Yet the *Odyssey* always pauses to narrate some part of the Trojan story and refers freely to a variety of older and contemporary Epic poems—*always excluding the Iliad*. [*The Homeric Odyssey*, 158; author's emphasis)

D. B. Munro is the most widely noted early proponent of this thesis in *Odyssey: Books 13–24* (Oxford, U.K.: Clarendon Press,1901), 325–27.

68. Here I agree generally with Nagy and specifically with Edwards, who writes: "It seems likely that the *Odyssey* poet was familiar with the *Iliad* at least as an oral text, composed of a relatively fixed song pattern, and formulated in the variable yet formulaic language of the epic tradition" (*Achilles in the* Odyssey, 8).

69. Edwards, *Achilles in the* Odyssey, 11–13.

70. See Adkins, *Merit and Responsibility*, 46–57, for his discussion of "competitive excellences." At the very least, if no formal competition was arranged, a singer would compete against his audience's expectations, as food and shelter were the rewards for a good song and a closed door the consequences of a poor one. See Fränkel, *Early Greek Poetry and Philosophy*, 12–13, on the Homeric bard's precarious existence.

71. Edwards, *Achilles in the* Odyssey, 13.

72. See, for example, its use at III.414 or XVIII.13.

73. Edwards, *Achilles in the* Odyssey, 44ff.

74. Here I disagree with Edwards, who views Achilles' words as "more of a continuation of his position in the *Iliad* than a reversal of it" (*Achilles in the* Odyssey, 51). Although Edwards is correct in noting that Achilles never explicitly chooses *kleos* over *nostos*, his acceptance of his fate (19.115–116) at the very least indicates an ambiguity between his two destinies that the *Odyssey* clearly settles.

75. Ehnmark, *The Idea of God in Homer*, 1.

76. Fränkel, *Early Greek Poetry and Philosophy*, 54.

77. Adkins, *Merit and Responsibility*, 13.

78. Dietrich, *Death, Fate, and the Gods*, 298.

79. Ehnmark departs from most interpretive accounts of the gods by dismissing the characteristic of immortality as ultimately defining. Because immortality results from a particular kind of nourishment—ambrosia and nectar—the gods do not *intrinsically* possess the quality of immortality in such a way that excludes the possibility of human immortality (*The Idea of God in Homer*, 1–2). It is a telling point, but also something of a tautology: the gods are immortal because they have access to immortal nourishment, but therefore they are not essentially immortal. Yet if this is the case, then why do humans not simply procure immortal nourishment? Why is the offer of immortality so precious to the few humans to whom it is extended? If it is not immortality itself that accounts for divinity, then at the very least immortality is an indivisible characteristic of the gods inasmuch as they are beings for whom immortal nourishment is accessible and permissible. Their immortality may be an effect, but it is one that is singularly divine.

80. Bruno Snell, *The Discovery of the Mind in Greek Philosophy and Literature*, trans. T. G. Rosenmeyer (New York: Dover, 1982), 30.

81. Dietrich, *Death, Fate, and the Gods*, 298

82. Adkins, *Merit and Responsibility*, 62.

83. Adkins, *Merit and Responsibility*, 65–66.

84. Ehnmark, *The Idea of God in Homer*, 93.

85. Ehnmark, *The Idea of God in Homer*, 93.

86. Here Adkins may be following Dietrich's formula, who writes of the *Odyssey* that Zeus "becomes concerned with justice among men along the same lines as the collective gods" (*Merit and Responsibility*, 336). Dietrich, like Eric Havelock (*The Greek Concept of Justice*, 123–92), seeks to distinguish the less moral *Iliad* from the more moral and explicitly just *Odyssey*.

87. See W. C. Greene, *Moira: Fate, Good, and Evil in Greek Thought* (Cambridge, MA: Harvard University Press, 1944), 14. As Greene writes of this curious relationship, "It is fair to say that on the whole Homer recognizes no essential conflict, as did certain later poets and philosophers, between the power of Fate and the will of Zeus (and other gods), between the remote power and the active agency. Both express the cause of events which man is powerless to alter, and it is only the demand of the story that determines whether the more abstract or the more vividly personified agent shall be invoked on a given occasion."

88. Havelock, *The Greek Concept of Justice*, 137.

89. Hugh Lloyd-Jones, *The Justice of Zeus*, 2d ed. (Berkeley: University of California Press, 1983), 9–21. Lloyd-Jones's criticism is shared by Norman Austin, who objects in particular to the anachronistic assumption of such an approach: "To concentrate exclusively on isolated words, however, produces an erroneous impression since, in fact, Homer is being judged according to his understanding of later general concepts. The assumption is that the only vehicle for concepts or categories is the individual word. We need rather to examine complexes of words to find the ways in which they relate to each other, and thus to find in their relations the general concepts" (*Archery at the Dark of the Moon*, 84–85).

90. Lloyd-Jones, *The Justice of Zeus*, 14.

91. Lloyd-Jones, *The Justice of Zeus*, 21. C. M. Bowra is perhaps the most noted proponent of this moral interpretation in his *Tradition and Design in the* Iliad (Oxford, U.K.: Clarendon Press, 1930), 19. This accords with his largely moralistic reading of the gods: "The gods watch over men's relations with each other, and if they are unjust, the guilty are punished" (*Tradition and Design in the* Iliad, 228). Redfield, following Milman Parry's *The Making of Homeric Verse*, 5, and C. H. Whitman's *Homer and the Homeric Tradition* (Cambridge, MA: Harvard University Press, 1958), 191, disagrees with this interpretation (*Nature and Culture in the* Iliad, 11).

92. Lloyd-Jones, *The Justice of Zeus*, 7.

93. Lloyd-Jones, *The Justice of Zeus*, 27.

94. No modern commentator conscious of the grave seriousness of rape and the violence against women can endorse Herodotus's easy dismissal of abduction; nevertheless, there is evidence, at least in the case of Helen's departure with Paris, that she left willingly with him.

95. See H. D. F. Kitto, *Poesis: Structure and Thought* (Berkeley: University of California Press, 1966), 133–148; and Clay, *The Wrath of Athena*, 213–246.

96. See B. Fenik, *Studies in the* Odyssey (Wiesbaden, Germany: Hermes Einzelschriften, 1974), 210. Fenik is equally incredulous at the unjustness of Poseidon's defense of Polyphemus: "The blinding was justified in terms of Homeric or any other morality: Odysseus and his men would have perished if they had not acted."

97. Clay's treatment of the meeting between Odysseus and Athena in Book 13 is authoritative. In her analysis she dismisses Athena's excuses and suggests that Athena's anger might actually have had as its source Odysseus's very intelligence, which ever threatens to muddy the border between man and god (*The Wrath of Athena*, 186–212).

98. Perhaps the most famous account of the *Telemachia's* interpolation is that of Wolfgang Schadewaldt in "Die beiden Dichter der *Odyssee*" (in *Die Odyssee* [Hamburg: Rovohlts Klassiker, 1958], 327–32), who nevertheless does not view the interpolation as inferior. For a unitarian defense, see generally Friedrich Eichhorn, *Die Telemachie* (Garmisch-Patenkirchen, Germany: Im Selbstverlag des Verfassers, 1973).

99. Clay, *The Wrath of Athena*, 233–34.

100. Nevertheless, as Kitto argues, the *agora* is not wholly a failure; on the contrary,

[t]he fact that the Assembly accomplishes nothing is the whole point. In the first book we saw the lawless behavior of the suitors within the palace, with Telemachus unable to check it. What Book II does for the poem is bring the lawlessness out of the seclusion of the palace and put it on the public stage: it is not a Greek idea that *adikia*, lawlessness, is a matter only of private conduct and consequence. Telemachus challenges the *polis* to deal with it, and the *polis* either cannot or will not. (*Poesis*, 138)

101. See David Bolotin, "The Concerns of Odysseus: An Introduction to the *Odyssey*," *Interpretation* 17 (1989): 41–57, for a fuller description of Odysseus's negative qualities, particularly his selfishness that tears him between desiring his own return and that of his companions.

102. Dimock, "The Name of Odysseus," 106–11.

103. Bolotin suggests as much: "Odysseus's awareness that the gods were not always able, and in some cases not even willing, to defend the cause of justice seems to have had a further consequence than merely teaching him to be more independent of them. It also seems to have helped weaken his own attachment to justice, and to have strengthened his own tendency to unscrupulous behavior" ("The Concerns of Odysseus," 46). See also Clay's *The Wrath of Athena*, 231, on this aspect.

104. Odysseus's gratuitous deception of his father Laertes is indicative of the difficulty he will have functioning in the peaceful community (24.244–79). Even though he quickly breaks down over the sight of his father's agony, there was no cause in the first place to perpetrate the ruse—the suitors are dead, and he already knows from the soul of his dead mother that Laertes is loyal to his son's memory (11.187–196). His cunning is now merely cruelty without cause.

105. Again, Bolotin points out Odysseus's difficulty with life on Ithaca: "To be sure, he rejoiced when he finally did obey Athena, but his delay in doing so makes us wonder whether Odysseus the warrior would ever become fully reconciled to the life of peace and prosperity that was ahead of him at home" ("The Concerns of Odysseus," 55).

106. This is also the conclusion of Aeschylus's trilogy, the *Oresteia*.

107. Yet even his response contains at base a childlike complaint:

She loves ruinous Ares
because he is handsome, and goes sound on his feet, while I am
misshapen from birth, and for this I hold no other responsible
but my own mother and father, and I wish they never had got me.
(8.309–312)

108. See Austin, *Archery at the Dark of the Moon*, 161; and Clay, *The Wrath of Athena*, 139–40.

109. See particularly the divine punishments of Tityos, Tantalus, and Sisyphus in Hades (11.576–600). Even those who unknowingly offend the gods' honor are subject to punishment, for example, Odysseus's treatment of Cyclops and Poseidon's wrath.

110. Clay, *The Wrath of Athena*, 231–32.

111. In "Homer and Democracy" (*The Classical Journal* 47 [1951–1952]: 338), Abraham Feldman, however, points out that Odysseus's words—"The rule of many (*polykoiranouai*) is not a good thing. Let us have one governor (*koiranos*), one chief (*basileus*)" (2.204–205)—are to be understood in the context of battle: "[Odysseus] was trying to restore military concord among the Greeks in despair and tumult who were getting ready for flight from Troy. . . . [It is] a plea for obedience on the battlefield to a single commander, to save energy for victory."

Although Feldman's article is somewhat dated in its reliance on then-contemporary anthropological evidence, his general argument—particularly the extent to which decision making in the epics is never simply tyrannical but is rather consensual—remains pertinent. For a more traditional if simplistic reading of these lines, see Hans Fenske, *Geschichte der politischen Ideen: Von Homer bis zur Gegenwart* (Frankfurt: Fischer Taschenbuch Verlag GmbH, 1987), 24.

112. This usage is also pointed out by Bolotin ("The Concerns of Odysseus," 57) and Clay (*The Wrath of Athena*, 235–36). See also Seth Benardete, *The Bow and the Lyre: A Platonic Reading of the Odyssey* (Lanham, MD: Rowman & Littlefield, 1997), 117–24. In his recent analysis of the *Odyssey*, Benardete also finds that the epic concludes with a strong affirmation of the ruling potential of the ordinary citizens of Ithaca.

CHAPTER TWO

Resolving the Ancient Quarrel between Poetry and Philosophy: Plato's *Odyssey*

The word, even the most contradictory word, preserves contact.

—Thomas Mann

Odysseus's journey begins in Ithaca and for a moment apparently ends there; but additional travels have been predicted for him by Teiresias, including a peaceful death possibly far from Ithaca and his family and *polis* (11.121–137). Much of the subsequent interpretation of Odysseus's *political* character implicitly takes a stance on Odysseus's fate, especially whether he is to be a political ruler or a wanderer. Does he tire of Ithaca, home, and family? (We might imagine that staid domestic life would quickly lose its charms for one who had seen things above and below the earth, one who had lived so intensely.) Or rather does he leave only to fulfill the prophecy, to guarantee finally for himself and his family a lasting peace with the gods and among humans? Is Odysseus finally political or antipolitical; and by adopting him in one guise or the other as a symbol for human admiration, what are the implications for political philosophy?

For Plato, Odysseus's political and protophilosophic qualities, represented especially through his concern for the institution of justice in political communities, his embrace of limits (especially that ultimate limit, human mortality), and his singular ability to order his soul along the lines described by Socrates in the *Republic* make him an attractive model for the new conception of the philosopher. Moreover, the tension between the two versions of Odysseus—one as the

81

pursuer of *nostos* and the securer of justice within a community of humans, and the other as the explorer abroad—mimics that tension that arises in the relationship between the philosopher and the city. In Odysseus, properly freed of the popular Homeric context of contemporary Athens that celebrated the warrior ethic, Plato finds a suitable analogue for many of those characteristics that suggest the philosopher's inherent majesty and yet also indicate his limitations. Odysseus's constant presence in the *Republic*, often in approving tones, confuses and deepens much of the attack on poetry and imitation and finally suggests the stark limitation of philosophy's rule over the city inasmuch as he—both product and producer of poetry and a dubious citizen—is elevated in the "Myth of Er" for his choice of the soul of a private man who minds his own business.

Writing and Reading

Given that a significant portion of the *Republic* is given over to a critique of poetry and its effects on politics, any analysis of that text must in some ways begin reflexively with a consideration of Plato's own form of writing, namely, the dialogue. The Platonic dialogue is shifting, protean, almost impenetrable; and no serious interpreter of the Platonic corpus has failed to note the difficulties of its interpretation. Hidden in the dialogic form, placed in the voice of a historical character named Socrates, inhabiting different settings with shifting audiences and emphases, the Platonic teaching is all but inaccessible.

In the dialogue *Phaedrus*, Plato suggests one of the paramount reasons for an elliptical style of writing, which involves a curious condemnation of writing generally:

> You know, Phaedrus, writing shares a strange feature with painting. The offsprings of painting stand there as if they are alive, but if anyone asks them anything, they remain most solemnly silent. The same is true of written words. You'd think they were speaking as if they had some understanding, but if you question anything that has been said because you want to learn more, it continues to signify just that very same thing forever. When it has once been written down, every discourse rolls about everywhere, reaching indiscriminately those with understanding no less than those who have no business with it, and it doesn't know to whom it should speak and to whom it should not. And when it is faulted and attacked unfairly, it always needs its father's support; alone, it can neither defend itself nor come to its own support. (275d–e)[1]

Writing is composed of objects frozen in time like those figures of a painting. Being questioned by a living audience, but existing in a crystallized form even beyond the author's death, writing is particularly susceptible to misinterpretation.

So, Socrates concludes with Phaedrus, if one must write, one should practice a form of writing with "intelligent words which are able to help themselves" (276e). Such writing engages in the "dialectic method," that very opaque form of writing that Plato practiced.

Such a critique on its face is straightforward: living beings can respond to questions and misinterpretations, whereas absent or dead ones cannot. Plato appears to make a somewhat mundane point hidden in the engaging story of the Egyptian invention of writing (274c–275b); that is, he conceals this argument within the discursive method he engages to avoid defenselessness. Yet shortly thereafter, Plato complicates this picture, extending the accusation not only to written speech but also to oral speech, in effect to the entire medium of language. His accusation applies also to the recitations of rhapsodes, delivered to sway people's minds, without opportunity for questioning and teaching (277e). Rhapsodes, the disseminators of ancient poetry (those performers who memorized the Homeric corpus and performed it dramatically at festivals and competitions), are, by dint of their unbroken performance, no more instructive than the defenseless written word and as susceptible to misinterpretation. And, as rhapsodes merely repeat verbatim the words of Homer, any purported teachings of the epic poet are also suspect.

As such, writing in itself is not to blame for defenselessness; rather, it is in the nature of language to be misunderstood from the time it leaves the lips or the pen to the time it is received by the ear or the eye.[2] Reception and interpretation of words almost always fail to recapture the original meaning of the writer or the speaker. Those philosophers who attempt to convey a true teaching are obstructed by the use of language and must practice a special form of writing. One must mimic the sensible husbandman, "planting the seeds he cared for when it was appropriate" (276b). Nonphilosophical teachers are therefore highly susceptible to delivering false teachings through ignorance or neglect of their audience.

It is notable that Plato concludes *Phaedrus* by expressly throwing into doubt the teachings of Homer, among other elocutionary, lyrical, and political authorities:

> Now you go and tell Lysias that we came to the spring which is sacred to the nymphs and heard words charging us to deliver a message to Lysias and anyone else who composes speeches, as well as Homer and anyone else who has composed poetry either spoken or sung, and third, to Solon and anyone else who writes political documents that he calls laws: If any one of you has composed these things with a knowledge of the truth, if you can defend your writing when you are challenged, and if you can yourself make the argument that your writing is of little worth, then you must be called by a

name derived not from these writings but rather from those things that you are seriously pursuing. (278b–d)

Traditional authorities—either poetic or political—that is, those authorities whose teaching is respected in part because of its antiquity and in part because it seems to contain a true teaching, must nevertheless be able to give an account for the words they let loose into the world. Only then can such a person properly be called "wisdom's lover—a philosopher" (278d).

In the *Apology*, Plato tests three such sources of authority in Athenian society—the politician, the poet, and the artisan—attempting to ascertain whether one might in fact prove the Delphic oracle false by revealing Socrates not to be the wisest man (21b–22e). The politician and the artisan are revealed not to possess wisdom: the politician only *seems* to be wise; the artisan does possess a definite kind of knowledge, a *techne*, but only a partial art that cannot be extended to include an encompassing wisdom of all things (21c–e; 22c–e). The art tested between these two is that of the poet, who singularly seems to possess wisdom; however, Socrates also observes that no poet can explicate the truth using language besides his poetically inspired words (22a–c). The poets, then, occupy a curious position in relation to true teaching: they fulfill half the Platonic requirement, knowing as they do a form of wisdom or truth; they fail that second requirement of explicating, or "defending," their words. As such, the poet is the most dangerous of the three, possessing a knowledge that is partial and that hence can easily be misconveyed or misused.

The wisdom conveyed by poetry is therefore dubious at best. Because it may contain a kind of truth, truth of a sort that is not easily conveyed through language and that is in fact in almost all cases *misconveyed* in the poetic medium, the truth contained therein may simply be quite irrelevant. Because of its easy misconstrual, poetry most often would seem to teach outright falsehoods. Yet Socrates makes an important comparison with the poets' art in the *Apology*: "Concerning the poets, I quickly recognized that they did not make [*poiein*] what they made by wisdom, but by a certain nature [*phusis*], and while inspired [*enthousiazontes*[3]], *like the diviners and those who deliver oracles*. For they also speak many beautiful things but they know nothing of what they speak" (22b; emphasis mine).[4] The comparison of the poets' art to that of prophets and oracles is most startling, occurring as it does in the midst of a test *about the truth of an oracle*. Contained, then, in this seeming dismissal of the poets' wisdom is at the same time an endorsement of their kind of knowledge; for in the very act of proving their wisdom to be suspect, Socrates also proves the truth of the oracle's mysterious pronouncement.[5] Socrates' form of inquiry is also a form of interpretation; not having the oracle at hand to "defend" its words, he must rather attempt through dialogue and questioning to interpret the cryptic meaning of the oracle. If the poets' art derives from the same source—divine inspiration—Socrates at the same time indicates to us that poetry must be at least as subject to this form of interpretation as oracular wisdom.

The comparison of the poets to the prophets and the givers of oracles allows us to begin distinguishing between what appear to be common targets in Plato's accusation against poetry, namely poets and rhapsodes. For the Athenians, the two were almost identical: great rhapsodes adapted their material for their own voices and meters, some evoking more fear, others more pity; they also functioned as leading interpreters of the great poets, particularly Homer and Hesiod.[6] If, according to Socrates' analogy, we can compare the poet to the oracle, then in this instance Socrates, as interpreter of the oracle, is in a position equivalent to that of a rhapsode. He is charged with interpreting the truth of the puzzling and opaque words of the oracle-poet. Socrates, in a sense, shows us in the *Apology* the philosophical approach to the rhapsodic art.

Elsewhere Socrates demonstrates how even the finest rhapsodes are incapable of proper poetic interpretation. In the dialogue *Ion* he questions Ion of Ephesus about the rhapsodic art, posing innocently as an ignorant questioner (a familiar pose) seeking enlightenment from a great teacher.[7] He praises Ion's art, in which

it is necessary to be busy with many good poets and above all with Homer, the best and most divine of the poets, *and to learn his thought thoroughly, not just his words.* . . . Because one could never be a good rhapsode if he did not understand the things said by the poet. *The rhapsode must be the interpreter of the thought of the poet to the listeners,* but to do this finely is impossible for the one who does not recognize what the poet means. (530b–c; emphasis mine)[8]

In seeming to praise Ion, Socrates rather abstracts the ideal practice of the rhapsodic art from its present practitioner. Ion claims to be the finest rhapsode, particularly for his ability to remember poetry and for his genius in performing those lines, qualities that, according to Socrates, are insufficient for the best rhapsode. Rather, a rhapsode must understand the thought of the poet and then be able to interpret that thought sufficiently to his listeners. Again, the dual requirement seen in *Phaedrus* reappears: if the poet's work contains truth, one must recognize it; but more, one must be capable of conveying that thought in nonpoetic, philosophic, and dialectical language. Yet given that rhapsodes are trained to perform the poems by rote, not to entertain conversation about the poet's words, their intimacy with the poem gives them no better access to the poem's truth than that possessed by a novice.[9]

Behind the apparent agreement between *Ion* and the *Apology* on the matter of the poet's incomprehension of his creation, a curious aporia lurks. If the oracle is also divinely inspired,[10] and Socrates as "interpreter" of that oracle seeks and finds its underlying truth in the *Apology*, then it would appear that a certain human "art" can be involved in the interpretive act, but an art that must follow that method prescribed by Socrates in *Phaedrus*—the dialogue and the dialectic. The divine source of poetry that otherwise "takes away the [poets'] intelligence [*nous*] and uses them as servitors along with soothsayers and diviners of the gods" (534d) is also ultimately a source of truth. Simply repeating the poet's words verbatim does not reveal the god's underlying meaning. One must rather grapple with divine language in human terms, much as Socrates does with the Delphic oracle, or as he likewise does in the apparent condemnation of the poets in the *Republic*. [11]

Reforming the Gods

The accusation against poetry in Books 2 and 3 of the *Republic* consists of two parts: first, that poetry that gives a "bad representation" of gods; second, that poetry that gives a "bad representation" of heroes (377e). Socrates expels the offensive poetry in that order: that concerning the gods first, and then the poetry about heroes. The gods, being prior to man, or paradigmatic of human behavior, must first be redefined and their stories retold before a reevaluation of humanity can occur. The story of Gyges has indicated that not only human beings possessing rings of invisibility are dangerous to the *polis*, but so are any supernatural beings who can undermine human standards, often invisibly, in pursuit of their own pleasures.[12] The challenge against justice by Glaucon and Adeimantus is not merely a human test; they ask Socrates why it would behoove a man to decline becoming a god in the Greek understanding. The question is whether human beings should consider justice as a standard of life at all.

Adeimantus lodges the first complaint against the poets, prompted by his brother's arguments about injustice to bring up the many examples of divine injustice offered by poetic authority (363e–365a). He makes a radical, even sacrilegious supposition:

> But if there are no gods, or if they have no care for human things, why should we care at all about getting away? And if there are gods and they care, we know of them or have heard of them from nowhere else than the laws [*nomoi*[13]] and the poets who have given genealogies; and these are the very source of our being told that they are such as to be persuaded or perverted by sacrifice, soothing vows, and votive offerings. Either both things must be believed or neither. (365d–365e)[14]

His is a curious formulation: the gods must be believed not to exist, or to exist only by convention and hence by *human* origin. In either case, the gods do not exist independent of human conception. Adeimantus combines atheists and the pious in one group: neither believes in the gods, and hence each is aware of the conventional origins of supposedly divine strictures. In either event, the lessons of poetry about the gods allow humans to pursue injustice with impunity, having recognized their conventional origin.

Socrates takes up the accusation but with careful modification, renewing Adeimantus's accusation of the gods in considering the ideal education of the guardians (377e–383c). Socrates' objection to poetry is similar to that of Adeimantus—that it offers an unethical education in justice to the young—but his solution is different. Socrates proposes neither fully denying the gods' existence nor making them wholly conventional; rather, by changing the conventions, he proposes to make their actual existence more acceptable, if negligible. He at once acknowledges the gods' conventionality in popular belief, but by forcing Adeimantus to measure the gods as they are portrayed to how they *should* be, Socrates maintains their existence in an ideal form. Specifically, the tales of the gods as related by Hesiod and Homer must be edited or removed altogether. It is hardly overstatement to suggest that Socrates recommends a rejection of almost the entire corpus of Greek theology, as that theology existed primarily through the work of those very poets.

It is curious that Socrates never claims that the present poetic representation of the poets is false, merely that it is "unacceptable." Indeed, he proceeds with the excision of poetic passages always on the condition that what is kept is morally instructive and what is cut out is morally disagreeable; questions of truth or falsehood are not at issue.[15] At one point Socrates argues: "It musn't be said that gods make war on gods . . . for it isn't even true—provided that those who are going to guard the city for us must consider it most shameful" (378b). Socrates appears to contend that Homer's tales are outright falsehoods; however, he goes on to condition this observation, suggesting that the tales are not true "provided" (or "if") the guardians are to act in a certain way. The stories of the gods will thus depend on their effect, not their validity. Similarly, because these stories are to be first told to children, any "hidden sense" that to an older listener would be edifying should likewise be rejected (378d–e). Socrates leaves open the possibility that adult listeners may be allowed to listen to poems with an ear to such a "hidden sense."

Like the regular citizens of Ithaca, human beings must act in all events as if the gods are just, lest human belief in a just universal order prove unfounded. But more than Homer, Plato here suggests that humans must take an active and conscious role in reforming the gods, not merely relying on their eventual commitment to justice, but in fact reformulating divine behavior in such a way that it conform to justice, even if not to the truth. In effect, the gods must be forced to conform to human formulations of justice if they are to be believed in; as stated by Adeimantus, either a conventional image of the gods is worshipped or none at all. Plato adopts the *Odyssean* solution, but to philosophic ends: the gods will conform to human expectations of justice, but humans will act preemptively, now controlling divinity through philosophy, not allowing the gods to control belief through invocation to the Muse. If the reformulation of the gods means that humanity is alone responsible for instituting justice politically, then it is no less true that the inspiration for such an act will not come from the Muses—as in the case of the poets—but from the philosopher alone.

The resulting portrait of the gods is one of utmost propriety, if not one of coldness. Although the gods will never act unjustly, will cease to war among themselves, will not be swayed by sacrificial offerings of appeasement, and will not incline to take human form to test the morals of humankind, nowhere does Socrates suggest that the gods will actively *reward* or *punish* men for justice or injustice. True to his word to Glaucon and Adeimantus, justice will not be recommended for its ability to procure divine rewards or to bring down divine sanctions. As Seth Benardete comments on these new gods: "The gods are as indifferent to friendship as they are to enmity. They are so much the models of self-sufficiency that they cease to be models of care. Indeed, since Socrates assigns them hypothetically a will only to deny them the possibility of exercising it, it is not clear whether they are meant to be alive. Perhaps they are beautiful but invisible statues."[16]

Education, including punishment and reward, is to be a wholly human affair. The gods may be appealed to in theory as a model for excellence and virtue, but their behavior will have no effect on nor implications for humanity. In the final estimation, Socrates has misled his charges: it is not the poets who are to be expelled in this first reformulation of poetry, but rather the gods.

Interpreting Heroism

The second reformation of poetry in Book 3, after that of the gods, concerns that of heroes or exceptional humans. The main difference between heroic humans and gods comes down to the fundamental fact that humans must die. Hence Socrates appropriately begins by discussing perhaps the greatest philosophic subject, the mortality of humanity. To engender decent citizens who, unlike Achilles in the underworld, must fear slavery more than death and, beyond that, to produce philosophic souls, humanity's greatest fear must be overcome. A full and conscious confrontation with death is necessary to gain the philosophic stance.

As Eric Voeglin writes, "Under the aspect of death the life of the philosophical man becomes for Plato the practice of dying; the philosophers' souls are dead souls . . . and, when the philosopher speaks as the representative of truth, he does it with the authority of death over the shortsightedness of life."[17] The fear of death, more than childhood stories of the gods, is the provenance of adults; thus, overcoming this fear must be directed at both "boys and men" (387b). As such, the poetic treatment of heroes must in some ways be more sophisticated for the more mature mind of the adult; there may be a "hidden sense" (cf. 378d) in these stories that was not to be found in the more straightforward treatment of the gods. In particular, in the curious dismissals of Homer's depictions of the afterlife, arriving at a hidden sense is unavoidable.

Socrates' method of dismissing Homer in Book 3 is most unusual, if not to say unjust. As Gadamer argues, one of Plato's strongest objections to poetry was the easy abuse to which it was subjected by purported authorities (such as was exercised by Ion): "Given the dominance of the spoken word in the Greek world, a poetic formulation taken out of context as creed or maxim went from the ear to the soul without the poet's overall intention defining and limiting its application."[18] Such a practice seems to underlie Socrates' objection to the "defenseless" written word in *Phaedrus*. Likewise, the fear of being used as an authority out of context would therefore indicate Plato's reason for adopting the discursive method, of placing his arguments in the guise of other characters, and thus making the summary of a "Platonic philosophy" supremely elusive.[19]

However, this is precisely the treatment that Homeric poetry receives at the hands of Socrates in Book 3 of the *Republic*. Socrates cites offensive passages out of context, contorting their meaning, even recommending their excision, when in fact an edifying moral accompanies the passage. His method is so outrageous that it invites us to check the accusation of immorality against the original text itself. As Leo Strauss observes: "Socrates almost literally invites us to reexamine the passages he purportedly cuts, in a sense turning our attention more closely to the poetic source even as he claims to expel it from his city. An old tactic of calling attention to certain passages by quoting them, even while condemning them, is undertaken by Socrates."[20] In so doing, Socrates initiates a new kind of interpretation of poetry, one that forces the careful reader to confront the ancient texts with renewed vigor and even to disagree with the words of Socrates as he or she begins to confront Socrates' meaning.

The most obvious invitation to reconsider the Homeric texts is offered through a series of quotations about the underworld that are considered by Socrates to be offensive (386c–387b). Seven quotations from Homer are offered; typically, whether they are from the *Iliad* or the *Odyssey* is not indicated. Their symmetrical ordering is noteworthy: the first, the middle, and the final quotes are from the *Odyssey*; the middle pairs are from the *Iliad*.[21] Concentrating on the citations (at 386c–387b) from the *Odyssey*, the first citation to be excised is that famous pronouncement of Achilles' in the underworld, who laments his death to the visitor Odysseus:

> I would rather follow the plow as thrall to another
> man, one with no land allotted to him and not much to live on,
> than be a king over all the perished dead.
> (11.488–491; 386c)

As suggested in chapter 1, this single pronouncement by Achilles marks an interpretive break between the *Iliad* and the *Odyssey*. Whatever the reason for Achilles' choice to battle Hector—and this passage indicates that it was likely his anger, not his commitment to the short, glorious life—it was never an altogether well-reasoned course of action. In Hades, amid the sifting souls of the dead, Achilles eternally bewails his rash action, preferring slavery to death—precisely that sentiment that is explicitly banished from the *Republic*. Yet, to omit this line destroys the dramatic and substantive difference between Achilles and Odysseus. By highlighting the offensiveness of Achilles' preference for enslavement, Socrates in fact calls attention less to the need for excising those exact words than to questioning the reverence of the hero who pronounced them. The edifying aspect of these lines is suggested inasmuch as this passage will be cited again by Socrates, curiously applied to the reluctance of the philosopher outside the cave to redescend in the Allegory of the Cave in Book 7.[22] Furthermore, it will additionally be adopted in an altered form by Socrates in the *Apology* (38d–e).

Likewise, the final citation of the seven (I will address the central one last because it can be argued that it is the most important) describes not Achilles but the souls of Penelope's suitors descending to Hades. Their fate is grim:

> And as when bats in the depth of an awful cave flitter
> and gibber, when one of them has fallen out of his place in
> the chain that the bats have formed by holding one another;
> so, gibbering, they went their way together, and Hermes
> the kindly healer led them along down moldering pathways.
> (24.6–10; 387a)

These souls are not the "heroes" in this instance, but rather the archetypal villains of the *Odyssey*, performing or intending to perform the most heinous acts against Odysseus and his family. It is strange, then, that shortly after citing this passage Socrates should state among the reasons for its removal that "for the decent man . . . being dead is not a terrible thing" and that he should not be lamented "as though he had suffered something terrible" (387d). The passage cited, however, does not refer to "decent" men; indeed, though bred as gentlemen, the suitors exhibit the worst features of aristocracy flouting justice. Thus, Socrates here proposes to excise a passage for reasons that do not wholly accord with the context from which it was taken.

The central citation of the seven, highlighted by the others, presents the existence of the sole sentient being among the souls in Hades: "He alone possesses understanding [*nous*]; the others are fluttering shadows" (10.495; 386d). The passage refers to Teiresias, the object of Odysseus's journey to the underworld. According to Homer, Teiresias is the only soul to have retained his "understanding" or "intelligence" (*nous*) in the underworld. Nevertheless, many other spirits speak with Odysseus; and Teiresias, like the others, must drink the ram's blood in the macabre ceremony that awakens the souls of the dead to speech (11.95–99). Teiresias's *nous*, then, does not differ in its initial manifestation from those others in Hades; but once "activated," his wisdom remains. Like the rest of the dead souls, he retains what was with him in life: for Achilles, it is his indignant anger; for Teiresias, his foresight and wisdom. Allan Bloom rightly notes this retention of one's mortal qualities, but he seemingly forgets that Socrates explicitly seeks to *excise* this passage, thus in a sense excising a recommendation of wisdom in mortal life. [23] Yet by citing this passage, both in its negative commentary on the afterlife of the "fluttering souls" and, more notably, in the positive mention of Teiresias's retention of wisdom, Socrates allows commentators like Bloom to extract a positive lesson from the passage, even as it poses as a negative example to those who would be more apt to fear its apparent lessons regarding the horrors of death. From the meaning of this purportedly censored passage, Socrates is eventually able to develop a more positive portrait of the afterlife, again in the Myth of Er in Book 10 where one's wisdom—or lack thereof—in the past life informs one's decision about the next.[24]

The conclusion that Socrates begins drawing an elusive positive lesson from the *Odyssey* in the early books of the *Republic* is further supported by the curious nature of the remaining citations from the *Odyssey* in Book 3. Among the passages of Homer that are recommended for removal is a passage from the *Odyssey*, declared by "the wisest of men" (meaning Odysseus), that claims that "the finest of all things" is the time when

the tables are loaded
with breads and meats, and from the mixing bowl the wine steward
draws the wine and carries it about and fills the cups.
(9.8–10; 390a–b)

Socrates accuses this passage of encouraging the physical and erotic appetites of the guardians, in opposition to the moderation that must be instilled in the excessive, unhealthy regime. Nonetheless, Socrates again deceives somewhat through the selectiveness of quotation: the passage cited is not so much a celebration of food and wine as a celebration of fellowship. The immediately preceding lines of the *Odyssey* read:

> Surely it is a good thing to listen to a singer
> such as this one before us, who is like the gods in singing;
> for I think there is no occasion accomplished that is more pleasant than when
>   festivity holds sway among all the populace,
> and the feasters up and down the houses are sitting in order and listening to the
>   singer.
> (9.3–8)

It is at first striking that Socrates skips these lines in choosing what is to be omitted, concentrating on the description of food and wine but implicitly accepting the preceding lines praising the hearing of poetry. The image of camaraderie and fellowship that is implicitly retained is itself reminiscent of two such moments in the *Republic*. The first is the closing description of the "healthy" city, or the "city of pigs" (in Glaucon's estimation) of Book 2: "Setting out the noble loaves of barley and wheat on some reeds or clean leaves, they will stretch out on rushes strewn with yew and myrtle and feast themselves and their children. Afterwards they will drink wine and, crowned with wreathes, sing of the gods. So they will have sweet intercourse with one another" (372b).

If Socrates recommends excising those florid passages of bounteous food and drink in Homer, then it would on its face appear that such passages must be excised from his own *Republic* as well. And such is apparently the case: for while the simple people of the first city sing praises to the gods, there is an unmediated aspect to their song—there is no poet.[25] Yet Socrates excises *not* the praise of the poet's song from the *Odyssey* but rather the praise of food and wine. Implicitly, then, if pictures of plentiful material repast are to be eliminated in the second city, the poets are to be allowed to remain. Even as Socrates rehearses the aspects of poetry that are to be rejected, it is suggested that the poet's song will be necessary to mediate the second city's citizens' relation to the gods, inasmuch as the immediacy of the first city has also been lost.[26]

The second arresting image hinted at by the purportedly excised image of gustatory excess from the *Odyssey* is, in fact, the framing discussion of the *Republic* itself, the dialogue of Socrates and the young men. Brought together with a promise of dinner (328a), they pass the night without food but deep in conversation. Although initiated through coercion, and viciously interrupted by the shameless Thrasymachus, the subsequent conversation is not unremiscent of the one described in the *Odyssey*, except that instead of the poet singing the praises of the gods, it is the philosopher praising justice.[27] The poet is allowed back into the second city in the guise of the philosopher, or the philosopher will find it necessary to employ poetry in the creation of that city. The very act of founding the city, the very dialogue of the *Republic*, would itself be suspect under Socrates' rules of excision; again a paradox arises that succeeds in calling more attention to the curiousness of Socrates' "censored" passages than their simple rejection would at first indicate.

This suspicion is almost too obviously confirmed through the next passage to be eliminated from the *Odyssey*: "Hunger is the most pitiful way to die and find one's fate" (12.342; 390b). In one of the most blatantly decontextualized passages yet cited, Socrates seems to indicate that the person's words damning hunger are a main lesson of the text, in this case the *Odyssey*. However, the speaker is not Odysseus; the words are those of Odysseus's second in command, Eurylochus, who is admonishing his men to disobey Odysseus's and the gods' order not to eat of the Sun god's herd. Eurylochus succeeds in his importuning over Odysseus's objections; of all the remaining Ithacans attempting to return from Troy, only Odysseus refuses to eat, despite his hunger.[28] The Sun god exacts his revenge on the impious: the last of Odysseus's ships is destroyed and its men drowned, with the exception of the one who did not eat. Socrates' suggestion to excise this passage is clearly outrageous; in context it instructs one that hunger or thirst is not the worst form of death, that the prudent, pious, and wise man will resist his hunger when necessary. The sense of Socrates' argument disagrees with the words he chooses to excise; in effect, Socrates reveals himself to be in agreement with the lesson of the *Odyssey*.

Through the last passage to be cited by Socrates, this implicit agreement with the *Odyssey* finally becomes explicit. Socrates earlier refuses to engage Adeimantus's suggestion to discover passages that one might positively use to educate the guardians, as they are "founders," not "poets" (379a). However, in one instance, while citing the *Odyssey*, Socrates breaks his word and gives an example of admirable poetry; he says: "But, if there are any speeches and deed of endurance by famous men in the face of everything, surely they must be seen and heard, such as 'Smiting his breast, he reproached his heart with a word. Endure, heart; you have endured worse before' " (20.17–18; 390d). This is the only *positive* example of instructive poetry offered by Socrates in his discussion of poetic education (against his stated intention not to offer one); thus, the importance of the virtue being recommended here is stressed. That virtue is generally moderation, the virtue shortly recommended by Socrates in Book 4 (moderation and justice being the only ones shared by all the classes in the city, although justice is an outcome, in part, of this shared moderation [432a]) and one that will be revealed to be among the most important of the philosophic qualities. Socrates also cites this single passage of the *Odyssey* as a positive example of endurance in the Homeric corpus; yet he cites it as simply an instance of those examples that "should be seen and heard" (ironically, praising in this case Odysseus's invisibility and silence). What Socrates in fact implicitly recommends is the entirety of the *Odyssey* itself, the epic poem par excellence of the enduring, prudent hero. Whereas the first citation from the *Odyssey* indicates that Socrates condemns the *Iliad*, this final one suggests that the *Odyssey* is to be retained.[29]

With the reformulation of the gods and the ancient heroes, Socrates concludes that only "human beings" remain—the city in speech will concern only these more humble creatures.[30] Yet if Socrates has arguably "expelled" the gods from the city, it is not so clear that the heroes have been expelled as opposed to being simply reevaluated. Socrates keeps the words of Odysseus rebuking his heart and any passage like it (390d). Later, in discussing the need for moderation and self-control in the Guardians, Socrates reaffirms his commitment to maintaining this passage, citing Odysseus's rebuke as an example of the higher, rational faculties taming the *thumos* (441b). Because now only human beings remain and Odysseus is shown to have been kept because of his qualities of moderation and self-control, Socrates indicates that Odysseus has in a sense been lowered in status— from "hero" to human being—but in doing so shows his esteem for Odyssean virtues. Whereas Achilles' godliness makes him too unstable and dangerous for the *polis*, Odysseus's embracing of his humanity makes him a candidate for Guardian, perhaps even philosopher.

Endurance is a prominent quality of the philosopher. Socrates' endurance on the battlefield is renowned.[31] The philosophic quality of endurance is reflected as well in Socrates' endurance of the coercion that initiates the conversation and in his greater endurance of the accusations of Athens's leading citizens and eventually his death sentence. If Socrates at various points equates a kind of endurance with philosophy—for endurance requires neither great strength nor beauty but firmness of soul—then he also points to the philosophical qualities of the long-enduring Odysseus.[32] Even while seeming to dismiss the content of the poem, Socrates succeeds in pointing anew at its more subtle qualities of instruction, those aspects that when quoted out of context may be objectionable, but when read with a more dialectic understanding of Homer indicate a more productive partnership between poetry and philosophy, indeed a form of philosophic poetry.

Achilles and Odysseus

Even though Plato is perhaps only implicitly dedicated to retaining, if reformulating, Odysseus's type of heroism in these early books of the *Republic*, Achilles fares less well in these pages. Odysseus is never mentioned explicitly by name in the critique of Homeric heroism,[33] even if his peculiar virtue is cited as a positive one by Socrates; on the other hand, Achilles' character is attacked explicitly by name. After criticizing the portrayal of heroes for fearing death, for lying, and for excess, Socrates begins a critique of the heroic love for money but ends by singularly condemning Achilles:

> "And for Homer's sake," I said, "I hesitate to say that it's not holy to say these things against Achilles and to believe them when said by others; or again, to believe that he said to Apollo,
>
> You've hindered me, Far-Darter, most destructive of all gods.
> And I would revenge myself on you, if I had the power;[34]
>
> and that he was disobedient to the river, who was a god, and ready to do battle with it. . . . It must not be believed that he did. The dragging around of Hector around Patroclus' tomb, the slaughter in the fire of the men captured alive: we'll deny that all this is truly told. And we'll not let our men believe that Achilles—the son of a goddess and Peleus, a most moderate man and third from Zeus, Achilles who was reared by the most wise Chiron—was so full of confusion as to contain within himself two diseases that are opposite to one another—illiberality accompanying love of money, on the one hand, and arrogant disdain for the gods and human beings on the other." (391a–c)

What begins expressly as an accusation against Achilles for "illiberality accompanying love of money" suddenly develops into a far more sweeping condemnation of Achilles' hateful relationship to humanity and divinity.

Socrates' more severe condemnation of Achilles unfolds most deviously, as he at first only circumstantially proves that Achilles is a lover of money. The examples he gives of this supposed Achillean quality are, in the first case, Achilles' acceptance of Agamemnon's gifts in order to return to the fighting (390e; *Iliad* IX.515–526; XIX.185–221) and, in the second instance, Achilles' apparent willingness to give up Hector's corpse in return for money (390e; *Iliad* XXIV.594). The startling aspect to both these accusations against Achilles is that they are simply not true in the sense Socrates wishes to convey: Achilles in fact *does* reject Agamemnon's gifts when offered by the Embassy in Book IX and only accepts them as inconsequential after the death of Patroclus.[35] Similarly, he accepts the gifts of Priam in return for Hector's body, describing the bounty as "not unworthy," but only after being ordered by Zeus to return the body and accept the gifts in the first place (*Iliad* XXIV.64–76). In each case Achilles only accepts money as a secondary concern, demonstrating at first an almost entire disregard for wealth.[36] He is motivated primarily by his passions, and mostly by his anger.

One might posit many possible reasons for Socrates' curious if unproven accusation against Achilles: one, perhaps, is that money is *not* a leading desire of the ancient heroes. Honor is, above all, their greatest desire; money and possessions are but the outward manifestation of that honor, not a value in themselves. Perhaps Socrates here attributes to the ancient poets a quality he wishes circumspectly to criticize among his contemporaries. Nevertheless, the preeminent explanation for Socrates' misleading accusation against Achilles is suggested by the very insignificance of the first accusation (Achilles' purported love of money) as compared to the second (his "arrogant disdain for gods and human beings"). The second, slipped suddenly into the main thesis of the first, is actually the most damning by far of all Socrates' critiques of the heroic code, and one that goes to the very essence of Achilles' character. His refusal to fight on the plains of Troy, his disobedience to god and man, and his very resistance to nature and divine limitations are finally those qualities that most define the heroic qualities of Achilles and give cause for widespread admiration of his character in Plato's Athens. By cushioning this most radical of critiques in an unsubstantiated accusation, Socrates begins to disassemble this ancient admiration of that very hero who is successively revealed to be his opposite and archenemy.

The dual movement of condemning Achilles and elevating Odysseus in the *Republic* is mirrored notably in Socrates' speech before the Athenian *demos*, the *Apology*. According to Eva Brann, the arguments and statements that compose the *Apology* in many respects represent not so much a "defense" of Socrates as an "offense" against Athens.[37] Clearly among the most "offensive" of these defenses is Socrates' claim to resemble the "son of Thetis," Achilles. Addressing an imaginary interlocutor who questions Socrates' awareness of the dangerous path he has set upon by choosing philosophy, Socrates responds:

> "According to your speech, those of the demigods who died at Troy would be paltry, both the others and the son of Thetis. Rather than endure anything shameful, he despised danger so much, that when his mother (a goddess) spoke to him he was eager to kill Hector—something like this, as I suppose: 'Son, if you avenge the murder of your comrade Patroclus and kill Hector, you yourself will die; for directly,' she declares, 'after Hector, your fate is ready at hand.' But when he heard this, he belittled death and danger, for he feared much more to live as a bad man and not to avenge his friends. 'Directly,' he declares, 'may I die, after I inflict a penalty on the one doing injustice, so that I do not remain here ridiculous beside the curved ships, a burden on the land.' Surely you do not suppose that he thought about death and danger?"[38] (28b–d)

Socrates' comparison of himself to the heroic Achilles must strike the jury as unusual. As Thomas West writes: "That Socrates should compare himself to Achilles is, of course, ludicrous. Before the judges stands an ugly old man of seventy who is about to be condemned to death. Achilles was the beautiful, strong youth whose courage and skill in battle had no equal."[39] The outrageousness of Socrates' claim here is then plainly shocking: he does no less here than to make Achillean heroism at the same time Socratic heroism.

Yet, Socrates' claims to the mantle of Achilles are not quite true here either. Indeed, one could say that the comparison does Socrates some disservice. Achilles flaunts death by the time of Patroclus's death, but up to that point he has revealed significant ambivalence about soldiering and the heroic life. There is some indication that he would prefer to live "the long, uneventful" life that is offered to him if he leaves the shores of Troy.[40] On the other hand, directly after invoking Achilles, Socrates notes his distinguished military service: he is indeed no Achilles, no hero, but he differs in one significant way—he never abandons his post (28e). The battles in which Socrates fought, moreover, do not compare to the victorious Trojan War; according to Thucydides, each was either an outright defeat or an inconclusive victory. Socrates' greatest virtue as a soldier was demonstrated more in his behavior during retreats than for his Achillean prowess against the enemy.[41] As such, he shows the distinctly non-Achillean quality of obedience—in any army, and especially a *democratic* army, the essential quality of a soldier and a citizen. The initial absurdity of the comparison Socrates invokes—he surely cannot compare to Achilles' nobility—begins to take on an opposite light. Achilles' cowardice—especially his fear of death—and his vainglorious and finally cruel method of warfare is a shoddy comparison to Socrates' quiet dignity. Achilles is in a sense *elevated* by the comparison; by reversing the audience's expectations, Socrates begins the delicate public process of reassessing the traditional reverence of Achilles.

The rhetorical question that Socrates poses to the Athenian jurors about Achilles—"Surely you do not suppose that he thought about death and danger?"—is revealed to be wholly ironic in light of the entire portrait of Achilles, particularly given his curse against death in Hades as portrayed in the *Odyssey*. This assessment differs decisively from leading interpretations of the *Apology*, most of which view Socrates' identification with Achilles as representing a Socratic approval of Achilles.[42] Among the most sensitive of these is that of J. Peter Euben in his superb treatment of ancient Greek tragedy and philosophy, *The Tragedy of Political Theory*. In his discussion of the *Apology*, Euben tries to maintain a tension between Socrates' identification with and his "critique and reconstitution" of Achilles: but in effect both these projects suggest that Socrates finally "keeps" Achilles as a source of reverence, however altered.[43] This is particularly confirmed by associating the two in their approach to death: "Like Achilles he [Socrates] accepts his fate willingly even though it means death."[44] The interpretive problem arises, then, when Socrates again allusively compares himself with Achilles, however this time clearly to Achilles' disadvantage. Facing the death penalty now, Socrates echoes the famous words of Achilles that he had banned in the *Republic* (386c): "But I have been convicted because I was at a loss, not however for speeches, but for daring and shamelessness. . . . But neither did I then suppose that I should do anything slavish because of the danger, nor do I now regret that I made my defense speech like this: I much prefer to die having made my defense speech like this, than to live like that" (38d–e).

Socrates *reverses* the curse of Achilles against death—unlike the lamentation in Hades in which slavery is preferable to death (11.488–491), Socrates professes a preference for death over slavery to the expectations of the *polis*. At the same time that he *rejects* the final stance of Achilles regarding his choice between life and death as propounded in the *Odyssey*, he *calls attention* to Achilles' ignoble speech as well. The very phrase that had been rejected in the *Republic* as unworthy for citizens to hear is now practically—however elliptically—recited for the Athenian *demos*. Socrates reveals that such passages have not been banished entirely but should be used carefully and instructively by the philosopher who seeks to use these negative examples as positive lessons.

The problem for commentators like Euben is how to square their prior suggestion that Socrates endorses Achilles' supposed embrace of death with this latter statement that effectively reveals Achilles' ignominy. Euben dispatches the problem in a footnote, stating:

> [Socrates] is also a rebuke to traditions of warlike virtue that have been built up around Achilles. It is interesting that in the last part of the last speech in the *Apology* Socrates obliquely reintroduces the analogy between himself and Achilles. Only it is now Achilles of the *Odyssey* and the passage where the greatest Greek hero would rather be a serf tilling the soil for another than rule over the dead (11.488–491). As Sallis rightly says (*Being and Logos*, pp. 62–63), Achilles here drops his heroic stance and "calls into question the world of the Homeric hero."[45]

Euben asserts that it must be *Achilles* who "drops his heroic stance" at the price of neglecting his earlier ambivalence about fighting in order to maintain the connection between Socrates and Achilles. Yet the action of the *Iliad* reveals that he never entirely embraced the heroic code to begin with: if his initial decision to withdraw from the battle derives from Agamemnon's breaking the heroic code, by the time of the Embassy in Book IX, Achilles has decided that living by that code is not enough if death is the consequence. It is *Socrates* who drops the *Achillean* stance and reveals in fact that all along the answer to the rhetorical question "Surely you do not suppose that he thought about death and danger?" has to be "*yes*."[46] In refusing to endorse Achilles' lamentation in Hades, Socrates rejects Achilles' stance and by extension embraces that of Odysseus—the hero who also chooses a long life but does not reject death when it comes. Achilles as an example of how to live the *philosophic* life is rejected from the outset, not just in these closing moments. His character all along is too driven by *eros*, by love, by apprehension, by rage—by *slavishness*—to be comparable to the philosophic character.

Besides the implicit comparison of Achilles and Odysseus in their approach to death, there is a particular point toward the end of the *Apology* in which it is further suggested that Odysseus is elevated by Plato, namely when Socrates names the souls that he wishes to meet in the afterlife. As Leo Strauss points out, there are two lists of names in the *Apology*—that of the friends of Socrates who are present at the trial (33d–34a) and that of the worthy souls in the underworld (40e–41c). On this first list is one of only three places in the dialogues in which Plato is mentioned by name. Plato's is the second-to-last name in the first list; Odysseus's is the second-to-last name in the second.[47] Although this comparison is suggestive, it is nevertheless also at first puzzling. For if throughout the *Apology* Socrates has been portrayed as the new hero displacing the old, one would have expected Plato to be compared to (or to have *compared himself* to) Homer. Plato is the new poet, hence the new educator, of Greece; Socrates is his main heroic character.[48] But Homer and Hesiod appear in the *center* of the second list, indicating their importance but not the explicit connection to Plato.

Plato is finally like Odysseus because he chooses to tell his own story, in a sense, to *become* a poet. Plato writes the dialogues, creating a character "Socrates" who is based on a real Socrates much as Odysseus creates a poem starring a character "Odysseus." If there is anywhere in Plato a repudiation of Socrates' refusal to write, one can perhaps find it here: the tales that Odysseus tells to the Phaiacians are not only tales that instruct, but also tales that will secure him a journey home and hence the opportunity to refound the political order of his home. The political philosopher attempts to create something *permanent*, even while recognizing that all regimes are flawed and destined for decay.[49] In telling his long story before the Phaiacians, Odysseus demonstrates how poetry—including describing cities in speech—is another form of immortality that is sanctioned by the gods for humanity.

The development of the "city in speech" in Plato's *Republic* seems to purposively recall another fanciful "city" in earlier Greek literature, that city imagined by Odysseus on "Goat Island." There, Odysseus's understanding of the exigencies of useful arts for the full development of political life similarly results in a strict division of labor. The social life of the Cyclopes, by comparison, resembles more extensively the defining features of that first city—"the city of utmost necessity"— outlined by Socrates and Adeimantus (396d–371e). Possessing only a rudimentary division of labor (it seems that no Cyclopes build houses, as they live in caves, nor do they have any knowledge of cooking, as creatures are eaten raw, but they do seem to know some arts of shepherding [cf. 370a–b]) and having no knowledge of shipping to permit imports and exports (cf. 370e), no currency (cf. 371b), no laborers (cf. 371e), no laws, nor finally even informal gatherings of storytelling and camaraderie outside the *oikos* (cf. 372b), the Cyclopes seem only to achieve the status of a "city of pigs."[50] Indeed, Odysseus's expression of surprise at the absence of development on the uninhabited island off the Cyclopes' shore stands at least as a precursor to Glaucon's disgust at hearing of life without "relish" in "the city of utmost necessity" (372c–d). Odysseus's longing, like that of Glaucon's, is not for "mere life" afforded by either immortality with Calypso or the narcotic existence on the island of the Lotus-eaters (which resembles in some ways the first, "healthy" city developed by Socrates and Adeimantus). Odysseus's disgust contains elements of material longing, political concerns, and philosophic inclinations, the combination of which, between Glaucon and Socrates, will go into building the second, "feverish" city and will allow for the inquiry into the nature of justice, which Plato permanently captures in telling the "story" of Socrates.

It should finally be recalled that among the few whom Odysseus spares during his heated revenge (22.344–380), one is a poet: so, too, by writing down the encounters of Socrates, "the myth is saved."[51] Plato here stops short of associating philosophy with Odysseus, although he will suggest this association more firmly at the conclusion of the *Republic* in the Myth of Er.

The New Poetry: The Myth of Er

The preceding examination of Plato's reassessment of ancient poetry, particularly his devaluation of Achilles and the *Iliad* in favor of Odysseus and the *Odyssey*, if it has been persuasive nevertheless leaves the major question unanswered: *why* is Odysseus to be considered worthy of our admiration and perhaps even to be considered as a precursor for the philosophic disposition? More than a summary reassessment of Plato's attitude toward poetry, the conclusion that Socrates is involved in a subtle but deliberate attempt to reevaluate the Homeric epics and to elevate the *Odyssey* and its hero over the *Iliad* and its hero leads one to a more sweeping interpretive conclusion about the *Republic's* recommendations for the philosopher. The preceding conclusions serve to alter the customary approach to the lessons offered by the "caves" of the *Republic*—not only that cave in the Allegory of the Cave in Book 7, but the underworld setting of the Myth of Er—

inasmuch as we find the new Odysseus both times prominently featured, as he also so often explored caves in the *Odyssey*.

As Eric Voeglin points out with accustomed sensitivity to resonance and myth in Plato's thought, three descents and ascents in the *Republic* are linked: (1) that initial descent by Socrates to the Piraeus ("I went down"—*katebēn*—is the first word of the *Republic*); (2) the ascent and descent of the philosopher in the Allegory of the Cave; and (3) the final descent and ascent of Er.[52] The image overarching each of these is that of Hades, or that lightless, lifeless cavern the portrayal of which Socrates purportedly excises in his reformulation of heroic courage in Book 3. Voeglin recognizes the theme of descent and ascent as one intentionally echoing that most famous journey to the underworld in Greek literature: "But above all it recalls the Homer who lets his Odysseus tell Penelope of the day when 'I went down [*katebēn*] to Hades to inquire about the return of myself and my friends' (23.252–253), and there learned of the measureless toil that still was in store for him and had to be fulfilled to the end (23.249–250)."[53] If the resonance of all these descents in the *Republic* recalls Odysseus's descent to Hades, then significantly the one descent in which Odysseus is mentioned by name—the Myth of Er—holds an interpretive key about the preceding images and, I will argue, about the ultimate viability of the *Republic*'s recommendations itself when the role of Odysseus in the Myth of Er is considered retrospectively in relation to the Allegory of the Cave in Book 7. The closing myth of the *Republic* finally and explicitly teaches us about how to understand the figurative and literal ascent and descent of human and philosopher. As ever with Plato, for whom Socrates' death marks a simultaneous ascent and descent of philosophy, we begin at the end.

The Myth of Er is perhaps the most curiously placed myth in the whole of the Platonic corpus: it effectively contradicts a major argument that has preceded it. Book 10 begins with the apparent expulsion of poetry because of its very *mimetic* nature, that is, its distance from reality itself (595a–608b), and then ends almost nonsensically with a poem of sorts—a myth about the afterlife witnessed by another and retold by Socrates (who has of course from the outset been narrating the entirety of the *Republic* to an unnamed listener a day after the fact [327a]). Socrates finally and strikingly admits that the expulsion of poetry is less than total, given the fact that the story of the "city in speech" and the search for justice must conclude with his own philosophic poetry about the afterlife.[54]

The tale, or so-called Myth of Er, is told purportedly by Er of Pamphylia who was killed in a war but comes back to life after twelve days just as he is to be burned on a funeral pyre. On coming back to life, he relates what transpired in "the other world" (614b). What startles about the so-called Myth of Er is that, having spent significant sections of the *Republic* apparently excising the poetry of Homer—including the comprehensive attack on poetry in the early portions of the same Book 10—the myth contains several revealing and complimentary allusions to the *Odyssey* in particular. Socrates begins his tale of Er with an allusion to the story that Odysseus tells the Phaiacians of his own journey home (*Odyssey*, 9–12), including the story of his descent to Hades (*Odyssey*, 11). The most significant and the last of the references to the *Odyssey* occurs during the description of the choices of lives by the souls in the afterlife, culminating in the choice made by the soul of Odysseus, who, it appears, is the only soul who chooses in a truly prudent, wise, and reflective manner. This most significant reference will be discussed at greater length later in this section.

The earlier reference to the *Odyssey* occurs at the outset of the myth, when Socrates denies that he will tell Glaucon "a story of Alcinous" (614b), as Odysseus's tale was commonly known.[55] What Socrates means by this claim is not entirely clear: at its least meaningful, he may merely be denying that he will make a long-winded tale.[56] More significant, unlike Odysseus's tale of the underworld, a tale of arbitrary punishment and general misery will not be portrayed. Rather, a tale of suitable deserts for lives of justice and injustice will be related; Socrates will not retell the old Homeric myth of the afterlife but will create a wholly new mythology more in keeping with the philosophical principles of life that he has just finished relating.

A further, more intriguing possibility remains: as in Book 3, when comparing the "Noble Lie" to a "Phoenician thing" (386c), Socrates may be referring again to that founding myth of the city in speech; but now (since in Book 10 he denies he will tell a "story of Alcinous," hence not a tale for Phaiacians), this latter myth will contain no untruths. The earlier "Noble Lie" sought to persuade the multiplicity of people introduced into the city after Glaucon's condemnation of the city of pigs that they shared a common origin; at the same time, it sought to place divine approbation on those differences arising from different inborn talents and subsequent training. The Myth of Er tells this same story after a fashion—it is not about the birth of humans and the genesis of the city, but rather about the death and afterlife of every mortal. All humans are to be equal in their finality: like that common birth, they will eventually meet a common fate in death.[57] Yet, now their differences will be distinguished according to their previous life-paths: if in the earlier "Noble Lie" human difference had to be justified by an appeal to heaven, in the afterlife differences will be a result of our own choices. There is no longer any need to lie: human differences and inequality are not divinely sanctioned, nor for that matter irreversible, but result from *human* decisions. As the myth relates, "A demon will not select you, you will select a demon. . . . The blame belongs to him who chooses; god is blameless" (617e).

If the "Noble Lie" suggests that our inequalities have a divine origin, and hence cannot be changed by human effort, the Myth of Er alternatively suggests that our differences are ultimately the result of our own decisions and hence can be undone or remade. Moreover, although our decisions in the afterlife are influenced by the habits of our previous lives, we begin from a standpoint of fundamental equality in the choices we make about the nature of our next life. As the "spokesman" (*prophētēs*) relates, there are many more "patterns" of lives than souls who will choose them; thus, in theory we all have the same possibility of choosing wisely (618a). Our equality is finally most fundamental, not our inequality, because even those most disadvantaged by previous habit and life-circumstances can still exercise wise choice if they can achieve "the capacity and knowledge to distinguish the good from the bad life, and so everywhere, and always to choose the better from among those that are possible" (618c).

This latter reference to the "Noble Lie," and the extent to which the gods are now absent from the new truth, also recalls the preceding discussion of poetry that concluded less in the expulsion of poetry than in the expulsion of the gods. As the "gods are blameless," Socrates explicitly reveals that the gods no longer exercise an arbitrary will over the lives of humans, as apparently they did in Homer. As portrayed in Book 2, they reign ethereally in heaven with no direct influence on the actions of people. As the end of the *Odyssey* suggests, humans will exercise control over the morality of the gods (since, in the case of the *Republic*, we will choose which poetic theology is beneficial for the city), not vice versa. Nevertheless, those who choose badly will still seek to blame their choice on anyone—"chance, demons, and anything"—rather than on themselves (619c). Injustice, even of one's own making, will still seek recourse to the existence of the gods, if only for someone to blame; this behavior mimics Zeus's complaint at the outset of the *Odyssey* (1.32–43) that humanity unfairly blames the gods for their own choices. The existence of gods, if only for the sake of false accusation, is finally more necessary for the unjust than the just.

After the souls choose the lives they will lead in their next incarnation, Er describes that each must have their choice confirmed by the Fates then make their way "through terrible stifling heat to the plain of Lethe." The heat blanketing *Lēthē*—the plain of forgetting—creates an enormous thirst, and "it was a necessity for each to drink a certain measure of the water [of Carelessness], but those who were not saved by prudence drank more than the measure. As he drank, each forgot everything." By drinking the water of Carelessness—an unavoidable step before rebirth—each soul is said to forget the entire motivation for choosing the present life, hence forever making each soul subject to the habituation of the life it chooses each time and never benefiting from the knowledge gained from previous lives. As Julia Annas observes, because "we are supposed to forget our previous incarnations anyway . . . , there is no reason to be depressed by the fact that nothing any individual does makes any difference to the eternal cosmic pattern."[58] According to this view, rather than suggesting the paramount importance of our choices, the myth suggests that we stand to learn very little from previous lives except the habituation of our immediately preceding life, a habituation that may in fact make it impossible for us to adequately reflect on the choices most important for determining our life paths.

Yet this conclusion overlooks an important detail: on the plain of Lethe, prudence (*phronesis*) may guide us to drink only the measure of water of Carelessness, not more than is our due. The same prudence we bring from our previous life, which assists us in our choice of our next life, may prevent us from forgetting as much as those souls without prudence, or assuming their same degree of "carelessness." The prudent soul may be enabled to remember more of what it has previously learned, especially the prudence that guided the soul to drink only that measure that was properly allotted.[59]

The ability to control our thirst, especially when it is the result of "stifling heat," may indicate more than merely prudence. Earlier in the *Republic*, Socrates has suggested that the ability to control one's impulse to drink more than one's measure is the sign not merely of prudence but of a properly ordered soul that intimates the possibility of a philosophic life. In Book 4, when discussing whether the properly ordered soul may be compared to the "city in speech" that they have created, Socrates claims that "the single man—with those same forms in his soul—thanks to the same affections as those in the city, rightly lays claim to the same names [of the virtues]" (435b–c). Thus, he concludes that the soul is governed in the same manner as the "city in speech" is governed: the "calculating" part governing the appetitive and irrational parts. To argue his point, Socrates makes the following points in his conversation with Glaucon, ones that are suggestive in light of the later details from the Myth of Er:

Insofar as [our desire] is thirst, would it be a desire in the soul for something more than that of which we say it is a desire? For example, is thirst . . . [a desire] for any particular kind of drink? Or isn't it rather that in the case where heat is present in addition to the thirst, the heat would cause the desire to be also for something cold as well . . . and where the thirst is much on the account of the presence of muchness, it will cause the desire to be for much, and where it's little, for little . . . (437d–e) Therefore, the soul of the man who's thirsty, insofar as it thirsts, wishes nothing other than to drink, and strives for this and is impelled toward it. . . . If ever something draws it back when it's thirsting, wouldn't that be something different in it from that which thirsts and leads it like a beast to drink . . . ? (439b) Isn't there something in their soul bidding them to drink and something forbidding them to do so, something different that masters that which bids?" (439c)

The "something" that differs from desire, according to Socrates, is "calculation" (*logismos*), which, when present in sufficient strength in the soul, is able to govern the appetites and desires (439d). Identifying this form of "calculation" with the "spiritedness" that is the defining feature of the "auxiliary" class, Socrates turns to poetic authority (in spite of the preceding critique of poetry in Books 2 and 3) for further evidence of the kind of governance that "calculation" can exercise over desire:

[Consider] the testimony of Homer that we cited in that other place somewhere earlier (i.e., 390d),

He smote his breast and reproached
his heart with word . . . (*Odyssey*, 20.17–18)

Here, you see, Homer clearly presents that which has calculated about better and worse and rebukes that which is irrationally spirited as though it were a different part. (441b–c)

Socrates had cited these lines earlier as evidence of the kind of poetry that should be preserved in the just city, indicating both that poetry was not to be completely expelled and that there was evidence even in the suspect Homeric texts of an edifying lesson—namely, the example of Odysseus's governance of his own appetites (390d). In the context of the discussion of thirst that preceded the citation of the *Odyssey* and in light of the importance of self-control over one's thirst in the afterlife on the plain of Lethe, the example of Odysseus is all the more notable given his exemplary ability to deny the temptations of food at certain points in his journey, notably when confronted by the Lotus-eaters and when wracked by hunger on the island of Thrinicia.

Further, the Homeric lines favorably cited by Socrates in Book 4 recall that moment when Odysseus, having returned from his journey, lies on the floor of his own home listening to the wanton revelry of the suitors and the traitorous maidservants. Though tempted by desire to act rashly and visit destruction on the defilers of his home, he governs his passion by recalling the moment when he resisted killing Cyclops in a similar rage, reasoning that were he to kill Cyclops, he and his men would be trapped in the cavern, as they would be unable to lift the stone covering the door. In effect, the governance of *logismos* is linked to *phronesis*: calculation works in the service of prudence (as in both instances he will successfully achieve his vengeance, if but a little later), just as prudence is fortified by calculation. One must know not only in what manner to act, but when and how. Socrates offers us the positive example of that soul who, in the Myth of Er, is able to act with *nous*, or intelligence, in exercising its choice.

Prior to arriving on the plain of Lethe, Odysseus's soul by lot (pure chance) has received the last choice of the lives witnessed by Er. His earlier habituation, as with the others, guides his choice: "From memory of [Odysseus's] former labors it had recovered from love of honor; it went around for a long time looking for the life of a private man who minds his own business; and with effort it found one lying somewhere, neglected by the others. It said when it saw this life that it would have done the same even if it had drawn the first lot, and was delighted to choose it" (620c). It is clear that Socrates intends us to admire Odysseus's soul for the choice he makes in the afterlife. In his warning that the souls should not pick rashly, the "spokesman" (*prophētēs*) announces, 'Even for the man who comes forward last, if he chooses intelligently [i.e., with *nous*] and lives earnestly, a life to content him is laid up, not a bad one. . . . Let not the one who is last be disheartened'" (619b). His "prophetic" announcement anticipates the choice of the soul of Odysseus, who by lot is fated to choose last but still finds the soul he would have chosen had he been designated to choose first. His soul searches "for a long time" (620c), obviously exercising more reflection than that first soul who rashly chose the life of the tyrant fated to eat his own children "and other evils" (619b). However, if we are to note that Odysseus's is among the only souls to act out of more than mere habituation from his last life, what is admirable about the particular life that the soul of Odysseus chooses is not altogether obvious. Socrates does not explicitly say that the soul of Odysseus chooses the life of the philosopher or that his choice will lead to the institution of the just city in speech. Rather, it is simply the fact that he chooses the life of "the private man who minds his own business" that is intended to elicit our admiration. If the method of Odysseus's soul's choice is notable for its singular reflection, the choice itself remains perplexing.

Many commentators on the Myth of Er do not pause to reflect on the grounds or rationale for admiring the particular life that the soul of Odysseus chooses.[60] Those few that have reflected on the grounds for Odysseus's soul's specific choice agree that it is noteworthy, but disagree on the grounds.[61] For example, Seth Benardete argues that "the experiences of Odysseus" might suggest the possibility of "freeing oneself from habit," but nevertheless concludes that Odysseus's soul does not intimate the possibility that one can choose the life of Socrates: "Socrates himself seems never to have been Odysseus. His *daimonion*, he said, was probably unique (496c, 4–5)."[62] On the other hand, Allan Bloom suggests that Odysseus's soul's choice *does* intimate a subsequent incarnation not only as a philosopher, but as Socrates: "The wise voyager Odysseus gains higher status [in the myth]. All he needed was to be cured of love of honor (a form of spiritedness), and he could live the obscure but happy life of Socrates."[63] In fine, the few interpretations of the *Republic* that attend to the content of Odysseus's soul's choice of lives do not long dwell on the reasons for their admiration, although there is agreement nonetheless that our admiration is warranted.

Yet why admiration should be forthcoming for the choice of "a private man who minds his own business" is elusive (620c). Bloom suggests that this choice intimates the life of Socrates; yet while the choice of a "private man" (i.e., one not actively involved in politics) hits the mark, one can hardly conclude from the description of Socrates' activities in the Platonic corpus that he is a man who "minds his own business." It depends, in large part, how one interprets the phrase "private man who minds his own business" (*bion andros idiōtou apragmonos*, 620c). Odysseus seems to choose exactly the life that most opposes his past history and seemingly his own disposition.[64] In the pages of the *Odyssey*, neither is Odysseus a private man (*idiōtēs*)—after all, he is king of Ithaca, even when he is absent from his island—nor does he "mind his own business." Indeed, minding one's own business requires one to avoid "being a busybody" (*polupragmonein*), or literally avoid "doing many things" (cf. 433d). Odysseus—he of "many ways" (*polutropos*)—is the supreme example of the human who does many things. Among the first things we learn of Odysseus is that "many were they [the men] whose cities he saw, whose minds he learned of ("*pollon d' anthropon iden astea kai noon egno*" [1.3]). The man who is neither private nor avoids "doing many things" is said to choose the seemingly opposite life when his soul is given the choice of all possible lives after death.

To fully understand the phrase "to mind one's own business," we must again recall an earlier conversation in Book 4 of the *Republic*. "Minding one's own business" is said to be the defining feature of justice in the "city in speech": each class will mind its own affairs without interfering in the affairs of any other class (433a). Thus the guardians will rule, the auxiliaries will defend, and the artisans and workers will produce. Because the city is to be understood as simply a larger version of the soul (368c–369a), Socrates goes on to say in Book 4:

> And, further, Glaucon, I suppose we'll say that a man is just in the same manner that a city too was just. . . . We surely haven't forgotten that this city was just because each of the three classes in it minds its own business. . . . [Further,] we must remember that, for each of us too, the one within whom each of the parts minds its own business will be just and mind his own business. (441d–e)

He concludes:

> But in truth, justice was, as it seems, something of this sort; however not with respect to a man's minding his external business, but with respect to what is within, with re-

spect to what truly concerns him and his own. He doesn't let each part in him mind other people's business or the three classes in his soul meddle with each other, but really sets his own house in good order and rules himself: he arranges himself, becomes his own friend, and harmonizes the three parts, exactly like three notes in a harmonic scale, lowest, highest and middle. (443c–d)

To prefer the life of one who "minds his own business" seems in the first instance to mean that Odysseus's soul prefers the life of the just man, one who has properly ordered his soul to "mind its own business," thereby charging "the calculating part to rule, since it is wise and has forethought about all our soul, and for the spirited part to be obedient to it and its ally" (441d). Because it would appear that the temptations to tyranny are overpowering in any but a private man (recall that the choice of the first soul is for the life of the tyrant (619b–c]), Odysseus's soul appears to make its choice secure in the knowledge that only "the private man who minds his own business" can continue to maintain a properly ordered, even just soul.

However, elsewhere in the *Republic* Socrates describes the life of this private, *apragmonon* man in different terms. In Book 6 he describes the response of the philosopher—now the proposed ruler of the just city in speech—who retreats from the "madness of the many" in order to preserve himself:

> Just like a human being who has fallen in with wild beasts and is neither willing to join them in doing injustice nor sufficient as one man to resist all the savage animals, one would perish before he has been of any use to city or friends and be of no profit to himself or others. Taking all this into the calculation, he keeps quiet and minds his own business—as a man in a storm, when dust and rain are blown about by the wind, stands aside under a little wall. Seeing others filled with lawlessness, he is content if somehow he himself can live his life here pure of injustice and unholy deeds, and take his leave from it graciously and cheerfully with fair hope. (496d–e)

This description of the private man who "minds his own business" goes beyond that one in Book 4, not only encompassing the earlier definition of one whose soul is properly ordered, hence just, but extending the definition to a philosopher who literally avoids being a busybody, that is, stays out of the affairs of others. Both the internal and the external senses are employed here: internally, the various parts of the philosopher's soul are said to "mind their own business" (hence indicating that perhaps only the philosopher can have the truly just soul); externally, the philosopher seeks to weather the violent storm of his polity by remaining apart from the violence of others. In the context of the choice of Odysseus's soul, what is unclear is whether Socrates intends us to understand the Myth of Er as recommending the life of one whose soul is internally ordered or who, adopting the stance of the philosopher in a storm, remains at a remove from the polity in which he lives.

Several specific life-paths resulting from the choice of the soul of Odysseus seem possible given these preceding definitions. As Benardete suggests, perhaps we are to understand Odysseus's soul's choice to resemble that of the prephilo-sophic private person with the well-ordered soul who is described in Book 4—a person who avoids rule but does not seem especially likely to pursue the philo-sophic life of Socrates. Perhaps we are to understand that Odysseus will return to life as a full-blown philosopher but will hang back from his society for fear of his life and philosophy, resembling more the philosopher described in the Allegory of the Cave in Book 7. Or perhaps Allan Bloom is correct that Er's tale leads us to conclude that Odysseus's next life will be that of Socrates, namely that of the private man whose soul is ordered, who does not seek public office, but who nevertheless "does many things." The myth and the passages describing the vari-ous ways that one can "mind one's own business" allow us to reach any of these conclusions without offering us evidence to conclude that any one is the most likely.

The Myth of Er in fact finally requires this uncertainty. In some respects, the myth bears some surface resemblances to the scenario that the philosopher John Rawls would later describe as "the veil of ignorance."[65] According to Rawls, the principles of a just society can be arrived at by imagining "a purely hypothetical situation," a thought-experiment in which individuals are only allowed severely limited knowledge about their personal circumstances.[66] He describes this ex-periment as one in which an individual occupies an "original position" behind a "veil of ignorance." With only scant information about the kind of world we will inhabit, the individual must choose what kind of society he or she would agree to enter given the various possibilities of actual wealth, poverty, talent, edu-cation, advantages, and disadvantages that will be the possession of the individual outside of the veil.[67] The souls in the Myth of Er are given a similar kind of choice, although not one in which souls seek to arrange the society in which they will live, but one in which the souls are charged with choosing the "pattern" of a life that they *must* lead once they have been reborn. While the "paradigm" of those lives will be known to the souls in greater or lesser degrees, they will have almost no knowledge of what kind of family, society, or polity they will enter, thus rep-resenting the reverse of Rawls's "veil of ignorance."

Of course, the choice of some lives necessitates a certain kind of society. For example, the first soul chooses the life of a tyrant, guaranteeing that the soul will live in an autocratic, unjust regime. This choice—made purely out of habitua-tion, without the necessary reflection to avoid the many evils of the tyrant's life—actually represents a narrowing of life possibilities for that particular soul. The soul that chooses without prudence will, in turn, be given no chance of exercising prudence once it assumes its new life. For the most part, however, the spokesman (*prophētēs*) seems to suggest that souls will choose only "patterns" of lives. As Jacob Howland observes, the existence of certain life-patterns "indicates that although each life is in some ways different from all others, individual human lives are not unique in their essentials."[68] Indeed, if each soul is initially responsible for choosing the life it will lead, the life it chooses will in turn come to govern the ordering of the soul that initially chose it. As the "spokesman" relates, "an ordering of the soul was not in them [i.e., the patterns of lives], due to the necessity that a soul become different according to the life it chooses" (618b). Each life will react differently and perhaps surprisingly on the soul that chooses it, potentially reordering the soul so that it will likely make a different choice when next it is presented with the lottery of lives in the afterlife.

Plato, unlike Rawls, seems to suggest that we can have more influence over the kind of life we will lead than over the kind of society in which we will live. When Socrates pauses for a moment to explain to Glaucon the significance of Er's tale, he concludes:

> Now here, my dear Glaucon, is the whole risk for a human being, as it seems. And on this account each of us must, to the neglect of other studies, above all see to it that he is a seeker and student of that study by which he might be able to learn and find out who will give him the capacity and the knowledge to distinguish the good from the bad life, and so everywhere and always to choose the better from among those that are possible. Thus he must know the effects, bad and good, of beauty mixed with poverty or wealth and accompanied by this or that habit of soul; and the effects of any particular mixture with one another of good and bad birth, private station and ruling office, strength and weakness, facility and difficulty in learning, and all such things that are connected with a soul by nature or are acquired. From all this he will be able to draw a conclusion and choose—in looking off toward the nature of the soul—between the worse and better life, calling worse the one that leads it toward becoming more unjust, and better the one that leads it to becoming juster. (618b–e)

In contrast to Rawls's argument that justice requires a fundamental *ignorance* of these substantive qualities that both govern the direction and become the goals of one's life, Socrates here argues that we must above all be concerned with how these qualities will allow us to distinguish the good from the bad life, between justice and injustice. By implication, the "veil of ignorance" may allow us to imagine what principles would be required for a just society, but it deprives us of the most necessary tools that would be required for making us desire to live a just life or desire a just society in the first instance.

Furthermore, Plato seems to suggest that part of the grounds for a soul's choice must be the expectation that one will be born in a vicious regime, but without abandoning an accompanying "fair hope" (*kalēs elpidos*) that one will be born into a fine city. As each soul makes its choice, it must be prepared to live like that philosopher amid the "wild beasts," protecting itself "under a little wall" from the ravages of the storm (496a–e). At the same time, although Socrates has agreed that preserving one's life in this manner would be "not the least of things" (497a), neither would it be "the greatest either." The "greatest" thing would be, according to Socrates, "to chance upon a suitable regime [for the philosopher]. For in a suitable one he himself will grow more and save the common things along with the private" (497a). Thus, the philosopher neither craves "to keep quiet and mind his own business" in every event nor seeks to remain a private man in all instances, but only in those situations that make it likely that his philosophy would "be of no profit to himself or others" (496d).

Most significantly, the choice of Odysseus's soul reflects the very prudence that made him praiseworthy during the consideration of poetry in Books 2 and 3 and that mark his ability to control his thirst on the plain of Lethe. Rather than unwisely choosing, either a soul that is not well governed or one that too fully anticipates the situation in which his life will unfold, Odysseus's soul chooses a life that will likely retain the ordering of his soul. Whether he becomes a philosopher or a "busybody" or even a Socrates will depend in large part on the situation into which he will be born. As when he achieves his homecoming, he arrives in the guise of a beggar—a seemingly "private man" who seeks to mind his own business, but one who awaits an opportunity, if presented, to be of profit to himself and to others. In effect, he chooses to remain a man "of many ways," but one, in all events, whose soul will be justly ordered.

Based on evidence in the Myth of Er, we can finally surmise what specific labors cured Odysseus of his love of honor. Given the many allusions to Odysseus's character to this point, Socrates refers specifically to those "labors" that most endorsed Odysseus's connection to humanity. Specifically, it is notable that of all the human souls mentioned by Er, only Odysseus's retains both his original human form and gender. One is reminded of his ability on Circe's island to resist being turned into a swine (unlike Adeimantus in the city of pigs), with the assistance of the gods and their knowledge of nature. His knowledge of nature permits him to retain his human form; through it he controls the bestial that commands the souls of most others. Likewise, his acknowledgment of human limitations and of his inexorable attachment to his family and people allows him to resist Calypso's offer of immortality. Odysseus is the man who declines both bestiality and divinity when offered—he remains human. At the same time, his exploration of the bestial and the divine parts of the human soul makes him finally the most philosophic and most wise of the ancient heroes: as such, he prepares the way for the next soul, almost certainly a just soul, and very likely the soul of a philosopher.

Odysseus, who reproved his heart and ordered its restraint, was earlier chosen as the one model of excellent poetry explicitly to be retained in the just city (390d). It must, however, be recalled that his rebuke to his passion occurs so that he might more successfully release his anger in the near future—the following day. His restraint serves as a means to the end of the violence he will release on the unjust community that has arisen in his absence. Once released, moreover, it proves difficult to restrain; Zeus and Athena combined must compel him not to continue the slaughter of townspeople. In Socrates' approval of Odysseus's restraint, a hint of the purpose of that restraint is also allowed—so, too, in the *Apology* does Socrates adopt the guise of one who will someday seek vengeance (38c–39d; esp. 39c). But the choice of the philosopher's soul also finally suggests that violence will cease to be a weapon of choice for the wise man; his weapon will be the pursuit of truth over the course of time, more unwieldy and less immediately effective, but also one that does not necessitate the intervention of the gods to cease its excesses, as is required in the case of violence.[69]

The preceding attacks on poetry, both in Books 2 and 3 and in Book 10, would have otherwise left us unprepared for Odysseus's elevation were it not for indications throughout that prepared for the explicit excellence of Odysseus in the Myth of Er. Inasmuch as Odysseus's choice reveals the depth of his wisdom and prudence and signifies the road of the philosopher, it also signals that the epics of Homer have finally been retained but will henceforth be read differently as Socrates has taught throughout. In attempting to excise passages and even in condemning the *mimesis* that misled people's emotions to identify with unworthy characters, Plato has demonstrated the impossibility of his suggestions while simultaneously indicating a new definition of heroism that appeals to human, not bestial or divine, elements of the human soul. The elevation of Odysseus in the Myth of Er finally points us back to the old epics, to seek there what Plato has already told us we might find there.

The Philosopher's Choice: Ascent or Descent

That Odysseus's soul chooses the potential life of a philosopher in the next life sheds light, in retrospect, also on the philosopher's relationship to the city. There is an appropriate coincidence in structure here between the *Odyssey* and the *Republic*. In the *Odyssey* we only find out the true significance of Odysseus's refusal of immortality (Book 5) later when Odysseus relates his descent to Hades (Book 11) that has nevertheless already taken place. Similarly in the *Republic*, Odysseus's choice of souls in Book 10 has significant implications for the philosopher's choice whether to redescend to the cave in Book 7.

The allegory portrays the philosopher's painful ascent from the false images and the darkness of the cave to the brilliant truth symbolized by the Sun (514a–521b).[70] Recently, a leading controversy about the cave's meaning centers on the question of whether the philosopher, once having reached the bright land of truth above the cave, would choose to return to the subterranean region and subsequently whether a philosopher would condescend to rule even if "citizens" of the cave could be persuaded to accept such leadership. One's answer to this question finally determines how one interprets the solution offered by the *Republic*: if the philosopher refuses to descend, the solution of the philosopher-king to the problem of justice proves impossible, and the *Republic* is a work about the "limits of the city";[71] alternatively, his voluntary descent would at least allow for the possibility of the "city in speech" to come into being.[72]

The cave image is the central image of descent and ascent in the *Republic*, occurring between the initial descent of Socrates to the Piraeus and the final descent of Er to the underworld. Significantly, it reverses the action of these other two ascents: rather than beginning above, descending, then reascending, the Allegory of the Cave begins below, describes the ascent of the philosopher, then posits the possibility of the philosopher redescending. Rather than the more positive action that describes the life, death, and rebirth, the Cave allegory describes the macabre deathlike existence in the cave, the true life afforded by ascent, and the unwilling return to the underworld. Little wonder that Allan Bloom and others rebel against the philosopher's purported requirement to redescend:

> It is true . . . that the potential philosophers must be compelled to leave the cave as well as return to it. But once out, they recognize how good it is to be out. They never see a reason to go back, and compelling them to go back is said to be good for the city, not the philosophers. If they thought it good to go back, they would not be good rulers. It is only by going out that they became aware that the kallipolis is a cave, nay Hades, and to be in it is as to be a shade.[73] (516d; 521c; cf. 386c)

Given the dank bleakness of Hades, it would apparently be in any human being's best interest to avoid redescent to death at any cost.

Bloom's argument, while comprehensible, is nonetheless more explicitly that of Glaucon than Socrates. It is Glaucon who objects to the compulsion required to force the philosopher's redescent and Socrates who defends its necessity:

> "Then our job as founders," I [Socrates] said, "is to compel the best natures to go to the study which we were saying before is the greatest, to see the good and to go up that ascent; and, when they have gone up and seen sufficiently, not to permit them what is now permitted."
> "What's that?"

"To remain there," I said, "and not be willing to go down again among those prisoners or share their labors and honors, whether they be slighter or more serious."

"What?" he said. "Are we to do them an injustice, and make them live a worse life when a better is possible for them?"

"My friend, you have again forgotten," I said, "that it's not the concern of law that any one class in the city fare exceptionally well, but it contrives to bring this about for the whole city, harmonizing the citizens by persuasion and compulsion, making them share with one another the benefit that each class is able to bring to the commonwealth. And it produces such men in the city not in order to let them turn whichever way each wants, but in order that it may use them in binding the city together." (519c–520a)

Glaucon, concerned now with personal gratification—as he was earlier in his rebellion against "the city of pigs"—offers a commonsense objection to the compulsion the philosopher faces.

Yet identifying with Glaucon's objections may not be unjustified inasmuch as Socrates himself suggests that the philosopher will desire to remain above. Socrates argues as much in his unusual and striking evocation of ancient poetry here in which he compares the philosopher to Achilles. The philosopher's reluctance to redescend is recalled through the lines recited by Achilles to Odysseus in the underworld—the very same that had been purportedly excised by Socrates in Book 3 (386c). Socrates asks Glaucon whether the philosopher, once freed, would prefer to be the most honored and knowledgeable man concerning the images in the Cave, or "rather, would he be affected like Homer says and want very much 'to be on the soil, a serf to another man, to a portionless man,' and to undergo anything whatsoever rather than to opine those things and live that way?" (516d). The philosopher, once away from the Cave, wishes the same fate as the deceased Achilles: he would prefer slavery to death. That statement, both earlier rejected by Socrates as unsuitable for the education of Guardians and later rejected by Socrates on the trial stand in the *Apology*, now is deemed a fitting response by the philosopher who refuses to redescend.

Socrates' philosopher here, an Achillean character, would of course refuse to reenter the cave, fearing death at the hands of the crowd and preferring the safety above; like the serf above the ground, life in the sunlight, no matter what its condition, is preferable to the darkness below.[74] The portrait of the philosopher here culminates a portrait of philosophy that is starkly barren of human concerns, even of humans. Plato's apparent attempt to eliminate all particularity results in a city of pure abstraction in which no purely *personal* satisfaction through family, friends, and finally even politics is possible. The rule of the philosopher based on perfect knowledge appears to be starkly inhuman, driven by mathematics and knowledge of the Forms, neither of which allows for distinctions between human individuals. In the words of Mary Nichols, "the tyrannical drive for absolute certainty and control ends in perfect horror."[75]

As will be the case in the *Apology*, Socrates appears at first to identify himself (here as the philosopher) with Achilles, only to distance that identification from himself. Recalling the initial descent of Socrates to the Piraeus, we find by comparison that his journey is quite voluntary: he seeks to instruct the young gentleman Glaucon. His motion, unlike that of the philosopher of the Cave, is one of descent to ascent; his movement is precisely the opposite of that philosopher who otherwise refuses to descend.[76] The opposite motion of the two types of philosophers also hints at another identity for Socrates in the Allegory of the Cave. The questions of precisely who frees the prisoner from the cave in the first instance and who subsequently compels him to return once freed remain unasked and unanswered. Yet the framing story of the *Republic* itself gives us a clue: Socrates must first descend to the Piraeus before the instruction of the young men can take place. Whereas in the first book it appears that Socrates is being "shackled," or arrested, by Polemarchus, in the end it is Socrates who literally frees them from opinion. He finally resembles more the mysterious person who *releases* the prisoner in the Cave, perhaps first by descending (voluntarily in this case) in order to teach another the truth that he has witnessed, and perhaps not to be alone. The descent of Socrates to the Piraeus, seeking in this case to instruct a young man and eventually a group of young men, proves itself to be the opposite of that reluctance demonstrated by the philosopher.[77]

Odysseus leaves Calypso's island because of an understanding of his limitations, his bond to humanity, and his desire for homecoming. One can only surmise that Socrates' incentive to descend to the Piraeus with Glaucon, much as in the *Crito* he refuses to cling to life at the cost of banishment, is finally much the same.[78] Glaucon, self-centered and anxious for happiness defined atomistically, views the philosopher's escape as exhilarating and final. Like Gyges's invisibility, the philosopher achieves perfect liberation. If Socrates is the unnamed character who frees the prisoners from the cave, then one of those prisoners is Glaucon. Having now tasted the heights to which philosophy aspires, Glaucon too easily tosses off the bondage of human limitations: his soul still longs for a form of tyranny, now the tyranny of philosophy, the absolute and total knowledge it promises. Socrates, perhaps deferring to Glaucon's limitations that have brought him to the point of becoming a Guardian but not a philosopher, seeks now to bring him back to the Cave, but realizing the limitation of comprehension he has now encountered in Glaucon's enthusiasm for life above—an Achillean reaction—he seeks to restrain him as Odysseus sought to restrain Achilles by reminding him of his mortal birthright and the demands of the stomach (*Iliad*, XIX.216–237). Where persuasion is not possible, the tyrannically inclined philosopher must be *com-*

pelled to return.[79] That he must be compelled to redescend finally reveals the moral poverty of this individual: completely self-absorbed and self-sufficient, in some respects he resembles Achilles in his tent—a distant, solitary, and even inhuman creature.

If, after the example of Odysseus and Socrates, the true philosopher is inclined to return to the cave willingly, there is still no indication that philanthropy is his motivation. Rather, the *Socratic* philosopher indeed seeks self-gratification; but coincidence and the human condition connect that gratification with the presence of others, not only other philosophers, but also students and friends—potential philosophers. The philosopher's descent is motivated, even compelled, by his *eros*, his love for both philosophy and the dialectic through which philosophy is pursued—but that love is both *particular* and *selfish*.[80] The evidence of the Platonic dialogues themselves, including the *Republic*, suggests that Socratic philosophy can only occur through the interplay with other voices and other perspectives and ultimately out of concern for teaching those about whom one cares.[81]

As such, notwithstanding the Socratic (or Odyssean) philosopher's choice to redescend, the question raised by Dale Hall remains: would the philosopher seek to *rule* the inhabitants of the Cave at the risk of his own life? Socrates admits that there is significant danger in the philosopher's redescent. The reception of that person who redescends by those remaining in the cave is not promising to the prospect of rule by the philosopher:

> And if he once more had to compete with those perpetual prisoners in forming judgments about those shadows while his vision was still dim, before his eyes had recovered, and if the time needed for getting accustomed were not at all short, wouldn't he be the source of laughter, and wouldn't it be said of him that he went up and came back with his eyes corrupted, and that it's not even worth trying to go up? And if they were somehow able to get their hands on and kill the man who attempts to release and lead up, wouldn't they kill him? (516e–517a)

Socrates, then, effectively condemns this philosopher to death in requiring him to rule openly and against the will of the cave-dwellers; Glaucon's reluctance, and the accusation of injustice against this solution, is comprehensible (520e). Like Achilles, he prefers even an apolitical life above the cave to rule below, especially because the prospects of rule seem dimmed by the greater likelihood of the philosopher's death at the hands of the cave-dwellers.

In pointing out the time required of the philosopher to reaccustom his eyes to the light, Socrates gives a clue about how the philosopher is to return: because those who remain in the cave long to kill him when he openly reveals his identity, he will have to remain disguised to them until his eyes have adjusted and he can speak to the cave-dwellers on their own terms and to their dimmer level of comprehension. Again, the image of the Socratic philosopher is Odyssean: unlike Agamemnon, who returns to his home in full array, ignorant of the changes that have taken place both to himself and to those he left behind, and hence who is immediately slain upon his return, Odysseus returns home in disguise, notably as a poor beggar. He accustoms himself to the situation on Ithaca before revealing himself: only then, after considerable difficulty, is political order reestablished in the *polis*. Socrates, also a wandering beggar of sorts, disguises himself as an ignorant man seeking wisdom from supposedly wise people in Athens. [82] Indeed, after suggesting the untenable proposition that philosophers openly rule upon their return from above, Socrates allows for the philosopher's avoidance of rule and hints at another role for the true philosopher:

> If you discover a life better than ruling for those who are going to rule, it is possible that your well-governed city will come into being. For here alone will the really rich rule, rich not in gold but in those riches required by the happy man, rich in good and prudent life. But if beggars, men hungering for want of private goods, go to public affairs supposing that in them they must seize the good, it isn't possible. When ruling becomes a thing fought over, such a war—a domestic war, one within the family—destroys these men themselves and the rest of the city as well. (520e–521c)

In seeming to dismiss the possibility that another such path of life exists that allows for the possibility of the "well-governed city" coming into being, Socrates in fact describes that very alternative. "Rich men" are now defined by their "good and prudent life," not their material holdings; "beggars" are characterized by their unleashed desires, not necessarily by their poverty. Socrates and Odysseus are now, by definition, "rich men," and the current rulers of Athens or Ithaca are "beggars." The disguises of Odysseus and Socrates as beggars hide their actual wealth; as such, they survive in the city until the time, if it comes, that their ruling virtues can be revealed without loss of their own lives. Death is to not to be avoided in its proper time, but neither is it to be prematurely embraced if possible.

Odysseus's self-revelation occurs with the assistance of the goddess and the likewise "rich" (but materially poor) swineherd and cowherd, all of whom assist him in his vengeance against the "poor" (i.e., greedy) suitors. However, Odysseus by himself is finally unable to reestablish political rule or even to halt the chain of violence without the aid of the gods. In trying to rule unphilosophically, he nearly destroys the city. Socrates, on the other hand, does not reveal himself until his guilt has been determined at his trial. Then outrageously he asks as his "punishment" a place at the table in the prytaneum (*Apology* 36d–37a). As such he claims himself more deserving of this reward than a man who wins the Olympic games, for "he makes you seem to be happy, while I make you be happy" (36d–

e). Like that rich man whose wealth is that of a "happy man" in the alternative to the philosopher-king, Socrates reveals that his life as a beggar and a private man—one that has allowed him to live in the city for over seventy years in disguise—is intimately connected with his attempt to make others "be happy." The alternative to the untenable life of the philosopher-king in the cave or the serf above who doesn't have sufficient *eros* is the life of Socrates, the private man, in Athens.

Only after Odysseus has been cured of his "love of honor" in the afterlife can he choose the life of the private man who minds his own business in the Myth of Er. His final inability to reestablish justice in Ithaca free of the beggar disguise reveals his attachment to power and honor manifested in the heroic code of vengeance now exacted against his own city. Indeed, his love of honor is alluded to by Plato in continuously referring to the lament of Achilles in the underworld. Achilles, who craves the life of a serf over that of a king, is provoked into this lament by Odysseus's praise of his position over the dead:

> "Achilles, no man before has been more blessed than you, nor ever
> will be. Before, when you were alive, we Argives honored you
> as we did the gods, and now in this place you rule mightily
> over the dead. Do not grieve, even in death, Achilles."
> [11.482–486]

It is initially Odysseus who finds Achilles' authority, even in Hades, so appealing as to provoke an angry response from Achilles' frustrated soul. It is curious, then, that Achilles' retort is a lesson to Odysseus's love of honor, teaching that to rule merely for the sake of ruling, in this case over dead souls, is not to be desired in itself. So we discover how even after excising Achilles' famous words in Book 3 of the *Republic* (386c)—the first to be disallowed to the hero—they reappear now in a more positive form in Book 7, not however for their embrace of slavery or fear of death, but for their rejection of honor and a ruling position at any cost. Such is the one lesson that the dead Achilles is able to offer Odysseus; hence Achilles' words meet with sudden new approval by Socrates who will reject ruling but will accept death nonetheless. In the Myth of Er, Odysseus's soul's choice of the private man who minds his own business is inspired "from the memory of its former labors" (620c): prominently and frequently alluded to among those labors is this final encounter with Achilles in Hades. Cured of the love of honor, Odysseus will not so readily relinquish the beggar's outfit, nor so quickly bring violence down on his own city. His *thumos* will now be tamed internally by a more philosophic self-reflection, not by the changeable orders of the gods.

Through Socrates' references to the *Odyssey*, a conclusion can be reached, on the one hand, that Socrates' provisional solution in which the philosopher becomes king is ironic, intended to reveal "the limits of politics." However, on the other hand, by equating the ascents and descents of the philosopher to Odysseus's own willingness to embrace death, the allegory also seems to indicate a certain commitment on the part of the philosopher, an ultimate willingness of the philosopher to return to the city, albeit now in another guise—that of a "beggar" whose wealth ultimately can be used to make the cave-dwellers not only "seem" better, but "be" better.

While Socrates points to the inherent weakness of the pure philosophic model portrayed in Book 7, culminating the three waves of paradox that have preceded it, at the same time Plato points to the limitations of the *Socratic* philosophic model. Socrates is finally *too* entwined in the particularity of the city and its citizens: his philosophy is bound by and to the individuals to whom he personally speaks. Plato, as a *writer* of philosophy, retains particularity through the dialogic form, but also indicates a more unified possibility through the presentation of a frozen and unchanging text. He cautions us throughout to tread carefully through its pages and to approach the interpretation of Platonic philosophy with the sensitivity that is absent in Ion. Despite finally siding with Socrates' acceptance of death by redescent, Plato also acknowledges a place for immortality in the philosophic pursuit, not above the cave, but written on its walls, all the way to the entrance to the Sun but back down as well. He, like Odysseus, knows how to tell a good story when he hears one.

Notes

1. Plato, *Phaedrus*, trans. Alexander Nehamas and Paul Woodward, in *Plato: Complete Works*, ed. John M. Cooper (Indianapolis, IN: Hackett, 1997). All citations to Platonic texts will be placed in the body of the text using the widely used "Stephanus numbers."

2. On the difficulty of conveying truth in human language, see the myth of the winged horses and the chariot in *Phaedrus* (246a–257b, esp. 247c). Plato adopts an even stronger stance in the possibly inauthentic *Seventh Letter*: "Moreover, because of the weakness of language . . . [one must be] as much concerned with making clear the particular property of each object as the being of it. On this account, no sensible man will venture to express his deepest thoughts in words, especially in a form which is unchangeable, as is true of written outlines" (trans. Glen R. Morrow, in *Plato: Complete Works*, 342e–343a).

The fact that Plato *does* attempt to set down philosophy in language, however opaque, that is "unchangeable" reveals his awareness of the limitations of his project.

3. From the verb *enthousiazein*, meaning literally "to have a god within."

4. Plato, *Plato's Apology of Socrates*, trans. Thomas G. West (Ithaca, NY: Cornell University Press, 1979).

5. Socrates makes this suggestion explicit in *Phaedrus*:

Third comes the kind of madness that is possession by the Muses, which takes a tender virgin soul and awakens it to a Bacchic frenzy of songs and poetry that glorifies the achievements of the past and teaches them to future generations. If anyone comes to the gates of poetry and expects to become an adequate poet by acquiring expert knowledge of the subject without the Muses' madness, he will fail, and his self-controlled verses will be eclipsed by the poetry of men who have been driven out of their minds. (245a)

Helmut Flashar notes that Plato does not explicitly condemn or dismiss poetic creation because of its origin in *enthousiasmos* when speaking in a political context:

> Nun ist es zwar höchst auffallend, daß im Staat mit keinem Wort vom Enthusiasmus des Dichters die Rede ist, aber daraus einen Widerspruch zum Ion und Phaidros oder einen Wandel in der Auffassung Platons zu konstruieren, verbietet schon die Tatsache, daß auch im Gorgias und im zweiten Buch der Gesetze, d. h. immer da, wo Platon kritisch sein muß, der Enthusiasmus ausdrücklich nicht erwähnt ist. (*Der Dialog Ion als Zeugnis Platonischer Philosophie* [Berlin: Akademie-Verlag, 1958], 107)

For a good general treatment of Plato on *enthousiamus* and the philosophers' reliance on "reasoned inspiration," see Robert Edgar Carter, "Plato and Inspiration," *Journal of the History of Philosophy* 5 (1967): 118.

6. Allan Bloom, *Giants and Dwarfs* (New York: Simon & Schuster, 1990), 125. Socrates expressly compares Homer and Hesiod to rhapsodes at 600d.

7. Long-standing approaches to *Ion* treated the dialogue with dismissiveness for its apparent light theme if not for its alleged spuriousness. A. E. Taylor's comment is typical: "Little need be said about this slight dialogue on the nature of 'poetic inspiration'" (*Plato: The Man and His Work* [New York: Meridian Books, 1956], 38). Of the few works devoted to discussing *Ion*'s themes, Allan Bloom's essay on *Ion* in *Giants and Dwarfs* (138–61) is among the most instructive.

8. Plato, *Ion*, trans. Allan Bloom, in Allan Bloom, *Giants and Dwarfs*, 124–37.

9. Plato suggests as much for poets as well in the *Apology*: "Now I am ashamed to tell you the truth, gentlemen, but still it must be told. For there was hardly a man present, one might say, who would not speak better than they about the poems that they themselves had composed" (22b). On the training of rhapsodes as purely memorizers of poetry, see Eric A. Havelock, *Preface to Plato* (Cambridge, MA: Harvard University Press, 1963), 44–49.

10. Compare with *Ion*, 534d.

11. The Athenian Stranger finally indicates a concurrence between poetry and philosophy in *The Laws* of Plato:

> As I look now at the speeches we've been going through since dawn until the present—and it appears to me that we have not been speaking without some inspiration from the gods—they seemed to me to have been spoken in a way that resembles in every respect a kind of poetry. . . . I don't think I would have a better model than this to describe for the Guardian of the Laws and Educator, or anything that would be better for him to bid the teachers to teach the children. (trans. Thomas L. Pangle [Chicago: University of Chicago Press, 1980], 811c–e)

Eric Voegelin emphasizes the centrality of this passage in the structure of the *Laws*:

> The discourse had begun "at dawn," and now, in the middle of the way (the passage is to be found actually at approximately the physical center of the *Laws*), the Athenian Stranger becomes aware that, under the divine guidance, "this compact discourse of his composition" has become "rather like a poem," that he has

created a form of spiritual poetry that most suitably will furnish the model for the sacred art of the new polis, the art in which the spirit will be kept alive.

Voeglin concludes, "The distention of the way between the beginning and the end in God thus becomes focused in the center of a divinely inspired poem, created at the solstice when Plato's life declines, marking an end and a beginning in the spirit's process." (Voeglin, *Plato* [Baton Rouge: Louisiana State University Press, 1966], 229)

12. Seth Benardete similarly concludes that "the gods are the model for Gyges" (Benardete, *Socrates' Second Sailing: On Plato's* Republic [Chicago: University of Chicago Press, 1989], 41).

13. *Nomoi* can also mean here and elsewhere "convention."

14. Plato, *The Republic of Plato*, 2d ed., trans. Allan Bloom (New York: Basic, 1991). Adeimantus is perhaps referring to a sophistic belief, often attributed to Critias, that the origin of the gods can be dated to a time when humans began to commit crimes in secret, whereupon a "wise and clever man invented fear of the gods for mortals, that there might be some means of frightening the wicked" (in *Ancilla to the Pre-Socratic Philosophers*, trans. Kathleen Freeman [Cambridge, MA: Harvard University Press, 1948], 158).

15. Elliot Bartky notes: "If Socrates is convinced that the Homeric teaching on the gods is false, he does not appear to be certain that his own teaching on the gods, although it is more correct in respect to the education of the soul and the city, is more true" (Bartky, "Plato and the Politics of Aristotle's *Poetics*," *The Review of Politics* 55 [1993]: 599). While I am hesitant to agree with Bartky's use of the word *false*, the general import captures the Socratic position. Compare with Socrates' admission of uncertainty about ancient things in *Republic*, 382d; see also *Laws*, 663d.

16. Benardete, *Socrates' Second Sailing*, 64.

17. Eric Voeglin, *The New Science of Politics: An Introduction* (Chicago: University of Chicago Press, 1952), 65–66; see also Voeglin, *Plato*, 10. See also Socrates' explicit connection of philosophy and death in *Phaedo*, 64a and 67e.

18. Hans-Georg Gadamer, *Dialogue and Dialectic: Eight Hermeneutical Studies on Plato*, trans. P. Christopher Smith (New Haven, CT: Yale University Press, 1980), 47.

19. Rosen writes:

It is entirely clear that Plato practices "esotericism" and that those who extract what they take to be Plato's theoretical views or "arguments" from their dialogical and poetic presentation are studying images of their own theoretical suppositions, but not Plato. I mean by this, not that arguments have no place in Plato, or in philosophy, but rather that one must be a poet as well as a philosopher in order to determine what are the Platonic arguments. Just as Homer is and is not Achilles, Odysseus, Helen and Andromache, so too Plato is and is not Socrates, Alcibiades, Protagoras and Diotima. (Stanley Rosen, *The Quarrel between Philosophy and Poetry: Studies in Ancient Thought* [New York: Routledge, 1988], 11)

20. Leo Strauss, *Persecution and the Art of Writing* (Chicago: University of Chicago Press, 1952), 24–25.

21. Allan Bloom incorrectly asserts that, of the seven quotations, "all but the central one have to do more or less directly with Achilles" ("Interpretive Essay," *The Republic of Plato*, 2d ed., trans. Allan Bloom [New York: Basic, 1991], 354). Of the four quotations from the *Iliad* (2, 3, 5, 6), only the fifth does not refer to Achilles but instead to Patroclus's soul parting from his body. Of the quotes from the *Odyssey*, the first is from Achilles' fa-

mous speech in the underworld, whereas the fourth and the seventh deal with Teiresias and the dead suitors, respectively.

22. At 516d: This seemingly positive reintroduction of Achilles' words, now applied to the potential philosopher-kings, is discussed later in this chapter.

23. According to Allan Bloom: "The central quote among the seven at the beginning of Book III refers to Teiresias, a man who was wise on earth and who alone among the shades in Hades still possesses prudence or wisdom. Perhaps even Homer suggests that wisdom can exempt a man from the miseries of Hades" ("Interpretive Essay," 357).

24. Notably, in the Myth of Er in Book 10, descriptions of harsh punishments and enviable rewards for one's vicious or admirable behavior on earth are reintroduced. Their less-than-total excision seems to indicate that the grounds for the ancient stories about the afterlife remain (614c–616a).

25. Poets and rhapsodes are not explicitly allowed into the city until the second, "feverish" city is established following Glaucon's objections to the first (373b).

26. Benardete makes a similar argument using a different passage from the Republic (389c5). The import is the same: "By the omission of the line, the poets are forthwith expelled, though by the same token they are allowed to stay" (Socrates' Second Sailing, 68).

27. Both Martha C. Nussbaum and J. Peter Euben are sensitive to Plato's constant interplay between the meaning in the dialogue and the existence of the dialogue itself. Between the two, there can be no final distinction between "form" and "content," even where they appear to be in opposition. See especially Nussbaum, The Fragility of Goodness: Luck and Ethics in Greek Tragedy and Philosophy (Cambridge, U.K.: Cambridge University Press, 1986), "Interlude 1"; and Euben, The Tragedy of Political Theory: The Road Not Taken (Princeton, NJ: Princeton University Press, 1990), chap. 8.

Paul Friedländer, on the other hand, dismisses much of the tension between content and form by making the content preeminent: "Thus this struggle with mimesis is, after all and primarily, also a struggle of Plato with himself, struggle of the philosopher against the poet, and therefore a form of watchfulness constantly exercised against himself and others" (Friedländer, Plato: An Introduction, trans. Hans Meyerhoff [Princeton, NJ: Princeton University Press, 1969], 124). It is my contention that the philosopher and the poet both watch one another's excesses.

28. See Darrell Dobbs ("Reckless Rationalism and Heroic Reverence in Homer's Odyssey," American Political Science Review 81 [1987], 491–508) for an excellent treatment on this passage. Eurylochus adopts a "rational choice" argument to persuade the men of the acceptability of eating; Odysseus, adopting a more human and humane form of decision making—like the one employed in deciding to leave Calypso's island—thereby survives.

29. Benardete reaches a similar conclusion: "Achilles never does or says anything that meets with his [Socrates'] approval; Odysseus is praised once but anonymously. The number of lines Socrates excises from Homer is not very great, but they are decisive, and with them goes the Iliad" (Socrates' Second Sailing, 65).

30. Iris Murdoch's The Fire and the Sun: Why Plato Banished the Artists ([Oxford, U.K.: Clarendon Press, 1977], 74) discusses Plato's preference for "the good man" over the "hero."

31. The Symposium, 219e–221c.

32. Admiration for Odysseus's restraint must be tempered by the recognition that Odysseus "endures" the abuses of the suitors so that he may fully unleash his vengeance when the proper time arrives. I will discuss the tension of this vengeful goal with the philosophic approach later in this chapter.

33. In fact, Odysseus's name appears only twice in the *Republic*, and of those, only one refers to Odysseus proper (at 620c in the Myth of Er; his appearance there will be discussed at greater length later in this chapter). The other mention occurs at 334b, in the discussion of Justice with Polemarchus in Book 1. There Socrates compares the just man to a "kind of robber" according to the definition of Simonides the poet: "For he admires Autolycus, Odysseus's grandfather on his mother's side, and he says he surpassed all men 'in stealing and swearing oaths.' Justice, then, appears to be a certain art of stealing." Autolycus is responsible for giving Odysseus his name and, according to W. B. Stanford (*The Ulysses Theme* [Oxford, U.K.: Basil Blackwell, 1963], chap. 1), serves as a model for his deceptive character as well. What is remarkable, then, in Socrates' accusation against the poet's praise of theft and lying is that "Odysseus's grandfather" and not simply "Odysseus" is negatively cited as a performer of trickery.

34. This two-line citation is from the *Iliad* XXII.15, 20. I have used Bloom's translation of the passage here.

35. The irrelevance of the gifts is stated most unequivocally by Achilles: "Son of Atreus, most lordly and king of men, Agamemnon, the gifts are yours to give if you wish, and as is proper, or to keep to yourself. But now let us remember our joy in warcraft" (XIX.146–148).

Directly after this speech, Odysseus rebukes Achilles for neglecting the hunger of the soldiers. See my discussion of this passage in chapter 1.

36. James M. Redfield, *Nature and Culture in the* Iliad: *The Tragedy of Hector* (Chicago: University of Chicago Press, 1975), 208. Allan Bloom, however, rightly notes that at a deeper level it is Achilles' concern for property that motivates the initial action of the *Iliad* inasmuch as "he does destroy his friends and countrymen because his possessions have been taken from him by the ruler. Such a man would make a poor citizen of the good regime which is being founded," notably with an absence of property ("Interpretive Essay," 356).

37. Eva Brann, "The Offense of Socrates: A Re-reading of Plato's *Apology*," *Interpretation* 7 (1978), 1–21.

38. Socrates significantly misquotes Homer here. The original reads:
> Straightway may I die. . . .
> Now therefore, seeing I return not to my dear native land,
> neither proved anywise a light of deliverance to Patroclus
> nor to my other comrades, those many who have
> been slain by godly Hector, but abide here by the ships
> an idle burden upon the earth.
> (18.98, 101–104)

Achilles mentions neither a "penalty" nor an injustice performed by Hector as supposed by Socrates. See Thomas G. West's comments ("Interpretation," in *Plato's Apology of Socrates*, 59–60, n. 79 and 155–56); see also Euben (*The Tragedy of Political Theory*, 219 n. 33, 225–26), and Seth Benardete ("Some Misquotations of Homer in Plato," *Phronesis* 8 [1963]: 173–78). By making Achilles concerned above all with the *justness* of his cause against Hector (a curious change by Socrates) and not simple revenge for Patroclus, Socrates effectively "domesticates" Achilles (West, "Interpretation," in *Plato's Apology of Socrates*, 156).

39. West, "Interpretation," in *Plato's Apology of Socrates*, 154.

40. *Iliad* 9.410–429. See my discussion of Achilles in chapter 1.

41. See Thucydides, *The Peloponnesian War* (trans. Thomas Hobbes, ed. David Grene

[Chicago: University of Chicago Press, 1989]), on the battles of Potideia (1.56–65), Amphipolis (5.6–10), and Delium (4.90–101). Socrates' military service, including his exemplary behavior during a retreat, are mentioned in *Symposium* (220d–221b) and *Laches* (189b). See West for a discussion of these battles in relation to Socrates' philosophic pursuit ("Interpretation," in *Plato's Apology of Socrates*, 162–63).

42. For example, Werner Jaeger, *Paideia: The Ideals of Greek Culture*, trans. Gilbert Highet, 3 vols. (New York: Oxford University Press, 1945), 1.262; Charles Segal, " 'The Myth Was Saved': Reflections on Homer and the Mythology of Plato's *Republic*," *Hermes* 106 (1978), 320–21; and West, "Interpretation," in *Plato's Apology of Socrates*, 160. In each case, these interpreters stress the similarity of Socrates' choice of death with the seeming resoluteness of Achilles after Patroclus's death. Diskin Clay ("Socrates' Mulishness and Heroism," *Phronesis* 17 [1972]: 53–60) also arrives at a positive identification between Socrates and Achilles through a clever and persuasive reading of a recurring "mule" (or mixed breed) image that applies to both Socrates and Achilles. One might respond, however, that although Socrates compares himself to a mule, Achilles' "half-breed" ancestry is rather traceable to a goddess. Hence, once again the comparison between the two is laughable if not for the continuous subtle indictment against Achilles. A notable exception to this approach is found in Bloom's brief discussion of the *Apology*, in which he recognizes that "Socrates' death and the mysterious power it reveals are the new model of the heroic and must replace the Achillean one" ("Interpretive Essay," 358).

43. Euben, *The Tragedy of Political Theory*, 218.

44. Euben, *The Tragedy of Political Theory*, 216.

45. Euben, *The Tragedy of Political Theory*, 220, n. 34.

46. Here I agree with Michael Brint (*Tragedy and Denial: The Politics of Difference in Western Political Thought* [San Francisco: Westview, 1991], 18), who recognizes the problems with Socrates' identification with Achilles, concluding that Socrates here is "consciously transforming the Homeric understanding of the heroic ethos." Brint, however, does not extend this insight to investigate Socrates' relationship to Odysseus in this passage.

47. Leo Strauss, *Studies in Platonic Political Philosophy* (Chicago: University of Chicago Press, 1983), 53.

48. West, "Interpretation," 157.

49. Diotima describes the compulsion felt by mortals to "engender" something immortal in the *Symposium* (206c–207c).

50. Compare to the description of the origins of the first city in *Laws*, which is explicitly compared to the prepolitical society of the Cyclopes, 679d–680e, esp. 680b.

51. This phrase (*muthos esōthē*) is used by Socrates in Book 10 (621b) to describe Er's revival on the funeral pyre and thus the preservation of what he witnessed in the afterlife. Plato has the same function in this respect in preserving his memories of Socrates. On the further significance of this distinction between Socrates and Plato, see Leo Strauss, *The City and Man* ([Chicago: University of Chicago Press, 1964], 52–53), and Mary P. Nichols, "The *Republic's* Two Alternatives: Philosopher-Kings and Socrates" (*Political Theory* 12 [1984]: 270–71).

52. Voeglin, *Plato*, 52–62.

53. Voeglin, *Plato*, 53.

54. Socrates acknowledges, even after having appeared to offer a categorical condemnation of poetry based on epistemological grounds, that "only so much of poetry as is hymns

to gods or celebration of good men should be admitted into a city" (607a). Recognizing Plato's final acceptance of some forms of poetry, Allan Bloom writes: "It is not, then, that poetry must be entirely banished but that it must be reformed. Book 10 begins with a criticism of Homeric poetry and ends with an example of Socratic poetry" ("Interpretive Essay," 427).

55. Bloom, "Interpretive Essay," 471, n. 13.

56. Bloom, "Interpretive Essay," 471, n. 13.

57. Accordingly, Er comes from Pamphylia, a man "of all tribes."

58. Julia Annas, An Introduction to Plato's Republic (Oxford, U.K.: Oxford University Press, 1981), 351. Annas considers the Myth of Er to be "a painful shock" marked by "vulgarity" (349).

59. Among the few scholars who note the difference between those souls that drink more than their share and those who exercise self-control is Bruce Lincoln, who has written, "Only if one is self-disciplined in the extreme and knowledgeable with regard to the river's pernicious effect will one be able to master the temptation to drink deeply. For Plato, it is only the philosopher who has such knowledge and self-control. . . . [Thus,] certain highly gifted individuals are able to reverse, or at least minimize, the river's effect and carry knowledge of tremendous importance back from the underworld" (Lincoln, "Waters of Memory, Waters of Forgetfulness," Fabula 23 [1982]: 21).

60. Most commentaries on the myth do not even specifically discuss Odysseus's soul's choice of lives. Among the lengthy commentaries on the Republic, neither Annas in An Introduction to Plato's Republic (349–53), nor C. D. C. Reeve in Philosopher-Kings: The Argument of Plato's Republic ([Princeton: Princeton University Press, 1988], 263–64), nor Daryl H. Rice in A Guide to Plato's Republic ([Oxford, U.K.: Oxford University Press, 1998], 116–17) explicitly discuss the choice of Odysseus's soul. Among shorter studies known to me that are specifically devoted to the Myth of Er, none addresses the choice; see Irwin C. Lieb, "Philosophy as Spiritual Formation: Plato's Myth of Er," International Philosophical Quarterly 3 (1963): 271–85; Hilda Richardson, "The Myth of Er (Plato, Republic 616b)," The Classical Quarterly 20 (1926): 113–33; and Griet Shils, "Plato's Myth of Er: The Light and the Spindle," L'Antiquité Classique 62 (1993): 101–14. Even Thayer's subtle and informative article analyzing the implications of the souls' choices of lives in the Myth of Er (regrettably) does not examine Odysseus's specific choice (H. S. Thayer, "The Myth of Er," History of Philosophy Quarterly 5 [1988]: (369–384). The other studies that emphasize the importance of choice elucidated in the myth (e.g., Annas, Reeve, and Lieb) also lack any analysis of what makes Odysseus's choice noteworthy.

61. Jacob Howland notes that Odysseus's soul's choice is admirable, stating that the myth allows us "to follow the heartening example of the soul of Odysseus" without analyzing what qualities of the life he chooses should elicit our admiration (Howland, The Republic: The Odyssey of Philosophy [New York: Twayne Publishers, 1993], 159).

62. Benardete, Socrates' Second Sailing, 229.

63. Bloom, "Interpretive Essay," 436.

64. Seth Benardete takes the opposite view when he writes, "Odysseus gives up the political life, but he does not give up anything else" (Socrates' Second Sailing, 228).

65. John Rawls, A Theory of Justice (Cambridge, MA: Harvard University Press, 1971), chap. 3, esp. pp. 136–42. The comparison between Rawls's "veil of ignorance" and the Myth of Er may seem jarring at first, but each shares a certain mythic formulation about life choices. On the mythic and poetic qualities of Rawls's "veil," see George Armstrong

Kelly, "Veils: The Poetics of John Rawls," *Journal of the History of Ideas* 57 (1996): 343–64.

66. Rawls, *A Theory of Justice*, 120.

67. Behind the veil of ignorance, we are disallowed knowledge of the following:

First of all, no one knows his place in society, his class position, or social status; nor does he know his fortune in the distribution of natural assets and abilities, his intelligence and strength, and the like. Nor, again, does anyone know his conception of the good, the particulars of his rational plan of life, or even the special features of his psychology such as his aversion to risk or liability to optimism or pessimism. More than this, I assume that the parties do not know the particular circumstances of their own society.

The features that are known to us are:

It is taken for granted, however, that they know the general facts about human society. They understand political affairs and the principles of economic theory; they know the basis of social organization and the laws of human psychology. (Rawls, *A Theory of Justice*, 137)

68. Howland, *The* Republic: *The Odyssey of Philosophy*, 156.

69. As West notes, Socrates does not personally pursue a violent revenge against those who condemn him to death, but he hints that others will not be so restrained: "Socrates' vengeance will be executed by human beings, who will continue the way of life he has discovered and who will carry forward the examinations and refutations of the Athenians and others. However, there will be this difference after Socrates is dead: his followers will be harsher than Socrates himself because they are younger. Socrates admits, then, a certain gentleness in himself." ("Interpretation," 226; cf. *Apology* 39c–d). Nevertheless, that harshness will not be expressly violent but rather will suggestively be manifested *poetically* by the immortalization of the Athenian's perfidy by the writer, Plato.

70. Good summaries of some of the more prominent interpretations of the Cave allegory can be found in Edward Andrew's "Descent to the Cave" (*The Review of Politics* 45 [1983]: 510–12) and Zdravko Planinc's *Plato's Political Philosophy: Prudence in the* Republic *and the* Laws ([Columbia: University of Missouri Press, 1991], 31–51).

71. This phrase is used both by Strauss (*The City and Man*, 138) and by Bloom ("Interpretive Essay," 408).

72. The thesis that the philosopher would refuse to redescend was primarily established by Leo Strauss and popularized by Allan Bloom in his "Interpretive Essay" appended to his translation. According to them, the city in speech is finally "against nature," not only because it seeks to abstract humans too completely from their own bodies and its inclinations, but also because it would sacrifice the philosopher's personal *eudaimonia* for the sake of the city (Strauss, *The City and Man*, 127; Bloom, "Interpretive Essay," 343–44, 373–74, 378, 380, 407–8, 411). The city in speech finally proves so unsatisfying to its members, especially the philosopher, that the solution to the question of justice is revealed to be wholly ironic, a sad admission that perfect justice is not available to imperfect and limited human beings.

In an interesting and revealing debate some years ago, Dale Hall attacked this thesis as mistaken, claiming that because of the city's "naturalness" the philosopher would descend in order to fulfill his existence as a human. One among the catalogue of arguments he brought to bear ("The *Republic* and the 'Limits of Politics,'" *Political Theory* 5 [1977]: 293–313) strikingly contradicted Strauss's and Bloom's main argument regarding the philosopher's *eudaimonia*: "the platonically just individual with an harmonious psyche will act for the good of others." Hall's conclusion that the philosopher will choose to redescend out of a sudden generalized love for humanity as well as the thesis that the philosopher is fulfilled *by nature* in the city are points that Bloom rejects.

Both Hall and Bloom, then, pointed to the issue of *training* as central to understanding the relation of the philosopher to the city: for Hall, the necessity for training the rational aspect of the soul or the city necessitates that the philosopher acts philanthropically on behalf of others; for Bloom, the necessity for training demonstrates that for the philosopher to rule on behalf of the city is finally against his nature inasmuch as it implants false desires. The best city is possible or impossible depending on whether the philosopher chooses or must be compelled to redescend. For Hall, the fact that the philosopher redescends willingly proves the realizability of the "city in speech"; for Bloom, the philosopher's reluctance indicates the city's ultimate impossibility.

73. Allan Bloom, "Response to Hall," *Political Theory* 5 (1977): 317.

74. I agree with Jacob Howland that the Cave is replete with imagery and echoes of the Odyssean descent (*The Republic*, 150–60). Socrates, in addition to comparing the philosopher to Achilles through repetition of the famous lament in Hades, also compares the philosopher's satisfaction above to that of one who has entered "the Isle of the Blessed" (519c). In the *Symposium* Phaedrus notes that Achilles lives in that idyllic place (179e— here called "son of Thetis"). The allusion may also refer to Menelaus, who alone of the Homeric heroes has been promised life in the Elysian fields. Any such allusion to Menelaus would additionally reveal the inhumanity of the philosopher (compare with my discussion of Menelaus in chapter 1).

75. Nichols, "The *Republic*'s Two Alternatives," 265; see also Sheldon S. Wolin, *Politics and Vision: Continuity and Innovation in Western Political Thought* (Boston: Little, Brown, 1960), chap. 2.

76. For the distinction here between the "philosopher" of Book 7 and Socrates himself, I rely heavily on the fascinating argument developed by Mary P. Nichols ("The *Republic*'s Two Alternatives").

77. The similarities between these various ascents and descents (summarized in the following figure) are striking and replete with unexplored resonances:

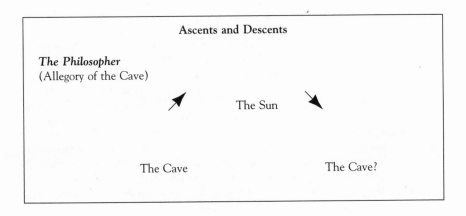

Ascents and Descents

The Philosopher
(Allegory of the Cave)

The Sun

The Cave   The Cave?

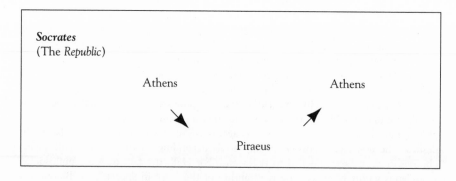

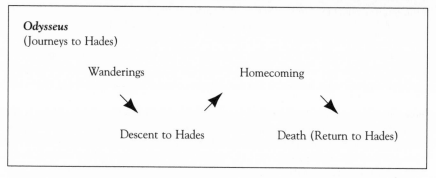

Socrates' descent, as well as the philosopher's ascent, mimics that motion of Odysseus's several ascents and descents to and from Hades. Odysseus, like Socrates, initially descends (one to Hades, the other to the Piraeus) and reascends; like the philosopher, Odysseus both ascends and descends (one from and to Hades, the other from and to the Cave). Odysseus's motions contain both versions of the ascent and descent; moreover, in a mixture of the motives of the philosopher, who must be compelled in both directions, and of the motives of Socrates, who goes and returns freely (after being compelled to stay in the middle), Odysseus's journey is composed both of compulsion and choice. He is first compelled to travel to the underworld to seek the wisdom of Teiresias by Circe, but later chooses to redescend to Hades eventually by refusing Calypso's offer of immortality. Once compelled, however, he shows no inclination of avoiding a redescent when offered. Odysseus proves more a model for Socrates, as Achilles appears as a model for the "philosopher."

Of additional interest is the fact that, in each instance, the final motion for each character—either ascent or descent—remains implicit or unstated but arguably follows from the preceding actions. Socrates does not return to Athens in the *Republic*, but we know he eventually does successfully "ascend." Likewise, Odysseus does not die and return to Hades in the text of the *Odyssey*, but his death is predicted in the underworld by Teiresias. Despite Socrates' arguments to Glaucon, we cannot be certain that the philosopher will willingly or otherwise return to the Cave, yet we are given enough evidence that he will be "compelled." Whether the true philosopher will be compelled externally by force or internally by the demands of his human nature is perhaps best answered by referring to the other two motions: both Socrates and Odysseus finally descend because of their connectedness to others, or their *eros*. On the erotic imperative to descend, see especially Andrew ("Descent to the Cave").

78. Xenophon's claim in his *Memorabilia* (III.vi) that Plato only takes an interest in Glaucon for the sake of "Plato, Glaucon's son, and Charmides" still attests to his concern for his friends, even if Glaucon is not one of them. Perhaps by the end of the discussion in the *Republic*, he does become a friend.

79. Perhaps Plato suggests that the philosopher above the cave is no true philosopher, but a caricature like that portrayed by Aristophanes in the *Clouds*. For Socrates, *the* condition of philosophy is an admission of ignorance: philosophy "has the character of an unfinished and unfinishable quest" (Bloom, "Interpretive Essay," 409). The Cave allegory is not only about the limits of politics, but about the limits of philosophy as well.

80. Cf. *Gorgias*, 481d–482a. There Socrates notes that his greatest loves at the moment are simultaneously Alcibiades and philosophy. Even though Alcibiades is more capricious or "fickle" than philosophy, they are not portrayed as opposites but rather as complements.

81. As Andrew persuasively argues, the same *eros* that motivates Socrates' descent to the Piraeus also motivates his entire approach to the philosophical life: "Because he was a true lover willing to die for his love, [he] is the liberator of the prisoners of the cave" ("Descent to the Cave," 522). On the irresolvable connection and tension between dialogue and philosophy, see Euben, *The Tragedy of Political Theory*, 264–69. See also Gerald M. Mara, *Socrates' Discursive Democracy: Logos and Ergon in Platonic Political Philosophy* (Albany: SUNY Press, 1997), chaps. 4 and 6.

82. Socrates' penury is highlighted at the outset of the *Republic*, where the wealthy young men promise to pay for Socrates in order to persuade Thrasymachus to speak (337d). Like Ion, Thrasymachus only speaks for the sake of material gain.

~

CHAPTER THREE

The Harrowing of
Rousseau's Emile

Is there not something worthy of Homer in my voyage?

—Jean-Jacques Rousseau; Geneva, 1754[1]

Adieu citizen—
and yet a hermit makes a very peculiar citizen.

—Denis Diderot to Rousseau, November 5, 1757

In *Emile, or On Education,* Rousseau renews the use of Homeric texts in a Platonic fashion—reaching back to both the *Iliad* and the *Odyssey* for ancient examples of heroic individuals—yet departs significantly from Plato's final assessment of Odysseus as an admirable political model. Rousseau, like Plato, initially appears to adopt Achilles as a model of the virtuous individual but abandons that example as insufficient after the first several books of *Emile,* concluding that the example of Achilles' *physical* prowess is more necessary during a child's education and that Achilles' propensity to anger—his lack of equanimity toward death, both his and others'—makes him inappropriate to the education of the natural man who accepts necessity. Rather, in Odysseus, Rousseau finds an ideal model for the mature Emile, both for his acceptance of death and—in a departure from the Platonic reading of the *Odyssey*—for his aspect as wanderer, implying the ability to depart when necessary from his family and his city. In Odysseus, Rousseau finds a model of the *promeneur solitaire,* that apolitical being in which he finally places his trust and hope for individual redemption.

Emile's "Negative Education": The Achillean Model

Rousseau begins *Emile* by immediately limiting the possibilities for the good education. From the outset we are confronted with the terrible truth governing the attempt to raise an excellent child: "all that one can do by dint of care is to come more or less close to the goal, but to reach it requires luck [*bonheur*]" (38; IV.246).[2] The happy outcome of *Emile* is largely the result of careful manipulation and planning by the tutor. Despite the claim that Emile will be educated according to nature (37–42), Rousseau admits that "to form this rare man, what do we have to do? Very much, doubtless" (41). The creation of natural man requires supreme artfulness. The natural education is not achieved "naturally"; Emile's upbringing is not, as Pierre Burgelin suggests, "une dénaturation naturelle,"[3] but rather an "unnatural renaturalization."[4]

The natural education is contingent entirely on luck of circumstances, on the coincidence of the lives of tutor and student. Emile is admitted to be "only a common mind [un esprit commun] . . . , [as] only ordinary men [les hommes vulgaires] need to be raised" (52; IV.266). An Emile is thus easily found, hence always available. The difficulty is clearly not only finding but initially also *creating* a tutor. Rousseau admits the problem is almost irresolvable:

> The more one thinks about it, the more one perceives the new difficulties. It would be necessary that the governor had been raised for his pupil, that the pupil's domestics had been raised for their master, that all those who have contact with him had received the impressions that they ought to communicate with him. It would be necessary to go from education to education and back to I know not where. How is it possible that a child be well raised by one who was not well raised himself? Is this rare mortal not to be found? I do not know [*"Je l'ignore"*]. But let us suppose this mortal found. (50; IV.263)

The solution to the near impossibility of finding such a tutor is finally assumed, albeit admitted to be exceedingly rare. Like the creation of Plato's Kallipolis, we witness more the creation of a natural child "in speech," one that is finally if not impossible, then highly unlikely. Rousseau, however, turns Plato on his head after a fashion: although the "city in speech" in *Republic* is nearly impossible to realize because it is against nature,[5] an Emile is so difficult to create because one must *recreate* nature. Only the existence of a naturally formed, almost autogenic tutor makes *Emile* realizable.[6]

Even the claim to *Emile*'s universality is severely limited. Rousseau claims that "wherever men are born, what I propose can be done with them" (35). Rousseau thus initially suggests that Emile's education is generalizable, hence everywhere and always applicable. Yet even the avoidance of all particularity—if such avoidance could be successfully accomplished, which is ever in doubt, especially considering the increasing encroachment of society—does not necessarily guarantee the success of *Emile*'s universality. Each tutor and each pupil is *already* a particularity, an individual. Rousseau must eventually admit such unavoidable particularity in considering the effect of the same words on even the same person: "How can one think that the same sermon is suitable to so many auditors of such different dispositions, so different in mind, humor, age, sex, station, and opinion . . . ? [A]ll our affections are so inconstant that there are perhaps not even two moments in the life of each man when the same speech would make the same impression on him" (319). Thus even the lessons of *Emile* are applicable alone to a particular Emile; part of its great lesson is for the individual tutor to regard the individuality of each pupil and appropriately alter each lesson.

What Rousseau proposes is the choice between the two educational possibilities: "One must choose between making a man or a citizen [*un homme ou un citoyen*], for one cannot make both at the same time" (39; IV.248). In choosing to make "a man," hence one according to nature, Rousseau must avoid all *particular*, necessarily national forms of education that would tie Emile to a place or a people (35). The citizen will be required to act within the specific cultural, religious, and political context demanded by the *moeurs* of each country: thus, the good Swiss citizen would make a bad French subject, and both would make a poorly educated "natural" man. The education of all possible good citizens would require as many books as there are countries, real and imagined, of which the *Social Contract* is one particular expression and from which the *Government of Poland* and *Project for a Constitution of Corsica* are necessarily departures. The initial sequestration of Emile from all external influences is an essential precaution in view of the easy corruption from universal man to particular citizen.

Yet, Emile is not to be a natural man raised in a pristine natural world. Other people inhabit the earth, the fall of one man from the State of Nature has led to the fall of all. Thus, Emile must be taught that property is privately held and fiercely protected; that people hurt and kill one another for no other reason than slights to amour propre; that entire systems of repression have been organized to enslave populaces. To the extent that it is possible, Emile will be kept free of all these vices of modern humanity, but the potential for his corruption is always present. Thus, the excellence of his education must be limited by the fact of other people's corruption. The movement of *Emile* is opposite of that of the *Second Discourse*: whereas the natural progress of history determines that humanity will begin in a state of nature and inevitably be corrupted by external accident as well as the internal quality of *perfectibilité* (*SD*, 149), *Emile* attempts to take a single human already living among corrupt civilizations and return him to a state of nature.[7] Such a project, if not against nature, then against history, is necessarily and exceedingly difficult.

Rousseau insists that "the first education ought to be purely negative. It consists not at all in teaching virtue or truth but in securing the heart from vice and the mind from error" (93). Emile's education is fundamentally preventative: he will be protected from the encroachments of the world, of other humans, of books, even of language, if possible. Rousseau advises his readers to "form an enclosure around your child's soul at an early date. Someone else can draw its circumference, but you alone must build the fence" (38). Through such protection, the child will receive an education of things, that is, of obstacles "in our control only in certain respects" (38).[8] In *Julie*, Rousseau writes that an ideal education "is to make [the student] feel . . . the heavy yoke of necessity that nature imposes on man" (OC, II.571).[9] A negative education is thus one that acknowledges limits to human control over the environment, seeking to foster resignation and a certain stoicism in the pupil. As Judith Shklar summarizes negative education,

> its aim is to make a self-sufficient adult who lives at peace with himself. To achieve this one must at all costs avoid trying to impose a foreign, social character upon the child. His natural self must not be inhibited in any way. On the contrary, everything must be arranged so that the child may learn everything that he has to know, without losing his natural characteristics. . . . "Negative education" is negative in that it prevents the imposition of an artificial, socially devised and socially oriented self upon the child.[10]

Nevertheless, Emile is also to be protected from "protection," or rather exposed to the harsh blows of the world. Rousseau especially criticizes mothers for their pampering of young children, a practice that will only encumber them later in life because they do not learn to accommodate themselves to the arbitrariness of fortune. "One thinks only of preserving one's child. That is not enough. One ought to teach him to preserve himself as a man, to bear the blows of fate, to brave opulence and poverty, to live, if he has to, in freezing Iceland or on Malta's burning rocks. You may very well take precautions against his dying. He will nevertheless have to die" (42). Thus, a mother who actively *exposes* her child to the hardening experience of Fortune finally assists her child more than by mere protection; even if the exposure does not add to the length of a child's life—which it may in fact well accomplish through a kind of hardening—the child will live more fully. "Men have been buried at one hundred who died at their birth. They would have gained from dying young; at least they would have lived up to that time" (42).

Shortly after chiding mothers for being overprotective, Rousseau suggests an alternative model of a mother willing to expose her child to difficulties. "Thetis, to make her son invulnerable, plunged him, according to the fable, in the water of the Styx. This allegory is a lovely one, and it is clear. The cruel mothers of whom I speak do otherwise: by dint of plunging their children in softness, they prepare them for suffering; they open their pores to ills of every sort to which they will not fail to be prey when grown" (47). Thetis, the mother of Achilles, sought unsuccessfully to make her child invulnerable through the bracing and desperate gambit of immersing him in the burning waters of the underworld. This harsh treatment is offered by Rousseau as an alternative to the "softness" to which most children are exposed.

This early allusion to the hero of the *Iliad* and the central problem of Achilles—whether to face death—presents two potential paradoxes within the context of *Emile* and even within the context of the immediate lesson Rousseau seeks to teach. The first paradox regards this allusion to a book. As though echoing his condemnation of the *Letter to D'Alembert*, Rousseau, in the next book after this first allusion to the *Iliad*, condemns book learning as unnecessary and even dangerous to a child (116–19, 159). Until the age of twelve "Emile will hardly know what a book is" (116). Several "educations" are occurring in *Emile*, then: not only the ongoing education of the fictive student Emile, but also a different education of the reader, who already has undergone an education in books, which must itself be corrected. Rousseau never proposes "going back" to a State of Nature once one has been corrupted by society. Rather, almost paradoxically, at that point one stands in greater need of what originally caused the corruption.[11] For one who already has been exposed to theater, the only cure is more theater. Even so, Rousseau's constant citation of books—whether used in support of his argument or as criticism of another theory—not only contains the *negative* lesson of preventing greater corruption, but also suggests a more positive *corrective* function. Rousseau, like Plato in the *Republic*, teaches his readers how to read anew.

This conclusion is particularly warranted given the second paradox of Rousseau's introduction of Thetis as an appropriate model for mothers. The purported lesson of Thetis's action—the steeling of a child through exposure to danger—is undertaken for precisely the reason Rousseau has already condemned, that is, the futile attempt at prolonging one's child's life. Thetis's action of hardening her child against fortune may be in itself admirable, according to Rousseau; but her intention and its effect is to create a false immortality for Achilles, to increase his longing for life at all costs. Rousseau's choice of a model here is most perplexing, given that it stands directly in contradiction to the central meaning of his lesson. Thus, his claim that the meaning of the allegory "is clear" is wholly misleading, even deceptive (47). His meaning in employing this contradictory lesson is far from clear.

If Thetis is admirable for her treatment of Achilles, Rousseau subsequently acknowledges that the result of her action removes any heroic claims for Achilles. His apparent invulnerability prevents him from possessing true courage. "It is the knowledge of dangers that makes us fear them; he who believed himself invulnerable would fear nothing. By dint of arming Achilles against peril, the poet takes from him the merit of valor; every other man in his place would have been an Achilles at the same price" (55). The overprotective mother creates a godlike entity who cannot know courage because he cannot know fear. One of the qualities that inspires great admiration for Achilles—his invulnerability—is thus rendered meaningless.

Nevertheless, Achilles is not fully invulnerable in actuality. Achilles must die, both by the prescriptions of the gods and because of his mixed birth to a mortal father. His mother's attempts to make him invincible leave him with a fatal flaw. The poignancy of her failed effort is obvious—as a goddess, Thetis is well aware that Achilles must die. As she bemoans in the *Iliad*,

"Ah me, my child. Your birth was bitterness. Why did I raise you?
If only you could sit by your ships untroubled, not weeping,
since indeed your lifetime is to be too short, of no length.
Now it has befallen that your life must be brief and bitter
beyond all men's. To a bad destiny I bore you in my chambers."
(I.415–420)

Rousseau acknowledges as much late in *Emile*, when again recalling the early image of the immersion in the River Styx, he laments: "But dear Emile, it is in vain that I have dipped your soul in the Styx: I was not able to make it everywhere invulnerable" (443).

Oddly, Rousseau points out two causes of weakness in Achilles that are not mutually compatible. On the one hand, Achilles' purported invulnerability leaves him incapable of courage. However, the method of his treatment in Styx, requiring his mother to cover his heel, reveals a critical vulnerability that should negate the former proposition.[12] He is either a godlike man who lacks simple courage or a mortal who carries a deadly flaw and can therefore act courageously. Because Achilles is fated to die and knows his fate in advance, it is apparent that the first proposition cannot be true, that Achilles cannot prima facie lack courage due to invulnerability. Considering the paradox more closely, one arrives at a subtle condemnation of Achilles by Rousseau, similar to that lodged by Plato in the *Republic*: all humans who possess invulnerability will lack courage. However, Rousseau elsewhere submits, Achilles is not invulnerable. Although this latter information negates the logic of the former, it does not dismiss the charge that Achilles lacked courage. Rousseau suggests that, even if one who is invulnerable cannot be brave, it does not necessarily follow that one who is vulnerable automatically possesses courage.

Each of the five books of *Emile* opens with an illustration from an ancient tale: the illustration of the first book depicts the moment that Thetis dips Achilles into the River Styx.[13] The accompanying text reads, "The illustration, which relates to the first book and serves as frontispiece to the work, represents Thetis plunging her son in the Styx to make him invulnerable" (36; OC, IV.869). The depiction captures Thetis's willingness to harden her child, her desperation to prolong her child's life at any cost, and, pathetically, highlights her grip on the child's ankle, thus revealing the final futility of her act. As a frontispiece, it also provides the broad thematic of the work, a theme to which Rousseau often returns—the education of Emile to face and accept his own death with resignation, to arrive at a stoic resignation before all necessity, particularly one's own mortality. The attempt of Thetis to prolong Achilles' life and Achilles' subsequent inability to face his death with ease and resignation suggest at the outset the limits of Emile's natural education and even pose a subtle precaution to parents and children to avoid the Achillean model.

Further evidence that Rousseau intends us to view Achilles as at least an ambiguous if not a *negative* model, inasmuch as he is so centrally featured from the outset of Emile's *negative* education, is Rousseau's stated intention that Emile's education is designed particularly to overcome *anger*. The very headnote to *Emile* is a citation from Seneca's *On Anger [De Ira]*: "We are sick with evils that can be cured; and nature, having brought us forth sound, itself helps us if we wish to be improved."[14] The natural education thus attempts to restore human equilibrium in the face of those frustrations that create anger. As Allan Bloom describes the problem of anger in *Emile*, "Anger is a self-indulgence bespeaking an incapacity to accept what happens to our hostages to fortune—friends, beloved, and family—a wanting to give protection to what is our own. In the accents of indignation it insists on justice where there is no justice. It is a much greater threat than the mere selfishness of the desires because it clothes itself in the appearance of morality."[15]

Anger is that passion that wells from human frustration over our weakness in the face of uncontrollable circumstances. In Mary Nichols's estimation, "It therefore indicates a man's dependence on others, whether it be to satisfy his desires or to acknowledge his dignity or worth."[16] Emile's education is explicitly directed at overcoming this frustration and, hence, the possibility of anger against his fate.[17]

Emile is to be protected not only from the outside world (due to its deleterious effects), but also, at least initially, from forming attachments that would produce anger against inevitable loss. Rousseau describes such a moment to be avoided, as when a lover receives a letter informing him of a tragedy: "A letter comes in the post; the happy man looks at it; it is addressed to him; he opens it, reads it. Instantly his aspect changes. He becomes pale and faints. Coming to, he weeps, writhes, moans, tears his hair, makes the air resound with his cries, seems to have a frightful fit of convulsions" (83). The recipient is like Achilles, who reacts with tears and threats when Briseis is taken from him by Agamemnon (*Iliad* I.349–363) and who later weeps and wails when confronted with the death of Patroclus:

> In both hands he caught up the grimy dust, and poured it
> over his head and face, and fouled his handsome countenance, and the black
> ashes were scattered over his immortal tunic. And he himself, mightily in his
> might, in the dust lay at length, and took and tore at his hair with his hands,
> and defiled it. . . .
> He cried out terribly, aloud, and his mother heard him.
> (XVIII.23–27, 35)

Anger is *the* defining feature of Achilles in his relationship to the humans and the gods; as the *Iliad* opens, "Sing goddess, the anger of Peleus' son Achilles,/ and its devastation, which put pains thousandfold upon the Achaians" (I.1–2). The disasters of the war, the tragedy of Hector and Achilles, occur largely as a result of Achilles' anger against Agamemnon because of his attachment to the slavegirl Briseis and his love of honor.

Emile, rather, is to avoid Achilles' example: "O man, draw your existence up within yourself, and you will no longer be miserable. Remain in the place which nature assigns to you in the chain of being. Nothing will be able to make you leave it. Do not rebel against the hard law of necessity; and do not exhaust your strength by your will to resist that law—strength which heaven gave you not for extending or prolonging your existence but only for preserving it as heaven pleases" (83).

Death, in particular, is to be faced with equanimity. Indeed, it is the very fact of our mortality that gives life its meaning and significance, unlike those immortal gods of Homer who look to humanity for respite. "If we were immortal, we would be most unhappy beings. . . . If we were offered immortality on the earth, who would want to accept this dreary present?" (82). Emile is to accept what is given, obey the strictures of nature, and watch the deaths of those around him with resignation, just as he is to face his own death.

The two lessons that Achilles provides in the first two books of *Emile* are, on the one hand, the purely "negative" (i.e., protective) lesson that mothers must "harden" their children without seeking to shield them from knowledge of their own death; and, playing on the word *negative*, the further lesson that Achilles' inability to control his anger presents an example to be *avoided*. If anywhere in the education there is a *positive* lesson, it is provided by way of the illustration of the second book (see figure 2). The accompanying text reads: "The illustration at the beginning of the second book represents Chiron training the little Achilles in running" (36). In addition to preparing his young charge for necessity and death, the first and second books also emphasize the *physical* training of a child (especially 124–141). Achilles—known by the epithet "swift"—is admirable in this strictly positive sense only inasmuch as his physical prowess is without peer. As such, his training by Chiron—beast below the waist—has emphasized his animality at the expense of moral training. Such a conclusion on the implicit value of Achilles' example is suggested by Rousseau himself. In elaborating on his distinction between positive and negative education, he described it thus to Christophe de Beaumont: "I call positive education that which tends to form the understanding before the proper time, and to give a child prematurely the knowledge of duties of a man. I call that negative education, which tends to perfect the corporeal organs, the instrument of our knowledge, and which prepares us for reasoning by exercising our senses" (OC, III.945).[18]

Inasmuch as Achilles provides an excellent physical education, he is an appropriate model for young Emile; his easily awakened anger, however, makes him less than ideal, and he is therefore dropped with the conclusion of the second book. Thus, for Rousseau the example of Achilles for the most part provides a *negative* education—how *not* to act when confronted with necessity, a model to be avoided. With the beginning of Emile's "second" education, Rousseau must look to another more prudent example, namely Odysseus. But, like Odysseus, before Emile can arrive "home" to wife and family, the tutor must first create the conditions for Emile's conveyance into society.

Emile's "Second Education": Reconciling Nature and Art?

"Positive education," as we have just seen, is inappropriate for the very young because it is "that which tends to form the understanding before the proper time, and to give a child prematurely the knowledge of duties of a man." Unlike negative education, which seeks to protect a child from social ties, positive education involves "the duties of a man," namely duties to other human beings. As Rousseau declares at the outset of Book V, with a conscious echo of Genesis 2:18, "It is not good for man to be alone" (357; see also 255, 327). There is a seeming contradiction between the two educations of Emile. The first, "negative" education, is aimed at keeping Emile separate from humans; the second, "positive" education, is intended to immerse him deeply in the affairs of others, as a husband, a father, and a citizen. Yet the first education serves the purpose of preparing him for the second: even when he becomes involved with others, he is to retain the stoic equanimity he learned in his first, negative education. Any apparent incongruity between the two educations is due to Rousseau's understanding of human development: whereas the passions are evident quite early in human life, reason is the last to develop.[19] Reason, properly prepared through the isolation of the child, results not in antisocial tendencies but rather in a morally healthy individual who is capable of living well among other people.

Emile's "second education" acknowledges that he can no longer be kept in isolation from the world.[20] If he is to be a "man," he must accept the "duties of a man," including work, religion, love, and citizenship. His connection to the rest of humanity is to be forged through his natural interest in the other sex once he has reached puberty. The fully reasoning man will be completed through the emotion of love. "We have made an active and thinking being. It remains for us, in order to complete the man, only to make a loving and feeling being—that is to say, to perfect reason by sentiment" (203). In *Emile*, Rousseau purposefully guides his young student's awakening feelings first to love a symbol of woman and finally to love an actual woman, Sophie, who has been raised especially for him. According to Bloom, Rousseau attempts to create a coincidence between two forms of maturation—the one physical and the other civic.[21] Rousseau tries "to make the two puberties coincide, to turn the desire for sexual intercourse into a desire for marriage and a willing submission to the law without suppressing or blaming that original desire" (17). Through *sublimation* of his natural desire, Emile will be brought entire and healthy into society.[22]

Such, at least, is the theory behind the tutor's efforts. Many attempts have been made to show that Rousseau is successful in this project: from Gustav Lanson, who argued that the education of Emile, made general, would result in a community akin to that described in the *Social Contract*;[23] to Asher Horowitz's more recent effort suggesting that *Emile* represents Rousseau's definitive effort to reconcile art and nature.[24] Indeed, Rousseau at the outset explains that, despite his recognition of the potential contradiction between the two educations, he nevertheless hopes to reconcile the education of "man and citizen": "There remains, finally, domestic education or the education of nature. But what will a man raised uniquely for himself become for others? If perchance [*peut-être*] the double object we set for ourselves could be joined in a single one by removing the contradictions of man, a great obstacle to his happiness would be removed" (41; IV.251).

From the outset Emile is intended for society, but without the contradictions that mar those people who are raised in and by it. Rousseau abandons his earlier recommendations in *Political Economy* for public education, rejecting the example of Plato's *Republic* not only because it is *public* education but because, according to Rousseau, it is not *political* (40).[25]

Yet despite attempts such as those by Lanson, Horowitz, and Paul Meyer to portray Emile's two educations as wholly complementary, an irreconcilable tension marks the transition of the negative to the second education and may account for Rousseau's use of the word *peut-être* in claiming to be able to combine the two. Emile, who has been thus far raised to avoid *dependency* on any other humans, is now to be instructed to involve himself in that most intense attachment of all: erotic love. "His first affections are the reins with which you direct all his movements. He was free, and now I see him enslaved. So long as he loved nothing, he depended only on himself and his needs. As soon as he loves, he depends on his attachments" (233). In attempting to create the good "man," Rousseau attempted to keep his student from forming attachments of dependency on any other human. Now, in attempting to join Emile to Sophie and, hence, to a family, a home, and a polity—in short, in attempting to educate the good citizen—Emile must be immersed in particularity, in attachments and bonds that potentially threaten his stoicism and resignation. He is to be both a "good man and a lover" (242), which, by definition according to the opening of *Emile*, is a contradiction.

Recalling the absence of stoicism demonstrated by the man who receives bad news through the mail, the tutor makes Emile undergo a test. Emile has fallen too fully in love with Sophie and, thereby, threatens his education in resignation. The tutor tells Emile that he has become a "slave" to his desires (443). Necessity requires one death from each mortal, a death that Emile can face with equanimity (83); however, having attached himself to Sophie, Emile now faces death twice (444). Realizing Emile's deepening attachment to Sophie, the tutor brings Emile a letter in which he learns (falsely) that Sophie has died. Instead of showing quiet acceptance, Emile "lets out a great cry, gets up, striking his hands together, and looks wild-eyed at me without saying a single word" (442). As Bloom perceptively notes, "This entire scene is a dramatic recapitulation of the deepest sources of our tradition. It is an explicit imitation of the *Iliad* where Agamemnon takes away Achilles' girl. . . ."[26] This comparison is shortly thereafter made explicit by Rousseau: "But, dear Emile, it is in vain that I dipped your soul in the Styx; I was not able to make it everywhere invulnerable. A new enemy is arising which you have not learned to conquer and from which I can no longer save you. . . . You were bound to nothing other than the human condition, and now you are bound to all the attachments you have given to yourself" (443). We learn only now that Thetis's attempt to make Achilles invulnerable, although perhaps admirable for its hardening qualities, did not and could not succeed in making the child invulnerable. His greatest weakness—overweening attachment and excessive anger—is now the weakness of Emile as well.

Emile must be separated from Sophie before he can be married. He must learn again to distance his attachment to her, at once to love her and yet not allow that love to chain him to her or to any other human. The model of Achilles—who loved too much, first Briseis, then Patroclus—must be dropped now in favor of the model of Odysseus. Emile must leave Sophie in order to travel, in order, after a fashion, to descend to the underworld in order to accept his mortality, but his alone.

The Odyssean Education: Harrowing Emile

The frontispiece of Book V of *Emile* (see figure 5) marks the transition from the early model of Achilles to that of Odysseus. The accompanying text reads: "The illustration at the beginning of the fifth book and the fourth volume represents Circe giving herself to Ulysses, whom she was not able to transform" (36). Standing at the beginning of the final volume of the original edition and hence representing the denouement of Emile's education, the final illustration depicts Odysseus with his sword drawn facing Circe, while in the background can be seen several pigs, hitherto crewmates of Odysseus. In the foreground is a fallen cup, indicating that Odysseus has already drunk the potion intended to turn him also into a swine, but, as instructed by Hermes—who rendered him immune—he now subdues Circe by force.[27] The illustration was well chosen by Rousseau, for it aptly represents the relationship Rousseau portrays between Sophie and Emile: that of the temptress and transformer against that of the detached male protected by nature.

At the outset of Emile's education in eros in Book IV, the tutor expresses quite how difficult this particular moment in Emile's life will be. Emile begs his master to "make me free by protecting me against those of my passions which do violence to me. Prevent me from being their slave; force me to be my own master and to obey not my senses but my reason" (325). In effect, Emile asks his tutor to force him to be free of those very bindings that will eventually tie him to family and city. The master replies: "How often you will curse the one who loves you when he finds himself forced to rend your heart in order to save you from the evils which threaten you! Just as Ulysses, moved by the Sirens' song and seduced by the lure of the pleasures, cried out to his crew to unchain him, so you will want to break the bonds which hinder you" (326).

The tutor represents the ropes that will hold Emile fast from the temptations of the Sirens, now representing not the knowledge of the gods but the temptations of the flesh, shortly to be incarnated by Sophie. Although Emile is to be joined to Sophie and through her to family and city because "it is not good for man to be alone," the tutor will also protect him from the irrationality of those passions, allowing him finally to escape them should it be necessary. He is to be bound by the tutor to the mast of reason, not to Sophie. Emile remains the stalwart and moderate man of self-restraint, like Odysseus, whereas Sophie is for the first, but not the last, time associated with the image of temptress who brings men to their doom.

The very meeting of Emile and Sophie is suffused with imagery from the *Odyssey*. As Emile and his tutor first enter the house of Sophie, having first imagined her and then searched for her, Emile remarks, "I believe I am living in Homer's time" (413). As he is first introduced to Sophie, Sophie's father continues in this Homeric vein: "'You appear to me to be a likeable and wise young man, and that makes me think that you and your governor have arrived here tired and wet like Telemachus and Mentor on Calypso's island.' 'It is true,' Emile answers, 'that we find here the hospitality of Calypso.' His mentor adds, 'And the charms of Eucharis.' But although Emile knows the *Odyssey*, he has not read *Telemachus*. He does not know who Eucharis is" (413–14).

Sophie's father greets him by referring to the opening pages of Fénelon's *Télémaque*, in which Odysseus's son Telemachus and Athena—disguised throughout the novel as Mentor—are washed ashore on the island of Calypso, much as Odysseus was earlier in the *Odyssey*. Fénelon's romance was written for Louis XIV's grandson and heir apparent; like *Emile*, it purports to be a definitive work in the education of children and was certainly a source of inspiration for *Emile*.[28] Emile's response to Sophie's father's literary reference is curious: having only read the *Odyssey*, he would know that in that epic Telemachus and Mentor never visit the island of Calypso. He mistakes the reference for Odysseus's landing on Calypso's island and, hence, believes himself to be Odysseus rather than Telemachus. In the *Télémaque*, as in the *Odyssey*, Calypso is captivated by each respective mortal man and offers each one immortality. In opposition to the *Odyssey*, in which Odysseus declines the goddess's offer without prompting, Telemachus must be advised by the wise Mentor (Athena) to be wary of the goddess and finally must be physically forced from the island to thwart his subsequent obsession with the nymph Eucharis.[29] Indeed, unlike his father, Telemachus sees no reason to leave the island and sees many reasons for staying: "Why do we not live on this island? Ulysses must be dead: he must have been buried a long time ago in the sea. Penelope, not seeing either him or me return, must have yielded to the solicitations of some of her suitors. . . . Do you count the immortality offered me by the goddess as nothing?"[30]

Mentor responds: "Alas! What would you do with an immortal life, without liberty, without virtue, and without glory? That life would only be so much the more miserable in being immortal, inasmuch as it would never end."[31] Telemachus must be taught by his tutor to appreciate the same reasons that his father originally left the island and not to succumb to the temptations of dangerous females.

Also, on Calypso's island, Telemachus falls for a waiting-girl, the nymph Eucharis, and must be again prompted by Mentor (Athena) to avoid immortal wiles.[32] Emile believes himself to be more like Odysseus—capable of avoiding the pitfalls of Calypso, or in this case Sophie. His tutor knows better, evoking the image of the seductive nymph Eucharis and implicitly the pliant Telemachus, who must continuously be guided by Mentor. As Telemachus finally declares once they escape from the island and his head begins to be cleared of Cupid's influence, "Vice can only be conquered by flight."[33] This is the lesson that Telemachus must learn from his encounter with Calypso and Eucharis, and, it is suggested, the same lesson that Emile must learn from his similar encounter with Sophie.

Sophie, in addition to her identification by Rousseau with Circe, the Sirens, and Calypso, herself often identifies with the nymph Eucharis. During the course of her education, she at one point develops an irrational need to be loved, so piercing that her mother suspects that something is amiss. Sophie admits to having read a book that has not been prescribed for her education.

> "Pity your unhappy daughter. Her sadness is without remedy. Her tears will never dry up. You want to know the cause. Well, here it is," she said, throwing the book down on the table. The mother took the book and opened it. It was the *Adventures of Telemachus*. At first she understood nothing of this enigma. But by dint of questions and obscure answers, she finally saw, with a surprise that is easy to conceive, that her daughter was the rival of Eucharis. Sophie loved Telemachus and loved him with a passion of which nothing could cure her. (404–405)

Hers has been, mistakenly, a sentimental education. Like Emile, who in the early stages of his education is only permitted to read Defoe's *Robinson Crusoe* in order to emulate solitary man on an island, Sophie is also prescribed one book: not the *Adventures of Telemachus*, but a household accounting handbook by Bertrand-François Barrême.[34] The *Telemachus* has fallen into her hands "by chance" (*par hazard*) (410; IV.769). Like Emile's education, one can succeed only through luck (*bonheur*) (38; IV.246); if Emile's education has by dint of fortune largely succeeded in making him a "man," in Sophie's case her education "by chance" has not been as lucky. According to Rousseau's definition of an ideal education for women, Sophie's is almost perfect but for the intrusion of a romantic novel. Not only is she associated with Circe, Calypso, and the Sirens by Rousseau—for as a woman, she represents, according to Rousseau, a temptation for men to lose their equanimity—she explicitly identifies *herself* with the nymph Eucharis and pines for the culmination of her imaginary love. Her sentimentality, if not properly controlled, threatens to endanger the equilibrium of their relationship.

Sophie, as woman, is both necessary and threatening to Emile. When it is obvious that he has become too attached to her, *too* much dependent on another human being and thus no longer fully capable of being a "man," Emile must receive his final lesson—he must be parted from Sophie and travel the world, thus also allowing him finally to receive a political education. As Emile embraces too much his relationship with Sophie and, hence by extension, the network of relationships that emanate from family to city and country, his education as universal man must again for a final time be reinforced. "I hold it to be an incontestable maxim that whoever has seen only one people does not know men; he knows only the people with whom he has lived. . . . Does it suffice for a well-educated man to know only his compatriots, or is it important for him to know men in general?" (451). The tutor proposes a "cosmopolitan" education: like Odysseus, Emile is meant to know of "many cities" and "the minds of men" in those cities (*Odyssey*, 1.3).

The tutor tells Emile that he has become a "slave" to his desires (443). Necessity requires one death from each human; by attaching himself to Sophie, however, Emile now faces death twice: "Everything on earth is only transitory. All that we love will escape us sooner or later, and we hold on to it as if it were going to last eternally. What a fright you had at the mere suspicion of Sophie's death. . . . Nature had enslaved you only to a single death. You are enslaving yourself to a second. Now you are in the position of dying twice" (444). His journey to all the various political regimes is to teach him to face his own death easily without immersing himself in the lives and deaths of others. Oddly, his political education is intended to result in his utter psychic separation from personal, familial, or political attachments. By coming to know the arbitrariness of all attachments and the inevitable demise of all persons and objects that one might hold dear, Emile learns to distance himself from the particular through an education in the universal. He is to become a "citizen" in name only, in effect by being a citizen of nowhere and everywhere.

Quite how this is accomplished is suggested by the nature of the political lesson Emile learns. The political education of Emile comprising a latter portion of Book V (455–471) is a succinct recapitulation of the *Social Contract*, which was published during the same year as *Emile*. Although supposedly a summary of Emile's journey, it takes more the form of a treatise, and, at that, one that has little to do with regimes as they are or were but as they should be. The formation of a general will is described (460), the only mechanism by which a government legitimately exists. The people who constitute the general will are the sovereign: "Inasmuch as the individuals have subjected themselves to the sovereign, and the sovereign authority is nothing other than the general will, we shall see how each man who obeys the sovereign obeys only himself, and how one is more free under the social pact than in the state of nature" (461). The sovereign body can thereafter enact specific pieces of legislation that must be put into effect by an executive body, which acts through reason or force as a substitute for the Sovereign (462). Having mentioned the formation of a regime through the General Will of the Sovereign and the need for a Magistrate, Rousseau points us in a footnote to the *Social Contract*.[35]

Rousseau directs us to the *Social Contract* at this point because within that text the relationship between the Sovereign and the Executive is more fully portrayed, including the tension between the two bodies, which is not fully limned in *Emile*. As Bertrand de Jouvenel has forcefully argued, the *Social Contract* tells a story not only about how to establish a legitimate government through the institution of a General Will, but also about how even this most excellent regime is destined to decay into, at best, an illegitimate and even tyrannical government.[36] Thus is Emile's political education essentially a lesson in mortality.

As de Jouvenel has argued, Rousseau's portrait of the sovereign and participatory democracy of the *Social Contract* is purely affective, like those of ancient Greece. A citizen populace must be able to see and hear one another to deliberate and decide; no representatives can be permitted to intervene in this direct governance.[37] Rousseau concludes that the state must necessarily be small because the larger the state grows, the less influence and power each citizen can exercise:

> Suppose the State is composed of ten thousand citizens. The Sovereign can only be considered collectively and as a body; but each member, as being a subject, is regarded as an individual: thus the Sovereign is to the subject as ten thousand to one. . . . If the people numbers a hundred thousand, the condition of the subject undergoes no change, and each equally is under the whole authority of the laws, while his vote, being reduced to one hundred thousandth part, has ten times less influence in drawing them up. . . . From this it follows that, the larger the State, the less the liberty. [SC, 61; see also *Emile*, 463–64]

Thus, except in those most intimate of city-states—an impracticality in modernity—the Sovereignty of citizens is largely rendered meaningless.

The result of this loss of effectiveness is dissatisfaction on the part of the citizens. In a small society, in which each individual's voice can be distinguished, conflicting claims can be sorted through and solutions devised that leave few if any dissatisfied. In larger States, where each individual's voice is rendered ineffectual, the resulting legislative process—although still legitimate in strictly democratic terms—nevertheless is unable to accommodate each person's individual desires. As de Jouvenel portrays this situation: "The same edicts seem to me the more oppressive, the less I have participated in their formulation; and my goodwill as a subject becomes correspondingly less. . . . The individual, lost in a greater crowd of citizens, feels less intensely his pride and sense of responsibility in participating, and when, as a subject, he receives his orders, they weigh heavily on him. He feels less free."[38]

The larger the population of States, Rousseau concludes, the more need there is of repressive measures as people begin to reject the edicts of the General Will that are no longer as "general" as formerly. With the growth of government comes the inevitable loss of freedom through rise of the Executive at the expense of the Sovereign.

Rousseau was not sanguine on the possibility of arresting this development; indeed, in the *Social Contract* he argues that this deterioration is "natural and inevitable" (SC, 88).[39] "The body politic, as well as the human body, begins to die as soon as it is born, and carries in itself the causes of its destruction. . . . The best constituted state will have an end; but it will end later than any other unless some unforeseen accident brings about its untimely destruction" (SC, 89). The imperatives of modern society, those toward complexity, urbanization, enlarging economies and empire—in short, those historical imperatives he first described in the *Second Discourse*—will inevitably force even excellent cities into inevitable decay toward tyranny.[40] Those "constructive" attempts to establish virtuous regimes—namely, his advice to Corsica and Poland—are fundamentally attempts to *prevent* the worst features of modern civilization from beginning its inevitable encroachment.[41] Rousseau was particularly hopeful in the case of Corsica because its limited boundaries at least dictated a limit to its population and, hence, the easier maintenance of democratic sovereignty (SC, 54; CO, 279). But even in Rousseau's most optimistic assessment, Corsica could only hope for a stay, and not improvement:

> You ask for a plan of government suitable for Corsica. It is asking for more than you think. There are peoples who, do what you may, are incapable of being well governed, for the law has no hold over them, and a government without laws cannot be a good government. I do not say that the Corsican people is in that condition. On the contrary, no people impresses me as being so fortunately disposed by nature to receive a good administration. But even this is not enough, for all things lead to abuses, which are often inevitable; and the abuse of political institutions follows so closely upon their establishment that it is hardly worthwhile to set them up, only to see them degenerate so rapidly. (CO, 277)

In short, the main thrust of Rousseau's political teachings, those embodied in the *Social Contract* and his later attempts to put those lessons into practice—if only to stave off the inevitable decline of regimes—is one that describes the mortality of even the best regimes.[42] *Such* is the lesson that Emile is to learn in his travels and his education in politics in Book V: in order to prevent an overwhelming attachment to Sophie—and through her, a too-great attachment to whatever regime he will join—he must be taught that, like Sophie, the city too will die.

Emile is to bring one book with him on his voyages to the cities of the world: finally he is to read the *Télémaque* of Fénelon (450). Yet the object of Emile's lesson is not the romantic education that Sophie gleaned illicitly by identifying with Eucharis; rather, he is to learn to resemble Telemachus, who himself is being educated to resemble his father Odysseus, to emulate his decisions (such as that allowing to escape Calypso's wiles) without having to be forced by Mentor. Inasmuch as the travels of Emile and his tutor are to be *political* lessons, those lessons will resemble as much as possible the lessons that Telemachus receives.

Many of Telemachus's lessons are intended to prepare him for the eventual kingship of Ithaca; as such, these lessons cannot be directly applicable to Emile—he is intended to be an anonymous citizen, not a recognized leader. As Rousseau disclaims, "Since Emile is not a king and I am not a god, we do not fret about not being able to imitate Telemachus and Mentor in the good that they did for men. No one knows better than we do how to keep in our place, and no one has less desire to leave it" (467). At various points in the *Adventures of Telemachus*, however, a more broadly applicable lesson is advanced that accords with the intentions of the tutor in his attempt to create a physical and psychic distance between Emile and Sophie.

One lesson in particular stands out. At one point, having arrived on the island of Crete, Telemachus participates with the other Cretans in answering a series of questions intended to discover who should be the next king. The question posed is, "Which is the freest of all men?" Some answer that the freest person would be a tyrant; a man of enormous wealth; a footloose bachelor; a savage; a newly freed slave; a dying man. Telemachus, answering last, stated, "The freest man is he who can be free even in slavery. In whatever country or condition one is, he is perfectly free, provided he fears the gods, and them only. In a word the truly free man is he who, detached from all, is to bid defiance to fear and all desire, is subject only to the gods and to his reason."[43] It is interesting that although this response (and others like it) wins Telemachus the offer of kingship, he declines it, thus demonstrating in effect his own freedom from temptations for glory (for, surely, the kingship of Crete would afford more glory and opportunity than his inherited seat in rocky Ithaca). This classically stoic lesson of *detachment* is the reason for Emile's education with the *Adventures of Telemachus*. At the conclusion of this political and literary education in detachment, Emile returns to reclaim his bride, not with a strengthened attachment to her and to his eventual city but with freedom from his dependence on her that he evinced before his journey.

His speech to his tutor after the two-year journey is marked by both acceptance and resignation. The lessons of temporariness have made him a man, thereby freeing him from citizenship: "Rich or poor, I shall be free. I shall not be free in this or that land, in this or that region; I shall be free everywhere on earth. All the chains of opinion are broken for me; I shall only know those of necessity" (472). The tutor's response to his pupil's culminating speech suggests the achievement of distinction: "Dear Emile, I am glad to hear a man's speech [*discours d'homme*] come from your mouth" (473; OC 4.857).[44] The education is completed: the tutor has kept his promise to create a man, not a citizen, a being capable of living *among* people but never becoming *of* them.[45] This includes a detachment not only from his fellow citizens and neighbors but ultimately, if necessary, from Sophie and his family as well. To her we now turn.

Sophie: La Nouvelle Circe

The case of Sophie has caused anger and consternation from many,[46] defensiveness and justification from some,[47] and everywhere has proven to be one of Rousseau's most enduring paradoxes. How could one so devoted to the furtherance of human freedom be so stubbornly insistent on the natural inferiority of women? How could one willing to describe through four long books the education of a child for freedom succumb in the final book to a long discussion of woman's education in obedience to her husband? Even though all critics are forced to agree that Rousseau's description of Sophie's education, at the very least, exists in contradiction to much of his philosophy and, at worst, finally mars any claim he might have to being a philosopher of freedom, few critics can agree on *why* Rousseau chooses the course he does, and some even refuse to ask the question.[48]

Penny Weiss is correct to contend that those treatments that ignore the problem of Sophie simply wear intellectual blinders: "This 'approach' to the problem treats Rousseau's views on the sexes as a detachable appendage to the main body of his thought, assuming that nothing essential to Rousseau's thought is revealed in those discussions, and implying that Rousseau's position on the sexes could be altered without consequences to the rest of his thought."[49] Moreover, one cannot simply dismiss Rousseau's ruminations as a reflection of the times because he was exposed to, and even at one time seemed to adopt, an early version of liberal feminism.[50] Rousseau is exceedingly self-conscious that his version of feminist education is not in keeping with certain tendencies of his time toward sexual equality.[51]

At one point, Rousseau insists that dependence, if it is to be avoided in the case of Emile, is inevitable for women: "Dependence is a condition natural to women, and thus girls feel themselves made to obey" (370). A woman is defined entirely by her sexuality, he insists, one rooted in the inevitability of nature:

> There is no parity between the two sexes in regard to the consequences of sex. The male is male only at certain moments. The female is female her whole life or at least during her whole youth. Everything constantly recalls her sex to her; and, to fulfil its functions well, she needs a constitution which corresponds to it. She needs care during her pregnancy; she needs rest at the time of childbirth; she needs a soft and sedentary life to suckle her children; she needs patience and gentleness, a zeal and an affection that nothing can rebuff in order to raise her children. She serves as the link between them and their father; she alone makes him love them and gives him the confidence to call him his own. How much tenderness and care is required to maintain the union of the whole family! (361)

Because a woman in this view always functions under the demands of her sexuality, she is naturally inferior to man in regard to any public function and, indeed, in regard to decisions in the household. The goal of her education is to make her attractive, faithful, and obedient to her husband.

These claims are startling and disturbing in themselves and all the more puzzling given Rousseau's previous treatment of woman's original condition in the state of Nature as described in the *Second Discourse*. There, women are effectively almost identical to men in capabilities and function; those differences in reproduction deemed in *Emile* to be determinative of sexual and social roles prove only a minimal hindrance to women in the state of Nature:

> It would be to commit a fallacy of those who, in reasoning about the state of Nature carry over into it ideas taken from Society, always [to] see the family assembled in one and the same dwelling and its members maintaining among themselves as intimate and as permanent a union as they do among us . . . ; whereas in this primitive state, without Houses or Huts or property of any kind, everyone bedded down at random and often for only a single night; males and females united fortuitously, according to chance encounters, opportunity, and desire, without speech being an especially necessary interpreter of what they had to tell one another; they parted just as readily.[52] The mother at first nursed her Children because of her own need; then, habit made them dear to her, she nourished them because of theirs; as soon as they had the strength to forage on their own, they left even the Mother; and since almost the only way to find one another again was not to lose sight of one another in the first place, they soon were at the point of not even recognizing each other. (SD, 153)

Even the mother's attachment to her child or children is tenuous; not based in nature, but rather only in habit, a woman nourishes her offspring only so long as is necessary and then wanders off once again wholly oblivious of them. The only *natural* condition of men and women is that of total independence and detachment from one another.[53]

Susan Moller Okin rightly notes that the relationship of Emile and Sophie resembles not so much that of that "natural" independence of primitive people just described in the *Second Discourse* as much as that of the later period, called by Rousseau "the golden age," in which families are based largely on a patriarchal basis.[54] Emile, who is educated to be detached from humanity, needs some anchor to tie him to the city. For *that* purpose Sophie is educated as a modern "woman." Her education is *relative* to Emile's: in and of itself it has no claims to excellence. Moreover, being destined for a *particular* family means, in fact, that Sophie's *natural* desire to procreate at will with any partner must be, after a fashion, educated out of her—hence, Rousseau's apparent obsession with the ability of the husband to know that the woman's children are in fact his own. Sophie's "natural" education in modernity does not at all resemble "natural" woman of the state of Nature.

That Sophie's education has to be considered as wholly relative to the successful education of the detached Emile is suggested by the fact that elsewhere Rousseau recommends wholly *different* types of education for women *relative to the end* at which one aims.[55] Just as Emile is educated to be a "man," and not a "citizen," Sophie is educated to be Emile's woman and not a *female* citizen. Such an education would require a wholly different sort of object: not devotion to husband and children, but total commitment to the city. The portrait of such a woman Rousseau located in Plutarch: a woman so devoted to the city that, when told that her sons were killed in war, would respond to the messenger: "'Yet this isn't what I asked you, vile slave, but rather how our country was doing." When he said that it was winning, she remarked, 'Then I gladly accept the deaths of my sons, too.' "[56] Like Emile, Sophie is not to be a "female citizen" (40), but rather a "woman."

Another form of education that Rousseau elsewhere recommends for women, remarkably, is the one that women receive in Plato's *Republic*: an education of equality with men (*Republic* V, 453a–464a). In a significant note in the *First Discourse*, Rousseau writes:

> I am far from thinking that this ascendancy of women is in itself an evil. It is a gift bestowed on them by nature for the happiness of Mankind; better directed, it might produce as much good as it nowadays does harm. We are not sufficiently sensible to the benefits that would accrue to society if the half of Mankind which governs the other were given a better education. . . . The reflections to which this subject lends itself, *and which Plato made in former times*, amply deserves to be more fully detailed by a pen worthy of modelling itself on such a master and of defending so grand a cause. [*FD*, 17–18n.; emphasis mine]

Such a suggestion is remarkable inasmuch as Rousseau explicitly rejects the Platonic education of women in the fifth book of the *Republic* as incompatible with his vision of the family in *Emile*: "As though the love of one's nearest were not the principle of the love one owes to the state; as though it were not by means of the small fatherland which is the family that the heart attaches itself to the large one; as though it were not the good son, the good husband, and the good father who make the good citizen!" (363).[57] Thus, according to the demands of *Emile*'s education, the family—through Sophie—serves to bind him to the city. For this reason, Plato's abolition of the family within the context of *Emile* is objectionable.

On the other hand, Rousseau does *not* explicitly object to Plato's education of women on the grounds of equality: "I am not speaking of that alleged community of women; the often repeated reproach on this point proves that those who make it against him have never read him" (362–63). Rousseau's objection to Plato's education, rather, is less that of the equal education of women than that of the problem in modernity of the abolishment of the family. As Judith Shklar observes, the family for Rousseau represents a buffer against the encroachments of modern civilization, much as do the institutions of civil religion and the censor in the *Social Contract*. "In these reflections Rousseau surely had a profound intuition of one of the functions that the primary family would fulfil in modern civilization: to shut out the public world and to protect its members against its pressures."[58] The Platonic education of women is therefore predicated on the account of the advance of history, not due to an inherent unnaturalness to educating women in the same method as men. Sophie must be educated as described in *Emile* not because it is the best education for Sophie but because it is the best education for Emile.

Unlike Emile, being a "woman" does not entail the absence of dependency as in the case of a "man," nor total devotion to the city, but rather total devotion and obedience to her husband. Emile's "natural" education more or less attempts to create a figure with a similar outlook as primitive man: detached, independent, and self-reliant. Sophie's "natural" education is aimed at producing the *exact opposite* of that female creature in the state of Nature. Sophie is to be obsessed with amour propre;[59] she is to be absorbed with her children and attractive to a single man; in effect, she is to be as far as possible from the state of Nature as conceived of by Rousseau. Fundamentally, woman's "nature" defined by her sexuality in *Emile* is entirely inconsistent with Rousseau's own pronouncements on the subject in the *Second Discourse*. He is as self-consciously guilty of importing socially constructed definitions of the "natural" into *Emile* as he accuses Hobbes of being in the *Second Discourse* (159–60). His reason for doing so, however, comes back to the subject of the book *Emile*: its purpose is to describe the education of natural *man* in modernity; part of that education requires an anchor—woman— in order that man can fulfill his role in society. Even as there is a contradiction between Emile's "negative" and "second" educations, a severe tension distorts the ends of Emile's and Sophie's respective educations—a tension of which Rousseau is well aware.

Sophie is not finally Penelope, the simple object of Odysseus's quest for home-coming, acknowledged as less beautiful and less perfect than the goddess Calypso, who offers Odysseus immortality. Rather, Sophie's implicit model is Circe, an enchantress, now a goddess as tantalizing and attractive as Calypso, and even more powerful for all her magic charms that Odysseus resists successfully through his knowledge of nature, but under which he subtly falls the longer he remains with her. His men must in the final instance remind him of his journey, upbraid him for his forgetfulness, and pull him away from the wiles of the tempting but dangerous enchantress. It is Circe who sends Odysseus to the underworld, just as it is Emile's great attraction to Sophie and his fear of losing her that prompts the tutor to send him to learn of the temporality of all humans and human institutions, even political institutions. If, however, Emile is to emulate Odysseus and learn the lessons of human mortality, Sophie is finally educated less to be the imperfect but nevertheless multifaceted Penelope—the spouse equal to Odysseus *polutropos*—than to be the unachievably perfect goddess. The frontispiece of Book V—picturing Odysseus resisting Circe's enchantments through his knowledge of nature—finally reveals not only how Emile is to learn his own form of defenses, but also the final inappropriateness of assuming Sophie's education is to be con-sidered as satisfactory inasmuch as Circe is her model—a dangerous if tempting goddess.

How well aware Rousseau was of this incompatible tension between the edu-cations of Emile and Sophie is demonstrated by the unfinished fragment, *Emile et Sophie, ou Les Solitaires*. Existing in apparent contradiction to the happy end-ing of *Emile*, *Emile et Sophie* documents the inevitable decay of the relationship between Emile and Sophie, much as the *Social Contract* documents the inevi-table decay of relations within a state. Yet, as we have seen, this decay was al-ready built into the premises of the relationship, one that finally exacts its toll, Rousseau admits, in his fragments *Emile et Sophie*. There can be no permanent association for Emile—neither family nor city—without Sophie's flawed educa-tion; yet the very flaws of that education doom that association.

Sophie has been educated not as a detached individual like Emile, but as a lover, one devoted to husband and family. Unlike Emile, she is not warned about experiencing more deaths than her own; indeed, her education dictates that her absorption with her family makes her supremely susceptible to devastation. This weakness of Sophie's education is pointedly revealed when the deaths of her parents and of her daughter shatter her fragile world: "She had ignored all the bitterness of life, she had not armed her sensitive and simple soul from its effects" (OC, IV.884).[60] Precisely that education through which Emile is to be anchored to the social and political world is the one that destroys Sophie. She has never been educated to avoid the model of Achilles.[61]

As for Emile, he is unequivocal about his new position in the world: "I thought I was seeing another sky, another earth, another universe; everything had changed for me" (OC, IV.894). "All of my attachments were broken or altered, all my duties were changed. I was becoming, so to speak, a new being" (OC, IV.899). Emile breaks those bonds that had held him to family, to city, and to State. His training in the "underworld" that prepared him to remain detached from the pains of mortal attachment serves him well: he figuratively returns to visit the river of Lethe and "the water of forgetfullness" (OC, IV.912). He forges his life among citizens but does not forget the education he received from his tutor: "I was becoming man by ceasing to be a citizen" (OC, IV.912).[62] In an echo of the lessons he learned from Fénelon (whose book the *Adventures of Telemachus* he was given when he was forced to leave Sophie the first time), during Emile's separation from Sophie, he is in fact enslaved and, recalling his stoic lessons, retains his psychic freedom while under the yoke of servitude.

If Emile finally demonstrates in *Emile et Sophie* that he is true to the teachings of his tutor, Sophie's behavior demonstrates the inevitable failure of her education. Sophie has been raised explicitly to avoid adultery, even in the most dangerous conditions of big cities. Sophie's virtue is a sort "that can be put to a test" in "big cities and among corrupt men" (383). Yet, in *Emile et Sophie*, the decision of Emile and Sophie to settle in Paris proves catastrophic for Sophie: following the deaths of her parents and daughter, in her bereavement, she engages in an adulterous relationship and becomes pregnant by another man (OC, IV.887–90). Emile admits that in the time between Sophie's mourning and her infidelity they had grown apart: "We weren't one anymore, we were two" (OC, IV.887). Given the imperatives of Sophie's education—total devotion to Emile—the resultant distance between them, largely a consequence of big-city corruption, but also of the fact that Emile is never to fully reciprocate her love, proves to be too great a contradiction for her. Her education now ineffective, she acts in direct opposition to all that she has been taught. The internal contradiction of their relationship inevitably appears, exacerbated by the pulls of Paris, but finally in keeping with the educational theories of *Emile*.

The irony of this result is not lost on commentators. As Pierre Burgelin has written, Sophie's education represents a "synthèse paradoxale."[63] The imperatives of Sophie's education demand the virtue of Penelope; yet Sophie's "nature" as a woman—that hedonistic, individualistic creature of the *Second Discourse*—makes her susceptible to the lusts of Eucharis, Circe, and Calypso. If Emile takes as his model in the later books of *Emile* that of Odysseus, Sophie is never explicitly compared to either Antiope, the virtuous woman of Fénelon's *Tèlèmaque* (Book XVII), or to Penelope, the model of the faithful wife. In setting forth the culmination of Emile's education through his travels to the underworld and by neglecting Odysseus's longing to return to his family and home out of *engagement* to his mortal loves, Rousseau fundamentally neglects Odysseus's great anchor and in many ways the source of his longing—his wife, Penelope. Sophie ultimately resembles more the examples of Helen and Clytemnaestra, the adulterous wives who cause ruin to home and city, rather than that example that would seemingly come quicker to mind for one so mindful of the *Odyssey's* example. Rousseau's failure to adopt the entire motivations of Odysseus in the underworld and on the island of Calypso is reflected in the final failure of Emile and Sophie to find happiness in mutual commitment.

Community versus Solitude: On Happiness and the Good

Susan Moller Okin argues that because only Sophie is unsuccessfully educated, the catastrophe of the marriage ends, if not well for Sophie, then at least respectably well for Emile. "The end of the story of Emile is not totally pessimistic either. Emile survives the abortive attempt to make him into a husband, father, and citizen, and becomes what he was always intended to be—a natural and autonomous man."[64] We do not have the conclusion of *Emile et Sophie* on which to base a surmise of what Rousseau finally "intended" Emile to be; but Okin correctly posits that, based on the education of *Emile*, Emile was always better prepared to be a man than a citizen and, indeed, better prepared for the blows of fate than Sophie was.

Nevertheless, one can legitimately question whether Emile is in the end any *happier* than Sophie. Autonomy from other people is a high ideal throughout the writings of Rousseau—as high an ideal as is the communion with others. Quite how one squares this further tension between the community and the individual in the writings of Rousseau remains, like many other paradoxes, perhaps irresolvable.[65] But, as in many other instances, Rousseau leaves certain clues and indications.

Within the text of *Emile*, Rousseau often discusses the topic of solitude. Emile is explicitly not to be alone: his happiness as a complete human being depends on the success of his relationship with Sophie and through her a relationship with family and city. "Emile is not *made* to remain always solitary. . . . Since he is *made* to live with men, he ought to know them" (327; emphasis mine). The *telos* of Emile, that for which he is *made* conventionally by the tutor, is to live together. Lacking that completion, Emile and all post–state of Nature humans are bereft and in a condition of emotional lack. Such would seem to be Rousseau's form of *eudaimonism*: in order for humans to achieve happiness in this life, they must share their existence with others. In the euphoric ending of *Emile*, the re-united couple are declared to be "happy lovers," their union blessed by the tutor, and now left on their own. Happiness has been achieved through the marriage of the lovers.

Although such completion results in human happiness, Rousseau neverthe-less suggests that solitude has its own, if different, advantages. In a notable foot-note, in response to a long-standing accusation by Diderot that "only the bad man is alone,"[66] Rousseau writes:

> The precept of never hurting another carries with it that of being attached to human society as little as possible, for in the social state the good of one necessarily consti-tutes the harm of another. This relation is in the essence of the thing, and nothing can change it. On the basis of this principle, let one investigate who is the better: the social man or the solitary man. An illustrious author says it is only the wicked man who is alone. I say that it is only the good man who is alone. If this proposition is less senten-tious, it is truer and better reasoned than the former one. If the wicked man were alone, what harm would he do? (105)

Solitude is preferable to one who would be *good* if not necessarily happy; indeed, even a wicked man cannot help but be good when he is rendered harmless by dint of his solitude. Rousseau here—speaking in a footnote, and hence for him-self and not as Emile's tutor—justifies the solitary existence for the same reason that he initially admired the state of Nature of the *Second Discourse*: if there is no joy or virtue, at least there is no wickedness.

Rousseau often lamented his lost happiness, the imagined community he would have joined had he not been fatefully locked outside of the walls of Geneva as a child.[67] In a sentiment often expressed, he writes in the *Confessions*: "I should have been a good Christian, a good citizen, a good father, a good friend, a good workman, a good man in every way. I should have been happy in my condition, and should perhaps have been respected. Then, after a life—a simple and ob-scure, but also mild and uneventful—I should have died peacefully in the bosom of my family" (CF, 51).

In short, he writes, he should have led "a happy . . . and obscure life" instead of undergoing the "misery" and finally the solitude of his existence (CF, 51). The happiness of obscurity among a family and community was for Rousseau an unachievable but never-forgotten ideal that provided his dreams of lost happi-ness. Yet, he also knew that even the most ideal of existing communities—like

Geneva—while affording happiness to those who could accept the limits set by its outer and inner walls, did by no means guarantee that its citizens would be "good." As with most people and places in his life, Rousseau's high-blown fantasies of Geneva were eventually dashed: "I was mistaken in my letter to D'Alembert. I did not believe that things had gone so far with us or that our morals were so 'advanced.' Our ills are henceforth without remedy."[68] Better finally to be a consistently good man in solitude than an occasionally happy man among inevitably degenerated people.[69]

There may be a form of happiness available to the solitary good man, but Rousseau admits that it is a happiness of a particularly *nonhuman* sort—the happiness of divinity. In the famous fifth walk of *Reveries of a Solitary Walker*, Rousseau concludes that a form of happiness *does* accompany solitude, indeed one more constant and accessible than that found among humans:

> What is the source of happiness in such a state [of solitude]? Nothing external to us, nothing apart from ourselves and our own existence; as long as this state lasts we are self-sufficient like God. The feeling of existence unmixed with any other emotion is in itself a precious feeling of peace and contentment which would be enough to make this mode of being loved and cherished by anyone who could guard against all the earthly and sensual influences that are constantly distracting us from it in this life and troubling the joy it could give us. (*SW*, 89)

Such a description complements the sentiments at various points of *Emile*, and more particularly *Emile et Sophie*, that solitude is desirable largely because it protects us from entanglements with others, namely those allowing for the possibility of "earthly and sensual" feelings and leading inevitably to wickedness. It is preferable to be "self-sufficient like a God."[70] Rousseau embraces the *autarkeia* that Aristotle in the *Politics* had rejected in his definition of humanity: "One who is incapable of participating or who is in need of nothing through being self-sufficient is no part of a city, and so is either a beast or a god" (1253a). In his solitude Rousseau reckons himself to be like a god, capable of transporting himself from earthly bounds and of communicating with "celestial spirits" (*SW*, 91).

Rousseau finally rejects the world, as it rejected him. Rather than be chained to the cities of men, he prefers to remain solitary, in communion with the divine rather than distracted by the earthly and human. He is tempted to use the ring of Gyges, to become "invisible and powerful like God" and to roam with impunity through the places of men without affecting or being affected by humans (*SW*, 101–3). If he refuses the ring, it is not because he does not crave the solitude and power it offers, but because it might make him do something of which he is yet unaware, something "foolish" among people rather than separate from them (*SW*, 103). Even were the ring of Gyges available, "it is still better to flee [people's] presence than to remain invisible in their midst" (SW, 103). The reference to Plato's *Republic* is not inadvertent here: Rousseau casts his lot with the philosopher of Plato's *Republic*, who prefers the purity of life above the Cave to the confusion and clamour of life below. Unlike Odysseus and Socrates, he will not redescend out of *eros* in order to exist in concert, if imperfection, with other people but rather chooses the rarefied air above the Cave, or life on Calypso's island, where unperturbed contemplation and peace is perpetually available. Perhaps not uncoincidentally, Rousseau wrote the *Reveries* while living on an island, an indication of his own "choice" to be contrasted with that of Odysseus, or even Telemachus.[71]

When Socrates asks Adiemantus what the basis of the first polity is, Adeimantus replies that it must be "need" (*chreia*)—"need" both in the physical sense, as the shoemaker needs a housemaker and the housemaker needs a toolmaker, and so forth, as well as associational needs of natural human sociability. Insufficient of itself—producing only a city of pigs—"need" nevertheless represents a positive force, a necessary step toward the higher goods of life such as justice, virtue, and philosophy. This same "need" also compels the philosopher to descend from the sunlit regions above the cave to find those who willingly or unwillingly can be freed from their chains. Rousseau's final embrace of the solitary existence of the philosopher is expressed through an opposite conception of "need" among humans.

Rousseau's theory of human need lies at the foundation of his theory of human corruption.[72] In the *Second Discourse* Rousseau describes the process by which humankind "progresses" from free and independent individuals to beings enslaved by human institutions and absorbed with *amour propre*. The singular force that propels humanity into this modern nightmare is "need":

> In a word, so long as they [savage humans] applied themselves to tasks a single individual could perform, and to arts that did not require the collaboration of several hands, they lived free, healthy, good, and happy as far as they could by their nature be, and continued to enjoy the gentleness of independent dealings with one another; *but the moment one man needed the help of another*; as soon as it was found to be useful for one to have provisions for two, equality disappeared, property appeared, work became necessary, and the vast forests changed into smiling Fields that had to be watered with the sweat of man, and where slavery and misery were soon seen to sprout and row together with the harvests. (*SD*, 177; emphasis mine)

Thus Rousseau attributes the basis of all subsequent human misery to the *unnatural* manifestation of human need that appears only late in human existence.[73]

Emile is a work designed explicitly to create a human being like that one originally of the state of Nature: one that has no need for others. As we have seen, even Emile's stated relationship with Sophie and, through her, to the city is a chain from which Emile can finally free himself in accordance with the principles of his education. In *Emile*, Rousseau writes: "The only one who does his own will is he who, in order to do it, has *no need* to put another's arms at the end of his own; from which it follows that the first of all goods is not authority but freedom. The truly free man wants only what he can do and does what he pleases. *That is my fundamental maxim.* It need only be applied to childhood for all the rules of education to flow from it" (84; emphasis mine). The moment of human enslavement—that moment when one human "needed" another—provides the key to Rousseau's "fundamental maxim."[74] Only by raising Emile to be freed of all bonds to humanity and only to bow to those of necessity (472)—those such as death, his own, of others, and of all political systems—can Emile be brought back to the condition of original nature.

In various of Rousseau's writings the family and the State represent some form of human redemption—in *Julie*, the family; and in the *Social Contract*, the State. Yet, as *Emile* suggests, those solutions are finally lacking in universal applicability. *Emile* is the only *comprehensive* work by Rousseau, containing theories of individual, familial, and political redemption; and although seeming to effect a reconciliation of the three, we have seen that the latter two prove in the end to be unsatisfactory. In the final estimation, Sophie and the family can hold forth no redemption because such would require a need or dependence on fleeting and mortal beings. Politics holds forth no redemption because it is too marked by the inevitability of decline. Even the most excellent regimes—such as that extremely unlikely one described in the *Social Contract*—are fated to pass away. The only secure promise of redemption in human life is individual and solitary existence without dependence on anyone or anything beyond the "necessary."[75] In a paradox finally both appropriate and baffling, Rousseau, the great political theorist of democracy and community, also proves to be one of the great theorists and proponents of isolated individualism. Like Odysseus of Teiresias's prediction, the Odysseus fated to leave his family and polity for new shores, and not the Odysseus of *nostos*, the stoic hero of Rousseau's imagination must bow only to necessity and must retain the ability to unencumber himself of all needs and affections beyond those that will allow him to leave, again and again.

Notes

1. These words appear in a set of notes by Rousseau describing a journey around the Lake of Geneva in September 1754. As I argue later in this chapter, they might more generally be applied to Rousseau's life journey. The citation is taken from Maurice Cranston,

Jean-Jacques: The Early Life of Jean-Jacques Rousseau, 1712–1754 (Chicago: University of Chicago Press, 1982), 345.

2. I use the following notations throughout this chapter: all numbered citations within the text of this chapter (e.g., 37–42 or 370) refer to page numbers in the Allan Bloom translation of *Emile, or On Education* (New York: Basic Books, 1979). The notation OC followed by a roman numeral and an arabic numeral (e.g., OC, IV.1) refers to the *Pléiade* edition of the *Œuvres Complètes of Rousseau*, 4 vols., ed. Bernard Gagnebin and Marcel Raymond [Paris: Gallimard, 1969], citing the volume and page number, respectively. Other works of Rousseau are abbreviated in the main text as follows:

CC—*Correspondences Complètes de J.-J. Rousseau*, 50 vols., ed. R. A. Leigh, (Madison: University of Wisconsin Press, 1965–1991).

CF—*The Confessions*, trans. J. M. Cohen (New York: Penguin, 1953).

CO—"Project for a Constitution of Corsica," in *Political Writings: Containing the Social Contract, Considerations on the Government of Poland, and Constitutional Project for Corsica*, trans. and ed. Frederick Watkins (New York: Nelson, 1953).

FD—"The First Discourse" ("Discourse on the Sciences and Arts"), in *The Social Contract and the Discourses*, trans. G. D. H. Cole (New York: Dutton, 1973).

LD—"Letter to M. D'Alembert on the Theater," in *Politics and the Arts*, trans. Allan Bloom (Ithaca, NY: Cornell University Press, 1960).

NH—*Julie, or the New Heloïse*, trans. and ed. Judith H. McDowell (University Park: Pennsylvania State University Press, 1968).

OL—"Essay on the Origins of Languages," in *The First and Second DiscoursesTogether with Replies to Critics and Essay on the Origin of Languages*, trans. Victor Gourevitch (New York: Harper and Row, 1986).

PE—"A Discourse on Political Economy," in *The Social Contract and the Discourses*, trans. G. D. H. Cole.

PN—"Preface to *Narcisse*," trans. Benjamin R. Barber and Janis Forman, *Political Theory* 6 (1978): 537–54.

SC—*The Social Contract*, trans. G. D. H. Cole (Buffalo, NY: Prometheus Books, 1988).

SD—"The Second Discourse" ("Discourse on the Origins of Inequality"), in *The First and Second DiscoursesTogether with Replies to Critics and Essay on the Origin of Languages*, trans. Victor Gourevitch, 1986.

SW—*Reveries of a Solitary Walker*, trans. Peter France (New York: Penguin, 1979).

Wherever possible I have attempted to use an accurate existing English translation of Rousseau's writings. A complete translation of Rousseau's works is forthcoming, but until its completion, much important supplementary material by Rousseau (notably many letters and notes) remains untranslated. In these instances, I have translated cited passages or have occasionally let the original stand in the notes, and I have cited from secondary sources in French.

3. Pierre Burgelin, *La Philosophie de l'existence de Jean-Jacques Rousseau* (Paris: Presses Universitaires de France, 1952), 476.

4. As such, Rousseau's paradoxical reliance on art to return to nature complicates Masters' observation that Rousseau replaces Plato's reliance on art with nature (Roger D. Masters, *The Political Philosophy of Rousseau* [Princeton, NJ: Princeton University Press, 1968], 104).

5. Leo Strauss, *The City and Man* (Chicago: University of Chicago Press, 1964), 127.

6. Rousseau admits in a letter that Emile was finally unrealizable. He writes to Cramer, "Vous dites très bien, qu'il est impossible de faire un Émile" (cited in Burgelin, *La Philosophie de l'existence de Jean-Jacques Rousseau*, 476).

7. This obverse relation between the *Second Discourse* and *Emile* is made succinctly by Burgelin: "L'historien du coeur humain offre un second *Discours sur l'Inégalité*, adapté cette fois à l'individu qui naît dans la société. [C'est un] *Discours* au négatif . . . " (Burgelin, *La Philosophie de l'existence de Jean-Jacques Rousseau*, 477).

8. Rousseau later writes: "Keep the child in dependence only on things. You will have followed the order of nature in the progress of his education. Never present to his undiscriminating will anything but physical obstacles or punishments which stem from the actions themselves and which he will recall on the proper education. Without forbidding him to do harm, it suffices to prevent him from doing it" (85).

9. Cited and translated by Asher Horowitz, *Rousseau: Nature and History* (Toronto: University of Toronto Press, 1987), 230.

10. Judith N. Shklar, *Men and Citizens: A Study of Rousseau's Social Theory* (Cambridge, U.K.: Cambridge University Press, 1969), 148. On "negative education," see also Pierre Burgelin (*La Philosophie de l'existence de Jean-Jacques Rousseau*, 494; and "The Second Education of Rousseau," *Yale French Studies* 28 [1961–1962], 107); and Maurice Cranston, *The Noble Savage: Jean-Jacques Rousseau 1754–1762* (Chicago: University of Chicago Press, 1991), 176–79.

11. Just as theater will afford necessary diversion to those living in big cities, so, too, Rousseau recommends "to leave be the academies, the colleges, the universities, the libraries, and the theaters; indeed, support them along with all the other entertainments that divert the wicked, and deter them from occupying their idleness with still more dangerous affairs" (*PN*, 551). See also his "Letter to Grimm," "Last Reply," "Letter About a New Refutation," and "Preface to a Second Letter to Bordes" (in *The First and Second DiscoursesTogether with Replies to Critics and Essay on the Origin of Languages*, trans. Victor Gourevitch 59–115; *OC*, III.59–110).

12. Joseph Cropsey, "The Human Vision of Rousseau," in *Political Philosophy and the Issues of Politics* (Chicago: University of Chicago Press, 1977), 317.

13. The illustrations appear on pages ii, 76, 164, 261, and 356 of the Bloom edition of *Emile*. Bloom notes that the accompanying explanations "are Rousseau's, who planned and commissioned the engravings. He considered them an integral part of the text" (481, n. 6). Rousseau himself was (as in most things relating to publication) exceedingly choosy regarding the plates and the accompanying words. In a letter to *Emile*'s publisher, Duchesne, he complained of even slight changes in the written text: "Mais je ne puis concevoir pourquoi vous avez fait effacer le mot *Thetis*, qui était sur la première, et qu'il convenait d'autant mieux d'y laisser, que chacune des d'autres à aussi le sien" (May 12, 1762; *CC*, 238). I include the illustrations as figures 1 through 5. See the appendix for reproductions of these illustrations.

14. This is Bloom's translation of the original latin (31). Bloom continues, "The work from which this is drawn, *On Anger*, is significant for Rousseau's intention. Anger is *the* passion which must be overcome, and his analysis of human psychology gives it a central place. It has pervasive and protean effects. His correction of education consists essentially of extirpating the roots of anger" (481, n. 2). See also Bloom's introduction to *Emile* (Allan Bloom, "Introduction," in *Emile, or On Education*, Jean-Jacques Rousseau, trans. Allan Bloom [New York: Basic, 1979], 11–13).

15. Allan Bloom, *Love and Friendship* (New York: Simon & Schuster, 1993), 135.

16. Mary P. Nichols, "Rousseau's Novel Education in the *Emile*," *Political Theory* 13 (1985): 536–37.

17. For example, Rousseau writes, "A child thus dominated by anger and devoured by the most irascible passions . . . is a despot" (87).

18. Cited and translated by Horowitz (*Rousseau: Nature and History*, 222). Rousseau also writes in *Emile*, "Since the body is born, so to speak, before the soul, the body ought to be cultivated first" (365).

19. Here Rousseau explicitly differs with Locke, who held reason should be trained from childhood. Rousseau contends, "To know good and bad, to sense the reason for man's duties, is not a child's affair" (90). See also *Julie*, Part V, Letter 3 (OC, II.571, passim).

20. For an overview of this "second education," see Burgelin, "The Second Education of Rousseau," 106–11.

21. Bloom, "Introduction," in *Emile, or On Education*, 25–26.

22. See particularly Allan Bloom's discussion of sublimation in *Love and Friendship*, 20–24, 61–62.

23. Gustav Lanson, "L'Unité de la pensée de Jean-Jacques Rousseau," in *Annales de la Société de Jean-Jacques Rousseau* 8 (1912): 22.

24. Horowitz, *Rousseau: Nature and History*, 207–53; according to Horowitz, Emile will easily become a productive member of society by virtue of his education, as he "will not separate communal and individual, public and private lives into antithetical spheres" (*Rousseau: Nature and History*, 245). Horowitz echoes much of Paul Meyer's earlier analysis of *Emile*, in which Emile's education will produce a perfectly acclimated citizen of whatever city in which he chooses to reside:

> Emile as an individual progresses from the freedom of the child of nature, restrained only by the laws of necessity, to a higher moral freedom through conscious submission to man-made law, and the formation of the community in the *Contrat social*, where freedom under law is established by a very similar ostensible renunciation of the individual's "natural" rights" (Meyer, "The Individual and Society in Rousseau's *Emile*," *Modern Language Quarterly* 19 [1958]: 112).

Both Horowitz and Meyer credit Rousseau with having achieved his stated goals of reconciling the individual and society, indeed, more successfully in *Emile* than through the collective community of the *Social Contract*.

25. "Do you want to get an idea of public education? Read Plato's *Republic*. It is not at all a political work, as think those who judge books by their titles. It is the most beautiful educational treatise ever written" (40). In quite another vein, Rousseau writes in *Political Economy*:

> From the first moment of life, men ought to begin learning to deserve to live; and, as at the instant of birth we partake of the rights of citizenship, that instant ought to be the beginning of the exercise of our duty. If there are laws for the age of maturity, there ought to be laws for infancy, teaching obedience to others: and as the reason of each man is not left to be the sole arbiter of his duties, government ought the less indiscriminately to abandon to the intelligence and prejudices of fathers the education of their children, as that education is of still greater importance to the State than to the fathers: for, according to the course of nature, the death of the father often deprives him of the final fruits of education; but his country sooner or later perceives its effects. Families dissolve, but the State remains. (*PE*, 136)

In the first version of *Sur L'Économie Politique*, Rousseau also writes of the father, "*Car ils pourroient en faire de très bon fils et de très mauvais citoyens*" (OC, III.1400).

If there is some moment of agreement between these sentiments and those of *Emile*, it is that the education of either a citizen or a man should in no instance be left to the parents of the child. As such, Rousseau actually agrees with Plato's *Republic*. However, his agreement takes on a peculiar character noted by Horowitz: "Just as Plato asks the reader of the *Republic* to discover the character of the just man in the larger characters of the just city, Rousseau in the *Emile*, which is in some ways an attempt to invert and supercede the *Republic*, asks his reader to find the character of the just city in the smaller figure of Emile. . . . " (Horowitz, *Rousseau: Nature and History*, 240–41).

26. Bloom, *Love and Friendship*, 135; also, Bloom, "Introduction," in *Emile, or On Education*, 26.

27. It is interesting that the illustration accompanying Book III (see figure 3) depicts Hermes "engraving the elements of science on columns" (36; 164). It is this knowledge of nature, the study of which humans call "science," that will allow him to find *moly* and to provide an antidote to Odysseus against Circe's spell. See *Odyssey*, 10.302–306, and my discussion in chapter 1.

28. It is worth noting that Fénelon also translated a significant portion of the *Odyssey*. On this work, see Jeanne-Lydie Goré, Introduction to *Les Aventures de Télémaque*, by François de Salignec de la Mothe Fénelon (Paris: Éditions Garniers, 1987), 56–61. Judith Shklar also notes Fénelon's influence on Rousseau (Shklar, *Men and Citizens: A Study of Rousseau's Social Theory* [Cambridge, U.K.: Cambridge University Press, 1969], 4–5).

29. Fénelon, *Les Aventures de Télémaque*, 1.124–126; 6.95–96.

30. Fénelon, *Les Aventures de Télémaque*, 6.84–85.

31. Fénelon, *Les Aventures de Télémaque*, 6.85.

32. Fénelon, *Les Aventures de Télémaque*, 6.239–241.

33. Fénelon, *Les Aventures de Télémaque*, 6.96.

34. A note to this reference in the *Pléiade* reads: "Sophie se destine à un homme, il vaut donc mieux qu'elle ait peu d'instruction, peu de préjugés, et soit formée par son mari. On ne lui a même pas donné *le Confiturier royal*, mais seulement *le Livre de comptes faits* (1682) de Barrême (1640–1703) pour l'initier à l'économie domestique. Par infortune, on l'a laissée lire *Télémaque*." (OC, IV.1663).

35. He writes: "Most of these questions and propositions are extracts from the treatise the *Social Contract*, itself an extract from a larger work that was undertaken without consulting my strength and has long since been abandoned. The little treatise I have detached from it—of which this is the summary—will be published separately" (462). See also *The Government of Poland*, 33–34 (chap. 7).

36. Bertrand de Jouvenel, "Rousseau's Theories of the Forms of Government," in *Hobbes and Rousseau*, ed. Maurice Cranston and Richard S. Peters (New York: Anchor, 1972), 484–97.

37. de Jouvenel, "Rousseau's Theories of the Forms of Government," 491.

38. de Jouvenel, "Rousseau's Theories of the Forms of Government," 492–93.

39. Similarly, in *Lettres Ecrites de la Montagne*, Rousseau writes:

The principle which determines the various forms of government depends on the number of members of which each is made up. The smaller the number, the stronger the government; the greater the number, the weaker the government, and since sovereignty *tends always to slacken*, government tends always to increase its power. Thus the executive body *must always* in the long run prevail over the legislative body; and when the law is finally subordinate to men, there remains nothing but slaves and masters, and the state is destroyed" (OC, III.808; cited by de Jouvenel, "Rousseau's Theories of the Forms of Government," 495; emphasis mine).

40. Bertrand de Jouvenel, "Rousseau, the Pessimistic Evolutionist," *Yale French Studies* 28 (1961): 83–96.

41. Shklar, *Men and Citizens*, 11–12; Arthur M. Melzer, *The Natural Goodness of Man: On the System of Rousseau's Thought* (Chicago: University of Chicago Press, 1990), 225–27.

42. Rousseau writes in the *Troisième Dialogue*, XXII:

But human nature does not move backwards, and never can we return to times of innocence and equality once we have departed from them: this is one of the principles which he [Rousseau, speaking of himself] most stressed. Therefore his aim could not be to bring back large nations and big States to their pristine simplicity, but only to arrest if possible the progress of those whose smallness and seclusion had preserved them from marching rapidly towards the perfection of society and the deterioration of the species. (Cited in de Jouvenel, "Rousseau, the Pessimistic Evolutionist," 10)

43. Fénelon, *The Adventures of Telemachus*, trans. Patrick Riley (Cambridge, U.K.: Cambridge University Press, 1994), 5.67.

44. See Etienne Brunet, *Index Concordance d'Emile ou de la Education* (Paris: Librarie Champion, 1977). Brunet notes in his Concordance to *Emile* that Emile's name is used more often in each successive book (I–10; II–35; III–45; IV–65; V–191). Even in the increased usage of his name, there is a suggestion that *Emile* becomes ever more Emile, culminating in the final book (lix).

45. I borrow this formulation from Masters, who writes, "Emile lives *in* civil society, but he is not *of* civil society" (*The Political Philosophy of Rousseau*, 11). Such a conclusion is drawn from the tutor's own words: "[Emile] has to know how to find his necessities in [cities], to take advantage of their inhabitants, and to live, *if not like them, at least with them*" (205; emphasis mine).

46. For example, see Susan Moller Okin, *Women in Western Political Thought* (Princeton, NJ: Princeton University Press, 1979), Part III; Helen Evans Misenheimer, *Rousseau on the Education of Women* (Washington, DC: University Press of America, 1981); and Penny A. Weiss, "Rousseau, Antifeminism, and Women's Nature," *Political Theory* 15 (1987): 81–98. Misenheimer's treatment is unfortunately marked and perhaps marred by a barrage of name-calling.

47. See William Boyd, *The Emile of Jean-Jacques Rousseau: Selections* (New York: Teachers College Press, Columbia University, 1966), 177; and J. H. Broome, *Rousseau: A Study of His Thought* (New York: Barnes & Noble, 1963), 98.

48. Misenheimer is content merely to catalogue Rousseau's "chauvinistic views" (*Rousseau on the Education of Women*, 50), and even Okin, in her excellent treatment in *Women in Western Political Thought*, does not push her conclusions as far as they demand. One exception to this is Joel Schwartz's excellent and thorough treatment of Rousseau's sexual politics (Schwartz, *The Sexual Politics of Jean-Jacques Rousseau* [Chicago: University of Chicago Press, 1984]).

49. Weiss, "Rousseau, Antifeminism, and Women's Nature," 82.

50. See his *Sur les Femmes* (II.1254–55), and consider his service as secretary for the early feminist thinker and great-grandmother of George Sand, Madame Dupin (Cranston,

Jean-Jacques Rousseau, 203–8). Cranston notes: "As recently as the autumn of 1980 there was offered at auction in Monte Carlo a substantial bound volume in the handwriting of Rousseau on the subject of feminism. It was evidently a series of notes that Mme Dupin had dictated to him, or had him copy from other authors' books" (206).

51. It is worth noting that one of Rousseau's great inspirations for *Emile*, Fénelon of the *Télémaque*, also wrote an early liberal tract *Traité de l'éducation des filles* (1687). Rousseau refers to this work by Fénelon in *Emile* (369, 492 n.10).

52. Here Rousseau includes a long footnote objecting in particular to Locke's contention in *Thoughts on Education* that families are wholly *natural* institutions (*SD*, n. 12, 221–25). Rousseau concludes, "Once the appetite is satisfied, the man no longer needs this woman, nor the woman this man. . . . One goes off in this direction, the other in that, and there is no likelihood that at the end of nine months they will remember ever having known one another" (*SD*, 224).

53. Rousseau is not always consistent on this point; indeed, in the *Social Contract* he writes, "The most ancient of all societies, and the only one that is natural, is the family." Nevertheless, I take Rousseau's arguments in the *Second Discourse* on the unnaturalness of the family to be definitive, as it is the most thoroughly devoted and sustained treatment of the "natural" in Rousseau's works. Even as he claims in the *Social Contract* that the family is natural, he qualified this contention in a way that is not in contradiction to the *Second Discourse*: "and even so the children remain attached to the father only so long as they need him for their preservation. As soon as this need ceases, the natural bond is dissolved. . . . If they remain united, they continue so no longer naturally, but voluntarily; and the family itself is then maintained only by convention" (*SC*, 14). This "natural" basis to the family resembles that initial urge by the mother to suckle her children; there is no emotional or moral background herein, merely the will for self-preservation.

54. Okin argues that Rousseau considered this age has yet to see the introduction of inequality (*Women in Western Political Thought*, 112–13, 199–220). I believe that Okin is mistaken on this point: by the time families have become established, property has been introduced and with it inequality (*SD*, 170). Moreover, Rousseau does not any longer claim that this age can be defined as "natural"; indeed, the introduction of language and families mark it as having departed from the state of Nature and having entered a very primitive civilized stage (*SD*, 152–53). That Rousseau considers the golden age of patriarchy to be the "happiest" of mankind (*SD*, 176) suggests more of Rousseau's personal preference than necessarily an inconsistency in his philosophy.

55. Here I disagree with Okin's contention that Rousseau only allows for one form of education for women (*Women in Western Political Thought*, 179). Even within *Emile* itself he describes the possibility of a "female citizen" (40) as I discuss later.

56. Plutarch, *Plutarch on Sparta*, trans. Richard J. A. Talbert (New York: Penguin, 1971), 160; cited in *Emile*, 40. Rousseau's admiration for Sparta, often in contrast to his disdain for Athens, is often in evidence (e.g., *FD*, 10; *LD*, 133–34). On Rousseau's conception of Spartan women, see Schwartz, *The Sexual Politics of Jean-Jacques Rousseau*, 52–55. Generally see Shklar, *Men and Citizens*, 14; and Mario Einaudi, *The Early Rousseau* (Ithaca, NY: Cornell University Press, 1967), 79, 101.

57. Similarly, in *La Nouvelle Heloïse*, Julie condemns the Platonic education of women as unnatural to the respective characters of the sexes (*NH*, 108). Here, too, as in *Emile*, the basis of society is to be the family (Shklar, *Men and Citizens*, 22–27).

58. Shklar, *Men and Citizens*, 27.

59. Rousseau writes: "It is important, then, not only that a woman be faithful, but that she be judged to be faithful by her husband, by those near her, by everyone. It is important that she be modest, attentive, reserved, and that she give evidence of her virtue to the eyes of others as well as her own conscience" (361). Nowhere is Emile to be held up to these relative standards.

60. The editor's note on this passage in the *Pléiade* reads: "Cette douleur insurmontable de Sophie monte une lacune dans son éducation par rapport a celle d'Émile: elle ne sait pas céder à la nécessité" (OC, IV.1712).

61. Indeed, Sophie is described in both *Emile* and *Emile et Sophie* as proud (alternatively *"fière"* or *"orgeilleuse"*: OC, IV.759, 889, 900). Her "proud" and "haughty" soul is not dashed, as has been Emile's from a young age, until the tragedy of both these deaths and her subsequent infidelity. After these devastations, she, too, undergoes something of a harrowing, though only after the culmination of her education and perhaps too late to have prepared her for the tragic nature of life. Nonetheless, Emile believes that "l'humiliation du remod adoucira cette âme orgeilleuse et rendra moins tiranique l'empire que l'amour lui donna sur moi; elle en sera plus soigneuse et moins fière . . . " (OC, IV.900–1). Like Achilles, she only "sweetens" her soul after her proud and haughty spirit has wrought destruction around her.

62. The editor's note on this passage in the *Pléiade* reads: "Rappelons qu'aprés la condamnation d'Emile, Rousseau avait renoncé à la bourgeoisie de Genève, le 12 mai 1763" (OC, IV.1723). This similarity between Emile and Rousseau will be discussed later.

63. Pierre Burgelin, "L'éducation de Sophie," *Annales de la Société Jean-Jacques Rousseau* 35 (1959–1962), 128. Also, Susan Moller Okin writes: "[Women] cannot be allowed to live in the patriarchal world, since there is no way they can fulfill the contradictory expectations it places on them. At least Rousseau allows that a man can be either an individual or a citizen. He does not allow a woman to be either" (*Women in Western Political Thought*, 194). Similarly, Joel Schwartz has written, "Sophie's education evidently fails here; she is seduced by an immoral man in the big city of Paris. But if her education fails, Emile's succeeds—he avoids the temptation to remain dependent upon Sophie" (*The Sexual Politics of Jean-Jacques Rousseau*, 96). Schwartz is finally not altogether in agreement with this thesis; he posits, based on some evidence of Rousseau's plans in *Emile et Sophie* to reunite the two lovers, that their respective educations finally "work." Because we do not have the remainder of *Emile et Sophie*, the point is largely moot; however, Schwartz's thesis fails to explain why Sophie's education fails in the first place, particularly regarding that aspect that has been most explicitly taught—the avoidance of adultery. For Schwartz's alternative argument, see *The Sexual Politics of Jean-Jacques Rousseau*, 96–98.

64. Okin, *Women in Western Political Thought*, 193–94.

65. Numerous commentators have discussed this tension in Rousseau. See, for example, Einaudi, *The Early Rousseau*, 151–65.

66. Diderot wrote this line in the play *Le Fils naturel*, which Rousseau rightly concluded was a commentary on Rousseau's decision to withdraw from society. On the circumstances and results of this accusation, see Cranston (*The Noble Savage*, 47–53). Rousseau's version can be found in the *Confessions* (OC, I.455–456).

67. See particularly Norman Jacobson's compelling treatment of this portentous moment in Rousseau's life and its influence on the development of his political thought in *Pride and Solace: The Function and Limits of Political Theory* (Berkeley: University of California Press, 1978), 97–100.

68. From a letter to Pastor Moultou, 1760, cited in Benjamin R. Barber, "How Swiss Is Rousseau?" *Political Theory* 13 (1985): 481.

69. Of course, many critics have observed that Rousseau would have found it difficult if not impossible to live even in his own ideally constructed communities. For example, Rick Matthews and David Ingersoll write:

> What is clear is that persons who had been exposed to modern society with its inequalities, its preponderance of *amour propre*, its extreme diversity, could *not* achieve happiness or a meaningful life under the Spartan model: "grass and nuts" are no longer nourishing. One cannot envision Rousseau existing in his proposed Corsican society—he knew too much, had been exposed to too many things, was a creation of modern society.

In Rick Matthews and David Ingersoll, "The Therapist and the Lawgiver: Rousseau's Political Vision," *Canadian Journal of Political and Social Theory* 4 (1980): 87–88.

70. One should compare this version of "happiness" with Rousseau's contention in *Emile* that "if we were immortal, we would be most unhappy creatures" (82).

71. Rousseau was living at this late point of his life on the Isle St.-Pierre, later renamed the Isle de Rousseau. Maurice Cranston, *The Solitary Self: Jean-Jacques Rousseau in Exile and Adversity* (Chicago: University of Chicago Press, 1997), 185.

72. I am much indebted to Arthur M. Melzer's analysis of "need" and "dependence" in Rousseau in the following discussion (Melzer, *The Natural Goodness of Man*, 70–85).

73. Melzer, *The Natural Goodness of Man*, 71.

74. Melzer writes: "[This] is truly Rousseau's 'fundamental maxim' because it shows that man's Fall did indeed occur at 'the moment one man needed the help of another.' It demonstrates how personal dependence has enslaved all civilized men and eventually destroyed the unity of their souls" (*The Natural Goodness of Man*, 74).

75. Masters comments: "Rousseau's 'romanticism' points to retired life in the family, and in the highest case to the *promeneur solitaire* as the good life for man" (*The Political Philosophy of Rousseau*, 90).

~

CHAPTER FOUR

Escaping the Dialectic: Vico, the Frankfurt School, and the *Dialectic of Enlightenment*

And surely the myths are, as a whole, false, though there is a truth in them too.

—Plato, *The Republic*, 377a

Responding to the *"Querelle des Anciens et des Modernes"* (The Quarrel of the Ancients and the Moderns) in its early stages, Rousseau's less-renowned contemporary, Giambattista Vico, attempted to establish a middle ground between the two positions, at once fixing the ancient authors in a definite historical context, but nonetheless arguing that no historical stage on the way toward modern civilization could ever be fully surpassed. Indeed, in his masterpiece *The New Science*, Vico contends that the enduring values contained in the myths of the ancients continue to exert a considerable moral force over modern civilization.[1] While warning that enlightenment criticism of ancient myths threatens to destroy the unacknowledged moral base of civilization, Vico attempts to curb the critical excesses demonstrated by such authors as Bacon, Descartes, Hobbes, and Spinoza and seeks to preserve the place of myth in civilization. Through an original examination of Homeric authorship, Vico demonstrates how important mythology remains in modernity and suggests that the *Odyssey*, representing the most advanced form of mythology, contained edifying elements that undergird the excellence of civilization.

The work of the Frankfurt School, particularly that of Max Horkheimer (who was an avid student of Vico) and Theodor Adorno in their masterpiece *Dialectic of Enlightenment*, remarkably adopt many of the themes initiated by Vico.[2] Responding against the atrocities of the Nazi regime, Horkheimer and Adorno locate much modern barbarity in the adoption of "enlightenment" principles, particularly those of instrumental reason and the mastery of nature. In a Vichean manner they contend that myth and enlightenment are inextricably linked; however, in a radical departure, they also assert that "enlightenment" principles were present throughout antiquity, indeed from the very inception of human consciousness. Thus, the ravages caused by enlightenment principles—particularly fascism and capitalism—can be found in an embryonic form in the art and practice of antiquity. Through a unique examination of Homer's *Odyssey*, Horkheimer and Adorno seek to locate enlightenment elements and attempt to show that there is no historical "progress" as such—only that "progress" has always been with us and is finally inescapable. However, the extent to which their interpretation is not wholly upheld by the text of the *Odyssey* suggests that their deep pessimism may not be entirely warranted.

By comparing the related but ultimately contradictory theories of Vico and the Frankfurt School, it can be shown that the "negative" or "critical" theories of Horkheimer and Adorno finally side with enlightenment, inasmuch as they deny myth a place of esteem in modernity, unlike Vico. Rather, their submerged sympathy for enlightenment can be located in their fundamental rejection of death—or more accurately, their rejection of the importance of death—in the lives, philosophies, and finally myths of human beings. Using their flawed analysis of the *Odyssey* as a starting point, I will contend that their inability or unwillingness to recognize Odysseus's acceptance of death reflects Critical Theory's own unwillingness to afford death, and hence the solace of myth, an appropriate place in modern philosophy. Their flawed interpretation of the *Odyssey*, although on many levels fascinating and even at times persuasive, nevertheless results in a flawed and empty political philosophy, one that ultimately must seek solace not in the *sensus communis* of shared myth but in the hollow cry of the lonely self. Horkheimer and Adorno continue a tradition as old as the post-Homeric cycles of epic poetry to return to the ancient themes of longing and limitation, the desire for immortality and death, the demands of the self and those of the *polis*, and the role of politics in negotiating these seemingly insurmountable divides. They deny, however, that the ancient epics finally give us guidance on how to navigate these choices and confrontations, and argue instead that no choice is available except renunciation and critique. I want to suggest, through a confrontation with their reading of the *Odyssey* especially, that they reject those resources without apprehending the possibilities those resources afford. Indeed, by posing their own analysis against that of Vico—who, I suggest, inspires their historicist and ahistoricist approach generally—the resources of ancient myth become more readily apparent.

Giambattista Vico and the "Discovery of the True Homer"

Because they are the first identifiable cultural and intellectual relic of the ancient Greek world, Homer's epics have served as a touchstone for many philosophers of history who seek to offer a panoramic explanation of history's direction. Depending on whether history is viewed as either degenerative (as in the case of Rousseau) or progressive (as with Hegel and Marx), the ancient epics are viewed as either a continuing source of wisdom or an example of childlike sentiments. Indeed, resorting to Homer as a source of historical knowledge significantly occurs in one of the first sustained works of historical investigation, that of Giambattista Vico.[3] Vico's formulation, which places the Homeric epics within a historical framework that is progressive, yet one that is at the same time curiously stagnant, proved to have a significant influence on the theories of the Frankfurt School.

First published in 1725 and appearing in its third and final edition in 1744, Giambattista Vico's *Principi di Scienza Nuova d'intorno alla Comune Natura delle Nazione* (*Principles of New Science Concerning the Common Nature of Nations*) represents perhaps the first sustained treatise on the progressive nature of history in postmedieval Europe. Max Horkheimer, in his 1930 *Habilitationsschrift* on the bourgeois philosophy of history, devotes his concluding section to Vico, calling him "*der erste wirkliche Geschichtsphilosoph der Neuzeit*" ("the first real modern philosopher of History").[4] Vico, reacting against the turn toward the natural sciences and a nature-based explanation of all phenomena—including human phenomena—initiates the famous formulation of human history that would serve as the basis of *Geisteswissenschaften*—the human sciences:

> But in the night of thick darkness enveloping the earliest antiquity, so remote from ourselves, there shines the eternal and never failing light of a truth beyond all questions: that the world of civil society has certainly been made by men and that its principles are therefore to be found within the modifications of our own human mind. Whoever reflects on this cannot but marvel that the philosophers should have bent all their energies to the study of the world of nature, which, since God made it, He alone knows; and that they should have neglected the study of the world of nations, or the civil world, which, since men had made it, men could come to know. (*NS*, 331)

This first "principle" of Vico's investigation, that the human mind can only know those institutions and practices created exclusively by human beings, serves as a fundamental basis to what Vico calls "the ideal eternal history," namely, a uniquely human history that is "traversed in time by the history of every nation in its rise, development, maturity, decline, and fall" (NS, 349). Vico's investigation into this movement of several exemplary "gentile nations" is thus driven by the assumption that seeming differences between cultures and nations are negligible, given the uniformity of each nation's universal historical pattern of development.[5]

For Vico, as for Rousseau, the origins of humanity hold the key to human understanding; and the historical aspect of those origins—their remoteness in time and their irretrievability—proves to be the defining universal feature of humanity. Indeed, there is a striking resemblance in the respective portraits of primitive humanity in Rousseau's Second Discourse and in Vico's New Science. Original humanity was conceived by Vico to be a race of "giants," inspired by the portrait of the Cyclopes in the Odyssey, living like Polyphemus's neighbors in a prepolitical and solitary bestial existence. Like Rousseau's primitive man, original humanity for Vico is also apolitical and by nature good (NS, 522); furthermore, in both instances, this original humanity is driven into prepolitical and finally political communities due to natural disasters, although in Vico this process is even more inevitable than Rousseau suggests: "For the giants, enchained under the mountains by the frightful religion of the thunderbolts, learned to check their bestial habit of wandering wild through the great forest of the earth, and acquired the contrary custom of remaining hidden and settled in their fields. Hence they later became the founders of the nations and the lords of the first commonwealths" (NS, 504; see also 377). Vico stresses this constant intertwining of original irrational impulse and rational outcomes: rather than founded through reasoned considerations of abstract political philosophy, the State is instead the inevitable result of the natural human tendency toward myth making. According to Vico, myth and civilization are inseparable.[6]

For Vico, poetry and poetic wisdom—the receptacle of myth—are "the master key" to understanding human origins and, by extension, human nature qua history (NS, 34, 368). Poetic wisdom differs from philosophic wisdom in two inseparable aspects: poetic wisdom is both cruder than philosophy—lacking any reflective or abstract quality—and at the same time more sublime than philosophy, given poetry's immediacy, its vividness, and indeed its ability to capture the entirety of the human experience afforded by its very vulgarity (NS, 361–63, 378, 383).[7] Human "nature" arises out of humanity's myth-making capacity, setting human history into motion and leading humankind toward more rational forms of inquiry and organization that nevertheless never fully lose their irrational origins.[8]

As expressed through poetry, myth is born out of a "deficiency of human reasoning," namely, early humanity's inability to provide rational and abstract reasons for the workings of nature. Instead, early humanity attributed the violence of thunderstorms to the anger of the god Jove (or his transnational counterpart [NS, 198]), thereby giving rise to religion.[9] The religious impulse, inseparable from its mythic and irrational origins, itself gives rise to moral order and thereby establishes the foundations for human institutions of justice. Through the Polyphemus tale in the Odyssey—that otherwise savage beast who devours humans raw—Vico brilliantly locates a seed of morality: inasmuch as the Cyclops knows of a prediction that Odysseus will put out his eye (Odyssey, 9.507–521), Vico deduces that "augurs certainly cannot live among atheists." Vico concludes: "Thus poetic morality began with piety, which was ordained by providence to found the nations, for among them all piety is proverbially the mother of all the moral, economic, and civil virtues" (NS, 503). Irrational myth leads to morality and thence inevitably to political institutions.

All of Vico's conjectures about the origins of humanity and human institutions are thus gleaned through the workings of ancient poetry—the repository of myth—and particularly the poems of Homer. Vico was apparently of two minds in his consideration of Homer. According to the base assumption underlying New Science—that human development arises from mythic dimensions and is captured in poetry—all human beings from all nations necessarily developed in a similar way and only differ with regard to specific human individuals who fulfill a preordained role. According to Vico's schema, Homer is but one poet, albeit a great one, whose verses capture the myths of human origins. Thus, in his Autobiography, Vico suggests that he concentrates on Homer as a paragon of poetic wisdom not because of an absence of poets in other cultures, but because he was born in Naples, "and not in Morocco."[10]

At the same time, there is something decidedly singular about Homer's place in Vico's philosophy. Indeed, not only does Vico concentrate on Western ideas and figures because he was born in the West and not the Orient, but because of his occidental origin, he "became a scholar."[11] This implied singularity of the West's philosophical heritage—or at least, that becoming a scholar in Naples appropriately paid homage to "the glory of his native city"—is also reflected in the unique position that Homer occupies in Vico's thought. Homer is considered by Vico to be, "of all the sublime, that is, the heroic poets, the first in the order of merit as well as in that age" (NS, 384). If poetry is "the master key" to uncovering the origins of human civilization, then Homer is by extension the master key to understanding poetry.

Vico commissioned a frontispiece for New Science that suggests the central importance of Homer to his enterprise.[12] The illustration (see figure 6) portrays a beam of light, seemingly emitted from an eye in heaven, and first illuminating a winged figure that represents "the metaphysic," as Vico preferred to call his "New Science." The light is further reflected, as Vico describes:

> The same ray is reflected onto the statue of Homer, the first gentile author who has come down to us. . . . The statue of Homer on the cracked base signifies the discovery of the true Homer. . . . Unknown until now, he has held hidden from us the true institutions of the fabulous time among the nations, and much more so those of the dark time which all had despaired of knowing, and consequently the first true origins of the institutions of the historic time. (NS, 6; cf. 41)

Thus Homer at once represents all poets who encapsulate myth within their ancient poems, awaiting "true" discovery by the metaphysic; and at the same time, Homer is singular, more than a representative but through his poems permitting the truest discovery of human origins.

Unstated by Vico, but implied both in the illustration and in the text of New Science proper, is another manner of interpreting this scene. The direction of the light is not entirely self-evident: thus, Homer at the bottom and not God above may be the origin of this "divine" light, illuminating the metaphysic of New Science and thence shedding light on God. As Vico himself notes, the gods are largely the invention of primitive cultures, and, above all, the poets of those primitive cultures, seeking an explanation for natural phenomena; the creative poet par excellence is Homer, from whom the West can credit its religious origins. Thus, the great ancient poets shed their light (through the discovery of the metaphysic of New Science) upon divinity, making the immortal gods comprehensible and in some ways responsible to humanity. Vico, the professor of linguistics, is aware of this role of poets as creators:

> In this fashion the first men of the gentile nations, children of the nascent mankind, created things according to their own ideas. But this creation was infinitely different from that of God. For God, in his purest intelligence, knows things, and, by knowing them, creates them; but they, in their robust ignorance, did it by virtue of a wholly corporeal imagination. And because it was quite corporeal, they did it with marvellous sublimity; a sublimity such and so great that it excessively perturbed the very persons who by imagining did the creating, for which they were called "poets," which is Greek for "creators." (NS, 376)

Unlike God, who "knows things" and is thus in some senses limited to a preexisting natural order or is perhaps simply the equivalent of nature, poets, through their imagination, can go beyond nature and, paradoxically, invent the very gods. Looking at the illustration from this perspective, one can view Homer as creator of the gods, of religion, and of all human institutions. The poets, and above all

Homer, are finally "the master key" for charting the creation of human nature itself.[13]

Given this central importance of Homer, Book III of *New Science*, "Discovery of the True Homer," is devoted to the quest. After having claimed that his "new science" was one that discovered "the common nature of the nations," Vico turns to a specific case study of the most ancient Greek poet to prove the universal validity of his system. By delineating the character and the historical background of the "True Homer," Vico is able to lay to rest the ongoing debate over the method of the epics' composition—the "Homer Question"—but more important, to make a final contribution to the question of religious and political origins.

In summary, those favoring the wisdom of the ancients attributed to Homer a refined genius and a source of irrefutable wisdom; those who viewed modernity as more advanced saw in Homer simple customs, barbarity, and outright falsehood. By defining "Homer" as either a single poetic genius or an invention that represented a largely accidental aggregate of existing poetry, each side sought to protect its prevailing view of Homer and, hence, of Greek culture as a whole.[14]

Despite the claim that he disagrees with Plato—indeed, to attribute unreflective admiration of Homer's wisdom to Plato is at best disingenuous on Vico's part—Vico proceeds with a critique of the Homeric epics that shares a great deal in common with Plato's critique both in the *Republic* and in the *Apology*. After listing various conventional immoral attributes of the gods and the heroes, such as their brute reliance on strength to resolve all conflicts and their pettiness, drunkenness, and inconstancy (*NS*, 781–85), Vico launches into a remarkable critique of Achilles that shares many features with those implied by Plato and, subsequently, by Fénelon and Rousseau:

> The same Achilles, even while impiously determined not to forgive a private injury at the hands of Agamemnon (which, grave though it was, could not justly be avenged by the ruin of their fatherland and of their entire nation), is pleased—he who carries with him the fate of Troy—to see all the Greeks fall to ruin and suffer miserable defeat at Hector's hands; nor is he moved by love of country or by his nation's glory to bring them any aid. He does it, finally, only to satisfy a purely private grief, the slaying of his friend Patroclus by Hector. (*NS*, 786)

To write what Vico considers to be such an admirable portrait of this self-absorbed hero means that the reader "must deny to Homer any kind of esoteric wisdom." Rather, "such crude, coarse, wild, savage, volatile, unreasonable or unreasonably obstinate, frivolous, and foolish customs [as contained in Homer's epics] . . . can pertain only to men who are like children in the weakness of their minds, like women in the vigor of their imaginations, and like violent youths in the turbulence of their passions" (*NS*, 787).

By attributing such childlike emotions to what he considers a childlike race of humanity, Vico attempts to refute theorists such as Hobbes who attributed to earliest humanity a civilized rationality such as that described in the State of Nature in *Leviathan*. At the same time, he seeks to refute the Cartesian and Hobbesian individualistic psychology, that "Epicurian" viewpoint, "a moral philosophy of solitaries."[15] Through his discovery of the "True Homer," Vico demonstrates the mythic origins of human civilization and also its basis in *sensus communis*—a phrase often translated as "common sense," but perhaps better understood as "communal sense."[16] By comprehending Vico's conception of *sensus communis*, we can fully appreciate the importance of Vico's discovery of the "True Homer" and, by extension, the inherited tension that this concept affords the Frankfurt School in *Dialectic of Enlightenment*.

Sensus communis is the underlying bond through which human decisions are made, societies built, and institutions organized. Unlike the enlightenment model, which posed individuals employing fully rational faculties to arrive at self-interested conclusions, Vico's conception of *sensus communis* was typically irrational but not necessarily haphazard; communal, not individualistic; and it developed out of the historical process of human life, although it was not necessarily progressive in character. As Vico describes, "human choice, by its nature most uncertain, is made certain and determined by the common sense [*sensus communis*] of men with respect to human needs or utilities, which are the two sources of the natural law of the gentes. Common sense is judgment without reflection, shared by an entire class of people, an entire nation, or the entire human race" (*NS*, 141–42).

Inasmuch as *sensus communis* is "judgment without reflection," it contains an irrational and almost accidental quality. Developments in human history and institutions are not necessarily intentional, although Vico denies that history can unfold in any manner other than as it has.[17] Thus, "Providence" or "Mind" orders human affairs, often "without human discernment or counsel and often against the designs of men" (*NS*, 342; also 1108).[18] In this regard, Vico describes a course of history that is not unlike that of Hegel's "cunning of history," a human-driven but not always intentional course of events.

Nevertheless, while *sensus communis* is often "judgment without reflection," judgment itself nevertheless continues to imply human intentionality. Just as poets are "makers" of human mythology, so are communities both the repositories and the continuing creators of human life. It is this sense of *sensus communis* that was understood by Hans-Georg Gadamer: "Sensus communis here obviously does not mean only that general faculty in all men, but the sense that founds community. According to Vico, what gives the human will its direction is not the abstract generality of reason, but the concrete generality that represents the community of a group, a people, a nation, or the whole human race. Hence the development of this sense of community is of prime importance for living."[19] Vico thus considers human civilization as communally created, mythologically inspired, and poetically captured.

"The Discovery of the True Homer" partakes of both these senses of *sensus communis*: namely its haphazard and accidental quality, but also its aspect as communally and intentionally created. Vico's discovery of the "true" Homer, as the greatest and most representative poet of antiquity, is the discovery not of the single figure who composed two great epics, but rather of the symbolic embodiment of the ancient communities of Greece itself. Expanding on Longinus's theory that the *Iliad* was written in Homer's youth and the *Odyssey* in his old age,[20] Vico attributes this movement not to an "individual" named Homer, but to a *sensus communis* within the general flow of history:

> That the reason why the Greek peoples so vied with each other for the honor of being his fatherland, and why almost all claimed him as a citizen, is that *the Greek peoples were themselves Homer*. . . . Thus Homer composed the *Iliad* in his youth, that is, when Greece was young and consequently seething with sublime passions, such as pride, wrath, and lust for vengeance, passions which do not tolerate dissimulation but which love magnanimity; hence this Greece admired Achilles, the hero of violence. But he wrote the *Odyssey* in his old age, that is, when the spirits of Greece had been somewhat cooled by reflection, which is the mother of prudence, so that it admired Ulysses, the hero of wisdom. (*NS*, 875, 879; emphasis mine)

Thus the *Iliad* is both the *reflection* and the *creation* of the "poetic" population of the most ancient Greece, the Greece of savage emotions and primitive customs; the *Odyssey* is the *reflection* and the *creation* of an already more civilized Greece, a Greece that has "progressed" to the point of valuing wisdom over strength, political solutions over violent ones. The spirit of each age penetrates its representative epics, both unconsciously "writing" the epics and "storing" them. For, as Vico states, "history cannot be more certain than when he who creates the things also narrates them" (*NS*, 349).

With the discovery of the "True Homer," Vico thus also arrives at his theory of history—at once a progressive yet curiously stagnant one. Vico clearly identifies a spirit of progress in the movement of history, symbolized most clearly by the movement from the savage *sensus communis* of the *Iliad* to the more refined concern for wisdom in the *Odyssey*. Yet, as we have seen, because myth is never fully separable from what succeeds it—neither the *Iliad* from the *Odyssey*, nor the initial irrationality of primitive man from the more philosophic rationality of modernity—"progressive" history can never escape its own past. Although progressive in its general aspect, history is nevertheless subject to reversals and even to collapse—a return to barbarity that forms the centerpiece of Vico's theory of "*ricorsi.*"[21] Indeed, the reversal of history's progress—the "return" to barbarity—is paradoxically contained within the very movement toward civilization. For as humanity's faculty of reason becomes more refined and critical, the relationship between humanity's mythic past and its rational present attenuates; and the salutary effects of myth—piety, justice, and *sensus communis*—are exhausted. The very progress of humanity creates conditions in which communities can no longer be maintained and therefore provokes a return to barbarity.[22]

This pattern of *ricorsi* (the return to primitivism after high civilization) significantly arises out of the most-advanced regime type of civilization—democracy—which, because of its tendency toward skepticism and self-interest, overcomes its own ancient basis in a mythologic *sensus communis*:

> But as the popular states became corrupt, so also did the philosophies. They descended into skepticism. . . . Thus they caused the commonwealths to fall from a perfect liberty into the perfect tyranny of anarchy or the unchecked liberty of the free peoples, which is the worst of all tyrannies. . . .
>
> But if the peoples are rotting in that ultimate civil disease and cannot agree on a monarch from within, and are not conquered and preserved by better nations from without, then providence for their extreme ill has its extreme remedy at hand. For such peoples, like so many beasts, have fallen into the custom of each man thinking only of his own private interests and have reached the extreme of delicacy, or better of pride, in which like wild animals they bristle and lash out at the slightest displeasure. Thus no matter how great the throng and press of their bodies, they live like wild beasts in a deep solitude of spirit and will, scarcely any two beings being able to agree since each follows his own pleasure or caprice. By reason of all this, providence decrees that, through obstinate factions and desperate civil wars, they shall turn their cities into forests and the forests into dens and lairs of men. In this way, through long centuries of barbarism, rust will consume the misbegotten subtleties of malicious wits that have turned them into beasts made more inhuman by the barbarism of reflection than the first men had been made by the barbarism of sense. (*NS*, 1102, 1106)

Ricorsi does not entail a return to conditions identical to humanity's original situation, nor do subsequent civilizations necessarily resemble their predecessors as progressive history once again resumes its course. Rather, this second era of primitivism is brought about by the "barbarism of reflection," resulting in a condition of greater "inhumanity" than previously. Because the newly devolved humanity does not possess the "barbarism of sense," that is, the barbarism that permits the creation of controlling myths and stories that give rise to justice, this "new" barbarism is more savage and long-lasting.[23]

Vico is himself curiously trapped between celebrating his discovery of history's movement—namely by trumpeting his discovery of the "True Homer"—and at the same time lamenting it. For in the very act of revealing myth's underlying centrality in modern civilization, Vico in some senses has joined those forces of "skepticism" who denigrate myth's place. By isolating mythology, one allows its universal recognition *as* mythology, that is, as *"mythos,"* an untruth or irrational tale. Vico simultaneously damns this process even as he—a late-Renaissance or early-Enlightenment figure—partakes of it. Indeed, his very treatment of the Homeric epics is symptomatic of this bind: by revealing that the epics are not the purposeful creation of a single and extraordinary genius, but rather the accidental repository of primitive peoples, Vico joins forces with those critics of the epics who sought to "diminish" ancient sources of supposed wisdom. Even while celebrating the presence of myth in antiquity, Vico joins in the "skeptical" or *critical* project of his era. As aptly described by Pietro Piovani, "The 'philological' interest in the genesis of things pays homage to their greatness, yet progressively strips them of their superficial glitter. In the childhood of mankind, glimpsed at its beginnings, there is nothing which does not become diminished in some way. The genetic way of knowing is a critical process."[24]

Even as Vico almost of necessity joins in the "diminishment" of ancient sources, it should be noted that Vico also allows for the ongoing positive influence of the ancient myths or *sensus communis* even in modernity. Because myth is always present in the rational civilizations of modernity, by recognizing the salutary aspects of myth, modernity by implication can benefit from its original civilizing force. The "poets" of antiquity—namely, according to Vico, the communities of antiquity—both judge "without reflection" and at the same time *create* poetry that, although unreflective, serves as a civilizing force. The poets of antiquity are thus, if only unconsciously, the most ancient of educators—a function that Vico explicitly recognizes: among the poets' labors is "to teach the vulgar to act virtuously, as the poets have taught themselves" (*NS*, 376). If, as Vico later suggests, the most ancient poets are in fact the communities themselves, then this "teaching" function is self-reflexive: through the mutual interaction of storytelling and myth making, members of a community "educate" themselves in virtue. And inasmuch as the *Iliad* (as we have seen) teaches little virtue through the poor example of Achilles, the most excellent lessons of antiquity's greatest poet is that of the "wisdom" demonstrated by the character of Odysseus.

Vico states throughout *New Science* that Homer is the greatest and most sublime of all the ancient poets; now has he revealed that the "true" Homer is in fact the ancient civilization of Greece itself. Homer's greatest educational epic is the more advanced and civilized *Odyssey*: by implication, if Greece is the most important "poet" of antiquity and if the *Odyssey* is its most important poem, then to the lessons of the *Odyssey* we can attribute most of modern humanity's virtues and vices. Inasmuch as ancient myth has constituted modern institutions and determinatively formed human "nature," then by logical extension one must turn to the *Odyssey* for evidence of modern humanity's origins. Vico does not pursue the implications of his theory. His main concern is to discover the "True Homer," not to engage in a textual analysis of the *Odyssey* and its mythic creation of modernity.[25] His only contextual evidence is that the relative antiquity of the *Iliad* and the relative modernity of the *Odyssey* can be proven by the respective vices and virtues of each epic's main characters, Achilles and Odysseus. The implications of his conclusion, however, did not escape Horkheimer and Adorno in their study of the *Odyssey* in *Dialectic of Enlightenment*. There, it is indeed through a sustained analysis of the Odyssean myths that the "master key" of modern civilization can be found. Thus, in many senses, their own project can be seen as an extension of the Vichean one.

Toward a "New" Philosophy of History: The Frankfurt School

The connection between Vico's *New Science* and the thought of the Frankfurt School is explicit in the case of Max Horkheimer and implicit in the work of its other members.[26] As already mentioned, Max Horkheimer—for years the head of the *Institut für Sozialforschung* (Institute for Social Research), both in its early years in Frankfurt and later in exile—as early as his postgraduate thesis noted the similarities between his own concerns and those of Vico.[27] Horkheimer and indeed all the members of the Frankfurt School were to find much resonance in Vico's rejection of the purely rational explanations for all human activity as propounded by early Enlightenment figures; in their simultaneous acceptance of human "nature" as historically constructed and rejection of history as necessarily progressive and ameliorative; and especially in their recognition that myth, society, and history are inseparably intertwined.[28] Vico's vision of human development through history—that it is the result of a halting and mostly irrational mixture of human intention, accident, and "Providence" that nevertheless does not guarantee history's "progressive" culmination—was finally almost indistinguishable from the thought of Horkheimer and Adorno.

In his 1930 postgraduate thesis, *Habilitationsschrift*, Horkheimer concludes in his study on the "Bourgeois Origins of the Philosophy of History" that Vico correctly posited that "human history began its course in a dark and terrible prehistory."[29] In opposition to enlightenment thinkers who viewed human development as following a rational and predictable course toward a definable and progressive end, Horkheimer agrees with Vico's theory that "moments of enlightenment in human history are, above all, mythological."[30] These mythic origins are not easily shrugged off once humanity has "progressed" toward more rational forms. As Horkheimer approvingly writes, "For Vico, distant mythological roots were a necessary primitive form of knowledge, from which our science has sprung."[31]

The recognition that "enlightenment" and "myth" are intertwined in human historical development—which would continue to reappear continuously in the thought of both Horkheimer and the entire Frankfurt School—indicates a significant departure from strictly materialist (i.e., Marxist) versions of history. Indeed, Marx himself also writes on the "mythic" origins of human history but rejects the idea that those origins exerted any control over future, "progressed" humanity. As he argues in the *Grundrisse*, humanity's mythic origins were a consequence of their irrational and nontechnological minds, in short, their "childishness." Once matured, humankind was no more susceptible to these childlike fears than was an adult subject to anxieties about the monsters under the bed. With particular attention to the epics of antiquity, Marx begins, undoubtedly correctly, by recognizing that certain narrative forms are subject to technological considerations: "Is Achilles possible with powder and lead? Or the *Iliad* with the printing press, not to mention the printing machine?" Marx, however, does not stop with that and concludes that the *human* concerns that undergird the epics are equally timebound: "Do not the song and the saga and the muse necessarily come to an end with the printer's bar, hence do not the necessary conditions of epic poetry vanish?"[32]

Marx recognizes that the epics of Homer still enchant: "They still afford us artistic pleasure and in a certain respect they count as a norm and as an unattainable model." Nevertheless, unlike Vico, Marx rejects the ongoing moral influence that myths exercise over modern civilization, rather arguing that human myths only applied to a specific historical era and could not be meaningfully recaptured: "A man cannot become a child again, or he becomes childish. . . . the Greeks were normal children. The charm of their art for us is not in contradiction to the undeveloped stage of society on which it grew. [It] is its result, rather, and is inextricably bound up, rather, with the fact that the unripe social conditions under which it arose, and could alone arise, can never return."[33]

Marx appears to suggest, on the one hand, that the social conditions that gave rise to the Homeric epic—the narrative and communal history of antiquity—no longer exist in the aftermath of Guttenberg's invention; but, on the other hand, Marx seems tempted to conclude that these material conditions also created the very *consciousness* of ancient man, a condition now surpassed. Whereas Vico and subsequently the Frankfurt School argue that humanity's mythic origins are never fully superseded and ever threaten to return ironically if humanity's rationality becomes too refined, Marx posits a significantly more unidirectional course of history, inevitably away from our childhood—one that still charms—but without the possibility of return in Vico's sense of *ricorsi*.[34]

As nominally "Marxist" thinkers, the conscious decision by the Frankfurt School to reject the Marxist vision of a progressive and intentional history culminating in the "dictatorship of the Proletariat" was, at the time, tantamount to secular sacrilege.[35] Indeed, coming of age in the rigid intellectual sphere of orthodox Marxism, many members of the Frankfurt School began only haltingly to move away from a strictly progressive view of History with the rise of Nazism in Germany. Horkheimer, often trapped between overweening optimism and resigned pessimism, still betrays evidence of hopefulness as late as 1934, writing, "The twilight of capitalism need not initiate the night of humanity, which, to be sure, seems to threaten today."[36] Yet, with the shadows of twilight (*Dämmerung*) finally deepening into "the night of humanity" over the course of the next ten years, Horkheimer and the entire Frankfurt School wholly reject any vision of a necessarily ameliorative course of history. In a marked turnabout, Horkheimer later writes: "There can be no formula which lays down once and for all the relationship between the individual, society, and nature. Though history cannot be seen as a uniform unfolding of human nature, the opposite fatalistic formula that the course of events is dominated by necessity independent of Man is equally naïve." [37]

Also to be rejected after a time was the very foundation of the Marxist theory of history, the theory that the motor of Progress was fired by the conflict between the classes. Becoming ever more Nietzschean in its condemnation of "mass-values," the Frankfurt School eventually rejected Marx's theory that the proletariat would inevitably overthrow the capitalist structure and form a revolutionary dictatorship.[38] As Horkheimer writes in the founding document of *Critical Theory*, "it must be added that even the situation of the proletariat is, in this society, no guarantee of correct knowledge. The proletariat may indeed have experience of meaninglessness in the form of continuing and increasing wretchedness and injustice in its own life. Yet, this awareness is prevented from becoming a social force. . . . Even to the proletariat the world superficially seems quite different than it really is.[39]

This elliptical and allusive conclusion, that "the world superficially seems quite different than it really is," reflects the growing suspicion by members of the Frankfurt School that the proletariat was being "co-opted" by the materialistic comforts afforded by capitalist society. Rather than encountering increasing poverty and alienation as Marx predicted, with the conclusion of World War II the material existence of the working class improved markedly and elicited widespread support for capitalist democracy. Thus, not seeing the world as "it really is"—one in which social and class injustice was being papered over by material goods and entertainment—the proletariat had ceased to be an actual or even theoretical ally in this reformulation of Marxist theory.[40] Horkheimer admits as much at the outset of *Critical Theory*:

> Since the years after World War II the idea of the growing wretchedness of the workers, out of which Marx saw rebellion and revolution emerging as a transitional step to the reign of freedom, has for long periods become abstract and illusory, and at least as out of date as the ideologies despised by the young. The living conditions of laborers and employees at the time of *The Communist Manifesto* were the outcome of open oppression. Today, they are, instead, motives for trade union organization and for discussion between dominant economic and political groups. The revolutionary thrust of the proletariat has long since become realistic action within the framework of society. In the minds of men, at least, the proletariat has been integrated into society.[41]

The Frankfurt School, in sum, ends by rejecting the foundation of Marxist theory, the belief, as Marx expresses it in the eleventh thesis on Feuerbach, that "the philosophers have only *interpreted* the world, in various ways; the point, however, is to *change* it."[42] The subordination of theory to practice, or rather, as Marx formulates, the need to "make the world philosophical," is viewed by the Frankfurt School as a fond wish betrayed by history. As history no longer has the proletariat to fuel a culminating revolution, we must now live in the "*Jetztzeit*" of a capitalist present.[43] The resignation of the Frankfurt School, that *praxis* can no longer reconcile the antinomies created by class conflict, nevertheless allows once more for the possibility of philosophy. As Adorno begins his late work, *Negative Dialectics*, in a bold rejection of the Marxist theory of *praxis*,

> Philosophy, which once seemed obsolete, lives on because the moment to realize it was missed. The summary judgment that it had merely interpreted the world, that resignation in the face of reality had crippled it in itself, becomes a defeatism of reason after the attempt to change the world miscarried. . . . A practice indefinitely delayed is no longer the forum for appeals against self-satisfied speculation; it is mostly the pretext used by executive authorities to choke, as vain, whatever critical thoughts the practical change would require.[44]

Despite its apparent adherence to Marxist theories, the Frankfurt School demonstrates more similarity to the historical theories of Vico than to those of Marx.[45] As Horkheimer suggests in his early writings on Vico, history could no longer be looked on as a benign, progressive force in human affairs; rather it had to be looked on as a force that could suddenly "return" humanity to the ever-present (or never-escaped) barbarism of its past. As Horkheimer writes elsewhere,[46] Vico correctly describes that the history of human society is in no way the product of human freedom, but is rather the natural result of blind and antagonistic forces. Inasmuch as human society is founded on such "blind and antagonistic forces," what are then explained by primitive humanity as myth—and continue to function on these implied foundations—are never absent from even the most rationalistic of eras. Moreover, the possibility that a *ricorsi* to a state of barbarity would occur precisely when humankind had reached the apex of modern reason was a conclusion shared by Horkheimer and Adorno. They describe their project as "nothing less than the discovery of why mankind, instead of entering into a truly human condition, is sinking into a new kind of barbarity."[47] In a radical departure from the Enlightenment belief in historical progress, Horkheimer and Adorno turn to the "enlightenment" to discover the very causes of the return to barbarity. These Vichean conclusions, that myth and enlightenment are necessarily and inescapably intertwined and that human history is not necessarily one of progress, form the central theses around which Horkheimer and Adorno build their masterpiece, *Dialectic of Enlightenment*.

The Entwinement of Myth and Enlightenment

Dialectic of Enlightenment (DE) is a dark and pessimistic book, written when Fascism was on the verge of defeat yet when the full extent of the Nazi regime's barbarity was being uncovered. There is no celebratory tone here extolling democracy's victory or the inevitability of the Nazi defeat. Rather, *Dialectic of Enlightenment* is a scathing critique of the whole of Western civilization, from its roots in the Homeric epics to its current incarnation as the liberal, commercial republic. The thesis of *Dialectic of Enlightenment*—that all of recognizable human history is infused with "enlightenment" and that "enlightenment is totalitarian" ("*Aufklärung ist totalitär*": DE, 6)—allows for no recourse from history, no transcendent island from which humanity can rest from the potential or actual barbarity written into enlightenment. According to Horkheimer and Adorno, the fascist moment is everywhere and always possible.

Vico's theory of the mythic origins of human civilization clearly informs *Dialectic of Enlightenment*; indeed, Vico's *New Science* is explicitly cited in referring to the movement from myth to abstract rationality that occurred in the "marketplace of Athens" (DE, 22). Yet Horkheimer and Adorno go far beyond Vico's considerations of the entwinement of myth and enlightenment, concluding not only that myth is ever-present in rational modernity, but that "enlightenment" was already present in humanity's mythic past: "Myth is already enlightenment; and enlightenment reverts to mythology" (DE, xvi). For Horkheimer and Adorno, "enlightenment" is not merely *the* Enlightenment: those elements most obviously identifiable with eighteenth- and nineteenth-century Enlightenment thought— science, rationality, and the mastery of nature are present in more or less identical form even in the very myths that precede the Enlightenment. Myth is not wholly irrational; Horkheimer and Adorno contend that evidence of "instrumental reason," which would dominate modern science, can be located as early as the epics of Homer.[48]

Like Vico, Horkheimer and Adorno also recognize that myth is inseparable from enlightenment. However, here again they push this Vichean thesis to a more radical conclusion. The Enlightenment, in its single-minded pursuit to discover nature's secrets, to objectify both humanity and nature under its searching and exploiting gaze, effectively creates a new mythic discourse: the tools of "enlightenment" claim to afford an all-encompassing explanation to human and natural phenomena. Just as primitive humanity invented Jove to explain thunder, modern humanity turns to science and instrumental reason to explain, among other things, beauty, human emotions, and politics. Horkheimer and Adorno write: "The human mind, which overcomes superstition, is to hold sway over a disenchanted nature. . . . What men want to learn from nature is how to use it in order to wholly dominate it and other men. That is the only aim. Ruthlessly, in spite of itself, the Enlightenment has extinguished any trace of its own self-consciousness. The only kind of thinking that is sufficiently hard to shatter myths is ultimately self-destructive" (*DE*, 4). This loss of "self-consciousness," the inability to think *critically* about one's own project, is tantamount to myth, to the unreflective belief in one's own explanations. Thus, not only does ancient myth linger in modernity (as in Vico's theory), but modern rationality in turn becomes a whole new mythic structure.

There is, then, a seeming lack of historical movement in *Dialectic of Enlightenment*, as implied by Horkheimer and Adorno's belief that myth and enlightenment are, in some senses, perpetually identifiable. Despite human claims that mythic belief has been superseded by enlightenment, Horkheimer and Adorno seek to demonstrate that myth is fundamentally inseparable from rationality. More radically, despite some attempts to attribute a progressive nature to history—such as Marx's rejection of the Homeric epics as somehow morally or materially inapplicable to modernity—Horkheimer and Adorno contend that enlightenment is already present in myth, notably evinced as a general tendency toward human mastery of nature. Although Horkheimer and Adorno do not intend to imply that the human condition, at least materially, has remained the same, they attribute a moral conformity throughout human history toward barbarity and fascism. Even the apparent achievement of human enlightenment through *the* Enlightenment has not secured an irrevocable human progress. As Vico also argues, the very harnessing of human reason creates the conditions for a return to barbarity, albeit in an even more savage form than the original: "the barbarism of reflection" (*NS*, 1106). In very similar language, Horkheimer and Adorno contend that "the prime cause of the retreat from enlightenment into mythology is not to be sought so much in the nationalist, pagan, and other modern mythologies manufactured precisely in order to contrive such a reversal, but in the Enlightenment itself . . ." (*DE*, xiii–xiv).

For Horkheimer and Adorno, as for Vico, there is no "history" per se but rather the movement from "prehistory" to "history," the latter a largely stagnant moment in which the mythic elements of "prehistory" are both substructurally present and ever-threatening to return. The very movement from prehistory to history is evinced through mythic retellings, as both *Dialectic of Enlightenment* and *New Science* contend by means of an analysis of Homer's epics. For both works, the turn to Homer is necessitated by the need to confront the very origins of Western civilization and to uncover there whatever continuities between past and present are hidden. Thus, Horkheimer and Adorno engage in a lengthy study of the *Odyssey* because it is "the basic text of European civilization" (*DE*, 46). Myth, for Horkheimer and Adorno as for Vico, was for ancient humanity a means of "report, naming, the narration of the Beginning; but also presentation, confirmation, explanation: a tendency that grew stronger with the recording and collection of myth" (*DE*, 8). Strongly connected with this explanatory function was also an educational one: "Narrative became didactic at an early stage" (*DE*, 8). Thus, an examination of the Homeric epics allows for both the discovery of "empirical" and "normative" elements, the simultaneous "collection" of myths and its "organization" into an educational structure (*DE*, 43). For Horkheimer and Adorno as for Vico, Western civilization is thus both a *reflection* and the conscious *creation* of these ancient myths.

Horkheimer and Adorno identify a communal element to the Homeric epics in particular, thereby sharing Vico's conclusion of the "Discovery of the True Homer" that the epics were the product of the whole of ancient Greece: "The epic narrative, especially in the most ancient of its various layers, clearly exhibits its close relation to myth: its component adventures have *their origin in popular tradition*" (*DE*, 43; emphasis mine). The movement from prehistory to history, described by Horkheimer and Adorno as "the retreat of the individual from the mythic powers" (*DE*, 46), is reflected by the relative moral development from the *Iliad* to the *Odyssey*. Although this movement is "already true of the *Iliad*," the more pronounced "interaction of prehistory and history . . . applies to the *Odyssey* in an even more drastic sense" (*DE*, 46). Thus, Horkheimer and Adorno focus their energies on the *Odyssey* because it is more representative of later "civilization," while nonetheless its mythic elements remain intact. As for Vico, the *Odyssey* is apparently a product of a relatively more "enlightened" Greece, communal in its composition, didactic in function, forming a textbook from which Western civilization took its cue.

However, by dint of the very similarity of Vico's *New Science* and Horkheimer and Adorno's *Dialectic of Enlightenment*, particularly regarding their approach and analyses of Homer, the differences evinced in their respective works are all the more striking. For Vico, myth is not simply an early attempt at explanation and dissolution of fear; myth also contains a *moral* aspect, derived from its creation through the *sensus communis* and hence serving a didactic function. As Vico argues in his "Discovery of the True Homer," the communal creation of the respective epics (early Greece's *Iliad* and later Greece's *Odyssey*) suggests that some degree of moral progress in the movement from prehistory to history is possible—particularly given the role of poets as educators in ancient society—and moreover that the *sensus communis* that created the *Odyssey* was to a large extent sufficiently advanced to exhibit the civilized qualities of "wisdom" and "prudence" (*NS*, 879).[49] Indeed, because the ancient myths contain an ethical core—that same moral underpinning that gave primitive humanity its religious sensibility and therefrom a will toward Justice—the continued presence of myth and of this *sensus communis* in modern civilization supports the moral institutions and private behaviors of modern humanity.[50] As Vico describes the presence of ancient myth in modernity, "the poetic speech which our poetic logic has helped us to understand continued for a long time into the historical period, much as great and rapid rivers continue far into the sea, keeping sweet the waters borne on by the force of their flow" (*NS*, 412). Revealing much with this naturalistic image, Vico suggests that the moral health and purity of modernity continues to depend on the strength of the "flow" of those ancient myths into the present.

When the modern impulse toward radical criticism of ancient practices and myths on the behalf of rationality becomes too complete—as exhibited in Vico's time by the works of Descartes, Spinoza, Bacon, and Hobbes—those unappreciated moral underpinnings are severed and "civilization" begins its *ricorsi* toward barbarism. Despite the seeming similarity of this thesis to that of Horkheimer and Adorno, Vico insists on a definite distinction between myth and enlightenment. The danger of modern Reason's pursuit of scientific Truth against irrationality is that it too easily overlooks the truth-bearing elements of Myth. Enlightenment threatens to bring on the "barbarism of reflection." Despite the "falsity" of myth, myth nevertheless contains a "truth" that is not entirely subject to rational examination. As Vico describes his project generally: "Vulgar traditions must have had public grounds of truth, by virtue of which they came into being and were preserved by entire peoples over long periods of time. It will be another great labor of this Science to recover these grounds of truth—truth which, with the passage of years and the changes in language and customs, has come down to us enveloped in falsehood" (*NS*, 149–50). To eviscerate the "falsehood" of myth as inherited by modernity threatens the destruction of myth's "public grounds of truth."[51] Vico seeks gingerly to reveal the mythic, however false, origins of human institutions in order to counteract the attack on mythology as deriving from the "communal sense" by Enlightenment thinkers.

Horkheimer and Adorno do not share with Vico this estimation of myth's continued importance. Indeed, as we have seen, because the vicious aspects of enlightenment are already present in myth, there is no strict differentiation possible between the two. Moreover, myth conveys not an underlying morality but merely *interests*, particularly those of the proto-bourgeois classes for whom they were written. Indeed, to a significant extent, myth is not only the attempt to explain the forces of nature, but also a widespread endeavor to *deceive* for the sake of proto-capitalist domination. This, then, is the primary "didactic" function of Homer's epics: to deceive, to dominate, and to exploit.

> What epic and myth actually have in common [is]: domination and exploitation. In the alleged genuineness of what is really the archaic principle of blood and sacrifice, there is already something of the bad conscience of deceit of domination proper to that national renewal which today has recourse to the primitive past for the purpose of self-advertisement. Aboriginal myth already contains the aspect of deception which triumphs in the fraudulence of Fascism yet imputes the same practice of lies to the enlightenment. But there is no work which offers more eloquent testimony of the mutual implication of enlightenment and myth than that of Homer. (*DE*, 45–46)

The "evident untruth in myths" (*DE*, 46) is nothing less than an effort by the property holders (such as Odysseus) to perpetrate dominion over the proletariat and to exploit their labor. Horkheimer and Adorno, far from merely tempering the historical theories of Marx, in fact take his theories one radical step further: rather than finding in history a gradual movement *toward* capitalist exploitation, Horkheimer and Adorno discover that *throughout the entirety of human history* fascist domination and capitalist exploitation were ever-present. And, unlike Marx's hopes for a proletariat revolution, Horkheimer and Adorno disallow the possibility for change, either within or transcending history: a world of fascism without end. Douglas Kellner has described *Dialectic of Enlightenment* as an "epic philosophy of history";[52] if so, however, it is a history strangely absent of movement, either of progress or regress.

In an effort to fix a starting point to humanity's inherent savagery, Horkheimer and Adorno—like so many political philosophers before them—turn to the *Odyssey* of Homer. Michael Shapiro notes that "the *Odyssey* is among those classics that has continued to attract commentators, most of whom have appropriated it as a vehicle for thinking about problems of the contemporary self and order."[53] Somewhat unconsciously formulated (albeit approvingly), the key aspect of Shapiro's description is that of *appropriation*. Horkheimer and Adorno do not so much seek to understand the *Odyssey* on the terms it demands of its readers as to transfer elements of modern and particularly critical theory to its ancient setting. The reading of the *Odyssey* by Horkheimer and Adorno is closely textual, but their conclusions depart radically from the explicit contents of the epic. Their analysis, then, marks a stunning departure from those that preceded it; their claims about the text, if true, suggest that political solutions to human problems are finally impossible. Thus, lest one too easily fall into a state of torpid resignation over the futility of human political action, their critical reading of the *Odyssey* calls for a critical evaluation.

A Critical Theory of the *Odyssey*

Their analysis startles. It is, without a doubt, one of the most original and controversial interpretations of the *Odyssey*, and indeed any ancient text, performed in this century. Those who study the work of the Frankfurt School consider it to be perhaps *the* centerpiece of Critical Theory. Indeed, David Held, in his valuable *Introduction to Critical Theory*, concludes his study with an appendix devoted solely to summarizing and placing in context Horkheimer and Adorno's study of the *Odyssey*. The singular value of this study, according to Held, "in contradistinction to a host of classical interpretations, [is] that Homer did not simply describe and praise the life and times of a Greek hero, [but rather] they [sic] sought to emancipate the writings of the first great poet of the Western world from ideology."[54] By implication, if Homer could be freed from "ideology"—namely the belief that ancient practices were uniquely remote and strange to modern ones—then the entirety of Western history would likewise be freed. In keeping with the grand tradition of political philosophy, by proving a particular view of Homer, one could consider such proof to be everywhere and always true.

Through a close examination of several episodes in the *Odyssey*, Horkheimer and Adorno glean several key themes. They contend that either the character of Odysseus or the action of the *Odyssey* proves that: (1) humanity is in a permanent state of conflict with nature, such that humanity continuously seeks nature's conquest and domination; (2) in the effort to dominate nature, human beings must at the same time practice repression of the self (or "self-renunciation") and of other human beings; and, (3) this drive to dominate self, humanity, and nature is born of humanity's ineluctable will toward self-preservation. There is an unmistakable resemblance between these central theses of *Dialectic of Enlightenment* and Freud's *Civilization and Its Discontents*: that humankind, in its effort to achieve civilized life, must effect through sublimation of desire and the "death instinct" a form of self-repression and the domination of others.[55] Where Freud sees this process in the transition of primitive tribalism to "modern" life, Horkheimer and Adorno pinpoint this action particularly in the Homeric episode in which Odysseus and his men pass by the Sirens.

The narrative of Odysseus and the Sirens exhibits "the entanglement of myth, domination, and labor (*die Verschlingung von Mythos, Herrschaft, und Arbeit*)" (*DE*, 32). The Sirens tempt Odysseus with the knowledge of "everything that ever happened on this so fruitful earth" (*Odyssey*, 12.191). To obtain this knowledge is tantamount to overcoming the alienation of humanity from nature; in effect, to achieve the knowledge of the Sirens is to lose the self in the Universal, akin to the narcotic trance afforded by the Lotus-eaters. Horkheimer and Adorno continuously note that the various episodes of Odysseus's journey always contain the threat of losing the self, either through death, narcotics, or magic. That Odysseus always successfully resists this temptation proves that he is the forerunner of capitalist man, the man of *Arbeit*.

Odysseus's resistance, however, does not come automatically nor easily. To lose the self is at once the temptation and the fear of all humanity, as Horkheimer and Adorno write concerning the Sirens' knowledge:

> The strain of holding the I [*das Ich*] together adheres to the I in all stages; and the temptation to lose it has always been there with the blind determination to maintain it. The narcotic intoxication which permits the atonement of deathlike sleep for the euphoria in which the self is suspended is one of the oldest social arrangements which mediate between self-preservation and self-destruction [*die zwischen Selbsterhaltung und vernichtung*]—an attempt of the self to survive itself. The dread of losing the self and of abrogating together with the self the barrier between oneself and other life, the fear of death and destruction, is intimately associated with a promise of happiness which threatened civilization in every moment. Its road was that of obedience and labor, over which fulfilment shines forth perpetually—but only as illusive appearance, as devitalized beauty. The mind of Odysseus, inimical both to his own death and his own happiness, is aware of this. (*DE*, 33–34)

The German word *Selbsterhaltung* nicely captures Horkheimer and Adorno's intention, explicitly meaning "self-preservation" but also implying a "holding back," and thus a word closely related to *Enthaltung*, or "abstinence." The very act of *preserving* the self at the same time necessitates a repression of the self through "obedience and labor"—the self is only preserved when it disallows itself the very pleasure of being a self. Thus Odysseus, the paramount "self" in ancient literature, seeks to avoid his own death (either literally or figuratively) by denying himself happiness.[56] Civilization is a state of discontent.

The solution that Odysseus devises on his approach to the Sirens reveals, with deep cynicism, his simultaneous will to preserve and to destroy his self and, at the same time, his position as oppressor. He can choose two possible courses of action, both involving repression to some extent, either self-inflicted or externally exerted. For his men, the "laborers" as Horkheimer and Adorno designate them, they must have their ears plugged and row without noting their surroundings. "The oarsmen, who cannot speak to one another, are each of them yoked in the same rhythm as the modern worker in the factory, movie theater, and collective" (DE, 36–37). Odysseus takes the other option: "He listens, but while bound impotently to the mast; the greater the temptation the more he has his bonds tightened—just as those burghers who would deny themselves happiness all the more doggedly as it drew closer to them with the growth of their own power" (DE, 34). The episode of the Sirens then encapsulates a proto-capitalist albeit mythic past: Odysseus is the factory boss, the crew its workers. Common humanity must work and does so at the command of its superiors; the superiors must also dominate, not through work but through a form of self-control that resembles being "bound impotently to the mast." No one is permitted happiness; even the song of the Sirens, once its temptation is "neutralized," becomes nothing more than "a mere object of contemplation—becomes art" (DE, 34).

Perhaps unconsciously, but almost unmistakably, this interpretation of the Sirens' episode evokes the imagery in the Allegory of the Cave of Plato's *Republic*. The content has been subtly altered, but the echoes are distinct. A mass of humans must sit face forward, viewing shadows on the wall (it is suggested, they might sit in a "movie theater"), going through motions prescribed by someone above them. Meanwhile, one among them is enabled to escape, to ascend to the realm above and gaze directly at the sun (or to know the world's knowledge through the Sirens' song). In Horkheimer and Adorno's version, the tension between the two human possibilities as Plato describes—the desire of the cave-dwellers to kill the freed man—is strangely absent. Rather, domination is thorough, either externally enforced or internally controlled. The truth that the light of philosophy claimed to reveal is reduced to a "mere object of contemplation," an aesthetic moment. Likewise, the possibility that the authority of philosophy might result in an ideal regime of Justice in Plato's estimation is wholly eliminated by Horkheimer and Adorno. Philosophy no longer allows for truth, only impotent contemplation; the philosopher can no longer selflessly rule, only selfishly dominate; and the cave-dwellers are no longer open to possible persuasion by the philosopher—neither through reason nor a "noble lie"—because their ears are plugged by wax. The possibility of even temporary Justice through politics has been replaced by perpetual Domination through capitalism and mass culture.

The interpretation of the Sirens' episode by Horkheimer and Adorno is plausible if strained. Odysseus does enlist his men to row deafly through the tempting sounds of the Sirens, but, one might easily conclude, he does so justifiably given that these same men have already demonstrated a lack of restraint in releasing the winds of Aeolus and will exhibit a similar lack of restraint by eating the kine of Helios (*Odyssey*, 10.38–49, 12.340–365). That Odysseus binds himself to the mast suggests his respect for and recognition of the temptation that all humans feel when offered the encompassing knowledge—or, as described in chapter 1 of this volume, the "immortal vision"—that the Sirens offer. Finally, Odysseus does not bind himself to prevent himself from experiencing happiness—indeed, the bonds insure his homecoming and, hence, his happiness—nor does he contemplate the Sirens' words as "art." The Sirens finally do *not* offer encompassing knowledge or immortal vision; they offer death to those who hubristically believe that such knowledge is possible for human beings. Odysseus recognizes that even the offer of such knowledge is tempting and thus, *in advance*, practices self-control in anticipation of his loss of control when within range of the Sirens' song. To interpret all forms of self-control as domination suggests two possibilities: either Horkheimer and Adorno view *all* forms of self-control as fundamentally suspect and, hence, favor a politically anarchist solution (which, in fact, they clearly do not); or they implicitly reject *all* rationality and rather appeal to a prerational, prehistorical past in which rational elements of self-control were unnecessary, given a purely animal reliance on instinct (akin to Rousseau's portrait of the state of Nature). This latter possibility, while not explicitly embraced by Horkheimer and Adorno, remains implicit both in this interpretation and in further analyses. In their rejection of both myth and enlightenment, they do not allow either rational or irrational solutions, but perhaps they imply *prerational* ones, humanity in a speechless condition of collective solitude.

Their condemnation of Odysseus's dedication to rational consciousness continues in their analysis of several subsequent episodes. Rightly so, Horkheimer and Adorno recognize a similarity between the episodes of the Sirens, Circe, and the Lotus-eaters, inasmuch as each offers mortal humans some form of unconsciousness, or the obliteration of self: "Whoever browses on the lotus succumbs, in the same way as anyone who heeds the Sirens' song or is touched by Circe's wand, . . . [to] oblivion and the surrender of will" (*DE*, 62). Discussing the temptation of oblivion provided by the Lotus-eaters, Horkheimer and Adorno tip their hand: although they do not necessarily approve of the "happiness of narcotic drug addicts," which the bliss of the Lotus-eaters resembles, their disapproval of Odysseus's rationally inspired resistance to the power of lotus proves stronger. Despite the resemblance of the Lotus-eaters to drug abusers, Horkheimer and Adorno also identify a positive aspect to their stoned state: without rational consciousness, there can be no domination and hence no capitalism or fascism. "Perhaps the tempting power prescribed to [lotus] is none other than that of regression to the phase of collecting the fruits of the earth and of the sea—a stage more ancient than agriculture, cattle-rearing, and even hunting, older, in fact than all production. . . . It points back to prehistory" (*DE*, 63–64). Prehistory is that stage in which no domination existed, neither thoughts of self-preservation nor individuation; only prehistory escapes the vicious dialectic of myth and enlightenment that Horkheimer and Adorno first identify in the *Odyssey*.

Rather than falling victim to this temptation of prehistory, Odysseus is condemned for resisting the attractions of oblivion. Given the choice between succumbing to the temptation of the Lotus-eaters, abandoning his men, or forcing them to leave the pleasures of oblivion, Odysseus chooses the route of most domination and least pleasure. "Odysseus's own action is immediate, and serves domination" (*DE*, 63). Arguably, the concern for the self-preservation of others entails the doling out of misery as well. He forces his stupefied, weeping men back aboard the ships; although death does not threaten them, they have relinquished their claim on humanity by "forgetting their homeland." Under the influence of the lotus, they would continue to live biologically, but human concerns—companionship, family, community—cease to exist. Defined through their relationships to others, their very selves cease to exist.

Odysseus is thus accused by Horkheimer and Adorno for valuing "self-preservation" above all else—not simply the preservation of life but, moreover, the preservation of *self*. As with Circe's curse, which changes humans to animals, not so much life as the human "self" is threatened:

> The mythic commandment to which [Odysseus's men] succumb liberates at the same time the repressed nature in them. . . . The repression of instinct that made them individuals—selves—and separates them from the animals, was the introversion of repression in the hopelessly closed cycle of nature. . . . The forceful magic, on the one hand, which recalls them to an idealized prehistory, not only makes them animals, but—like the idyllic interlude of the Lotus-eaters—brings about, however delusive it may be, the illusion of redemption. (*DE*, 70)

"The repression of instinct" is responsible for making prehistoric human animals into human selves, and is by implication the cause of all human misery occurring in the form of self- and other-domination. Even if the magic of Circe—or the narcotic of lotus or the song of the Sirens—only provides "the illusion of redemption," that is, a falsely realized return to prehistory, this "delusive" return is preferable to the domination actuated by Odysseus's will to self-preservation. Inasmuch as this preservation requires the dimming of the temptation for oblivion—often meaning purely animalistic and sensual pleasure—self-preservation is viewed as the equivalent of self-domination, or by extension (for those who do not have Odysseus's strength to resist) the domination of others. The very foundation and continuing maintenance of political community, according to this logic, is founded on the will to dominate and exploit; to be preferred is the animalistic unconsciousness of "prehistory." Odysseus's men are at least rendered harmless, whereas Odysseus, driven by self-preservation, must act within the flow of history, necessitating violence, repression, and domination.[57]

The centrality of importance that self-preservation as equated with domination plays is most fully manifested in Horkheimer and Adorno's analysis of the Cyclops episode. Claiming that he is "No-man" (*Udeis*, and hence a pun on *Odysseus*), Odysseus denies the self that until then he had been so adamant on maintaining. The dangers involved in denying this identity have been apparent in the preceding episodes with the Lotus-eaters, with Circe, and with the Sirens: Odysseus as "nobody" endangers his rationalistic self. "He who calls himself Nobody for his own sake and manipulates approximation to the state of nature as a means of mastering nature, falls victim to *hubris*" (*DE*, 68). To approach the state of nature by denying the self is, dialectically, to seek to master nature: Odysseus evaporates his identity not through magic or drugs, but through the excessive rationality of a trick, a play on words. The very attempt, *rationally and consciously*, to deny his identity demands rational recognition. Hence, Odysseus must subsequently reveal his identity and endanger his life and the lives of his companions. Self-preservation endangers the physical self but makes one superior to mere nature. To reassert identity after artificially denying it is to master nature.

Horkheimer and Adorno presume throughout their analysis that Odysseus's intention is one of self-domination and mastery of nature. Yet, fissures in their analysis are evident, suggesting finally that the "dialectic of enlightenment" may not be as iron-clad as suggested. Odysseus's relationship with nature, as seen in chapter 1 of this volume, is ever subject to more ambiguity than is granted by Horkheimer and Adorno. In particular, Odysseus's fashioning of the olive trunk into the marriage bed—the combination of both nature and artifice—is brushed off with uncharacteristic lightness by Horkheimer and Adorno. They attribute Odysseus's fashionings to be that of "a proto-typical bourgeois—the with-it hobbyist" (*DE*, 74). Not bothering to concentrate too deeply on the implications of Odysseus's handiwork, they miss entirely the simple refusal of Odysseus to "dominate" nature rather than to accommodate the human convention of marriage within a natural framework.

By extension, their neglect of the Calypso episode suggests their further insensitivity to the possibility of human relationships not first and foremost informed by power and domination. By refusing Calypso's offer of immortality, Odysseus arguably preserves his self by refusing to relinquish himself to a changeless immortal existence (in keeping with Horkheimer and Adorno's analysis). Yet the barren recognition that his decision entails his own death, particularly inasmuch as he has already seen his fate through his visit to Hades, suggests the limits of Horkheimer and Adorno's argument. Indeed Odysseus is drawn to preserve his

self in opposition to the offer of immortality by Calypso; but that very self is finally defined not in the narrow, even liberal fashion suggested by Horkheimer
and Adorno as a calculating, self-maximizing entity, but rather as a self existing
in a network of relationships: a "situated" self. To *tempt* death in the pursuit of
self-preservation is one thing; to *embrace* one's own death is quite another, such
that the strains between self-preservation and self-obliteration implicit in
Odysseus's decision to refuse immortality are not comprehensible without considering the strong considerations of community that Odysseus shares.

Notwithstanding these interpretive differences, in the final estimation,
Horkheimer and Adorno offer a plausible if unattractive and at times misleading
interpretation of the *Odyssey*. Like Plato and Rousseau before them, Horkheimer
and Adorno turn to Homer's *Odyssey* both to locate the origin of humanity (or
at least *their* particular view of humanity) and to illustrate the universality of their
theory. Like Plato, they perceive in the *Odyssey* the beginnings of unanswered
political problems, particularly those involving the strained relationship of humanity and nature. And much like Rousseau's description of "the natural goodness of man," Horkheimer and Adorno intimate that in humanity's prehistory
there was no tension between man and nature—said differently, no alienation—
but that already evinced at the dawn of civilization is a selfish and proto-bourgeois creature whose only concern was the accrual and justification of private
property.[58] Where Horkheimer and Adorno differ from these preceding (if partial) interpretations of the *Odyssey* is in their relentless rejection of any redeeming quality to Odysseus, to the characters that inhabit the *Odyssey*, and to the
story itself. The only value to be recovered in reading Homer is overwhelming
evidence that capitalist and fascist elements in human history have been present
since the most distant antiquity. The political lesson of the *Odyssey* is purely
negative: in renouncing Marx's version of history, Horkheimer and Adorno in
fact give a wider sweep to Marx's vision than he had anticipated, finding throughout the course of history a story of exploitation and domination rather than its
gradual rise. Marx is rejected only to be universalized. But given the very universality of this vision and this stagnant version of human history, the Marxist solution—revolution brought about through the process of history—is also rejected.
A particularly vicious and unforgiving portrait of human nature is the result of
Horkheimer and Adorno's analysis of Homer's *Odyssey*.

The Limits of a Purely Critical Theory

Despite the implicit and even Rousseauian preference in Horkheimer and
Adorno's interpretation of the *Odyssey* for prehistory, as with Rousseau, there is

no consideration of "return." As Horkheimer wrote in 1947: "We are the heirs, for better or for worse, of the Enlightenment and technological progress. To oppose these by regressing to more primitive stages does not alleviate the permanent crisis they have brought about. On the contrary, such expedients lead from historically reasonable to utterly barbaric forms of social domination. The sole way of assisting nature is to unshackle its seeming opposite, independent thought."[59]

"Historically reasonable" forms of domination are preferable to "barbaric" forms; here Horkheimer still betrays a dimmed but continuous faith that the enlightenment project can cure itself of its own pathologies. At the outset of *Dialectic of Enlightenment*, Horkheimer and Adorno clearly reveal their preference for enlightenment, despite its vicious aspects: "We are wholly convinced—and therein lies our *petitio principii*—that social freedom is inseparable from enlightened thought" (*DE*, xiii). In the final estimation, the benefits accruing from the Enlightenment's project of freedom is worth preservation; the project of Critical Theory is to transform the enlightenment from within, rather than seeking its overthrow through revolution.[60]

Critical Theory, then, does not to seek return to prehistory, nor to mythic preenlightenment; rather it attempts to identify those mythic aspects inherent in the enlightenment project and through such self-conscious identification to overcome them. Thus, while the "dialectic" of myth and enlightenment would seem initially to suggest their inseparability, there is a continuous presumption on the part of Horkheimer and Adorno that myth can be separated from enlightenment through critical reason and thus that enlightenment can be cleansed of its unattractive contents. "If enlightenment does not accommodate reflection on this *recidivist element* ("*rückläufige Moment*"), then it seals its own fate" (*DE*, xiii; emphasis mine). The "recidivist element" (or, in the literal German, "stepping back") to which Horkheimer and Adorno refer is clearly mythology itself—the "charlatanism and superstition" that infests enlightenment thought.[61] The seemingly inevitable dialectic is in fact more of a pathology that careful surgery can cure: revealing their wholehearted preference for rationality, however critical, Horkheimer and Adorno finally stand fully revealed as children of the enlightenment.[62]

This grudging and at times submerged alliance with the enlightenment is at the basis of Horkheimer and Adorno's misinterpretation of the *Odyssey*, particularly where it touches upon the subject of facing death and human community. The Enlightenment's attempt to rationalize away all human fears is limited by its confrontation with the fact of human death.[63] The attempt to dissolve human fear is acknowledged by Horkheimer and Adorno to be perhaps the most important part of the enlightenment project: "In the most general sense of progressive thought, the Enlightenment has always aimed at liberating men from fear (*Furcht*) and establishing their authority [*sie als Herren einzusetzen*]," states the first line of the text (*DE*, 3). These two projects—liberation from fear and establishment of authority—as Horkheimer and Adorno's subsequent analysis makes clear, are not necessarily compatible: the establishment of modern authority, most gruesomely characterized by the Nazi regime but also undergirding theories of the State arising from the state of Nature in Hobbes and Locke, is finally *reliant* on human fear and the drive toward self-preservation.[64] Horkheimer and Adorno hope, in an unexplained fashion other than through "critical reason," to break this relationship, freeing humanity from fear and at the same time from authority and domination.

Christian Lenhardt, in an otherwise sympathetic treatment of *Dialectic of Enlightenment*, notes the problem posed by Horkheimer and Adorno's attempt to rationalize away human fear: "The question is therefore whether, with all the continuity linking enlightenment and myth, there is not an element which has dropped out of the historical dialectic. This element is the fear of death. No theory can desubjectivize fear. . . . The *Dialectic of Enlightenment* I think wrongly implies that fear and panic are the psychic accompaniments of everyday life in an age of computerized welfare."[65] Horkheimer and Adorno avoid a discussion of human fear of death, emphasizing that human fear in modernity no longer must confront such primal natural forces inasmuch as modern humanity is sheltered by protecting technologies. Even Odysseus, it is implied, seeks self-preservation only to continue his domination in the world; Odysseus's actual decision to embrace death such that he can return to Ithaca cannot be a motivation in Horkheimer and Adorno's limited worldview. Where human relationships are only defined by patterns of domination, it is literally impossible to credit Odysseus's decision to "return" to the underworld as a means of rejoining human community.

Death, according to the Frankfurt School, is not a subject meriting philosophical attention.[66] As intimated by their lack of analysis, even unawareness, of the significance of Odysseus's embrace of death, the problem of human death is one that a purely "critical theory" cannot apprehend. Indeed, Adorno attempts to dismiss the problem with which death confronts philosophy, significantly adopting two not entirely compatible tactics. In a section entitled "Dying Today" in his study *Negative Dialectics*, he first scoffs at the terror induced by approaching death as nothing more than a bourgeois attitude enhanced by the surrounding consumer culture:

> As the subject lives less, death grows more precipitous, more terrifying. The fact that it literally turns them into things makes them aware of reification, their permanent death and the form of their relations that is partly their fault. The integration of death in civilization, a process without power over death and a ridiculous cosmetic procedure in the face of death, is the shaping of a reaction to this social phenomenon, a

clumsy attempt of the barter society to stop up the last holes left open by the world of merchandise.[67]

Mortality is but another object of "reification" in the capitalist arsenal, in and of itself empty of meaning or significance. Death as experienced by humanity in "civilization"—since the inception of human consciousness according to the argument of *Dialectic of Enlightenment*—has always been a manipulated "social phenomenon."

Shortly thereafter, Adorno suggests that, rather than being a trite consumer product, death is finally so sublime as not to be subject to human understanding.

[I]t is impossible to think of death as the last thing pure and simple. Attempts to express death in language are futile, all the way into logic, for who should be the subject of which we predicate that it is dead, here and now. Lust—which wants eternity, according to a luminous word of Nietzsche—is not the only one to balk at its passing. If death were that absolute which philosophy tried in vain to conjure positively, everything is nothing; all that we think, too, is thought into the void; none of it is truly thinkable.[68]

Central to Adorno's rejection of death as an object of human contemplation is the repeated observation that death is ultimately not *comprehensible*, neither "in language," nor through "logic," nor finally "thinkable." Thus Adorno rejects the premise that makes Odysseus's refusal of Calypso's offer of immortality, and his commitment to homecoming, so extraordinary: "All this ideological mischief probably rests on the fact that human consciousness to this day is too weak to sustain the experience of death, perhaps even too weak for its conscious acceptance."[69] The very "conscious acceptance" that motivates Odysseus's choice— emphasized by his knowledge of the afterlife—can be perceived by Adorno as nothing more than "ideological mischief."

Connected to this fundamental inability to "think" about death is the implicit rejection of myth. Rational philosophy has always approached the limits of its perception when considering death; therefore, philosophers such as Plato necessarily resorted to myth in order to comprehend human eschatology. The Myth of Er, in particular, is such a "philosophic" attempt to connect justice with inevitable mortality, an attempt that escapes purely rational considerations. Horkheimer and Adorno, despite their misgivings about enlightenment, finally reject myth as nothing more than falsehood, a deception of the powerful propounded for the weak. Yet because of their very inability to recognize the powerful attraction that myth (or in Arendt's term, "enacted stories") continues to hold even in an era of enlightenment, Horkheimer and Adorno are finally rendered speechless in the face of death.[70] The absence of analysis accorded to Odysseus's embrace of death for the sake of human fellowship is indicative of this "silence."

This silence is even more ominous in the echoes of Adorno's speechlessness in the historical shadow of Auschwitz and reveals the limitations of a demythologized worldview. Almost as a personal epigram, Adorno writes: "To write poetry after Auschwitz is barbaric" ("*Nach Auschwitz ein Gedicht zu schreiben, ist barbarisch*").[71] Adorno's choice of words here is revealing: not merely the offensive existence of Auschwitz itself, but even an attempt to capture the atrocity of the concentration camps in words is considered barbaric—precisely that condition, in *Dialectic of Enlightenment*, to which mankind was "returning," as opposed to achieving a "truly human condition" (*DE*, xi). Poetry—the verbal medium that, from Homer until the present, has captured both the ineffable beauty of the world but also its horrors, making life and death somehow more comprehensible to humanity—is rejected by Adorno as "barbaric" in a post-Auschwitz world. Adorno rejects poetic attempts to comprehend human barbarity as *itself* barbaric because "critical intelligence cannot be equal to this challenge as long as it confines itself to self-satisfied contemplation."[72] Poetry, according to Adorno, is nothing but an aesthetic pastime capable only of "self-satisfied contemplation." Because of his inability to see that mythic substructures have a *healing* and *therapeutic* quality (and not merely a deceptive and dominating one) and that poetry has historically indulged less in "self-satisfied contemplation" than it has attempted to capture and interpret those mythic elements—not the least of which is to confront death—Adorno necessarily rejects any positive quality to the poetic enterprise. Sadly, for Adorno, to remain speechless before the horror of Auschwitz is finally preferable to "barbaric" attempts to confront human horror through language.

If Horkheimer and Adorno ultimately reject myth as offering any solace to human beings in a post-Enlightenment world, at the same time their commitment to enlightenment is also dubious, at least in any form that is commonly recognizable. At the outset of *Dialectic of Enlightenment*, although they clearly side with enlightenment, they state that the enlightenment as manifested in modernity "already contains the seed of the reversal universally apparent today" (*DE*, xiii). That "seed" was evident as early as Homer's epics, particularly in the instrumental reason wielded against nature by Odysseus. Enlightenment thought, though preferable to Horkheimer and Adorno than "mythic" thought, finally cannot offer political solutions to perennial human problems without resulting in the evisceration of nature and the domination of humanity already present in humanity's earliest "mythology."

Although the names of Horkheimer and Adorno, along with Marcuse, are often and perhaps justifiably associated with the student protest movements of the late 1960s,[73] it is revealing that Horkheimer and even more so Adorno repudiated any identification with the student movement.[74] The rallying cry of the students to engage in "participation"—that age-old dream of universal activity in political life—met with particular skepticism on the part of Adorno.[75] In a far more "Platonic" understanding of the division between theory and practice than Plato allowed, Adorno criticized calls for "participation" precisely because such political activity interfered with the purity of contemplation—now not merely "poetic" contemplation, but the contemplation of critical reason: "Being consumed, swallowed up, is indeed just what I understand as 'participation' [mitmachen] which is totally characteristic for the new anthropological type—the lack of curiosity. No longer wanting to know anything new, above all anything that is open and unguarded."[76] Rather than the "consumption" of "mitmachen," Adorno continuously called for a philosophy of "nicht-mitzumachen," nonparticipation that would afford peaceful contemplation.[77] The alternative to enlightenment and myth, Adorno suggested, was solitude.[78]

Solitude in the face of the enormities of human terror, atrocity, and malevolence is indeed that to which Adorno finally retreats. More than the "elitist" Plato—whose version of the Odyssean philosopher-king suggests an engagement in human affairs—and more than Rousseau—who, in spite of his ambivalence toward human community and solitude, at least holds human community as a political ideal—Adorno in his demythologized, derationalized world can only admit the possibility of intellectual retreat.

> The best mode of conduct, in the face of all this still seems an uncommitted, suspended one: to lead a private life, as far as the social order and one's own needs will tolerate nothing else, but not to attach weight to it as to something still socially substantial and individually appropriate. "It is even part of my good fortune not to be a house-owner," Nietzsche already wrote in the Gay Science. Today we should have to add: it is part of morality not to be at home in one's home.[79]

The only home that Adorno ultimately sanctions is the "home" created by the solitary scholar through his writings:

> In his text, the writer sets up house. Just as he trundles papers, books, pencils, documents untidily from room to room, he creates the same disorder in his thoughts. They become pieces of furniture that he sinks into, content or irritable. He strokes them affectionately, wears them out, mixes them up, re-arranges them, ruins them. For a man who no longer has a homeland, writing becomes a place to live.[80]

This new morality of homelessness is directly related to Horkheimer and Adorno's inability to credit Odysseus's homecoming with anything more than cynical materialist motives. Human community is impossible because human relationships are always tainted with instrumental rationality. Because they reject any form of legitimate "mythic" social composition, like that suggested by

Vico, Horkheimer and Adorno in turn reject any form of accompanying "rationality" that is more communal and associative. On the other hand, Vico envisioned a form of rationality that he called "poetic logic," precisely that form of "poetic" truth that Adorno rejects. For Vico, in distinction from his Enlightenment contemporaries, there is no strict division between *mythos* and *logos* (myth and rationality).[81] Indeed, the *mythos* that preceded *logos* allowed enlightenment to develop, what Vico calls "esoteric wisdom":

> As much as the poets had first sensed in the way of vulgar wisdom, the philosophers later understood in the way of esoteric wisdom; so that the former may be said to have been the sense and the latter the intellect of the human race. What Aristotle said of the individual man is therefore true of the race in general: *Nihil est in intellectu quin prius fuerit in sensu.* That is, the human mind does not understand anything of which it has had no previous impression. (*NS*, 363)

The "previous impression" that gives life to "esoteric" or enlightened wisdom is that "sense" derived from "vulgar wisdom," or the *sensus communis*, the associational rationality that at the same time served as the foundation and moral underpinnings of early human communities. Vico seeks to recommend this more associative form of reasoning, which he calls "*mente,*" one that does not consider the self as an isolated individual but rather as one situated in a network of existing relationships.[82] Vico condemns those who "pursue nothing but their own private interests, which divide men."[83] Thus was Vico critical of Epicurean and Stoic philosophies of "solitaries," of "idlers inclosed in their own little garden . . . , of contemplatives who endeavor to feel no emotion," equally applying to the philosophies of Descartes and Hobbes, and to Horkheimer and Adorno as well.[84]

Horkheimer and Adorno are aware of Vico's arguments and to a limited extent adopt certain of his approaches—particularly in positing the intermingling of myth and enlightenment, as seen earlier. However, their ultimate rejection of myth and their ambivalence toward the enlightenment leave them only a realm of negative or critical individualism.[85] Adorno, realizing the impasse his rejection of myth had brought him, goes so far as to retract his previous condemnation of poetry: "Perennial suffering has as much right to expression as a tortured man has to scream; hence it may have been wrong to say that after Auschwitz you could no longer write poems."[86] Despite his attempt to retract, Adorno ends by equating poetry to the scream of a tortured man, finally as hopeless and inarticulate a sound. For all of his attempts to avoid the conclusions to which his rejection of the world led him, Adorno finally can only identify writing, or the realm of pure philosophy, as the only pursuit that could leave a man guiltless. Thus is the whole of the political philosophy of the Frankfurt School finally curiously antipolitical, convinced as its members ultimately were that human problems were at once caused by politics but beyond the therapy of politics. Were Horkheimer and Adorno given the choice of Odysseus, to remain in immortal and innocent bliss with Calypso or to return to the sometimes unpleasant but endlessly sublime variety of humanity—to achieve *nostos*, homecoming—one wonders whether they would have had the courage to follow the example of Odysseus, an example they did not acknowledge or value. Their very blindness to the possibilities of politics resembles the blindness of Cyclops, who also lived in an apolitical world, a solitary cave-dweller.

Notes

1. Giambattista Vico, *The New Science of Giambattista Vico*, trans. Thomas Goddard Bergin and Max Harold Fisch (Ithaca, NY: Cornell University Press, 1948). References to *New Science* will be demarcated by the letters NS followed by paragraph numbers devised by Fausto Nicolino found in the Bergin and Fisch translation of *New Science*. All references to *New Science* refer to the third edition of 1744. My interpretation of Vico owes considerable debt to Joseph Mali's *The Rehabilitation of Myth: Vico's* New Science (Cambridge, U.K.: Cambridge University Press, 1992), as should be apparent from subsequent citations.

2. Max Horkheimer and Theodor Adorno, *Dialectic of Enlightenment*, trans. John Cumming (New York: Continuum, 1991).

3. Mario Einaudi, for one, rightly noted the similarities between Rousseau and Vico:
As Rousseau raises history to such a lofty position among human sciences, he is forging a link with Vico, both the early Vico (the defender of humane sciences) and the Vico of the *New Science* (the champion of history, because we know what we do), whose final version was even then in the making. There is the same polemical note against scientific education at the expense of a humanistic one; the same complaint against the attempt to make of man, who is a moral being, a machine subjected to the rules of mathematical thinking; the same conclusion: the placing of history on the highest rung of the ladder of human sciences, as history was the creation of man and therefore the most certain and valuable tool available to man and through which man would know himself. (Einaudi, *The Early Rousseau* [Ithaca, NY: Cornell University Press, 1967], 67)

4. Max Horkheimer, *Anfänge der bürgerlichen Geschichtsphilosophie*, in *Gesammelte Schriften*, 10 vols. (Frankfurt am Main, Germany: S. Fischer Verlag, 1988), 252.

5. For a good discussion of Vico's rejection of Cartesian natural sciences, see Mali, *The Rehabilitation of Myth*, chap. 1. On Vico's "ideal eternal history," see Robert Caponigri, *Time and Idea: The Theory of History in Giambattista Vico* (South Bend, IN: University of Notre Dame Press, 1953), chap. 6; and Robert Nisbet, "Vico and the Idea of Progress," in *Vico and Contemporary Thought*, ed. Giorgio Tagliacozzo, Michael Mooney, and David Phillip Verene, 2 vols. (Atlantic Highlands, NJ: Humanities Press, 1976), I.235–47.

6. Henry Tudor correctly notes that Vico reverses the contemporary practice of searching for *rational* explanations underlying myths and instead argues that *irrational* myths underlie rational civilization (Tudor, *Political Myth* [New York: Praeger, 1972], 21).

7. Caponigri, *Time and Idea*, 168–73.

8. Mali writes: "[Vico] was most emphatic in his contention that our modern 'civil world' was not only created by the poetic fictions of the first men, but still consists in them—insofar as their fictions permeate all our social practices: they persist in linguistic metaphors, religious myths, marital and burial rites, national feasts, and all the anonymous and collective customs we live by" (*The Rehabilitation of Myth*, 88).

9. Vico apparently excludes the Hebraic and Christian religions from this otherwise universal explanation for the rise of gentile religions, claiming that only the Hebraic line of descent from Noah escaped the devolution into the race of Giants (*NS*, 313). See Mali, *The Rehabilitation of Myth*, 74–76.

10. Giambattista Vico, *The Autobiography of Giambattista Vico*, trans. Max Harold Fisch and Thomas Goddard Bergin (Ithaca, NY: Cornell University Press, 1981), 85.

11. Vico, *Autobiography*, 85.

12. The frontispiece was only included in the third edition of *New Science*. It was designed by a local artist, Domenico Vaccaro, with personal assistance from Vico (Peter Burke, *Vico* [New York: Oxford University Press, 1985], 30). The illustration is included in the appendix, figure 6.

13. Such a theory of human "self-creation" would be in keeping with Renaissance theories of an undefined and thus self-created human nature. See especially Pico della Mirandolla's essay *On the Dignity of Man*, which Vico admired (Vico, *Autobiography*, 132).

14. On the extent and importance of the "Homeric Question" during Vico's lifetime, especially as it served as a centerpiece in the "Quarrel of the Ancients and the Moderns," see Mali, *The Rehabilitation of Myth*, 190–202.

15. Vico, *Autobiography*, 122.

16. Mali rightly rejects this inevitable translation of *sensus communis* as "common sense" and suggests instead "collective sense" (*The Rehabilitation of Myth*, 124). However, given the negative political implications of "collectivism," I prefer the translation "communal sense," which captures its local and cooperative meaning.

17. Leon Pompa differentiates between two types of "common sense" forwarded by Vico. The first type, which he calls "absolute common sense," comprises the universal underpinnings found in all human society, "i.e., the beliefs that there is a provident divinity, that the passions ought to be controlled and moderated (or that one ought to pursue a moderate life), and that the human soul is immortal" (Pompa, *Vico: A Study of the New Science*, 2d ed. [New York: Cambridge University Press, 1990], 34). The second type is termed "relative common sense" and consists of "those beliefs that belong to a nation . . . at some determinate period in its history, which are therefore also common to all nations at some point in their histories" (35). In effect, while a subtle difference between the two types of "common sense" can be interpolated, they nevertheless both contain a universal yet simultaneous communal or particular quality—they are shared at some historical stage by all humans but exist temporally only within specific communities. Hence, *sensus communis* is the embodiment of human nature as it unfolds over the course of time.

18. There is much debate about the meaning of "Providence" and "Mind" in Vico's science; Caponigri includes a good general discussion (*Time and Idea*, chap. 5); also see Isaiah Berlin, "Vico and the Ideal of the Enlightenment," in *Vico and Contemporary Thought*, 262–63.

19. Hans-Georg Gadamer, *Truth and Method* (New York: Crossroads Publishing, 1986),

20. Alasdair MacIntyre (*After Virtue*, 2d ed. [South Bend, IN: University of Notre Dame Press, 1984]) similarly lights on this "communitarian" aspect of Vico's thought:

It was Vico who first stressed the importance of the undeniable fact, which is becoming tedious to reiterate, that the subject matters of moral philosophy at least— the evaluative and normative concepts, maxims, arguments, and judgments about which the moral philosopher enquires—are nowhere to be found except as embodied in the historical lives of particular social groups and so possessing the distinctive characteristics of historical existence. (265)

20. Longinus writes in On the Sublime (in Classical Literary Criticism, trans. T. S. Dorsch [New York: Viking Penguin, 1965], 113): "It was, I suppose, for the same reason that, writing the Iliad in the prime of life, he filled the whole work with action and conflict, whereas the greater part of the Odyssey is narrative, as is characteristic of old age. . . . As though the ocean were withdrawing into itself and remaining quietly within its own bounds, from now on we see the ebbing of Homer's greatness as he wanders in the realms of the fabulous and incredible." On Longinus's influence on Vico, see Mali, The Rehabilitation of Myth, 158.

21. On Vico's concept of ricorsi, see Caponigri (Time and Idea, chap. 7) and generally Nisbet's "Vico and the Idea of Progress" and Berlin's "Vico and the Ideal of the Enlightenment."

22. Nisbet writes: "We had better, before we think of Vico as an early Hegel, bear in mind the significant difference that in Vico, unlike Hegel, there is a clear recognition of deterioration as a fixed phase of the process of change, one, moreover, brought about by the selfsame elements of reason which in the beginning had generated advancement" ("Vico and the Idea of Progress," 244).

23. For an informative discussion of the "barbarism of sense" and the "barbarism of reflection," see Donald Phillip Verene, Vico's Science of the Imagination (Ithaca, NY: Cornell University Press, 1981), chap. 7.

24. Pietro Piovani, "Apoliticality and Politicality in Vico," in Vico's Science of Humanity, ed. G. Tagliacozzo and D. P. Verene (Baltimore: Johns Hopkins University Press, 1976), 406. For an excellent discussion of this "critical" aspect of Vico's era and his own ambivalence toward it, see Mali, The Rehabilitation of Myth, 210–28.

25. Caponigri, Time and Idea, 191.

26. The problem of examining the "thought" of a group of theorists is problematic. While the Institut für Sozialforschung contained a well-defined core of theorists whose work was guided by the Institut's mission and was often collaborative, such as Horkheimer and Adorno, other theorists are less easily catagorized, in particular Walter Benjamin (who was officially never a member of the Institut) and Herbert Marcuse (who was a member but who, some contend, never fully broke with Heidegger and whose work reflected more Freudian concerns than that of the others). George Friedman (The Political Philosophy of the Frankfurt School [Ithaca, NY: Cornell University Press, 1981]), argues that, inasmuch as these four theorists formed the core of the Frankfurt School and inasmuch as that School was self-defined as collaborative and guided by a common mission, it would be an injustice not to examine their works as fundamentally connected. As my main interest in this study is to examine the use of the Odyssey in Horkheimer and Adorno's Dialectic of Enlightenment, a collaborative spirit will also be assumed, especially in the case of Horkheimer and Adorno. As Horkheimer writes of their respective work, "our philosophy is one" (Horkheimer, Eclipse of Reason [New York: Oxford University Press, 1947], vii). Although I will be peripherally concerned with the contributions of Benjamin and Marcuse—particularly where it appears that their statements can clarify the thought of Horkheimer and Adorno—their work is nevertheless of less centrality to this study. With these caveats in

mind, I will refer to a singular "Frankfurt School" and their "Critical Theory" throughout this study.

27. The influence of Vico on Horkheimer's thought is well documented in Martin Jay, *The Dialectical Imagination: A History of the Frankfurt School, 1923–1959* (Boston: Little, Brown, 1973), 49, 257. See also the articles by Fred Dallmayr ("'Natural History' and Social Evolution: Reflections on Vico's *Corsi e Ricorsi*") and Joseph Maier ("Vico and Critical Theory"), both in *Vico and Contemporary Thought*, and the articles by Jean-Louis Chiss ("Horkheimer face à Vico: la problématique du precurseur") and Gerard Dessons ("Horkheimer et le materialisme historique de Vico"), both in *Critique de la Theorie Critique: langage et histoire* (ed. Henri Meschonnic [Saint-Denis, France: Presses Universaires de Vincennes, 1985]), which explicitly examine the link between Vico and the Frankfurt School. Although these articles cover much the same ground as I do, none of them notes the centrality of Homer both to Vico and to Horkheimer and Adorno in *Dialectic of Enlightenment*.

28. Maier provides a full "list" of similarities between Vico's thought and that of the Frankfurt School ("Vico and Critical Theory," 188–89); I have chosen to emphasize only those that are of specific interest to this study. Maier additionally notes that even though only Horkheimer explicitly wrote about Vico, the other members of the School were equally concerned with these themes, as gleaned either directly from Vico or through a historical lineage traceable from Lukács, Sorel, and Croce, among others ("Vico and Critical Theory," 189–90).

29. "*Das Menschengeschichte beginnt seine Laufbahn in einer dunklen and furchtbaren Urgeschichte,*" Horkheimer, "*Anfänge der bürgerlichen Geschichtsphilosophie,*" *Gesammelte Schriften*, 258.

30. "*Erklärungsmomente für die menschliche Geschichte . . . [sind] vor allem die Mythologie,*" Horkheimer, *Gesammelte Schriften*, 258.

31. "*Für Vico war ferner die Mythologie eine notwendige primitive Vorform der Erkenntnis, aus der unsere Wissenschaft entsprungen ist,*" Horkheimer, *Gesammelte Schriften*, 261.

32. Karl Marx, *Grundrisse*, in *The Marx-Engels Reader*, 2d ed., ed. Robert C. Tucker, trans. Martin Nicolaus (New York: Norton, 1978), 246.

33. Marx, *Grundrisse*, 246.

34. Von Staden argues that Marx's appreciation for the ancient Greeks contradicts his fervent antiromantic stance and is the result of the influence of the long-standing Romantic idealization of antiquity. Von Staden refers to this turn toward the idealization of Greece's childlike attraction as a "Viconian twist" (Heinrich Von Staden, "Nietzsche and Marx on Greek Art and Literature: Case Studies in Reception," *Daedelus* 105 [Winter 1976]: 83). Nevertheless, while Marx shares Vico's view of antiquity as humankind's "childhood," Von Staden must also recognize that Marx eliminates the possibility of "return": "It must be stressed, however, that Marx, like many Romantics (Herder, the later Schiller, etc.), is far from espousing a theory of recurrence: the Garden is not the City, Eden is not the New Jerusalem, Arcadia is not Utopia" (85).

35. Jay, *The Dialectical Imagination*, 40, 256; Susan Buck-Morss, *The Origin of Negative Dialectics: Theodor W. Adorno, Walter Benjamin, and the Frankfurt School* (New York: Free Press, 1977), 24 ff.); Friedman, *The Political Philosophy of the Frankfurt School*, 57 ff..

36. Cited by Jay, *The Dialectical Imagination*, 40. Paul Connerton also notes Horkheimer's early adherence to a belief in scientific and historical progress (Connerton, *The Tragedy of Enlightenment: An Essay on the Frankfurt School* [Cambridge, U.K.: Cambridge University Press, 1980], 62).

37. Max Horkheimer, *Critical Theory: Selected Essays*, trans. M. J. O'Connor (New York: Herder and Herder, 1968), 202.

38. Karl Marx, "Critique of the Gotha Program," in *The Marx-Engels Reader*, ed. Robert Tucker (New York: Norton, 1978), 538.

39. Horkheimer, *Critical Theory*, 213-14.

40. Michael Greven points out that the absence of the proletariat revolution was to dominate the early research of the Frankfurt School:

> In der ersten Phase der "Frankfurter Schule" nach der Errichtung des Instituts für Sozialforschung unter dem Direktorat von Max Horkheimer stand daher die wissenschaftliche Erforschung der Frage im Vordergrund, warum die Marxschen Prognosen über die Entwicklung des Proletariats im Kapitalismus sich als unzutreffend erwiesen hätten. . . . Die Kritische Theorie der "Frankfurter Schule" [findet] außerhalb der Theorie selbst keinen Begründungsanspruch auf historische Wahrheit mehr. (*Kritische Theorie und historische Politik: Theoriegeschichtliche Beiträge zur gegenwärtigen Gesellschaft* [Opladen, Germany: Leske & Budrich, 1994], 24–25)

41. Horkheimer, *Critical Theory*, vi. The general point of the Frankfurt School's departure from Marxist theories of history is almost universally noted. A good summary is provided by S. E. Bronner and Douglass MacKay Kellner (Introduction to *Critical Theory and Society: A Reader*, ed. Bronner and Kellner [New York: Routledge, 1989], 8):

> [The Frankfurt School] increasingly distanced themselves from the traditional Marxist position which claimed that socialist revolution was inevitable and that historical progress would necessarily lead from capitalism to socialism. Henceforth, the critical theorists' relation to Marxism would become more ambivalent and complex. Thus . . . , individuals like Horkheimer would eventually abandon Marxism altogether for a form of mystical irrationalism derived from Schopenhauer and Nietzsche.

Both Herbert Marcuse and Walter Benjamin shared Horkheimer's suspicion that a socialist revolution prompted by the proletariat was not forthcoming. See Marcuse in *Soviet Marxism* (Boston: Beacon, 1964), 106; and Benjamin, "Theses on the Philosophy of History," in *Critical Theory and Society: A Reader*, 259.

42. Karl Marx, "Theses on Feuerbach," in *The Marx-Engels Reader*, 145. Despite the popular interpretation that Marx wholly repudiates theory in favor of practice, a more "dialectical" interaction of theory and practice is intended. As Peter Singer describes Marx's intention: "the problems of philosophy cannot be solved by passive interpretation of the world as it is, but only by remoulding the world to resolve the philosophical contradictions inherent in it" (Singer, *Marx* [New York: Oxford University Press, 1980], 32).

43. The phrase "*Jetztzeit*" was coined by Walter Benjamin in his seminal essay "Theses on the Philosophy of History" (in *Critical Theory and Society: A Reader*). Benjamin suggests that time is "filled with the presence of the now," the inescapable embeddedness of the past in the present. Benjamin's essay is a critique of traditional Marxism, which, so often concerned with new future time, turned history into a "homogenous, empty time" (260).

44. Theodor Adorno, *Negative Dialectics*, trans. E. B. Ashton (New York: Seabury, 1973), 3.

45. It should be added, however, that many Marxist theorists see in Vico's historical theory a precursor to that of Marx. For a critique of this view, see Eugene Kamenka, "Vico and Marxism," in *Giambattista Vico: An International Symposium*, ed. Giorgio Tagliacozzo

and Hayden V. White (Baltimore: Johns Hopkins University Press, 1969). John O'Neill, however, attempts to revive this connection (O'Neill, "On the History of the Human Senses in Vico and Marx," in *Vico and Contemporary Thought*). Although there are many similarities between the two theorists—including their profound recognition of history in the creation of human society and the importance of class conflict as an engine of politics—there nevertheless remain definitive differences. Perhaps most notable is, as discussed earlier, Vico's theory of *ricorsi*, implying that the past is never wholly superseded (and hence that the future can never "transcend" human history). Moreover, while there is a "Providential" aspect to history for both thinkers, Vico's theory of history does not allow for a culmination. As Isaiah Berlin argues, "[for Vico] there is no vision of the march of mankind toward final perfection, whether inspired by a conscious realization of it (as the optimistic *philosophes* hoped was the case) or driven by hidden but beneficent forces" ("Vico and the Ideal of the Enlightenment," 262).

46. "*Noch keineswegs die Produkte der menschlichen Freiheit, sondern natürliche Resultanten des blinden Wirkens anagonistischer Kräfte sind*" ("Zum Problem der Voraussage in den Sozialwissenschaften," in Horkheimer's *Gesammelte Schriften*, vol. 3, 155).

47. Adorno and Horkheimer, *Dialectic of Enlightenment*, xi. Dallmayr also notes this shared belief in the recurrence of barbarity both in Vico and in Horkheimer and Adorno ("'Natural History' and Social Evolution," 204–10).

48. Horkheimer elsewhere contends that such "enlightenment" thought was also present as early as the first chapters of Genesis in the Bible (*Eclipse of Reason*, 63, 104).

49. Again, Gadamer offers a succinct summary of this point: "For Vico . . . the *sensus communis* is the sense of the right and the general good that is to be found in all men, moreover, a sense that is acquired through living in the community and is determined by its structures and aims" (*The Idea of Good in Platonic-Aristotelian Philosophy*, trans. P. Christopher Smith [New Haven, CT: Yale University Press, 1986], 22).

50. In an appendix to *New Science* in which Vico sets forth the *practical* benefits of his discoveries, he states that one of the principles of *New Science* was that "we must respect the common judgment of all men—the common sense (*sensus communis*) of mankind. . . . So long as the peoples keep to good customs, they do decent and just things rather than talk about them, because they do them instinctively, not from reflection" (Giambattista Vico, *Practic of the New Science*, in *Giambattista Vico's Science of Humanity*, ed. Giorgio Tagliacozzo and Donald Phillip Verene [Baltimore: Johns Hopkins University Press, 1976], 1406).

51. In a manner similar to that of Vico, Leszek Kolakowski describes myth's truth-bearing capacity:

> values inherited under a binding function of authority are being inherited in their mythical form; they are not being inherited as information about social or psychological facts (that this or that happens to be thought valuable) but precisely as information regarding what is or is not a value. The idols of the tribe govern in an inescapable manner: a complete emancipation from them springs from a tyranny of another illusion. Universal godlessness is utopia. Myths that teach us that something simply is good or evil cannot be avoided if humanity is to survive.

In *The Presence of Myth*, trans. Adam Czerniawski (Chicago: University of Chicago Press, 1989), 25.

52. Douglass Kellner, *Critical Theory, Marxism, and Modernity* (Cambridge, U.K.: Polity Press, 1989), 87.

53. Michael J. Shapiro, "Politicizing Ulysses: Rationalistic, Critical, and Genealogical Commentaries," *Political Theory* 17 (1989): 10.

54. David Held, *Introduction to Critical Theory: Horkheimer to Habermas* (Berkeley: University of California Press, 1980), 401. More recently, Christopher Rocco has also offered a summary of Horkheimer and Adorno's analysis of the *Odyssey* as evidence of their perspicacity and, ironically, their sympathy for ancient conceptions of politics (Rocco, *Tragedy and Enlightenment: Athenian Political Thought and the Dilemmas of Modernity* [Berkeley: University of California Press, 1997]; 201–8.

55. Sigmund Freud, *Civilization and Its Discontents*, trans. Joan Riviere (New York: Doubleday, 1930). Leszek Kolakowski notes the similarity between *Dialectic of Enlightenment* and *Civilization and Its Discontents* ("The Frankfurt School and Critical Theory," in *Foundations of the Frankfurt School of Social Research*, ed. Judith Marcus and Zoltán Tar [New Brunswick, NJ: Transaction Books, 1984], 110).

56. Horkheimer writes in *Eclipse of Reason*: "One may say that the life of the hero is not so much a manifestation of individuality as a prelude to its birth, through the marriage of self-preservation and self-sacrifice. The only one of Homer's heroes who strikes us as having individuality, a mind of his own, is Ulysses . . . " (130).

57. Connerton writes: "The exploitation of external nature for the purpose of freeing man from subjection to it strikes back in the repression of man's instinctual nature. . . . This means that, in the interest of self-preservation, the self is engaged in constant inner struggle to repress many of its own natural drives" (*The Tragedy of the Enlightenment*, 67).

58. The similarity between "prehistory" in *Dialectic of Enlightenment* and Rousseau's "State of Nature" (and specifically *not* Marx's "aboriginal communism") is noted by Christian Lenhardt ("The Wanderings of Enlightenment," in *On Critical Theory*, ed. John O'Neill [London: Heinemann, 1976], 39).

59. Horkheimer, *Eclipse of Reason*, 127.

60. Kellner writes: "It is not clear whether Horkheimer and Adorno intend to carry out an immanent critique of enlightenment thought or break with enlightenment rationality altogether" (*Critical Theory, Marxism and Modernity*, 89). Although I share Kellner's uncertainty about Critical Theory's final judgment toward enlightenment thought, I think the evidence of these preceding quotations at least proves that Horkheimer and Adorno do not set out explicitly to reject enlightenment, whatever their subsequent hesitations.

61. Horkheimer, *Eclipse of Reason*, xiii. Elsewhere Horkheimer refers to myth as nothing more than "superstition and paranoia" (*Eclipse of Reason*, 30). He contends that "the effects of the philosophical revival of Christianity are not so different from those of the revival of heathen mythology in Germany" (*Eclipse of Reason*, 65)—thereby equating the former effects with the latter ones that resulted in Nazi Germany.

62. Indeed, David Held notes that Horkheimer and Adorno express sympathy with Positivism only insofar as it, too, attempts to dismiss mythology from human beliefs (*Introduction to Critical Theory*, 162).

63. However, even here Enlightenment figures attempted to "reason" away at least the fear of death. See Michael Ignatieff's compelling description of David Hume's refusal to sanction last rites and a Christian burial (*The Needs of Strangers* [New York: Penguin, 1985], 83–103).

64. Another member of the Frankfurt School (before a break in the 1940s), Erich Fromm, captured this modern phenomenon most trenchantly in his *Escape from Freedom*

(New York: Holt, Rinehart &Winston, 1941). For a discussion of Fromm's relationship with the Frankfurt School, see Jay, *The Dialectical Imagination*, 88–100.

65. Lenhardt, "The Wanderings of Enlightenment," 51.

66. In the following discussion, I am indebted to George Friedman's critique of the Frankfurt School's approach to mortality (*The Political Philosophy of the Frankfurt School*, 279–301). Although his critique focuses mainly on the work of Herbert Marcuse, his analysis applies equally to Horkheimer and Adorno, particularly, as I argue, as it reflects on their interpretation of the *Odyssey*.

67. Adorno, *Negative Dialectics*, 370.

68. Adorno, *Negative Dialectics*, 371. It is significant that Adorno here cites Nietzsche's aphorism that "Lust (or Joy) wants eternity." This aphorism was also cited in connection with the theme of death by Marcuse in *Eros and Civilization: A Philosophical Inquiry into Freud* (Boston: Beacon, 1955), 112. As Friedman summarizes Marcuse's interest in Nietzsche's aphorism, "Marcuse founders on the heart of his problem: joy cannot have eternity. Suffering may be a means for gratification, but the end of suffering is death and the end of all sensation" (*The Political Philosophy of the Frankfurt School*, 283–84). Marcuse, favoring *eros* over *thanatos*, finally suggests that, in some unstated fashion, death will be overcome:

> The struggle for existence then proceeds on new grounds and with new objectives: it turns into the concerted struggle against any constraint on the free play of human faculties, against toil, disease and death. Moreover, while the rule of the performance principle was accompanied by a corresponding control of the instinctual dynamic, the reorientation of the struggle for existence would involve a decisive change in this dynamic. Indeed, such a change would appear as the prerequisite for sustaining progress. We shall presently try to show that it would affect the very structure of the psyche, alter the balance between Eros and Thanatos, reactivate tabooed realms of gratification, and pacify the conservative tendencies of the instincts. A new basic experience of being would change the human existence in its entirety.

In a more extreme fashion but one compatible with Adorno, Marcuse finally seeks a "revolution" from within the individual psyche, one that will maximize human pleasure by means of avoiding, abandoning, or finally overcoming death altogether.

69. Adorno, *Negative Dialectics*, 369.

70. See Arendt's *The Human Condition* for a discussion of "enacted stories" (161–67).

71. Theodor Adorno, *Prismen: Kulturkritik und Gesellschaft* (Frankfurt am Main, Germany: Suhrkamp, 1955), 22.

72. Adorno, *Prismen*, 22.

73. The "justifiable" association of the Frankfurt School with the student movement is provided by Friedman (*The Political Philosophy of the Frankfurt School*, 13–26) and Held (*Introduction to Critical Theory*, 13, 363).

74. Martin Jay writes: "By 1951, Adorno had ruled out the possibility of any collectivity being on the side of truth and located the residue of those progressive social forces in the critical individual. In later years, this led to a denial that student radicals or other nascent 'negative' groups were legitimate social forces on the side of true change" (*The Dialectical Imagination*, 292). See also Adorno's comments in a 1969 interview entitled "Kritische Theorie und Protestbewegung" in *Gesammelte Schriften*, vol. 20, 398.

75. Horkheimer was also skeptical of calls for participatory democracy for the same reason he came to reject the possibility of a proletarian revolution: the co-optation of the masses (*Eclipse of Reason*, 28).

76. From Adorno, "Notizen zur neuen Anthropologie," 1942. Cited and translated by Buck-Morss, *The Origin of Negative Dialectics*, 189.

77. Adorno's and indeed the whole of the Frankfurt School's commitment to *nicht-mitzumachen* is documented by Jay (*The Dialectical Imagination*, 291) and Buck-Morss (*The Origin of Negative Dialectics*, 189–92).

78. Friedman, *The Political Philosophy of the Frankfurt School*, 66-67. Horkheimer, too, was skeptical of political activism where it might interfere with philosophical contemplation: "The concentrated energies necessary for reflection must not be prematurely drained into the channels of activistic or nonactivistic programs" (*Eclipse of Reason*, 184).

79. Theodor Adorno, *Minima Moralia*, trans. E. F. N. Jephcott (London: NLB, 1951), 39.

80. Adorno, *Minima Moralia*, 87.

81. Vico in fact finds a philological identification between *mythos* and *logos*: " 'Logic' comes from *logos*, whose first and proper meaning was *fabula*, fable, carried over into Italian as *favella*, speech. In Greek the fable was also called *mythos*, myth . . . " (*NS*, 401).

82. For a discussion of *mente* in opposition to Enlightenment rationality, see Mali, *The Rehabilitation of Myth*, 91.

83. Vico, *Practic of the New Science*, 1409.

84. Vico, *Autobiography*, 122.

85. Many commentators have criticized Horkheimer and Adorno for their exclusive negativity. Among them are George Steiner, who asked of Horkheimer and Adorno's project, "Where is the actual program for a mode of human perception freed from the 'fetishism of abstract truth?'" (*In Bluebeard's Castle*, 139). More critical are Leszek Kolakowski's comments regarding *Dialectic of Enlightenment*: "The authors do not offer any way out of the state of decadence. They do not say how man can become friends with nature again, or how to get rid of exchange value and live without money and calculation. Failing a positive Utopia, [their] final response to the human condition can only be an inarticulate cry" ("The Frankfurt School and Critical Theory," 111, 114). Perhaps most damning is the otherwise restrained critique of Jürgen Habermas, who was an intimate student of both Horkheimer and Adorno: "Their critique [is] so far reaching that the very project of Enlightenment offers hardly any prospect of escape from the constraints of instrumental rationality" (Jürgen Habermas, "The Entwinement of Myth and Enlightenment: Re-Reading *Dialectic of Enlightenment*," *New German Critique* 26 [1982], 18). Habermas, despite his sympathies with Horkheimer and Adorno, realizes that the relentless sweep of their critique ultimately leaves them no recourse for action or reform in the political arena. For some reasons behind Habermas's critique of Horkheimer and Adorno, see Peter Hohendahl, "The Dialectic of Enlightenment Revisited: Habermas' Critique of the Frankfurt School," *New German Critique* 35 (1985): 3–26.

86. Adorno, *Negative Dialectics*, 362.

~

CHAPTER FIVE

Against Cosmopolitanism: Resisting the Sirens' Song

I love a hundred times better the poor Ithaca of Ulysses,
than a city shining through so odious a magnificence.
Happy the men who content themselves with the pleasures
that cost neither crime nor ruin!

—Fenélon, *Lettre sur les occupations de l'Académie Française*

We are not presented with Odysseus's choice. Immortality is not an option for those of us not becalmed on enchanted islands populated by divinities. Yet how we view such an offer, how we finally regard the relative attractions or disadvantages of such an offer, whether we praise or question Odysseus's choice, may have implications beyond the sheer brute fact that immortality is not our lot. For it seems that Odysseus's choice reflects a whole range of commitments regarding human limits—most obviously limits on life itself, but also limits that human affections demand; limits on the range of those affections themselves, to human designs, to ambitions, to optimism; limits on the extent to which humanity can or should seek to conquer nature. The embrace of death is representative of an embrace of an array of limiting features to human existence, and the admission that we would be incapable of making, or unwilling to make, Odysseus's choice, might give us pause as to what other implications that stance would entail.[1]

To begin to appreciate Odysseus's choice, or alternatively to condemn it, at least requires the recognition of its significance, something that Horkheimer and Adorno cannot credit, given their philosophic inability to recognize its implications. Yet with the realization that their condemnation of the *Odyssey*—and their attempt to link "enlightenment" and "myth" in a wholly inextricable manner—

fails to appreciate this least "enlightened" aspect of Odysseus, a space opens for its reconsideration in light of contemporary debates on limits and human potential within a global context. The Odyssey itself appears to provide a corrective to the Frankfurt School's *understanding* of the Odyssey by offering the possibility of a politics outside the desperate trap of modernity described by Horkheimer and Adorno. If this is the case, as I have argued, then it needs must be asked whether the alternative that Horkheimer and Adorno reject, the alternative of Enlightenment itself, remains a viable preference to the limitations that antiquity appears to recommend, particularly those limitations of human longing that the Odyssey seems to endorse. If there is a choice to be made between myth and enlightenment, between the attractions of a particular place and of the limited and limiting goal of *nostos* on the one hand, and appeals to universality of reason and transcendence that lie at the core of Enlightenment theory on the other, does the Odyssey represent one option over the other or in fact suggest that these alternatives may represent a false choice?

I want to suggest the latter, albeit with recognition that the attempt to wend one's way in the center between Scylla and Charybdis is of course impossible. As the tale in the Odyssey relates—a lesson that is often overlooked by those who assume that the tale teaches us to take the middle course—lest one be sucked altogether into the prevailing current, one must favor instead the less dangerous course, if only but a little. So, one of the crucial lessons of the Odyssey on this question suggests that the choice may be too stark; on another level the ancient text also recognizes that a choice must be made nevertheless. Between enlightenment and myth, between universal and particular, there is a choice, although a choice that needs must recognize the attractions and the pitfalls of each. In the end, I will suggest, the Odyssey seems to recommend a course of "limited transcendence," a transcendence of which humans are aware and even to which they can aspire, but of which finally they must also be wary and that they must reject when it tempts them to total transcendence of what Homer understands to be the human condition. I will suggest that this form of "limited transcendence" is exemplified in some of the actions and the choices of Odysseus, especially those that reveal the simultaneous attractions of the cosmopolitan alternative and the requirements of partiality that bind us to particular places and particular people.[2] These latter requirements, the Odyssey finally suggests, keep us fully human and represent the only avenue by which justice can finally be achieved, not through dedication to universal or cosmopolitan knowledge inasmuch as this knowledge threatens to attenuate our connections, devotion, and duties to humanity, especially to the humblest and least powerful of our fellow citizens.

The question of whether particularity is to be preferred to universality is of

course played out in many different debates in contemporary political philosophy. To pursue an earlier examination of the "culture wars" with which this study
began, of special interest are recent responses to the multicultural challenge in
the wake of the end of the Cold War. Primarily in the face of the devolving
nationalisms of the post-Soviet era following the fall of the Berlin Wall in 1989,
thinkers who shared some of the same political aspirations of multicultural critics nevertheless became uncomfortable with disconcerting similarities between
the renewed politics of ethnic and national strife and arguments about ethnic
and racial identity forwarded by colleagues in the academy. A renewed fascina-
tion with the origins of liberalism during the Enlightenment, of the promise of
equal status and equal rights, of universal reason, of the overcoming of religious
superstition, and of the possibility of cosmopolitan citizenship found new support among a wide range of scholars whose initial impetus was a rejection of
multiculturalism's critiques linked to a desire to retain the aspirations of the traditional Left.

Echoing older laments that the true universalism of the Enlightenment has
been betrayed, such as Julien Benda's *Betrayal of the Intellectuals*,[3] are recent authors ranging from sociologist Todd Gitlin, discussed already in the Introduction
for his own accusations of "betrayal" by those on the Left, to historian David
Hollinger, who calls for a new cosmopolitanism in an era of postethnicity. In *The
Twilight of Common Dreams*, Gitlin for one regrets the embrace by the Left of a
form of particularism that betrayed the older Enlightenment ideal of universalism, especially a form of cosmopolitanism that stressed the commonalities of
human beings over the differences of ethnicity, gender, race, or nationality. The
competing universalisms in the wake of the Left's betrayal of Liberalism hold less
appeal and more danger, from Gitlin's perspective: either the universalism preva-
lent among some on the Right, the "rhetoric of global markets and global freedom" that has about it "something of the old universalist ring" or the renewal of
an even older universalism than that of the Enlightenment emanating from religious impulses around the world.[4] If the first is worrisome for the false universalism that reduces us primarily to consumers rather than to citizens, the second
is equally worrisome, less for its purported attempt to convey a universal message
than for its actual practice of excluding "the infidel, the secularist, the modernist
blasphemer."[5] Instead, Gitlin recommends a form of universalism that allows us,
on the one hand, to overcome any differences that either religious or "multicultural" divisions may portend—"to agree to limit the severity of [our] differences"—even while, on the other hand, it enables us to "pound the table and
claim the uniqueness of our communities.[6] Only by limiting the embrace of those
identities that only partially define us and by instead focusing on that part of our

common human identity that binds us, Gitlin contends, can the Left reengage in a politics that hopes to address true conditions of injustice not only within universities but throughout the world as well.

Sharing Gitlin's concerns about the overdetermined nature of identity according to either ethnicity, race, or gender is David Hollinger, for whom the very openness of identity that modernity affords leads less to the easy assumption of identity along ethnic or cultural lines than to a situation of postethnicity. Due especially to shifting identities that would allow, for example, Alex Haley to identify his "roots" as much with his white Irish forebears as with his black African ancestors, as well as with the various heritages that compose America more generally, such as that democratic heritage arising from America's documentary history of the Declaration of Independence and the Constitution, Hollinger suggests that the more appropriate perspective for the twenty-first century is one of "cosmopolitanism," which he distinguishes from both universalism and pluralism.

In contrast to universalism, which Hollinger suggests seeks to find a common ground where multiculturalists would be inclined to find only difference, cosmopolitans do not seek to identify all people as either fundamentally distinct or similar, but rather to identify them as receptive to "recognition, acceptance, and eager exploration of diversity."[7] Cosmopolitans are "diversity-appreciating" in outlook and view such diversity as a simple fact; universalists, by contrast, actively seek to create unity despite existing diversity and ultimately must view such diversity more as a problem than as a simple fact. On the other hand, cosmopolitans differ from pluralists in that pluralists tend to view human beings first as members of groups, rather than as individualists, and cosmopolitans, by contrast, view people primarily as individuals for whom group identity is potentially shifting and evolving. Thus, according to Hollinger, pluralists grant privilege especially to already-established groups, assuming the existing landscape of human relations to be the norm; cosmopolitans, alternatively, are "willing to put the future of every culture at risk through the sympathetic but critical scrutiny of other cultures."[8]

Although Hollinger's formulation is compelling, to an extent he attempts to draw too fine a distinction between cosmopolitans and universalists, on the one hand, and between cosmopolitans and pluralists, on the other. Even though he is intent on creating an ideal type of cosmopolitan, there is no denying that a cosmopolitan, however defined, continues to place a priority on the universal over the particular (or else cosmopolitan would cease to mean anything), even if the cosmopolitan continues to appreciate diversity in the world. Indeed, there is less tension between "cosmopolitan" and "universalist," as Hollinger defines them, than he suggests, especially considering the distinction Hollinger draws between the cosmopolitan and the pluralist. Regarding the pluralist, the cosmopolitan concludes that group affiliation *can* be a problem, hence drawing on the critical perspective of what Hollinger describes as "universalist"; yet equally so, regarding the universalist, the cosmopolitan concludes that plurality must have a place. In effect, the cosmopolitan as described by Hollinger shifts between the two poles, evoking a more universalist stance in response to pluralism and a pluralist stance in response to universalism. However, in effect, his definition of cosmopolitanism does not depart radically from the original understanding that he argues is not present (i.e., its universalist orientation), inasmuch as group or patriotic identity, whether our own or someone else's, is something to be regarded as wholly unnatural, changeable, even finally discardable. Although a cosmopolitan by Hollinger's lights can *appreciate* difference, even acknowledge that it is ineradicable at some level, a cosmopolitan can always transcend such differences by an act of volition or will, by *choice*. Such is at base the fundamental assumption of liberal cosmopolitanism, whether defined as universalist or not.

This aspect is seen most clearly in the work of the preeminent proponent of cosmopolitanism during this period, Martha Nussbaum. Originally formulating her defense of cosmopolitanism in a 1994 *Boston Review* article entitled "Patriotism and Cosmopolitanism," which was later collected with various replies in the 1996 collection *For Love of Country* and recently reiterated in her 1997 book on liberal education, *Cultivating Humanity*, Nussbaum has been in the forefront of reasserting the Stoic and Enlightenment ideal of cosmopolitanism.[9] Nussbaum finds particularly appealing the stance of Diogenes Laertius, who declared himself to be "a citizen of the world."[10] The import of this phrase, for Nussbaum, is not to *extirpate* our citizenship of any particular place but, as she puts it, to reveal that our more "fundamental" and "primary" allegiance is with the human race, not any particular group thereof, from which we derive generalizable moral obligations and a universal conception of justice.[11]

Although Nussbaum stresses that the Stoics recognized our dual identities— the one identity deriving from "the local community of our birth," the other from "the community of human argument and aspiration"—it is this latter community to which we owe our primary allegiance because, she suggests, only this latter allows us to overcome the limitations of perspective and prejudice that the former forces upon us.[12] Nussbaum recognizes that the latter community of the *cosmos* is the more *volitional* of the two: whereas our birth community is an "accident," an arbitrary place where any human being might have been born but only particular humans *happen* to occupy, the latter condition of universal humanity is something that we can choose to theorize and to accept. At the same time, even Nussbaum must acknowledge that the very fact of our common humanity is at some level arbitrary; after all, we did not choose to be human any more than we chose to be born in any particular place. Thus, in a footnote she writes: "I am surprised that none of my critics have asked why I focus on the moral claim of the human species, and they appear to neglect the claims of other forms of life. From this direction one could imagine a serious challenge to my position, one that I have not yet answered."[13] The challenge she imagines undoubtedly would force her either to articulate an inherent dignity solely inhering in the human creature or to extend her analysis to include sentient and perhaps even all living creatures. In any event, most fundamental to Nussbaum's recommendation is the insistence that arbitrariness be lifted from our identities, that we seek rather the fundamental sameness that attends the human or sentient condition—what she insists is our shared human dignity—regardless of any underlying distinction that may at first seem to separate us.[14] We can *choose* between our identities: the one to which we should afford priority is the more universal, as it removes contingency and accident, which for Nussbaum almost always prevent apprehension of justice and morality.[15]

Like Gitlin, she resists multiculturalism's appeals to particularity as preeminent over the false claims of reason and enlightenment: Nussbaum favorably cites, in addition to the Stoics, the philosophy of that archrationalist and cosmopolitan, Immanuel Kant.[16] However, like Hollinger, Nussbaum resists calling for a kind of "universalism" that eliminates difference: while occasionally she speaks as if we should concentrate only on underlying similarities of human beings and argues at some points that "we should recognize humanity and its fundamental ingredients, reason and moral capacity, wherever it occurs and give that community of humanity our first allegiance," at others she insists that a cosmopolitan education should concentrate on exploring the uniqueness of other cultures and traditions.[17] However, she also shares Hollinger's criticism of "pluralism," insisting that we are in the first instance always individuals, never primarily part of a group. She asserts that we should "give our first allegiance to no mere form of government, no temporal power, but to the moral community made up by the humanity of all human beings."[18] The presumption, of course, is a familiar one in liberal theory, viewing government as fundamentally unnatural, even inherently wicked, but *humanity* as potentially good, either as individuals or in its universal incarnation.[19] Thus, Nussbaum is able to adhere to an individualist worldview that she combines simultaneously to a fictive idea of "world community" deriving from the inherent morality of our human attributes.

In Nussbaum's most explicit description of the connection between the cosmopolitan and the citizen of a particular place, Nussbaum writes of "concentric circles" that capture the series of obligations defining a given human being. Stating that a cosmopolitan does not "propose the abolition of local and national forms of political organization and the creation of a world state," nevertheless she believes that we must view our relations with particular people against the backdrop—and standard—of humanity generally:

> The first [circle] is drawn around the self; the next takes in one's immediate family; then follows the extended family; then, in order, one's neighbors or local group, one's fellow city dwellers, one's fellow countrymen. . . . Beyond all these circles is the largest one, that of humanity as a whole. Our task as citizens of the world, and as educators who prepare people to be citizens of the world, will be to "draw the circles somehow toward the center," making all human beings like our fellow city dwellers. In other words, we need not give up our special affections and affiliations and identifications, whether national or ethnic or religious; but we should work to make all human beings part of our community of dialogue and concern, showing respect for the human wherever it occurs, and allowing that respect to constrain our national and local politics.

On the one hand, Nussbaum asserts that we must form our universal relationships to emulate the intimacy of our particular ones, while at the same time "constraining" actual relationships located in our "national and local politics" by means of appeal to universal standards. This is the dream—perhaps even fantasy—of classical cosmopolitanism, to make the universal particular and the particular universal.[20]

Cosmopolitanism, in its ancient, Enlightenment, and contemporary manifestations, and despite slight differences among them, is marked by several fundamental shared features. The first is its preference for universality. Notwithstanding Hollinger's correct reservation that cosmopolitanism does not necessarily seek the homogenization of the world according to a universal standard (although some versions do, notably varieties of Marxism), cosmopolitanism can acknowledge a pluralist cultural universe while insisting that certain features of human existence apply across national and cultural boundaries. Cosmopolitanism simultaneously stresses the need to study other cultures with the toleration to resist condemnation of different practices; at the same time, however, it is fully expected that a result of that examination will be, as Nussbaum suggests, a "drawing together" of the circles when we come to realize the common features of humanity uniting us. Those features are our shared rationality, a universal morality (expressed, among others, by Kant in his formulation of "the kingdom of ends"), and a fundamental human dignity. Above all, cosmopolitanism stresses that the universal is a *priority* over the particular and that in all instances a choice can and should be made for transcendence of the limitations of locality.

To varying degrees, cosmopolitans also exhibit a confidence in science and technology to conquer natural challenges to human penury and to break down physical barriers separating humans[21] and a belief in progress, not only in the ability of science to ameliorate humanity's material and political condition but also in its moral capacities. Cosmopolitans often evince the certitude that irrational religious beliefs, often manifested in persecution and intolerance, will give way to either the willingness to forgo religion altogether or to a naturalistic or deistic piety that offers a moral code without accompanying threats of punishment from a divine being or a class of clerics to enforce them. Informing all of these beliefs, cosmopolitans exhibit an underlying certainty that all of these outcomes can be effected by a properly designed educational approach, rationally conceived, widely disseminated, universally applicable, and irresistible in its effect once its teachings were moved from the elite intellectual arena to the populace at large.[22]

Critics of cosmopolitanism, often disagreeing among themselves, nevertheless agree in rejecting many and at times all of these defining features of cosmopolitanism. Respondents to Nussbaum's original article ranged in their critiques from Benjamin Barber's conditioned patriotism to Gertrude Himmelfarb's claims of American universalism; from Nathan Glazer's insistence that loyalty has actual physical limits to Michael McConnell's invocation of Burkean "little platoons"; from Michael Walzer's gentle reminder that cosmopolitanism is as much prone to political abuse as patriotism to Anne Norton's telling critique that cosmopolitanism may simply be another variety of particularism. Coming exclusively from neither the Left nor the Right, these critiques were almost uniformly informed by a mistrust both in the practicability of a cosmopolitan worldview—summarized in Harvey Mansfield's dismissive response that although "Martha Nussbaum is one of the most eminent female philosophers of our time . . . , when it comes to politics she's a girl scout"—and more often than not in its desirability if such a worldview comes at the cost of weakening people's ties to local affiliations and loyalties.[23]

Often, then, a stark choice is presented: cosmopolitanism or patriotism; universality or particularity; locality or humanity. Yet ancient reflection on human aspirations and personal duties suggests at least that this choice may be too stark, too severe. The *Odyssey* in several moments intimates that if at some level such a choice is finally unavoidable, the choice that most retains our connection to humanity must be informed by what draws us to the human condition generally and finally beyond humanity.

Nostalgia: "Homecoming" and the "Longing Born of Separation"[24]

To ask whether the *Odyssey* can shed light on contemporary debates about cosmopolitanism versus its opposite—defined by cosmopolitans as "nationalism," but by its supporters more positively as "communitarianism" or "patriotism"[25]—would appear to engage is an anachronistic inquiry. The very concept of *kosmou politēs*—"citizen of the world," a phrase coined by Diogenes the Cynic in the fourth century B.C.—would have represented a contradiction in terms in the Homeric world, inasmuch as a citizen, or *politēs*, is necessarily a member of a city, or *polis*. Yet, in discussing the relative merits of cosmopolitanism and nationalism, the *Odyssey* has often been cited as exhibiting some of the original motivations that came to inform both cosmopolitanism and the critique of that universal perspective. For example, in his 1973 essay "A Case for Patriotism," John Schaar contrasted the *Odyssey* and its theme of homecoming—"the central motif of patriotic discourse"—with the "melancholy figure of the lone wanderer, or . . . the Stoic whose 'my home is everywhere' meant he had a home nowhere."[26] Even critics of cosmopolitanism have at times recognized the profound tension that lies at the heart of the *Odyssey* between the attractions of homecoming and the mysteries of the unknown, between patriotism and cosmopolitanism, and between departure and return. As the poet Robert Pinsky observes, "The paradoxical ideal of reconciling the pull of the home and of market, the patriotic and the cosmopolitan, is an underlying energy of the *Odyssey*, epic of seagoing pirate-traders who believed both in venturing out on Poseidon's ocean . . . and in coming home to Ithaca."[27]

At the outset of the *Odyssey*, we are told that Odysseus has seen untold marvels of the world: "Many were they [the men] whose cities he saw, whose minds he learned of" (*pollōn d' anthrōpōn iden astea kai noon egnō*—1.3). Of all the heroes who fought in Troy, Odysseus most fully embodies that first injunction toward achieving a cosmopolitan education as recommended by Nussbaum and most other proponents of cosmopolitanism—that a cosmopolitan education "must be a multicultural education, by which I mean one that acquaints students with some fundamentals about the histories and cultures of many different groups."[28] Yet, it is curious that we are told shortly thereafter that this undeniably "multicultural" experience did not succeed in making Odysseus long for a community composed of citizens of the world but instead might be said to have had the opposite effect—to make him pine for *nostos*, to return to a particular place and a particular people.

> Then all the others, as many as fled sheer destruction,
> were at home now, having escaped the sea and fighting.
> This one alone, longing for his wife and his homecoming [*nostou*],
> was detained by the queenly nymph Kalypso, bright among goddesses,
> in her hollowed caverns, desiring that he should be her husband.
> (1.11–15)

Only in Book 5 do we learn the extent of the sacrifice that Odysseus makes:

Calypso not only offers to make Odysseus her husband but also accompanies the invitation of matrimony with an offer that few mortals ever encounter, that is, the possibility of immortal life. I have already discussed many of the implications of Odysseus's refusal of this offer in chapter 1; here I would merely like to reflect on the extent to which Odysseus's refusal also suggests a stance of suspicion toward what might be called proto-cosmopolitanism, or a form of transcendence, that nevertheless he recognizes as holding attractions as well as dangers.

When we join Odysseus in the midst of his ninth year of wandering, we encounter a man who consistently turns down Calypso's astonishing proposals but also a man who has found both Calypso and presumably those proposals enticing at some point. It is important to note not only that Odysseus refuses the offer of immortality, but also that he does so having acknowledged fully the attractions of Calypso and her island. Although we are told that his eyes are "never wiped dry of tears" (5.152) and that he is to be found often sitting at the edge of the sea longing for a means by which to return to Ithaca, we are also told that he "wept for a way home since the nymph was no longer pleasing to him" (5.154)—meaning, of course, that at one time she *was* pleasing to him. In light of our later discovery that Odysseus remains for a year with Circe, despite her promises to perpetrate no further evils against him (which would seem to preclude the spinning of a spell that forces Odysseus to remain against his will), and only leaves upon being approached by his men and challenged not to forget his desire to return to Ithaca, it comes as little surprise that while on the island of Calypso, for at least some time, he finds the bounty of her immortal offerings and the pleasure of her bed to be irresistible.

Even though the many varieties of pleasure and ease offered by both Calypso and Circe prove appealing, in their purely physical aspect they resemble more the temptations of endless torpor with which the Lotus-eaters tempt Odysseus's men than the presumed attractiveness of universality or cosmopolitanism.[29] However, in addition to the attractions of longevity and the sexual aspects of Odysseus's temptation by the goddesses, one perceives how life among the goddesses also intimates not the unconsciousness accompanying the Lotus but the expanded consciousness that seems to be the lot of the gods. As we learn upon Hermes' arrival on Calypso's island, the gods instantly recognize one another; moreover, there is no point in dissembling their thoughts or words because they are able to perceive the true purpose and intentions of each other.[30] Indeed, Hermes is the source of many of these revelations concerning divine apperception. As we have seen previously, not only do the gods know one another and each other's thoughts instantly, but they possess the ability of instant apperception of nature itself: Hermes is able to apprehend the "nature" of the moly plant even though its true attributes lie hidden to Odysseus (10.302–306). In these many small pictures of divine sight, a larger portrait appears suggesting that divine vision comes closest to that to which humans aspire when they speak of a vision of the whole, the ability to envision a comprehensive picture of existence that transcends their own shortcomings and limitations born of ignorance, partiality, or prejudice. In short, the gods seem to have the ability to see as *cosmopolitans*, as true citizens of the universe, to see through the apparent divisions and cultural accretions to the "nature" of things, to apprehend others truthfully and instantly, and to understand the undercurrents of human and divine existence from a point above, and not as mere participants caught in its many currents and tides.[31]

As discussed earlier, this divine vision is a tempting one: Tithonus especially but also Orion and Iasion fall prey to the attractions of the immortals and the temptations of transcendence, always at the dreadful price of death and outright destruction, however. If Odysseus does not know of this particular fate often awaiting mortals who seek more than their lot, he does seem able to resist Calypso's offer of immortality, mostly due to his own distaste for the repetitive emptiness of existence on Ogygia. If a year's infinite pleasure on Circe's island proves multifarious enough not to weary, seven years of similar titillation with Calypso is more than enough to alert Odysseus that an eternity of the same would represent less the ultimate reward than perpetual torment. Existence among humanity, if mortal and restricted in its vision, is also curiously fuller and more "real" than that bloodless universality offered by Calypso. Even Hermes senses as much as he lights on Calypso's island, lamenting that he did not wish to make the journey to the godforsaken (if not goddessforsaken) island, where

there is no city of men nearby, nor people
who offer choice hecatombs to the gods, and perform sacrifice.
(5.101–102)

Although life on Calypso's lonely island apparently represents the more obviously attractive option, having tasted the emptiness of divine existence, Odysseus reaffirms his longing to return "back to my house and see the day of my homecoming" (5.220).

Odysseus's decision remains remarkable, however, not only given the later revelation that he has descended to Hades—and hence knows the final horrors of mortal existence, the inescapability of death, and its attendant miseries in eternal lamentation—but also that he knows the overwhelming attractiveness of transcendence that he seems to reject in his refusal to accept divine immortality. For, prior to the offer of immortality, Odysseus has been tempted by the prospect of "cosmopolitan" vision in as pure a manner as ever described in human experience. A short time before he reaches Calypso's island in a shipwreck, he first sails by the island of the Sirens, who afford him the most severe temptation of his entire perilous journey. As Charles H. Taylor observes, "There is, indeed, only one occasion when he consciously wishes to yield to a temptation, even though he knows it would mean his destruction. Despite Circe's explicit warning of the mortal danger, he wishes to stop and hear the Sirens' song. Because he takes the precautions Circe has advised, he is unable to yield, but it is instructive that this one time he wishes he could."[32]

What is the content of this most irresistible temptation? Taylor stresses the first part of the Sirens' song, in which they promise to reveal "the great glory of the Achaeans." For Taylor, the crux of the temptation is a full realization of Odysseus's identity, which is what often comes under threat by temptations of unconsciousness, but which is in this instance a temptation offered to secure final knowledge of his own identity. This may be correct as far as it goes, but this reading wholly misses the second and, finally, more intriguing promise offered by the Sirens:

> for we know everything that the Argives and the Trojans
> did and suffered in wide Troy through the gods' despite.
> Over all the generous earth we know everything that happens.
> (12.189–191)

Not only, then, do the Sirens offer to confirm what Odysseus already knows, but they also hold forth the temptation of all the many things that he does not and cannot possibly know. Each person who passes by the Sirens' island and takes time to listen to their comprehensive song comes away "a wiser man" (*pleiona eidos*—12.188). What the Sirens essentially promise is to lift that veil of darkness that limits human vision, that imperfect vision that allows only partial or mistaken knowledge of those things we directly encounter. In the place of our fragile and incomplete knowledge, the Sirens promise Odysseus the sight of the gods, that vision of Zeus that in the *Iliad* is described as *pleiona eide*, an expansiveness of apprehension that the Sirens promise to those who listen as well (XIII.355).

For this expanded vision, Odysseus uniquely strains and submits to temptation. Yet we also know that the promise is in fact an illusion. The Sirens may indeed know all that passes on the bountiful earth and even may be able to disclose it to the passing sailor as he strives to reach their barren island; but we also know that in the course of that desperate effort, any man who tries to realize the Sirens' offer will meet a calamitous fate. Odysseus has tied himself to the mast in order to hear their song but to avoid the fate that awaits those mortals who pass by the Sirens without knowing the dangers accompanying their song. He singularly knows those dangers, since Circe has related:

> You will come first of all to the Sirens, who are enchanters
> of all mankind and whoever comes their way; and that man
> who unsuspecting approaches them, listens to the Sirens
> singing, has no prospect of coming home and delighting
> his wife and little children as they stand about him in greeting,
> but the Sirens by the melody of their singing enchant him.
> They sit in their meadow, but the beach before it is piled with boneheaps
> of men now rotted away, and the skins shrivel upon them.
> (12.39–46)

Odysseus, who is so often notable for his ability to hold himself back from temptations that divert him from *nostos*—those many offerings that would overcome the *algos* that seemingly separate humanity from a greater comprehension of the whole through either the loss of consciousness represented by the effects of Lotus or a form of hyperconsciousness offered by the Sirens—in the case of the Sirens shows how ultimately tempting, and devastating, the offer of "expanded vision" is to the human who craves knowledge of the whole. Of all the many challenges confronting Odysseus in his long journey home, not the vengeance of Poseidon, not the barbarism of Cyclops or the Laestrogonians, not the wiles of Circe or the immortality offered by Calypso, bring him to a moment of total succumbing as does the song of the Sirens.

Knowledge of all that passes on the bountiful earth appeals for its comprehensiveness. Similar to arguments in favor of cosmopolitanism, the knowledge of the whole attracts especially due to the promise of a fundamental knowledge, that vision of *phusis* that is otherwise only accorded to the gods. The Sirens offer to Odysseus an encompassing knowledge of what makes humanity, and perhaps all of existence, a singular whole. From our limited perspective, we tend to see only the many distinctions that culture and history accord to people separated by distance and time; the Sirens, on the other hand, have a global knowledge that comprehends diversity and allows a glimpse of underlying unity. What startles about Odysseus's response to this knowledge is how much this global knowledge undermines his actual sympathies to human beings. Odysseus exhibits a complete lack of awareness of those corpses described by Circe lying about the shore of the Sirens' island, "boneheaps of men now rotted away, their skin shrivel[led] upon them." At no point in *Odysseus*'s description of the actual passage of his ship past the island of the Sirens does he acknowledge that he had perceived the rotting bodies of similarly tempted humans: we know of them only from Odysseus's recitation of *Circe's* description, not from Odysseus's recollection of his moment before the Sirens. It is as if, in the midst of his own enchantment, entranced by the overwhelming attraction to the promise of universal knowledge, Odysseus is no longer able to see either the true effects of that temptation or even the mortality of his fellow humans, the fundamental similarity that is seemingly promised by the knowledge of the Sirens but that in fact lies before him unseen on the shore.

In some respects, Odysseus's total succumbing before the Sirens reflects deep ambivalence about homecoming (or remaining at home), the uncertainty of his devotion to justice, and the deep tension between the promise of transcendence and the possibilities of commitment. Seth Benardete has observed in damning terms that Odysseus's "greatest and deepest desire is not for home, but for knowledge. Odysseus can resist the enchanting speeches of Calypso, which offer him immortality, but he cannot resist the enchantment of omniscience, and he is willing to give up his life for the chance. Justice is not at the heart of his nature."[33] Odysseus's inability to apprehend the true commonality of humanity when confronted by the Sirens, which is exhibited both by his willingness to sacrifice his homecoming and by an absence of pity toward fellow humans who have fallen, seems to be the concomitant result of the very temptation toward an unachievable and misleading comprehensive knowledge. If Odysseus is able to resist the temptation of immortality offered by Calypso precisely *because* of his acknowledgment of a shared fate and underlying similarity with his fellow mortals—as indicated by his recognition of Penelope's limitations, especially her mortality, compared to Calypso's eternal splendor—then by contrast, in succumbing to the Sirens' appeal of *pleiona eidos* he forgets his mortality and the mortality of those around him, literally becoming unable to *see* the *actual* humans who have fallen before him in his vain effort to comprehend the totality of humanity.[34]

However, what is lost in Benardete's condemnation of Odysseus's abandonment of justice and of his utter forgetfulness of both his and others' needs and limitations is the fact that Odysseus is only able to survive this callous moment because he has *previously* ordered himself bound. This is the same character who, escaping Cyclops, seeking *kleos*, announced his name and taunted the more powerful because he had not, in Plato's words, been cured of "his love of honor." However, before the Sirens, he heeds Circe's warning to have himself bound, in effect reflecting a commitment to law, those external restraints that are necessary for limited and easily tempted mortals in the pursuit of justice. Thus, to anticipate his own weakness reflected in his respect for Circe's warning, Odysseus reflects what may be construed as a commitment to a higher form of justice, which, even while occurring amid his ultimate temptation, reflects his more fundamental commitments to homecoming and to the pursuit of justice on Ithaca.

Cosmopolitan vision is something of a Siren's song: irresistible to those who open their ears to it, but finally diverting in its true effects and damaging to the actual relations among existing people, ultimately threatening to undermine the possibility of achieved justice in communities of humans in the pursuit of imagined universal justice for the community of humanity. If the Sirens threaten to divert Odysseus finally and irrevocably from his homeward journey and to turn him entirely from the concerns of humanity—including concerns for justice—it is later, when confronted with the choice of Calypso, that Odysseus seems to reassert his humanity by reference to humans and to rededicate himself to the push homeward that will culminate in the reestablishment of justice in Ithaca.

The Temptations of Temptation

Of course, this sequential reading may render the answer too simply and far too definitively than the text will allow. After all, Odysseus does return and poignantly recaptures the erotic love that binds him to Penelope (23.300–309); he does vanquish the suitors, and—with the assistance of Athena and the final intervention of Zeus—he does put Ithaca on a just footing, setting the stage for the rule of Telemachus. We also know, however, that he must leave Ithaca in accordance with the prediction of Teiresias, that he must journey to a land whose people cannot distinguish between an oar and a winnowing fan, and that he will finally die "by agency" of—either at or from—the sea. Has Odysseus been cured of the temptations of the Sirens? Has he overcome the seemingly eternal longing for transcendence, to know "everything that happens"? Does not his own savagery in the treatment of the suitors, in the severe punishment of the serving girls, and the grisly execution of Melanthius contradict anything that might be said about his tenderness toward Telemachus, Eumaeus, Penelope, or Laertes (only after treating even his father with some unnecessary cruelty of deception)? Has Odysseus become fully capable of seeing the rotting corpses surrounding the feet of the Sirens, or, if forced to travel past their island again on subsequent journeys, would he overlook them again, diverted from human sympathies to see only the dream of knowledge?

Dante, like Rousseau, seemed to think that Odysseus is not wholly cured of his love of knowledge but continues his journey after his homecoming. Dante understood that the pure love of knowledge, the pursuit of "experience," represented a concomitant rejection of his commitments to people. As Ulysses himself relates from the flames in the *Inferno*,

Neither fondness for my son, nor
reverence for my aged father, nor the due love
which would have made Penelope glad, could
conquer in me the longing that I had to gain
experience of the world, and of human vice

and worth.
(Canto 26, 94–99)

At the foot of a mountain that likely ascends to "Paradiso" itself, Ulysses urges his men:

to this so brief vigil of our
senses that remains to us, choose not to deny
experience, following the sun, of the world
that has no people. Consider your origin: you
were not made to live as brutes, but to pursue
virtue and knowledge.
(Canto 26, 114–120)

This proves to be a call that leads to their final destruction as punishment for their hubris.[35]

A telling understanding of Odysseus's continued *algos*, his incurable "longing," despite even the achievement of *nostos*, is rendered in touching detail by the contemporary Greek poet C. P. Cavafy in the poem "Ithaka":

Hope the voyage is a long one.
May there be many a summer morning when,
with what pleasure, what joy,
you come into harbors seen for the first time;
may you stop at Phoenician trading stations
to buy fine things,
mother of pearl and coral, amber and ebony,
as many sensual perfumes as you can;
and may you visit many Egyptian cities
to gather stores of knowledge from their scholars.

Keep Ithaka always in your mind.
Arriving there is what you are destined for.
But do not hurry the journey at all.
Better if it lasts for years,
so you are old by the time you reach the island,
wealthy with all you have gained on the way,
not expecting Ithaka to make you rich.

Ithaka gave you the marvelous journey.
Without her you would not have set out.
She has nothing left to give you now.

And if you find her poor, Ithaka won't have fooled you.
Wise as you will have become, so full of experience,
you will have understood by then what these Ithakas mean.[36]

One wonders if Odysseus is content with his lot, whether he even comes to regret his decision—if not constantly, at least occasionally during times of ennui, when the demands of ruling become burdensome or the wrinkles adorning Penelope's and his own faces deepen and spread. The satirist Lucian, for one, thought that Odysseus must have come to regret his choice: indeed, in a fanciful letter written to Calypso, he imagined Odysseus lamenting his situation, "thoroughly sorry to have given up my life with you and the immortality which you offered me. Therefore, if I get a chance, I shall run and come to you."[37]

As the Sirens episode reminds us, humans may successfully resist the temptations of knowledge, the cosmopolitan gaze, the transcendent opportunity of divine sight; but the temptation nevertheless remains and, above all, it is a *temptation*, constant, irking, never fully overcome. There is something *desirable* about transcendence, a longing that even our *eros* for particular people and our commitments to justice cannot overcome. To deny the fact that such temptation exists—to deny that a real *choice* is presented to Odysseus or to humans generally—is to deny that most anciently described longing to see beyond the horizons that limit our sight, to place ourselves so firmly in the world of *limits* that we forget aspirations beyond what "these Ithacas really mean." It is quite ironic that the embrace of a world defined only by limits and the absence of longings beyond the apparent can breed pride in the recognition of our own humility.[38]

It is curious that the view that transcendence holds little fundamental appeal to humanity is to be found in the writing of Martha Nussbaum—not now in her recent discussions of cosmopolitanism, but in a profoundly sensitive reading of the *Odyssey* that, focusing on Calypso's offer of immortality and Odysseus's denial, deeply appreciates the dangers posed to existing human bonds by the temptations of the divine and transcendent. At some level her reading of the *Odyssey* in the essay entitled "Transcending Humanity" seems to exist at profound tension with her later writings on cosmopolitanism (although, I will suggest later, there is a continuity to be detected).[39] Nussbaum, who in her recent writings on cosmopolitanism poses the priority of *humankind* over particular *humans*, in focusing especially on Odysseus's decision to decline Calypso's offer of immortality finds instead a recommendation of homecoming opposed to the transcendence offered by Calypso. Faced with the choice—like that of Achilles—for a long, uneventful life with Calypso or a short, glorious one with Penelope, Odysseus apparently does not hesitate (unlike Achilles). Rather, according to Nussbaum, he chooses "the whole human package: mortal life, dangerous voyage, imperfect mortal aging woman. He [chooses], quite simply, what he is."[40]

One understands Nussbaum here: Odysseus confirms his position as human opposed to the divine option offered by Calypso. Yet, to a large extent, Nussbaum seems to understate the magnitude of that decision, indeed to deny an actual choice was made. Can one simply choose to be what one already is? To be what one is neglects both the option of what one is not—clearly attractive to Tithonus—and the thought that what one thinks one is does not fully comprehend the full range of longings of the human experience, the possibility that one can "be" more than what one "is." Such a reading neglects not only the evidence that Tithonus longs for immortality—hence, that transcendence "is," or can be, as much a part of the human experience as its conscious denial—but, tellingly, also the temptations to which Odysseus succumbs before the Sirens, which Nussbaum neglects to discuss. For Nussbaum, there would seem to have been no actual *choice*, because she cannot credit the longing for transcendence in the first place; she wholly ignores the very attractions of *becoming* a god.[41] If Odysseus can only choose that which he *is*, then he is presented no real choice at all. Such a view is finally *too* limited, too disregarding of widening horizons, and seems refuted by the descriptions of the frequent, if mostly unhappy, human temptation to transcend humanity.

Transcendence, then, is not as wholly strange or unavailable to Odysseus as Nussbaum suggests in her account of the *Odyssey* (just as it seems too strange and unavailable in her account of cosmopolitanism), at least not from the perspective of human craving. As the examples of both Tithonus (who tragically but wholeheartedly accepts immortality) and Odysseus (before the Sirens) reveal, transcendence may be wholly inappropriate for humans, at some essential level undermining what it means to be *human*; but paradoxically, at least one recognized feature of "humanity" in antiquity *is* the overwhelming but dangerous temptation to transcend our human estate. Part of being human means to long to be more than human, even if we stand to lose our humanity in the pursuit. Our natures as human are more divided than Nussbaum indicates in her analysis—one that quite rightly stresses the "otherness" of "external" transcendence, but that does not credit its attraction nonetheless. The choice that Odysseus makes on Ogygia in refusing Calypso's long-standing offer of immortality reveals a centrally important feature of the human brush with transcendence. Not only is such transcendence foreign to being human at some level, but in the struggle to ascertain which is more centrally human—our aspirations or our limitations—the choice for the latter in many ways deepens our commitments to *humans* in ways that a devotion to "humanity" or to the "divine" cannot. Curiously, the lack of recognition by Nussbaum of the attractions of divine transcendence while considering Odysseus's choice seems intimately related to her subsequent downgrading of commitments to particular *humans*, as opposed to the priority of "humanity," in her later writings on cosmopolitanism. Altogether absent in Nussbaum's own sympathetic treatment of Odysseus is the absence of doubt, of misgiving, of curiosity, of the sense that Odysseus—having heard the Sirens, descended to Hades, tasted the moly plant, slept with Calypso—will never be wholly content with the limits of the human condition, even if (*pace* Lucian) he continues to view his choice as correct.

Odysseus's choices, especially that one made on Calypso's island, do suggest that the encounter with transcendence can be limited, without denying its dangers and attractions. In the first instance, one can detect "limited transcendence" in Odysseus's own embrace of human infirmity—his devotion to Penelope and Ithaca—an infirmity that is underscored by the dangerousness of comprehensive knowledge or divine vision whenever humans encounter it. This limit is not automatically recognized: before the Sirens, Odysseus shows significantly less resistance to the dream of transcendence than he does with Circe or Calypso, who themselves offer a form of transcendence nearly irresistible to most mortals. Once human infirmity is embraced, however, a form of transcendence proves possible, but only on a limited basis. Transcendence is possible to imperfect humanity as a glimpse, not as a way of being. Thus, Odysseus does hear the song of the Sirens, however momentary in nature. He does remain with Circe for one year and with Calypso for seven. He does journey to the underworld and see there the fate of all humanity. His momentary contact with the divine and chthonic affords him glimpses of a comprehensive knowledge that is reserved for the gods but that is briefly perceptible to those who are open to its existence yet wary of its overarching temptations. In this sense, Odysseus asserts human aspiration for comprehensive knowledge even as he denies its full possibility, siding with "humanity"—in Nussbaum's account—without denying the attractions of the divine.

The second manner in which transcendence is limited relies on this first. An embrace of human limits suggests that the encounter with transcendence, if successfully resisted at some level, deepens human commitments to partiality, namely to the places from which we come, the people with whom we regularly concert. Whereas Nussbaum sees Odysseus's choice as exhibiting only his commitment to "humanity," it is in fact more the case that Odysseus denies the divine estate because of *humans*. Nussbaum's view disregards Hannah Arendt's observation that "men, not Man, live on the earth and inhabit the world."[42] The limitation that this observation represents, Homer suggests, results for two reasons. First, knowing the final inaccessibility of transcendence, we view more realistically the limitations placed on our senses and the finite extent to which we can extend the realm of our senses. The admission of our limitations, which is often only possible having made contact with transcendence or even its possibility—an encounter that reveals the true extent of our limitations—can have the unexpected effect *not* of making us crave for the inaccessible transcendent, but rather of making us cast our lot more firmly with those who surround us, those with whom we can reasonably pursue justice in the more limited fashion possible for humanity. Second, inasmuch as the encounter with transcendence reveals our similarities most profoundly not from a global perspective, but from an awareness of our shared limitations, especially our fragile mortality, our sense of commonality with other humans is correspondingly deepened, allowing us to see likeness even where the evidence of our senses suggests only differences.

The effect of Odysseus's travels is not a deepening of Odysseus's dedication to his fellow citizens of the world, as might be predicted by Gitlin or Hollinger or Nussbaum, but rather quite the opposite: in recognizing his own limitations, he comes to see a likeness especially to those he would otherwise not usually see, the people before his eyes who most desperately need a person of Odysseus's talents and wiles to help them in their pursuit of justice in Ithaca. Acknowledging the limits of what one can rightly perceive has the concomitant effect of comprehending those with whom one is connected through *eros*, the people closest to one's senses and self—not only one's family, but also fellow citizens and even those whose own prospects are most limited. Much of the tale of Odysseus's encounters on his return to Ithaca is infused with his own sense of human limitations, of the ever-present possibility that even the greatest man can be brought down easily and swiftly by a whim of the gods or fate.[43] Odysseus is not alone in this understanding: it is perhaps a lesson that has been deepened by his encounters during his homecoming, but it is not one that is only available to those who are able to become true cosmopolitans, those who see "many cities" and who learn of "many minds" (1.3). Even the humblest of humans—perhaps especially the humblest—can encounter not only the fragility of human existence, but also the possibility of something greater, and hence yearn too for a realization of justice. This yearning is most conspicuously found at the conclusion of the *Odyssey* in the encounter with the simple swineherd, Eumaeus.

Eumaeus is obviously a special character for Homer: he is, among the many characters who populate the *Iliad* and the *Odyssey*, the only character whom Homer refers to directly as "you," some fifteen times all told. He is thus, in some senses, the person for whom the *Odyssey* is written, paradigmatic of an ideal audience. It is a poem intended for the ordinary people as this unique use of "you" reveals, people who work at times in seemingly futile situations and who seek order and decency from the universe around them. Notwithstanding his ordinary status in the epic, Eumaeus is also remarkable for his apparent similarity to Odysseus. When Odysseus, disguised as a beggar, first encounters Eumaeus, Odysseus weaves a fable (one he will tell some five times to various people, always with some differences) in which he claims to have been born a wealthy man's son who has fallen on bad times, even at one point almost being sold into slavery (14.192–359). We discover shortly thereafter that Eumaeus is truly the person Odysseus claims to be: born the son of a king, abducted from his home as a child by a duplicitous servant, and at a tender age sold into bondage to Odysseus's father Laertes—Eumaeus is a highborn man brought low by fate and fortune. Odysseus, through his disguise and by means of his lie, becomes indistinguishable from Eumaeus in *fact*. The questions this peculiar resemblance begs us to consider are: what is the reality of their similarities, and what is mere appearance? Knowing as we do that Odysseus is in fact highborn posing as one lowborn and that Eumaeus at least at the outset appears solely as lowborn but is, in fact, equally highborn, we are forced to ask whether appearances or even one's apparent status can tell us about a person's nobility or inherent virtues. The similarities of the highest and the lowest bring us closer to an understanding of a shared human condition.

Odysseus responds to this tale of woe in a revealing manner, bemoaning the sad fate of Eumaeus, but being thankful that Eumaeus has now found a good home, unlike the fate that Odysseus supposedly suffers:

> But beside the sorrow Zeus has placed some good for you, seeing
> that after much suffering you came into the house of a kindly
> man, who, as he ought to do, provides you with victuals
> and drink, and the life you lead is a good one. But I come to you
> only after much wandering in the cities of people.
> (15.488–492)

Odysseus views his own long journey as a curse compared to Eumaeus's seemingly unenviable status as a bondsman and as servant to the suitors' endless appetites. To be a wanderer adrift in the world is worse than the good life that Eumaeus apparently leads; and but for the absence of Odysseus—who ruled once with justice, according to Eumaeus—one thinks Eumaeus might well agree with that assessment, notwithstanding his misfortune.

Eumaeus's understanding of the situation of humanity relative to the gods is similar to that of Odysseus's. Eumaeus often expresses the fragility of the human condition, the impotence of people in the face of fate, and the inscrutable plans of the gods. Yet that realization does not give over to resignation or rage, but rather to an acceptance of the obligations that this understanding of the human condition leads one to recognize between one's fellows who are equally limited and frail. As Eumaeus says to the "beggar" Odysseus during their first encounter,

> Stranger, I have no right to deny the stranger, not even
> if one came to me who was meaner than you. All vagabonds
> and strangers are under Zeus, and the gift is a light and dear one
> that comes from us, for that is the way of us who are servants and forever filled
> with fear when they come under the power of masters
> who are new.
> (14.56–61)

Eumaeus understands his condition as one that is potentially shared by any human informed by the fear of the suddenness that any situation can change for the worse. Further, Eumaeus recognizes the protection that Zeus accords to all humans, even the most desperate, despite—or perhaps because of—Eumaeus's vast distance from the concerns of the gods, in contrast to the divine status of Poseidon's son, Polyphemus, who views with contempt and cruelty the claims of guest-strangers.

Eumaeus's understanding of how his own position in the world connects him to others is clearly not a "class" condition any more than it is a result of one's relative expectations in the world. There is more in common between the beggar Iros and the gentleman suitor Eurymachos and more similarity between Odysseus and Eumaeus than one might expect if class and status were determinative of one's worldview. One might suppose that the exposure to the fragility of the human situation makes Eumaeus and Iros more kindred; but although the beggar Iros knows the deep misfortune to which humanity is subject, he nevertheless treats the disguised Odysseus with contempt and humiliation. Homer does not tell us why some people interpret their situation differently, how some people embrace the human limits that connect us to those around us and impel us toward the pursuit of justice and others turn bitter and ruthless toward others, especially the less fortunate. It seems, however, to be an appreciation of the middle position of humanity—the condition of simultaneously longing for more than one can have and committing to what one does have—that marks the dispositions of an Odysseus and a Eumaeus, making them at once appreciative of the limits of human longing yet aware of the possibilities for human decencies and even justice among a community of kindred.

The Final Limit

The acceptance of death is the acceptance of utmost limits. Humanity pushes at most other limits that nature imposes, even apparently overcoming some from time to time; but as Sophocles acknowledges in the "Ode to Man" in *Antigone*, "Only death, from death alone [man] will find no rescue."[44] Of course, it makes no difference whether we accept our deaths or not: our demise is inevitable. What the attitude of acceptance entails, however, is a whole range of acceptance of limitations: negatively stated, limitations to hubris and overweening ambition; more positively, those limitations that make us aware of our fundamental equality to other humans who also face death, that focus our attention on what can be done in concert with others, and that cause us to cherish the living as we make our inevitable journey toward death.

To accept death is to repeat Odysseus's contemplation of Calypso's offer of immortality as he confronted it: seriously, poignantly, perhaps desirously, but finally deciding against its temptations. It is most paradoxical that, as the reason for Odysseus's choice of death reveals, namely *nostos*, the embrace of our mortality does not separate us from others—as assuredly our actual entombment will—but, in life, deepens our affections and provokes shared remembrance and the desire to enshrine memory in story and song.[45] Acceptance of death links generations, affords us a longer term view of life's continuities, helps us to see beyond our momentary desires (revealing their stark insignificance), and yet, at the same time, makes us realize that our mortal condition is the fundamental condition that we share with all others, hence confirming the underlying equality of what our human condition entails.

Death is portrayed as nothing if not horrific in the *Odyssey*. In the *Nekyia* (the descent to Hades in Book 11), Odysseus is portrayed standing above a pit of steaming sheep's blood with sword drawn to fend off the innumerable spirits who would drink the vile brew. It is as if the spirits are drawn to corporeal fluids in order to assuage their inability to embrace one another. Death separates, turns humanity insubstantial, makes us as solitary and alone as individuals described in any State of Nature scenario. Nevertheless, in Odysseus's confrontation with the dead, Homer shows how an encounter with mortality as harrowing as Odysseus's actually results in a deepening of his commitments not only to those he loves, but also to those who would seem otherwise insignificant and unworthy of one's attention or friendship.[46] This dynamic is shown with particular poignancy in a series of episodes somewhat startling for its unusualness: the death of Elpenor that shortly precedes Odysseus's journey to the underworld, his presence as the first soul that Odysseus encounters while in Hades, and the burial of his body on Odysseus's return to the land of the living (10.552–560; 11.51–83; 12.9–15).

Elpenor is an insignificant and wholly forgettable figure in the epic, previously one of the nameless figures who works on Odysseus's boat anonymously rowing as he silently gazes homeward. Yet, on the day that Odysseus and his companions are to descend to Hades, Elpenor emerges from his anonymity when, following an evening of drunkenness, he awakens on the roof of Circe's palace and, descending the ladder, loses his balance, striking the ground "so that his neck bone / was broken out of its sockets, and his soul went down to Hades" (10.559–560).[47] Only a few of Odysseus's companions are named at any point, usually due to their excellence (e.g., Polites, "the leader of men, who was best and dearest to me of my friends" [10.224]) or for the purpose of making competing claims to Odysseus's claims to rule (e.g., Eurylochos's insistence that they eat the kine of Helios [12.279–293]). Elpenor, by contrast, is notable for his lack of notability: he is, Odysseus relates, "the youngest man, not terribly powerful in fighting or sound in his thoughts" (10.552–553). Elpenor's death, while tragic, does little to advance the story; his presence in Hades, narratively speaking, merely diverts the reader from the true purpose of the journey, which is Odysseus's interview with Teiresias. One is tempted to agree with the "analytic" interpretation of Denys Page, who views the presence of Elpenor as a convenient bridge between the worlds of life and death and as a figure who provides a transition between the bulk of the *Odyssey* and what Page takes to be the interpolation of the *Nekyia*, but by himself an uninteresting and discardable character.[48]

However, this dismissive interpretation altogether misses the poignancy of the meeting between Odysseus and Elpenor and of the exchange there that foreshadows Odysseus's choice for mortality as confirmation of his commitments to family and polity. Odysseus has descended without realizing that Elpenor has died: in keeping with Elpenor's insignificant status, his absence goes wholly unnoticed. As the most recent soul to descend to Hades—and as an unburied soul—Elpenor stands closest to the entrance of Hades and is the first soul that Odysseus encounters. Seeing him, realizing he has died, Odysseus addresses him in anguished tones:

> I broke into tears at the sight of him, and my heart pitied him,
> and so I spoke aloud to him and addressed him in winged words:
> "Elpenor, how did you come here beneath the fog and the darkness?
> You have come faster on foot than I could in my black ship."
> (11.55–58)

In Odysseus's recognition of the swiftness of Elpenor's journey is an implicit comparison of the length of time it has already required and will yet take to return to Ithaca and the comparable brevity of our final journey to our true "homeland." Odysseus's pity for Elpenor implies a sadness about the finality of that journey, not only for the previously nameless but also for himself and all mortals.

Elpenor responds by asking Odysseus to give his body rightful burial. Yet he extracts this promise not only by reminding him of the traditional curse that will result should his body be left exposed (a curse that the action of *Antigone* aptly reveals), but also by reminding Odysseus of his own obligations to others, to those who bore him, to those he has chosen to love, and to those he will leave behind:

> But now I pray you, by those you have yet to see, who are not here,
> by your wife, and by your father, who reared you when you were little,
> and by Telemachus whom you have left alone in your palace;
> for I know that after you leave this place and the house of Hades
> you will put back with your well-made ship to the island, Aiaia;
> there at that time, my lord, I ask that you remember me,
> and do not go and leave me behind unwept, unburied,

when you leave, for fear I might become the god's curse on you;
but burn me there with all my armor that belongs to me,
and heap up a grave mound beside the beach of the gray sea,
for an unhappy man, so that those to come will know of me.
(11.66–78)

By naming Odysseus's three most-beloved living relatives, Elpenor reminds Odysseus of his duties to the living and by extension to those who die, even one as insignificant as he.

The invocation of Odysseus's father in order to provoke pity and to remind Odysseus of his obligation even to one as lowly as Elpenor is particularly striking, given its similarity to Priam's invocation of Achilles' father Peleus as he pleads with Achilles—the man who killed and maimed his son—for the body of Hector that he might give him a rightful burial: "Achilles like the gods [*theois epieikel' Akhilleu*], remember your father, one who / is of years like mine, and on the door-sill of sorrowful old age."[49] The invocation of his father's own infirmity and approaching death and by extension of Achilles' own mortal lot provokes profound and newly discovered pity in Achilles:

So [Priam] spoke, and stirred in the other a passion for grieving
for his own father. He took the old man's hand and pushed him
gently away, and the two remembered, as Priam sat huddled
at the feet of Achilles and wept now for manslaughtering Hektor
and Achilles wept now for his own father, now again for Patroclus.
(XXIV.508–512)

In each case, the pity invoked by remembrance of a dying generation, and a reminder of our own inevitable journey, succeeds in bringing seemingly divided people together: Achilles is moved to hold Priam's hand, and, in an eerily similar scene, Odysseus—who is not recorded as having spoken to Elpenor during his life—is similarly moved to share remembrance and fleeting contact with Elpenor now that he has died:

So we two stayed there exchanging our sad words, I on
one side holding my sword over the blood, while opposite
me the phantom of my companion talked long with me.
(11.81–83)

Reminding Odysseus of the ones that are yet "unseen," those whom he cherishes, Elpenor, like Priam, recalls the deep commitments that motivate Odysseus, reminding us, too, of the links that our own mortality forges to the deaths of those we love, and extends that consideration beyond our own fears to a concern for that fate we share with even the least noticed, the most anonymous, the previously unnamed. Elpenor's request that an oar be raised over his burial mound foreshadows the task that Teiresias will shortly reveal to Odysseus, that he must carry an oar far inland, to a place where an implement of the sea will be mistaken for a fan. If the oar in this latter instance will become, in the words of Seth Benardete, a reminder that "there is a god who presides over something you cannot see," in the case of Elpenor, the oar is to remind us that here lies a human who was barely seen in life but whose life nevertheless mattered and whom other men mourned and remembered.[50] The poet is careful that we know that Elpenor is not forgotten when Odysseus and his crew return from Hades. Immediately on the morning following their return from Hades, Elpenor is buried by the crew that remains:

> Then we cut logs, and where the extreme of the foreland jutted
> out, we buried him, sorrowful, shedding warm tears for him.
> But when the dead man had burned and the dead man's armor, piling
> the grave mound and pulling the gravestone to stand above it,
> we planted the well-shaped oar in the very top of the grave mound.
> (12.11–15)

The poet notes that the burial mound lies on a bit of land that juts out into the water, so that any passing ship may see there the grave site of a man who was not forgotten and know that others mourned his passing. The presence of Elpenor's honored grave site forms a profound contrast to the unburied and unseen bodies of those who lay scattered around the island of the Sirens. If the invocation of loved ones reminds us more extensively of our commitments to other humans and recalls us to the limits of our human estate, Odysseus's inability to "see" the rotting bodies beneath the Sirens demonstrates the dangers of transcendence, even acknowledging its ultimate attraction.[51]

Accepting death shows our awareness of limits, an acknowledgment of our feebleness, and our participation in the continuities of nature, no matter what alienation our technology can buy. To resist death, to attempt to overcome that final and inevitable human limitation, is to pursue the mastery of nature to its extreme but unavoidable conclusion. The *Odyssey* shows us how old this most elusive and subversive dream is and how the gods eventually exact their punishment.

The *Odyssey* also shows that death is indeed to be feared: the spirits of the underworld cannot be touched by Odysseus; even their words are strange and incomprehensible. As Homer understood death, it meant the freezing of all one's attributes and characteristics at the moment of death: thus Achilles remains bitter, Agamemnon bewildered, Ajax furious. Death, it seems, can only be overcome in life through being *polutropos*, many-sided, such that death's frozen quality can be thawed by variegated brilliance. Odysseus does not seek immortality through mastery, or *hubris*, but rather as a human, fully and magnanimously many-sided. Perhaps the key to comprehending Odysseus's quality of *polutropos* is that, having embraced death, he seeks to deny it its final victory. Through poetry and politics and home, he stakes his claim to life.

This aspect is wholly overlooked by Horkheimer and Adorno, who find little with which to sympathize in the *Odyssey*. Not comprehending the import of Odysseus's refusal of Calypso's offer of immortality, they can only portray a caricature of the besotted hero scrambling to increase his real estate holdings and gold reserves. For Horkheimer and Adorno, there is not, nor can there be, nobility in life: after Auschwitz, poetry is dead, philosophy is failed, and the only recourse is the negative dialectic of one's own solipsistic heart. Rousseau affords us a more positive vision of the *Odyssey*'s political potential, but only in order to undermine the continuity of politics, and even the family and love. Rather than finding a story that seemingly tells of homecoming, Rousseau finds an example by which to teach his pupil how to avoid the obligations and perhaps complications that adhere to human relations.

Of the several versions of Odysseus that have been examined—Odysseus the proto-capitalist acquirer, Odysseus the "Emilian" wanderer, Odysseus who is alternatively the cosmopolitan and the patriot—in respect to understanding Homer's teachings about limits and aspirations, it must be concluded that Plato was among the most sensitive interpreters of the *Odyssey*. Despite his accusations against poetry, Plato concludes by portraying Odysseus as possessing a philosophic understanding, as one who accepts his death, who redescends to the Cave having first witnessed the wonders of the world and those beyond the world, and only after being cured of his "love of honor." Plato's understanding of the relation of philosophy and poetry finally best captures the idea of limited transcendence, one that holds forth the possibility of transcending the limits of the cave, but in acknowledging that possibility nevertheless recognizes that the culmination of such a dream is also nightmarish.[52] By accepting human limits we not only commit to improving conditions within the cave, but also acknowledge that there is no truly human life outside the cave. Nevertheless, Plato suggests in his many images of ascent that we should continue to glance upward at the entrance, trying to glimpse in rare moments the light above or to hear the echoes of a song about knowledge and even to entertain the possibility of divinity, however unlikely its fulfillment by the Sirens. Like Odysseus, our journey may not end in Ithaca, but Ithaca remains the goal of those who would remain human.

Notes

1. My teacher Wilson Carey McWilliams has written, "The willingness to die is an ultimate guarantee of moral standards, of purposes, and of the self; it establishes control over the tendency of the passions to seek survival at all costs, not excluding the destruction of the ego, the identity, of man" (McWilliams, *The Idea of Fraternity in America* [Berkeley: University of California Press, 1973], 43). By contrast, Martha Nussbaum—whose view of "cosmopolitanism" will be contrasted with the more limited perspective of Odysseus—asks and answers the following question: "Who, given the chance to make a spouse or child or parent or friend immortal, would not take it? (I would grab it hungrily, I confess at the outset)" (Nussbaum, "Transcending Humanity," in *Love's Knowledge: Essays on Philosophy and Literature* [Oxford, U.K.: Oxford University Press, 1990], 368).

2. The notion of "limited transcendence" is a variation of and draws on Drew A. Hyland's understanding of Platonic philosophy as one of "finite transcendence" (Hyland, *Finitude and Transcendence in the Platonic Dialogues* [Albany, NY: SUNY Press, 1995]).

3. Julien Benda, *The Betrayal of the Intellectuals*, trans. Richard Aldington (Boston: Beacon, 1955), 60.

4. Todd Gitlin, *Twilight of Common Dreams: Why America Is Wracked by Culture Wars* (New York: Metropolitan Books, 1995), 84, 86.

5. Gitlin, *Twilight of Common Dreams*, 86. See also Benjamin R. Barber, *Jihad v. McWorld* (New York: Times Books, 1995), and Richard Falk's essay "Revisioning Cosmopolitanism" (in *For Love of Country: Debating the Limits of Patriotism*, by Martha C. Nussbaum, ed. Joshua Cohen [Boston: Beacon, 1996]) for an exploration of the false cosmopolitanism of the market.

6. Gitlin, *Twilight of Common Dreams*, 209.

7. David A. Hollinger, *Postethnic America* (New York: Basic Books, 1995), 84.

8. Hollinger, *Postethnic America*, 85.

9. On the extent to which Enlightenment authors, ranging from the *philosophes* to Benjamin Franklin, relied on earlier Stoic expressions of cosmopolitanism, see Thomas J. Schlereth's *The Cosmopolitan Ideal in Enlightenment Thought* (South Bend, IN: University of Notre Dame Press, 1977), xvii–xxv.

10. Martha C. Nussbaum, "Patriotism and Cosmopolitanism," *Boston Review* 19, no. 5 (October/November 1994): 4; Nussbaum, *The Fragility of Goodness: Luck and Ethics in Greek Tragedy and Philosophy* (Cambridge, U.K.: Cambridge University Press, 1986), 6; Nussbaum, *Cultivating Humanity* (Cambridge, MA: Harvard University Press, 1997), 52.

11. Nussbaum, *Cultivating Humanity*, 52.

12. Martha C. Nussbaum, "Patriotism and Cosmopolitanism," in *For Love of Country: Debating the Limits of Patriotism*, ed. Joshua Cohen (Boston: Beacon, 1996), 7.

13. Martha C. Nussbaum, "Reply," in *For Love of Country: Debating the Limits of Patriotism*, ed. Joshua Cohen (Boston: Beacon, 1996), 151, n. 12. Perhaps here Nussbaum is thinking of potential objections by thinkers such as Peter Singer, who forwards a definition of all sentient creatures, including animals, as "persons" in his controversial book *Practical Ethics* (Cambridge, U.K.: Cambridge University Press, 1979).

14. Nussbaum, *For Love of Country*, 9.

15. Nussbaum, *Cultivating Humanity*, 60. She writes, "Stoic texts show repeatedly how easy it is for local or national identities and their associated hatreds to be manipulated." That is, all local affiliations *necessarily* and *unavoidably* give rise to "associated hatreds,"

which can only be overcome by an appeal to universal reason that transcends such emotional attachments.

16. See, e.g., Nussbaum, *For Love of Country*, 13; *Cultivating Humanity*, 59, 61.

17. Nussbaum, *Cultivating Humanity*, 58–59; *For Love of Country*, 9–10.

18. Nussbaum, *For Love of Country*, 7.

19. Nussbaum acknowledges this form of liberalism to be more Kantian—and perhaps Rawlsian—than the classic liberalism of Hobbes or Locke, which assume a fundamental human viciousness, albeit also distrusting the motives of governments.

20. Nussbaum, *Cultivating Humanity*, 59, 60–61. For a critique of this view, see McWilliams, *The Idea of Fraternity in America*, 95–111.

21. John Dewey is a good example of this belief in the dual benefits of science for both material and political ends, among many others. See my essay "Havel, Rorty, and the Democratic Faith of John Dewey," *Social Research* 66 (Summer 1999): 577–609.

22. In addition to Nussbaum's own recommendations for a cosmopolitan education (*Cultivating Humanity*, chap. 2), see D'Alembert's famous "Preface" to Diderot's *Encyclopedia: Selections by Diderot, D'Alembert, and a Society of Men of Letters* (trans. Nelly S. Hoyt and Thomas Cassirer [Indianapolis, IN: Bobbs-Merrill, 1965]) as well as Rousseau's *Emile, or On Education* (trans. Allan Bloom [New York: Basic, 1979]), in which a child is to be educated as a "man," not as a "citizen." On all of these features of cosmopolitanism as pursued during the Enlightenment, consult more generally Schlereth, *The Cosmopolitan Ideal in Enlightenment Thought*.

23. Most of the mentioned replies appeared in the volume of Nussbaum's *For Love of Country*. The response of Harvey Mansfield, "Foolish Cosmopolitanism," as well as Anne Norton's essay "Cosmopolitan Seductions," appeared only in the original *Boston Review* debate. *Boston Review* 19 (October/November, 1994), 10, 11.

24. The word *nostalgia* is a combination of *nostos*, meaning "return" or "homecoming," and *algia* (from *algos*), meaning "grief or longing, a feeling of separation, the sense of pain and loss from something lacking."

25. For a spirited defense of patriotism against those who confuse it with nationalism, see Maurizio Viroli, *For Love of Country: An Essay on Patriotism and Nationalism* (Oxford, U.K.: Oxford University Press, 1995).

26. John H. Schaar, "The Case for Patriotism," in *American Review*, vol. 17 (New York: Bantam, 1973), 63.

27. Robert Pinsky, "Eros against Esperanto," in *For Love of Country*, ed. Joshua Cohen (Boston: Beacon, 1996), 86.

28. Nussbaum, *Cultivating Humanity*, 68.

29. On the relationship of these assorted pleasures to the threats to Odysseus's consciousness and finally return to the realm of the human, see Charles H. Taylor's fine article, "The Obstacles to Odysseus's Return: Identity and Consciousness in *The Odyssey*," (*The Yale Review* 50 [1960–1961]: 569–80).

30. See 5.77–80 describing Calypso's instantaneous recognition of Hermes and 5.97–98, in which Hermes acknowledges that because he is questioned by a goddess, he must speak truthfully. Of course, the gods can be diverted if they are not attentive and can on occasion even hide their identities from one another; but to accomplish this latter obfuscation requires extraordinary devices, such as the cap of invisibility donned by Athena and the golden cloud sheltering Zeus and Hera described in the *Iliad* (V. 845; XIV. 344–345).

31. As described in chapter 1 above, Jenny Strauss Clay's discussion of the differences between mortal and divine apprehension seems to me to be authoritative. See Clay, *The Wrath of Athena* (Princeton, NJ: Princeton University Press, 1983), chaps. 1 and 3.

32. Taylor, "The Obstacles to Odysseus's Return," 573.

33. Seth Benardete, *The Bow and the Lyre* (Lanham, MD: Rowman & Littlefield, 1997), 99.

34. Fyodor Dostoevsky notes this phenomenon in *The Brothers Karamazov* (trans. Richard Pevear and Larissa Volokhonsky [New York: Knopf, 1992]) when Ivan observes that the more one loves humanity, the less one cares for people in near proximity (part 2, chap. 4: "Rebellion"). Gilbert and Sullivan in a lighter vein capture this paradox in a verse from the *Gondoliers*: "When everyone's someone, then no one's anybody."

35. Dante Alighiere, "Inferno," in *The Divine Comedy*, vol. 1, trans. Charles Singleton (Princeton, NJ: Princeton University Press, 1970).

36. C. P. Cavafy, "Ithaka," in *Collected Poems*, rev. ed., ed. George Savidis, trans. Edmund Keeley and Philip Sherrard (Princeton, NJ: Princeton University Press, 1992), 36–37.

37. Lucian, "A True Story II," trans. A. M. Harmon, in *Lucian*, vol. 1 (Cambridge, MA: Harvard University, Loeb Classical Library), 341. In some regards, Lucian's dismissal of Odysseus's choice resembles Homer's treatment of Achilles' choice in the *Iliad* by revealing his regrets during the confrontation in the *Odyssey* between Odysseus and Achilles in the underworld (11.465–540). What each of these instances suggests is that regret may be built into the most resolute decision of this kind, even if we know that the choice we made is likely the correct one.

38. This paradox is wonderfully captured by Benjamin Franklin, who, while trying to practice each virtue of a list he created, discovered that in the process of practicing humility he noticed that "no one of our natural passions is so hard to subdue as *Pride*. Disguise it, struggle with it, beat it down, stifle it, mortify it as much as one pleases, it is still alive, and will every now and then peep out and show itself. . . . For even if I could conceive that I had compleately overcome it, I should probably be proud of my Humility" (Franklin, *Autobiography*, in *Writings* [New York: Library of America, 1987]: 1393–94).

39. "Transcending Humanity," 365–91. The essay was originally written in response to Charles Taylor's review (*Canadian Journal of Philosophy* 18 [1988]: 805–14) of Nussbaum's *The Fragility of Goodness*.

40. Nussbaum, "Transcending Humanity," 366.

41. Nussbaum, "Transcending Humanity," 376.

42. Hannah Arendt, *The Human Condition* (Garden City, NY: Doubleday, 1959), 9. Christopher Lasch makes a similar point when he writes, "We love particular men and women, not humanity in general" (*The True and Only Heaven* [New York: Norton, 1991], 36).

43. Perhaps no other passage captures this better than the one in which Odysseus warns the beggar Iros of the fragility of human life:

> Of all creatures that breathe and walk on the earth there is nothing
> more helpless than a man is, of all that the earth fosters;
> for he thinks that he will never suffer misfortune in future
> days, while the gods grant him courage, and his knees have spring
> in them. But when the blessed gods bring sad days upon him,
> against his will he must suffer it with enduring spirit.
> For the mind in men upon earth goes according to the fortunes

the Father of Gods and Men, day by day, bestows upon them. (18.130–137)

44. Sophocles, *Antigone*, in *The Three Theban Plays*, trans. Robert Fagles (New York: Penguin, 1984), 77.

45. The idea of shared remembrance, of course, is drawn from Hannah Arendt's discussion of death and remembrance in *The Human Condition*.

> The organization of the *polis* . . . is a kind of organized remembrance. It assures the mortal actor that his passing existence and fleeting greatness will never lack the reality that comes from being seen, being heard, and, generally, appearing before an audience of fellow men, who outside the *polis* could attend only the short duration of the performance and therefore needed Homer and "others of his craft" in order to be presented to those who were not there. (176–77)

46. John E. Seery, in a probing and very funny book about death, suggests how such visits to the underworld serve to reinforce our connections to others: "Underworldly accounts have been particularly good at providing a sense of linkage between past and present, for recollecting in the land of the dead the memories of lost lovers, neglected parents, and vanquished enemies" (*Political Theory for Mortals* [Ithaca, NY: Cornell University Press, 1996], 34).

47. Seth Benardete notes that Elpenor climbed to the roof in the first place in search of cool air (*psuckhos*), but in the process loses his soul (*psuche*) (*The Bow and the Lyre*, 91).

48. Denys Page writes, "Aimless anecdotes about insignificant persons are not at all characteristic of the *Odyssey*." Page finds the only justification for the story is that "it forms a link between the story of Circe and the story of the Visit to Hades," and he suggests furthermore that "this link too was subsequently forged in order to connect two separate narratives"—between the *Odyssey* and the interpolated *Nekyia* (Page, *The Homeric Odyssey* [Oxford, U.K.: Clarendon Press, 1955], 44).

49. See also my discussion in chapter 1 of the several instances in which Achilles' mortal father is invoked in order to remind him of his mortal condition and hence his connections to other people. Because Achilles is here explicitly described as "like the gods," Priam here seeks also to remind him of his own mortal origins as well.

50. Benardete, *The Bow and the Lyre*, 93.

51. Elpenor is remembered in another significant way as well: by including him in the story of his journey to the Phaiacians (Odysseus is telling his own story here), which is "preserved" artistically by the epic poet, Elpenor is remembered every time the epic poem is subsequently told or read. Indeed, Elpenor has found a form of immortality other than remembrance itself, reappearing often in the pages of poetry and literature. See Nasos Vaghenàs, "Elpenore: l'anti-Ulisse nella litteratura moderna," in *Ulisse: archaeologia dell'uomo moderno*, ed. Pietro Boitani and Richard Ambrosini (Rome, Italy: Bulzioni Editore, 1988).

52. Similarly, Gerald M. Mara writes of Plato: "In the language of the image of the cave, . . . [Plato] reminds us that a complete, permanent ascent to the sunlight is impossible, while [also warning] us against confusing the cave with everything that is important" (Mara, *Socrates' Discursive Democracy: Logos and Ergon in Platonic Political Philosophy* [Albany, NY: SUNY Press, 1997], 241).

APPENDIX

~

Illustrations

All captions are from Rousseau, "Explanation of the Illustrations," *Emile*, trans. Allan Bloom (New York: Basic Books, 1979), 36.

Figure 1 *Emile*: "The illustration, which relates to the first book and serves as frontispiece to the work represents Thetis plunging her son in the Styx to make him invulnerable."

Figure 2 *Emile*: "The illustration at the beginning of the second book represents Chiron training the young Achilles in running."

Figure 3 *Emile*: "The illustration at the beginning of the third book and the second volume represents Hermes engraving the elements of the sciences on the columns."

Figure 4 *Emile*: "The illustration, which belongs to the fourth book and is at the beginning of the third volume, represents Orpheus teaching men the worship of the gods."

Figure 5 *Emile*: "The illustration at the beginning of the fifth book and the fourth volume represents Circe giving herself to Ulysses, whom she was not able to transform."

Figure 6 Vico's *New Science*: Frontispiece.

Bibliography

◡

Adkins, Arthur W. H. *Merit and Responsibility: A Study in Greek Values*. Chicago: University of Chicago Press, 1960.

Adorno, Theodor W. *Gesammelte Schriften*. Edited by Ralf Tiedemann. 23 vols. Frankfurt am Main, Germany: Suhrkamp, 1972.

———. *Minima Moralia*. Translated by E. F. N. Jephcott. London: NLB, 1951.

———. *Negative Dialectics*. Translated by E. B. Ashton. New York: Seabury, 1973.

———. *Prismen: Kulturkritik und Gesellschaft*. Frankfurt am Main, Germany: Suhrkamp, 1955.

Alighieri, Dante. *The Divine Comedy*. Translated by Charles S. Singleton. Princeton, NJ: Princeton University Press, 1970.

Amory, Anne. *Homeric Studies*. Yale Classical Studies, vol. 20. New Haven, CT: Yale University Press, 1966.

Andrew, Edward. "Descent to the Cave." *The Review of Politics* 45 (1983): 510–35.

Annas, Julia. *An Introduction to Plato's* Republic. Oxford, U.K.: Oxford University Press, 1981.

Arendt, Hannah. *Between Past and Future*. New York: Viking, 1968.

———. *The Human Condition*. Chicago: University of Chicago Press, 1958.

Aristotle. *Nicomachean Ethics*. Translated by H. Rackham. Loeb Classical Library. Cambridge, MA: Harvard University Press, 1926.

———. *The Politics*. Translated by Carnes Lord. Chicago: University of Chicago Press, 1984.

———. *Politics*. Translated by H. Rackham. Loeb Classical Library. Cambridge, MA: Harvard University Press, 1932.

Augustine. *The Confessions of St. Augustine*. Translated by Rex Warner. New York: New American Library, 1963.

Austin, Norman. *Archery at the Dark of the Moon: Poetic Problems in Homer's* Odyssey. Berkeley: University of California Press, 1975.

Autenrieth, Georg. *A Homeric Dictionary*. Translated by Robert P. Keep. Revised by Isaac Flagg. Norman, OK: University of Oklahoma Press, 1958.

Barber, Benjamin R. *An Aristocracy of Everyone: The Politics of Education and the Future of America*. New York: Ballantine Books, 1992.

———. "How Swiss Is Rousseau?" *Political Theory* 13 (1985): 475–95.

———. *Jihad vs. McWorld*. New York: Times Books, 1995.

———. "Rousseau and Brecht: Political Virtue and the Tragic Imagination." In *Artistic Vision and Public Action*, edited by M. McGrath. New York: Marcel Dekker, 1978.

———. "Rousseau and the Paradoxes of the Dramatic Imagination." *Daedalus* 107 (Summer 1978): 79–92.

251

Barthes, Roland. "The Death of the Author." In *Image, Music, Text*, translated and edited by Stephen Heath. New York: Hill and Wang, 1977.

Bartky, Elliot. "Plato and the Politics of Aristotle's *Poetics*." *The Review of Politics* 55 (1993): 589–619.

Beiner, Ronald. *What's the Matter with Liberalism?* Berkeley: University of California Press, 1992.

Benardete, Seth. *The Bow and the Lyre: A Platonic Reading of the* Odyssey. Lanham, MD: Rowman & Littlefield, 1997.

———. *Socrates' Second Sailing: On Plato's* Republic. Chicago: University of Chicago Press, 1989.

———. "Some Misquotations of Homer in Plato." *Phronesis* 8 (1963): 173–78.

Benda, Julien. *The Betrayal of the Intellectuals*. Translated by Richard Aldington. Boston: Beacon, 1955.

Benjamin, Walter. "Theses on the Philosophy of History." In *Critical Theory and Society: A Reader*, edited by S. E. Bronner and Douglass MacKay Kellner. New York: Routledge, 1989.

Bennett, William J. *The De-valuing of America: The Fight for Our Culture and for Our Children*. New York: Simon & Schuster, 1992.

Berkowitz, Peter. "Nietzsche's Ethics of History." *The Review of Politics* 56 (Winter 1994): 5–27.

Berlin, Isaiah. "Vico and the Ideal of the Enlightenment." In *Vico and Contemporary Thought*, edited by Giorgio Tagliacozzo, Michael Mooney, and David Phillip Verene. Atlantic Highlands, NJ: Humanities Press, 1976.

Beye, Charles Rowan. *The Iliad, the* Odyssey *and the Epic Tradition*. New York: Doubleday, 1966.

Bloom, Allan. *The Closing of the American Mind: How Higher Education Has Failed Democracy and Impoverished the Souls of Today's Students*. New York: Simon & Schuster, 1987.

———. *Giants and Dwarfs*. New York: Simon & Schuster, 1990.

———. "Interpretive Essay." In *The Republic of Plato*, 2d ed., translated by Allan Bloom. New York: Basic Books, 1991.

———. Introduction to *Emile, or On Education*, by Jean-Jacques Rousseau. Translated by Allan Bloom. New York: Basic Books, 1979.

———. Introduction to *Politics and the Arts: Letter to M. D'Alembert on the Theatre*, by Jean-Jacques Rousseau. Translated by Allan Bloom. Ithaca, NY: Cornell University Press, 1960.

———. *Love and Friendship*. New York: Simon & Schuster, 1993.

———. "Response to Hall." *Political Theory* 5 (1977): 315–30.

Boitano, Pietro. *The Shadow of Ulysses: Figures of a Myth*. Translated by Anita Weston. Oxford, U.K.: Clarendon Press, 1994.

Bolotin, David. "The Concerns of Odysseus: An Introduction to the *Odyssey*." *Interpretation* 17 (1989): 41–57.

Borges, Jorge Luis. "Kafka and His Precursors," translated by James E. Irby. In *Labyrinths: Selected Stories and Other Writings*, edited by Donald A. Yates and James E. Irby. New York: New Directions, 1962.

Bork, Robert H. *The Tempting of Politics*. New York: Basic Books, 1990.

Bowra, C. M. *Tradition and Design in the* Iliad. Oxford, U.K.: Clarendon Press, 1930.

Boyd, William. *The Emile of Jean-Jacques Rousseau: Selections*. New York: Teachers College Press, Columbia University, 1966.

Brandwood, Leonard. *A Word Index to Plato*. Leeds, U.K.: W. S. Maney & Son Limited, 1976.

Brann, Eva. "The Offense of Socrates: A Re-reading of Plato's *Apology*." *Interpretation* 7 (1978): 1–21.

Brennan, William J., Jr. "The Constitution of the United States: Contemporary Ratification." Speech given on October 12, 1985.

Brint, Michael. *Tragedy and Denial: The Politics of Difference in Western Political Thought*. San Francisco: Westview, 1991.

Bronner, S. E. *Ideas in Action*. Lanham, MD: Rowman & Littlefield, 1999.

———. *Socialism Unbound*. New York: Routledge, Chapman and Hall, 1990.

Bronner, S. E., and Douglass MacKay Kellner. Introduction to *Critical Theory and Society: A Reader*, edited by S. E. Bronner and Douglass MacKay Kellner. New York: Routledge, 1989.

Broome, J. H. *Rousseau: A Study of His Thought*. New York: Barnes & Noble, 1963.

Brunet, Etienne. *Index Concordance d'Émile ou de la Education*. Paris: Librairie Champion, 1977.

Buck-Morss, Susan. *The Origin of Negative Dialectics: Theodor W. Adorno, Walter Benjamin, and the Frankfurt School*. New York: Free Press, 1977.

Burgelin, Pierre. "L'éducation de Sophie." *Annales de la Société Jean-Jacques Rousseau* 35 (1959–1962): 113–30.

———. *La Philosophie de l'existence de Jean-Jacques Rousseau*. Paris: Presses Universitaires de France, 1952.

———. "The Second Education of Rousseau." *Yale French Studies* 28 (1961–1962): 106–11.

Burke, Edmund. *Reflections on the Revolution in France*. 1790. Reprint, New York: Dutton, Everyman's Library, 1964.

Burke, Peter. *Vico*. New York: Oxford University Press, 1985.

Caponigri, A. Robert. *Time and Idea: The Theory of History in Giambattista Vico*. South Bend, IN: University of Notre Dame Press, 1953.

Carter, Robert Edgar. "Plato and Inspiration." *Journal of the History of Philosophy* 5 (1967): 111–21.

Cavafy, C. P. *Collected Poems*. Rev. ed. Edited by George Savidis and translated by Edmund Keeley and Philip Sherrard. Princeton, NJ: Princeton University Press, 1992.

Chiss, Jean-Louis. "Horkheimer face à Vico: la problématique du précurseur." In *Critique de la Théorie Critique: langage et histoire*, edited by Henri Meschonnic. Saint-Denis, France: Presses Universaires de Vincennes, 1985.

Clarke, Howard. *Homer's Readers: A Historical Introduction to the Iliad and the Odyssey*. Newark, DE: University of Delaware Press, 1981.

Clay, Diskin. "Socrates' Mulishness and Heroism." *Phronesis* 17 (1972): 53–60.

Clay, Jenny Strauss. *The Wrath of Athena: Gods and Men in the Odyssey*. Princeton, NJ: Princeton University Press, 1983.

Condorcet, (Marie-Jean-Antoine-Nicolas Cavitat) Marquis de, "Sketch for a Historical Picture of the Progress of the Human Mind" (1793), in *Condorcet—Selected Writings*, edited by Keith Michael Baker (Indianapolis, IN: Bobbs-Merrill, 1976).

Connerton, Paul. *The Tragedy of Enlightenment: An Essay on the Frankfurt School*. Cambridge, U.K.: Cambridge University Press, 1980.

Cooper, John M., ed. *Plato: Complete Works*. Indianapolis, IN: Hackett, 1997.

Cranston, Maurice. *Jean-Jacques: The Early Life of Jean-Jacques Rousseau, 1712–1754*. Chicago: University of Chicago Press, 1982.

———. *The Noble Savage: Jean-Jacques Rousseau, 1754–1762*. Chicago: University of Chicago Press, 1991.

———. *The Solitary Self: Jean-Jacques Rousseau in Exile and Adversity*. Chicago: University of Chicago Press, 1997.

Cropsey, Joseph. "The Human Vision of Rousseau." In *Political Philosophy and the Issues of Politics*. Chicago: University of Chicago Press, 1977.

Dallmayr, Fred R. "'Natural History' and Social Evolution: Reflections on Vico's *Corsi e Ricorsi*." In *Vico and Contemporary Thought*, edited by Giorgio Tagliacozzo, Michael Mooney, and David Phillip Verene. Atlantic Highlands, NJ: Humanities Press, 1976.

Darnton, Robert. *The Great Cat Massacre*. New York: Anchor Books, 1972.

Dejean, Joan. *Ancients against Moderns: Culture Wars and the Making of a Fin de Siècle*. Chicago: University of Chicago Press, 1997.

Demos, Raphael. "A Fallacy in Plato's *Republic?*" In *Plato II: Ethics, Politics, and Philosophy of Art and Religion*, edited by Gregory Vlastos. New York: Anchor Books, 1971.

Deneen, Patrick J. "Friendship and Politics, Ancient and American." In *Friends and Citizens: Essays in Honor of Wilson Carey McWilliams*. Lanham, MD: Rowman & Littlefield, 2000.

———. "Havel, Rorty, and the Democratic Faith of John Dewey." *Social Research* 66 (Summer 1999): 577–609.

Derrida, Jacques. *Of Spirit: Heidegger and the Question*. Translated by Geoffrey Bennington and Rachel Bowlby. Chicago: University of Chicago Press, 1989.

Dessons, Gérard. "Horkheimer et le matérialisme historique de Vico." In *Critique de la Théorie Critique: langage et histoire*, edited by Henri Meschonnic. Saint-Denis, France: Universaires de Vincennes, 1985.

Diderot, Denis. *Encyclopedia: Selections by Diderot, D'Alembert, and a Society of Men of Letters*. Translated by Nelly S. Hoyt and Thomas Cassirer. Indianapolis, IN: Bobbs-Merrill, 1965.

Dietrich, B. C. *Death, Fate, and the Gods*. London: Athlone Press, 1965.

Dimock, George E., Jr. "The Name of Odysseus." In *Homer: A Collection of Critical Essays*, edited by George Steiner and Robert Fagles. Engelwood Cliffs, NJ: Prentice Hall, 1962.

———. *The Unity of the Odyssey*. Amherst, MA: University of Massachusetts Press, 1989.

Dobbs, Darrell. "Reckless Rationalism and Heroic Reverence in Homer's *Odyssey*." *American Political Science Review* 81 (1987): 491–508.

Dodds, E. R. *The Greeks and the Irrational*. Berkeley: University of California Press, 1951.

Dorter, Kenneth. "The *Ion*: Plato's Characterization of Art." *The Journal of Aesthetics and Art Criticism* 23 (1973): 65–78.

D'Souza, Dinesh. *Illiberal Education: The Politics of Race and Sex on Campus*. New York: Free Press, 1991.

Dunbar, Henry. *A Complete Concordance to the Odyssey of Homer*. Revised by Benedetto Marzullo. Hildesheim, Germany: Georg Olms Verlagsbuchhandlung, 1962.

Eagleton, Terry. *Literary Theory: An Introduction*. Minneapolis, MN: University of Minnesota Press, 1983.

Early Greek Poetry and Philosophy. Translated by Moses Hadas and J. Willis. Oxford, U.K.: Oxford University Press, 1975.

Edwards, Anthony T. *Achilles in the Odyssey: Ideologies of Heroism in the Homeric Epic*. Konigstein, Germany: Verlag Anton Hain Meisenhem GmbH, 1985.

Ehnmark, Erland. *The Idea of God in Homer: Inaugural Dissertation*. Uppssala, Sweden: Almquist & Boltrycken, 1935.

Eichhorn, Friedrich. *Die Telemachie*. Garmisch-Patenkirchen, Germany: Im Selbstverlag des Verfassers, 1973.

Einaudi, Mario. *The Early Rousseau*. Ithaca, NY: Cornell University Press, 1967.

Eliot, T. S. "Tradition and the Individual Talent." In *Selected Essays*. New York: Harcourt, Brace & World, 1932.

Elshtain, Jean Bethke. *Augustine and the Limits of Politics*. South Bend, IN: University of Notre Dame Press, 1995.

———. *Public Man, Private Woman*. Princeton, NJ: Princeton University Press, 1981.

———. *Real Politics*. Baltimore: Johns Hopkins University Press, 1997.

Elster, Jon. *Ulysses and the Sirens: Studies in Rationality and Irrationality*. Rev. ed. New York: Cambridge University Press; Editions de la Maison des Sciences de l'Homme, 1984.

Ely, John Hart. *Democracy and Distrust: A Theory of Judicial Review*. Cambridge, MA: Harvard University Press, 1980.

Euben, J. Peter. *Corrupting Youth: Political Education, Democratic Culture, and Political Theory*. Princeton, NJ: Princeton University Press, 1997.

———. *The Tragedy of Political Theory: The Road Not Taken*. Princeton, NJ: Princeton University Press, 1990.

Falk, Richard. "Revisioning Cosmopolitanism." In *For Love of Country*, edited by Joshua Cohen. Boston: Beacon Press, 1996.

Feldman, Abraham B. "Homer and Democracy." *The Classical Journal* 47 (1951–1952): 337–45.

Fénelon, François de Salignac de la Mothe. *Les Aventures de Télémaque*. Edited by Jeanne-Lydie Goré. Paris: Éditions Garnier, 1987.

Fenik, B. *Studies in the Odyssey*. Wiesbaden, Germany: Hermes Einzelschriften, 1974.

Fenske, Hans. *Geschichte der politischen Ideen: Von Homer bis zur Gegenwart*. Frankfurt: Fischer Taschenbuch Verlag GmbH, 1987.

Finley, M. I. *The World of Odysseus*. Rev. ed. New York: Viking Penguin, 1979.

Fish, Stanley. "The Common Touch." In *The Politics of Liberal Education*, edited by Darryl J. Gless and Barbara Herrnstein Smith. Durham, NC: Duke University Press, 1992.

Flashar, Hellmut. *Der Dialog Ion als Zeugnis Platonischer Philosophie*. Berlin: Akademie-Verlag, 1958.

Flaumenhaft, Mera J. "The Undercover Hero: Odysseus from Light to Dark." *Interpretation* 10 (1982): 9–41.

Foucault, Michel. *The Foucault Reader*. Edited by Paul Rabinow. New York: Pantheon, 1984.

———. *The Order of Things*. Anonymous translator. New York: Random House, 1973.

Frame, Douglas. *The Myth of Return in Early Greek Epic*. New Haven, CT: Yale University Press, 1978.

Fränkel, Hermann. *Early Greek Poetry and Philosophy: A History of Greek Epic, Lyric, and Prose to the Middle of the Fifth Century*. Translated by Moses Hadas and James Willis. New York: Harcourt Brace Jovanovich, 1973.

Franklin, Benjamin. *Autobiography*. In *Writings*. New York: Library of America, 1987.

Freeman, Kathleen, ed. and trans. *Ancilla to the Pre-Socratic Philosophers*. Cambridge, MA: Harvard University Press, 1983.

Freud, Sigmund. *Civilization and Its Discontents*. Translated by Joan Riviere. New York: Doubleday, 1930.

Friedländer, Paul. *Plato: An Introduction*. Translated by Hans Meyerhoff. Princeton, NJ: Princeton University Press, 1969.

Friedman, George. *The Political Philosophy of the Frankfurt School*. Ithaca, NY: Cornell University Press, 1981.

Fromm, Erich. *Escape from Freedom*. New York: Holt, Rinehart & Winston, 1941.

Gadamer, Hans-Georg. *Dialogue and Dialectic: Eight Hermeneutical Studies on Plato*. Translated by P. Christopher Smith. New Haven, CT: Yale University Press, 1980.

———. *The Idea of Good in Platonic-Aristotelian Philosophy*. Translated by P. Christopher Smith. New Haven, CT: Yale University Press, 1986.

———. *Truth and Method*. New York: Crossroads Publishing Company, 1986.

Galston, William A. *Liberal Purposes: Goods, Virtues, and Diversity in the Liberal State*. Cambridge, U.K.: University of Cambridge Press, 1991.

Germain, Gabriel. "The Sirens and the Temptation of Knowledge." Translated by George Steiner. In *Homer: A Collection of Critical Essays*, edited by George Steiner and Robert Fagles. Englewood Cliffs, NJ: Prentice Hall, 1962.

Geuss, Raymond. *The Idea of Critical Theory: Habermas and the Frankfurt School*. Cambridge, U.K.: Cambridge University Press, 1981.

Giroux, Henry A. "Liberal Arts Education and the Struggle for Public Life: Dreaming about Democracy." In *The Politics of Liberal Education*, edited by Darryl J. Gless and Barbara Herrnstein Smith. Durham, NC: Duke University Press, 1992.

Gitlin, Todd. "The Left, Lost in the Politics of Identity." *Harper's* 287 (September 1993): 16–20.

———. *Twilight of Common Dreams: Why America Is Wracked by Culture Wars*. New York: Metropolitan Books, 1995.

Gless, Darryl J., and Barbara Herrnstein Smith, ed. *The Politics of Liberal Education*. Durham, NC: Duke University Press, 1992.

Goré, Jeanne-Lydie. Introduction to *Les Aventures de Télémaque* by François de Salignac de la Mothe Fénelon. Paris: Éditions Garnier, 1987.

Greene, W. C. *Moira: Fate, Good, and Evil in Greek Thought*. Cambridge, MA: Harvard University Press, 1944.

Greven, Michael. *Kritische Theorie und historische Politik: Theoriegeschichtliche Beiträge zur gegenwärtigen Gesellschaft*. Opladen, Germany: Leske Budrich, 1994.

Griffen, Jasper. *Homer on Life and Death*. Oxford, U.K.: Clarendon Press, 1980.

Habermas, Jürgen. "The Entwinement of Myth and Enlightenment." *New German Critique* 26 (1982): 13–30.

Hall, Dale. "The *Republic* and the 'Limits of Politics.'" *Political Theory* 5 (1977): 293–313.

Hamilton, Alexander, John Jay, and James Madison. *The Federalist*. New York: Modern Library, n.d. 1787.

Hanson, Victor Davis, and John Heath. *Who Killed Homer?* New York: Free Press, 1998.

Havelock, Eric A. *The Greek Concept of Justice: From Its Shadow in Homer to Its Substance in Plato*. Cambridge, MA: Harvard University Press, 1978.

———. *Preface to Plato*. Cambridge, MA: Harvard University Press, 1963.

Heidegger, Martin. *Poetry, Language, Thought*. Translated by Albert Hofstadter. New York: Harper & Row, 1971.

Held, David. *Introduction to Critical Theory: Horkheimer to Habermas*. Berkeley: University of California Press, 1980.

Hepp, Noémi. *Homère en France au XVIIe Siècle*. Paris: Librairie C. Klincksiek, 1968.

Herodotus. *The History*. Translated by David Grene. Chicago: University of Chicago Press, 1987.

Herzfeld, Michael. *The Poetics of Manhood: Contest and Identity in a Cretan Mountain Village*. Princeton, NJ: Princeton University Press, 1985.

Hohendahl, Peter. "The Dialectic of Enlightenment Revisited: Habermas' Critique of the Frankfurt School." *New German Critique* 35 (1985): 3–26.

Hollinger, David A. *Postethnic America*. New York: Basic Books, 1995.

Holmes, Stephen. *The Anatomy of Antiliberalism*. Cambridge, MA: Harvard University Press, 1993.

Homer. *The Iliad*. Translated by A. T. Murray. 2 vols. Loeb Classical Library. Cambridge, MA: Harvard University Press, 1924–1925.

———. *The Iliad*. Translated by Richmond Lattimore. Chicago: University of Chicago Press, 1951.

———. *The Iliad*. Translated by Robert Fitzgerald. New York: Anchor Press/Doubleday, 1974.

———. *The Odyssey*. Translated by A. T. Murray. 2 vols. Loeb Classical Library. Cambridge, MA: Harvard University Press, 1919.

———. *The Odyssey*. Translated by Richmond Lattimore. New York: HarperCollins, 1965.

———. *The Odyssey*. Translated by Robert Fitzgerald. New York: Doubleday & Company, 1961.

Horkheimer, Max. *Critical Theory: Selected Essays*. Translated by M. J. O'Connor. New York: Herder and Herder, 1968.

———. *Eclipse of Reason*. New York: Oxford University Press, 1947.

———. *Anfänge der bürgerlichen Geschichtsphilosophie*. In *Gesammelte Schriften*. 10 vols. Frankfurt am Main, Germany: S. Fischer Verlag, 1988.

Horkheimer, Max, and Theodor W. Adorno. *Dialektik der Aufklärung: Philosophische Fragmente*. In *Gesammelte Schriften*, vol. 3, by Theodor W. Adorno. Frankfurt am Main, Germany: Suhrkamp, [1944] 1981.

———. *Dialectic of Enlightenment*. Translated by John Cumming. New York: Continuum, 1991.

Horowitz, Asher. *Rousseau: Nature and History*. Toronto: University of Toronto Press, 1987.

Howland, Jacob. *The Republic: The Odyssey of Philosophy*. New York: Twayne Publishers, 1993.

Hunter, James D. *Culture Wars: The Struggle to Define America*. New York: Basic Books, 1991.

Hyland, Drew A. *Finitude and Transcendence in the Platonic Dialogues*. Albany, NY: SUNY Press, 1995.

———. "*Republic*, Book II, and the Origins of Political Philosophy." *Interpretation* 16 (1988): 247–61.

Ignatieff, Michael. *The Needs of Strangers*. New York: Penguin, 1985.

Jacobson, Norman. *Pride and Solace: The Functions and Limits of Political Theory*. Berkeley: University of California Press, 1978.

Jacoby, Russell. *The End of Utopia: Politics and Culture in an Age of Apathy*. New York: Basic Books, 1999.

Jaeger, Werner. *Humanistische Reden und Vorträge*. 2d ed. Berlin: Walter de Gruyter, 1960.

———. *Paideia: The Ideals of Greek Culture*. 3 vols. Translated by Gilbert Highet. New York: Oxford University Press, 1945.

Jay, Martin. *The Dialectical Imagination: A History of the Frankfurt School, 1923–1950*. Boston: Little Brown, 1973.

Jouvenel, Bertrand de. "Rousseau, the Pessimistic Evolutionist." *Yale French Studies* 28 (1961): 83–96.

———. "Rousseau's Theories of the Forms of Government." In *Hobbes and Rousseau*, edited by Maurice Cranston and Richard S. Peters. New York: Anchor Books, 1972.

Kamenka, Eugene. "Vico and Marxism." In *Giambattista Vico: An International Symposium*, edited by Giorgio Tagliacozzo and Hayden V. White. Baltimore: Johns Hopkins University Press, 1969.

Kellner, Douglass. *Critical Theory, Marxism, and Modernity*. Cambridge, U.K.: Polity Press, 1989.

Kelly, George Armstrong. *Idealism, Politics, and History: Sources of Hegelian Thought*. Cambridge, U.K.: Cambridge University Press, 1969.

———. "Veils: The Poetics of John Rawls." *Journal of the History of Ideas* 57 (1996): 343–64.

Kennedy, George A. "Classics and Canons." In *The Politics of Liberal Education*, edited by Darryl J. Gless and Barbara Herrnstein Smith. Durham, NC: Duke University Press, 1992.

Kimball, Roger. *Tenured Radicals: How Politics Has Corrupted Our Higher Education*. New York: Harper and Row, 1990.

Kirk, G. S. *The Songs of Homer*. Cambridge, U.K.: Cambridge University Press, 1962.

Kitto, H. D. F. *Poesis: Structure and Thought*. Berkeley: University of California Press, 1966.

Kolakowski, Leszek. "The Frankfurt School and Critical Theory." In *Foundations of the Frankfurt School of Social Research*, edited by Judith Marcus and Zoltán Tar. New Brunswick, NJ: Transaction Books, 1984.

———. *Main Currents of Marxism: Its Origins, Growth, and Dissolution*. Translated by P. S. Falla. 3 vols. New York: Oxford University Press, 1978.

———. *The Presence of Myth*. Translated by Adam Czerniawski. Chicago: University of Chicago Press, 1989.

Labarbe, Jules. *L'Homère de Platon*. Liège, France: Faculté de Philosophie et Lettres, 1949.

Lanson, Gustav. "L'Unité de la pensée de Jean-Jacques Rousseau." *Annales de la Société de Jean-Jacques Rousseau* 8 (1912): 22.

Lasch, Christopher. *Haven in a Heartless World*. New York: Basic, 1977.

———. *The Revolt of the Elites*. New York: Norton, 1995.

———. *The True and Only Heaven*. New York: Norton, 1991.

Lattimore, Richmond. Introduction to *The Iliad*, translated by Richmond Lattimore. Chicago: University of Chicago Press, 1951.

———. Introduction to *The Odyssey*, translated by Richmond Lattimore. New York: HarperCollins, 1991.

Lenhardt, Christian. "The Wanderings of Enlightenment." In *On Critical Theory*, edited by John O'Neill. London: Heinemann, 1976.

Lesher, J. H. "Perceiving and Knowing in the *Iliad* and *Odyssey*." *Phronesis* 26 (1981): 2–24.

Levinson, Sanford. *Constitutional Faith*. Princeton, NJ: Princeton University Press, 1988.

Liddell, Henry George, and Robert Scott. *A Greek–English Lexicon*. Revised by Henry Stuart Jones and Roderick MacKenzie. Oxford, U.K.: Clarendon Press, 1990.

Lieb, Irwin C. "Philosophy as Spiritual Formation: Plato's Myth of Er." *International Philosophical Quarterly* 3 (1963): 271–85.

Lincoln, Bruce. "Waters of Memory, Waters of Forgetfulness." *Fabula* 23 (1982): 19–34.

Lloyd-Jones, Hugh. *The Justice of Zeus*. 2d ed. Berkeley: University of California Press, 1983.

Longinus. *On the Sublime*. In *Classical Literary Criticism*, translated by T. S. Dorsch. New York: Viking Penguin, 1965.

Lord, A. B. *The Singer of Tales*. Cambridge, MA: Harvard University Press, 1960.

Mabbot, J. D. "Is Plato's *Republic* Utilitarian?" In *Plato II: Ethics, Politics, and Philosophy of Art and Religion*, edited by Gregory Vlastos. New York: Anchor Books, 1971.

MacIntyre, Alasdair. *After Virtue*. 2d ed. South Bend, IN: University of Notre Dame Press, 1984.

———. *A Short History of Ethics*. New York: Macmillan, 1966.

Mahoney, Timothy A. "Do Plato's Philosopher-rulers Sacrifice Self-interest to Justice?" *Phronesis* 37 (1992): 265–82.

Maier, Joseph. "Vico and Critical Theory." In *Vico and Contemporary Thought*, edited by Giorgio Tagliacozzo, Michael Mooney, and David Phillip Verene. Atlantic Highlands, NJ: Humanities Press, 1976.

Mali, Joseph. *The Rehabilitation of Myth: Vico's New Science*. Cambridge, U.K.: Cambridge University Press, 1992.

Mansfield, Harvey C., Jr. "Foolish Cosmopolitanism." *Boston Review* 19 (October/November 1994), 10.

———. "The State of Harvard." *The Public Interest* 100 (1990): 113–23.

Mara, Gerald M. *Socrates' Discursive Democracy: Logos and Ergon in Platonic Political Philosophy*. Albany, NY: SUNY Press, 1997.

Marcuse, Herbert. *Eros and Civilization: A Philosophical Inquiry into Freud*. Boston: Beacon Press, 1955.

———. *Soviet Marxism*. Boston: Beacon Press, 1964.

Marx, Karl. "Critique of the Gotha Program." In *The Marx-Engels Reader*, 2d ed., edited by Robert C. Tucker, translated by Martin Nicolaus. New York: Norton, 1978.

———. *The Grundrisse*. In *The Marx-Engels Reader*, 2d ed., edited by Robert C. Tucker, translated by Martin Nicolaus. New York: Norton, 1978.

———. "Theses on Feuerbach." In *The Marx-Engels Reader*, 2d ed., edited by Robert C. Tucker, translated by Martin Nicolaus. New York: Norton, 1978.

Masters, Roger D. *The Political Philosophy of Rousseau*. Princeton, NJ: Princeton University Press, 1968.

Matthews, Rick, and David Ingersoll. "The Therapist and the Lawgiver: Rousseau's Political Vision." *Canadian Journal of Political and Social Theory* 4 (1980): 83–99.

McWilliams, Wilson Carey. "Democratic Multiculturalism." In *Multiculturalism and American Democracy*, edited by Arthur M. Melzer, Jerry Weinberger, and M. Richard Zinmar. Ithaca, NY: Cornell University Press, 1998.

———. *The Idea of Fraternity in America*. Berkeley: University of California Press, 1973.

Melzer, Arthur M. *The Natural Goodness of Man: On the System of Rousseau's Thought*. Chicago: University of Chicago Press, 1990.

Meyer, Paul H. "The Individual and Society in Rousseau's *Emile*." *Modern Language Quarterly* 19 (1958): 99–114.

Misenheimer, Helen Evans. *Rousseau on the Education of Women*. Washington, DC: University Press of America, 1981.

Munro, D. B., ed. *Odyssey: Books 13–24*. Oxford, U.K.: Clarendon Press, 1901.

Murdoch, Iris. *The Fire and the Sun: Why Plato Banished the Artists*. Oxford, U.K.: Clarendon Press, 1977.

Nagy, Gregory. *The Best of the Achaeans: Concepts of the Hero in Archaic Greek Poetry*. Baltimore: Johns Hopkins University Press, 1979.

———. *Comparative Studies in Greek and Indic Meter*. Cambridge, MA: Harvard University Press, 1974.

Nelson, Cary. *Manifesto of a Tenured Radical*. New York: New York University Press, 1997.

Nichols, Mary P. "The *Republic*'s Two Alternatives: Philosopher-Kings and Socrates." *Political Theory* 12 (1984): 252–74.

———. "Rousseau's Novel Education in the *Emile*." *Political Theory* 13 (1985): 535–58.

Nisbet, Robert. "Vico and the Idea of Progress." In *Vico and Contemporary Thought*, edited by Giorgio Tagliacozzo, Michael Mooney, and David Phillip Verene. 2 vols. Atlantic Highlands, NJ: Humanities Press, 1976.

Nussbaum, Martha C. *Cultivating Humanity: A Classical Defense of Reform in Liberal Education*. Cambridge, MA: Harvard University Press, 1997.

———. *For Love of Country: Debating the Limits of Patriotism*. Edited by Joshua Cohen. Boston: Beacon Press, 1996.

———. *The Fragility of Goodness: Luck and Ethics in Greek Tragedy and Philosophy*. Cambridge, U.K.: Cambridge University Press, 1986.

———. *Love's Knowledge: Essays on Philosophy and Literature*. Oxford, U.K.: Oxford University Press, 1990.

———. "Patriotism and Cosmopolitanism." *Boston Review* 19, no. 5. (October/November 1994): 3–6.

Oakeshott, Michael. *Rationalism in Politics and Other Essays*. London: Methuen, 1962.

O'Brien, Conor Cruise. *On the Eve of the Millennium: The Future of Democracy through an Age of Unreason*. New York: Free Press, 1994.

Okin, Susan Moller. *Women in Western Political Thought*. Princeton, NJ: Princeton University Press, 1979.

O'Neill, John. "On the History of the Human Senses in Vico and Marx." In *Vico and Contemporary Thought*, edited by Giorgio Tagliacozzo, Michael Mooney, and David Phillip Verene. Atlantic Highlands, NJ: Humanities Press, 1976.

Pachter, Henry. *Weimar Etudes*. New York: Columbia University Press, 1982.

Page, Denys. *Folktales in Homer's Odyssey*. Cambridge, MA: Harvard University Press, 1973.

———. *The Homeric Odyssey*. Oxford, U.K.: Clarendon Press, 1955.

Pangle, Thomas L. *The Ennobling of Democracy: The Challenge of the Postmodern Age*. Baltimore: Johns Hopkins University Press, 1992.

———. Introduction to *Studies in Platonic Political Philosophy* by Leo Strauss. Chicago: University of Chicago Press, 1983.

Parry, Adam. *The Langage of Achilles and Other Papers*. Edited by Hugh Lloyd-Jones. Oxford, U.K.: Clarendon Press, 1989.

———. "The Language of Achilles." *Transactions and Proceedings from the American Philological Association* 87 (1956): 1–7.

Parry, Milman. *The Making of Homeric Verse*. Edited by Adam Parry. Oxford, U.K.: Clarendon Press, 1971.

Partee, Morriss Henry. "Plato's Banishment of Poetry." *The Journal of Aesthetics and Art Criticism* 29 (1970): 209–22.

Pinsky, Robert. "Eros Against Esperanto." In *For Love of Country*, edited by Joshua Cohen. Boston: Beacon Press, 1996.

Piovani, Pietro. "Apoliticality and Politicality in Vico." In *Vico's Science of Humanity*, edited by G. Tagliacozzo and D. P. Verene. Baltimore: Johns Hopkins University Press, 1976.

Planinc, Zdravko. *Plato's Political Philosophy: Prudence in the Republic and the Laws*. Columbia, MO: University of Missouri Press, 1991.

Plato. *Plato: Complete Works*, edited by John M. Cooper. Indianapolis, IN: Hackett, 1997.

———. *Euthyphro, Apology, Crito, Phaedo, Phaedrus*. Translated by Harold North Fowler. Loeb Classical Library. Cambridge, MA: Harvard University Press, 1914.

———. *Ion*. Translated by W. R. M. Lamb. Loeb Classical Library. Cambridge, MA: Harvard University Press, 1925.

———. *Ion, or on the* Iliad. Translated by Allan Bloom. In *Giants and Dwarfs*. New York: Simon & Schuster, 1990.

———. *Laches, Protagoras, Meno, Euthydemus*. Translated by W. R. M. Lamb. Loeb Classical Library. Cambridge, MA: Harvard University Press, 1924.

———. *Laws*. Translated by R. G. Bury. 2 vols. Loeb Classical Library. Cambridge, MA: Harvard University Press, 1926.

———. *The Laws of Plato*. Translated by Thomas L. Pangle. Chicago: University of Chicago Press, 1980.

———. *Lysis, Symposium, Gorgias*. Translated by W. R. M. Lamb. Loeb Classical Library. Cambridge, MA: Harvard University Press, 1925.

———. *Plato's* Apology of Socrates. Translated by Thomas G. West. Ithaca, NY: Cornell University Press, 1979.

———. *The Republic*. Translated by Paul Shorey. 2 vols. Loeb Classical Library. Cambridge, MA: Harvard University Press, 1935.

———. *The Republic of Plato*. 2d ed. Translated by Allan Bloom. New York: Basic, 1991.

Plutarch. *Plutarch on Sparta*. Translated by Richard J. A. Talbert. New York: Penguin, 1971.

Pompa, Leon. *Vico: A Study of the New Science*. 2d ed. New York: Cambridge University Press, 1990.

Postlethwaite, N. "The Continuation of the *Odyssey*: Some Formulaic Evidence." *Classical Philology* 76 (1981): 177–87.

Pratt, Mary Louise. "Humanities for the Future: Reflections on the Western Culture Debate at Stanford." In *The Politics of Liberal Education*, edited by Darryl J. Gless and Barbara Herrnstein Smith. Durham, NC: Duke University Press, 1992.

Prendergast, Guy Lushington. *A Complete Concordance to the* Iliad *of Homer*. Revised by Benedetto Marzullo. Hildesheim, Germany: Georg Olms Verlagsbuchhandlung, 1962.

Pucci, Pietro. *Odysseus Polutropos*. Ithaca, NY: Cornell University Press, 1987.

Ramsey, Warren. "Voltaire and Homer." *Publications of the Modern Language Association* 66 (1951): 182–96.

Rawls, John. *A Theory of Justice*. Cambridge, MA: Harvard University Press, 1971.

Redfield, James M. *Nature and Culture in the* Iliad: *The Tragedy of Hector*. Chicago: University of Chicago Press, 1975.

Reeve, C. D. C. *Philosopher-Kings: The Argument of Plato's Republic*. Princeton, NJ: Princeton University Press, 1988.

Rehnquist, William H. "The Notion of a Living Constitution." *Texas Law Review* 54 (1976): 693–706.

Rice, Daryl H. *A Guide to Plato's Republic*. Oxford, U.K.: Oxford University Press, 1998.

Richardson, Hilda. "The Myth of Er (Plato, *Republic* 616b)." *The Classical Quarterly* 20 (1926): 113–33.

Robinson, Philip E. J. *Jean-Jacques Rousseau's Doctrine of the Arts*. New York: Peter Lang, 1984.

Rocco, Christopher. *Tragedy and Enlightenment: Athenian Political Thought and the Dilemmas of Modernity*. Berkeley: University of California Press, 1997.

Rohde, Erwin. *Psyche: The Cult of Souls and Belief in Immortality among the Greeks*. Translated by W. B. Hollis. New York: Harcourt, Brace, 1925.

Rosen, Stanley. *The Ancients and the Moderns: Rethinking Modernity*. New Haven, CT: Yale University Press, 1989.

———. *The Quarrel between Philosophy and Poetry: Studies in Ancient Thought*. New York: Routledge, 1988.

Rousseau, Jean-Jacques. *The Confessions*. Translated by J. M. Cohen. New York: Penguin, 1953.

———. *Correspondences Complètes de J.-J. Rousseau*. Edited by R. A. Leigh. Madison: University of Wisconsin Press, 1969.

———. "A Discourse on Political Economy." In *The Social Contract and the Discourses*, translated by G. D. H. Cole. New York: Dutton, 1973.

———. *Emile, or on Education*. Translated by Allan Bloom. New York: Basic Books, 1979.

———. *The First and Second Discourses Together with the Replies to Critics and Essay on the Origin of Languages*. Edited and translated by Victor Gourevitch. New York: Harper & Row, 1986.

———. *Government of Poland*. Translated by Willmore Kendall. Indianapolis, IN: Hackett, 1985.

———. *Julie, or the New Heloïse*. Translated and edited by Judith H. McDowell. University Park, PA: Pennsylvania State University Press, 1968.

———. "De L'Imitation Théatrale: Essai Tiré des Dialogues de Platon." *Oeuvres de J.-J. Rousseau*. Vol. 11. Paris: Chez E. A. Lequien, 1821.

———. *Œuvres Complètes*. Edited by Bernard Gagnebin and Marcel Raymond. 4 vols. Paris: Bibliothèque de la Pléiade, 1969.

———. "Letter to M. D'Alembert on the Theater." In *Politics and the Arts*, translated by Allan Bloom. Ithaca, NY: Cornell University Press, 1960.

———. "Preface to *Narcisse*." Translated by Benjamin R. Barber and Janis Forman. *Political Theory* 6 (1978): 537–54.

———. "Project for a Constitution of Corsica." In *Rousseau: Political Writings: Containing the Social Contract, Considerations on the Government of Poland, and Constitutional Project for Corsica*, edited and translated by F. M. Watkins. New York: Nelson, 1953.

———. *Reveries of a Solitary Walker*. Translated by Peter France. New York: Penguin, 1979.

———. *The Social Contract*. Translated by G. D. H. Cole. Buffalo, NY: Prometheus Books, 1988.

Rucker, Darnell. "Plato and the Poets." *The Journal of Aesthetics and Art Criticism* 25 (1966): 167–70.

Rüter, Klaus. *Odysseeinterpretationen: Untersuchungen zum ersten Buch und zur Phaiakas*. Göttingen, Germany: Vandenhoek & Ruprecht, 1969.

Sabine, George. *A History of Political Theory*. 4th ed. Hinsdale, IL: Dryden Press, 1973.

Sachs, David. "A Fallacy in Plato's *Republic*." In *Plato II: Ethics, Politics, and Philosophy of Art and Religion*, edited by Gregory Vlastos. New York: Anchor Books, 1971.

Sandel, Michael J. *Democracy's Discontent*. Cambridge, MA: Harvard University Press, 1996.

———. *Liberalism and Limits of Politics*. New York: Cambridge University Press, 1982.

Saxonhouse, Arlene W. *Fear of Diversity: The Birth of Political Science in Ancient Greek Thought*. Chicago: University of Chicago Press, 1992.

———. "The Tyranny of Reason in the World of the Polis." *American Political Science Review* 82 (1988): 1261–75.

Schaar, John H. "The Case for Patriotism." *American Review* 17 (1973): 59–99.

Schadewaldt, Wolfgang. "Die beiden Dichter der *Odyssee*." In *Die Odyssee*. Hamburg, Germany: Rovohlts Klassiker, 1958.

———. *Von Homers Welt und Werk: Aufsätze und Auslesungen zur Homerischen Frage*. Leipzig, Germany: Koehler & Amelang, 1944.

Schlereth, Thomas J. *The Cosmopolitan Ideal in Enlightenment Thought: Its Form and Function in the Ideas of Franklin, Hume, and Voltaire, 1694–1790*. South Bend, IN: University of Notre Dame Press, 1977.

Schwartz, Joel. *The Sexual Politics of Jean-Jacques Rousseau*. Chicago: University of Chicago Press, 1984.

Seery, John E. *Political Theory for Mortals: Shades of Justice, Images of Death*. Ithaca, NY: Cornell University Press, 1996.

Segal, Charles. " 'The Myth Was Saved': Reflections on Homer and the Mythology of Plato's *Republic*." *Hermes* 106 (1978): 315–36.

Shapiro, Michael J. "Politicizing Ulysses: Rationalistic, Critical, and Genealogical Commentaries." *Political Theory* 17 (1989): 9–32.

Shils, Griet. "Plato's Myth of Er: The Light and the Spindle." *L'Antiquité Classique* 62 (1993): 101–14.

Shklar, Judith. *Men and Citizens: A Study of Rousseau's Social Theory*. Cambridge, U.K.: Cambridge University Press, 1969.

Singer, Peter. *Hegel*. New York: Oxford University Press, 1983.

———. *Marx*. New York: Oxford University Press, 1980.

Smith, Rogers M. "All Critters Great and Small: Critical Legal Studies and Liberal Political Theory." *Laws, Courts, and Judicial Process Newsletter* (APSA) 3 (1986): 2.

Snell, Bruno. *The Discovery of the Mind in Greek Philosophy and Literature*. Translated by T. G. Rosenmeyer. New York: Dover, 1982.

Sophocles. *Antigone*. In *The Three Theban Plays*, translated by Robert Fagles. New York: Penguin, 1984.

Stanford, W. B. *The Ulysses Theme*. Oxford, U.K.: Basil Blackwell, 1963.

Starobinski, Jean. *Jean-Jacques Rousseau: Transparency and Obstruction*. Translated by Arthur Goldhammer. Chicago: University of Chicago Press, 1988.

Steiner, George. *In Bluebeard's Castle: Some Notes toward the Redefinition of Culture*. New Haven, CT: Yale University Press, 1971.

Strauss, Leo. *The City and Man*. Chicago: University of Chicago Press, 1964.

———. *Liberalism Ancient and Modern*. Ithaca, NY: Cornell University Press, 1989.

———. *Natural Right and History*. Chicago: University of Chicago Press, 1950.

———. *Persecution and the Art of Writing*. Chicago: University of Chicago Press, 1952.

———. *Studies in Platonic Political Philosophy*. Chicago: University of Chicago Press, 1983.

————. *What Is Political Philosophy? and Other Studies*. Chicago: University of Chicago Press, 1959.

Strong, Tracy B. *The Idea of Political Theory: Reflections of the Self in Political Time and Place*. South Bend, IN: University of Notre Dame Press, 1990.

Taylor, A. E. *Plato: The Man and His Work*. New York: Meridian Books, 1956.

Taylor, Charles. *Sources of the Self*. Cambridge, MA: Harvard University Press, 1989.

Taylor, Charles H. "The Obstacles to Odysseus' Return: Identity and Consciousness in *The Odyssey*." *The Yale Review* 50 (1960–1961): 569–80.

Thayer, H. S. "The Myth of Er." *History of Philosophy Quarterly* 5 (1988): 369–384.

Thornton, Agathe. *People and Themes in Homer's Odyssey*. London: Methuen, 1970.

Thucydides. *The Peloponnesian War*. Translated by Thomas Hobbes. Edited by David Grene. Chicago: University of Chicago Press, 1989.

Tudor, Henry. *Political Myth*. New York: Praeger, 1972.

Unger, Robert Mangaberia. "The Critical Legal Studies Movement." *Harvard Law Review* 96 (1983): 563.

Vaghenàs, Nasos. "Elpenore: l'anti-Ulisse nella litteratura moderna." In *Ulisse: archaeologia dell'uomo moderno*, edited by Pietro Boitani and Richard Ambrosini. Rome, Italy: Bulzioni Editore, 1988.

Van Nortwick, Thomas. *Somewhere I Have Never Traveled: The Second Self and the Hero's Journey in Ancient Epic*. New York: Oxford University Press, 1992.

Verene, Donald Phillip. *Vico's Science of Imagination*. Ithaca, NY: Cornell University Press, 1981.

Vernant, Jean Pierre. "Travail et nature dans la Grèce ancienne." *Journal de psychologie* 52 (1955): 18–38.

Vico, Giambattista. *The Autobiography of Giambattista Vico*. Translated by Max Harold Fisch and Thomas Goddard Bergin. Ithaca, NY: Cornell University Press, 1985.

————. *Practic of the New Science*. Translated by Thomas Goddard Bergin and Max Harold Fisch. In *Giambattista Vico's Science of Humanity*, edited by Giorgio Tagliacozzo and Donald Phillip Verene. Baltimore: Johns Hopkins University Press, 1976.

————. *The New Science of Giambattista Vico*. Translated by Thomas Goddard Bergin and Max Harold Fisch. Ithaca, NY: Cornell University Press, 1948.

Viroli, Maurizio. *For Love of Country: An Essay on Patriotism and Nationalism*. Oxford, U.K.: Oxford University Press, 1995.

Vlastos, Gregory. "Justice and Happiness in the *Republic*." In *Plato II: Ethics, Politics, and Philosophy of Art and Religion*, edited by Gregory Vlastos. New York: Anchor Books, 1971.

————, ed. *Plato I: Metaphysics and Epistemology*. New York: Anchor Books, 1971.

Voeglin, Eric. *The New Science of Politics: An Introduction*. Chicago: University of Chicago Press, 1952.

————. *Plato*. Baton Rouge: Louisiana State University Press, 1966.

Von Staden, Heinrich. "Nietzsche and Marx on Greek Art and Literature: Case Studies in Reception." *Daedelus* 105 (Winter 1976): 79–96.

Walzer, Michael. *Interpretation and Social Criticism*. Cambridge, MA: Harvard University Press, 1987.

Weil, Simone. "The *Iliad*, or Poem of Force." In *Revisions*, ed. Stanley Hauerwas and Alasdair MacIntyre. South Bend, IN: University of Notre Dame Press, 1983.

Weiss, Penny A. "Rousseau, Antifeminism, and Women's Nature." *Political Theory* 15 (1987): 81–98.

West, Thomas G. "Interpretation." In *Plato's* Apology of Socrates, translated by Thomas G. West. Ithaca, NY: Cornell University Press, 1979.

Whitman, C. H. *Homer and the Homeric Tradition*. Cambridge, MA: Harvard University Press, 1958.

Williams, Bernard. *Shame and Necessity*. Berkeley: University of California Press, 1993.

Wolin, Sheldon S. *Politics and Vision: Continuity and Innovation in Western Political Thought*. Boston: Little, Brown, 1960.

———. *The Presence of the Past: Essays on the State and the Constitution*. Baltimore: Johns Hopkins University Press, 1989.

Yack, Bernard. *The Longing for Total Revolution: Philosophic Sources of Social Discontent from Rousseau to Marx and Nietzsche*. Berkeley: University of California Press, 1992.

Index

Achilles, 50–58; dipping of, 137, 244; and heroic code, 76n59; and nature, 76nn61–62; in *Odyssey*, 55–57; Plato on, 90, 94–100; Rousseau on, 131–39, 141; versus Socrates, 96–98, 124n42; training of, 139, 245; Vico on, 175–76

Achilles' shield, 40, 63, 68

Adkins, Arthur W. H., 56, 58–60, 73n25, 77n70

Adorno, Theodor, 30–31, 169–70, 183–89, 237; critique of, 195–202, 210n85

adultery: of Aphrodite and Ares, episode of, 67–68; Rousseau on, 154, 166n59

Agamemnon, 46, 74n45

Aigisthos, 63

Ajax, 74n43

amorality, Odysseus and, 65–66

Andrews, Edward, 129n81

anger: of Achilles, 54; of Athena, 47, 78n97; of Odysseus, 65–66; Rousseau on, 137–38, 161n14

Annas, Julia, 103–4, 125n58

Apology (Plato), 84, 96–98

appetite: Horkheimer and Adorno on, 193–94; Odysseus and, 33–34, 52, 71n14; Plato on, 91–93, 104–6, 125n59; Teiresias on, 44

appropriation, 188–89

Arendt, Hannah, 12, 71n16, 198, 229, 241n45

Argos, 37

Aristotle, 3, 34–35, 72n17

artifice: and immortality, 41; and nature, 38–41; Rousseau on, 139–42

artisan, Plato on, 84

Athena: anger of, 47, 78n97; in Ithaca, 64–65

Austin, Norman, 33, 38, 47–49, 78n89

autonomy, 15; Aristotle on, 35; Rousseau on, 155, 157

Bacon, Roger, 169, 187

barbarism: Horkheimer and Adorno on, 170, 185, 199; Vico on, 177–78, 187

Barber, Benjamin, 6, 218

Barrême, Bertrand–François, 144

Barthes, Roland, 21n8

Bartky, Elliot, 121n15

beasts: Achilles as, 55; and nature, 35–38; Rousseau on, 139

bed episode: Horkheimer and Adorno on, 194; nature and artifice in, 38–40

Benardete, Seth, 87, 106, 109, 224, 236

Benda, Julien, 213

Benjamin, Walter, 204n26, 206n41, 206n43

Bennett, William J., 4

Berlin, Isaiah, 206n45

Beye, Charles Rowan, 75n52, 76n59

bie (force), 51

Bloom, Allan: on canon debate, 9, 22n13; on *Iliad*, 123n36; on Plato, 91, 106–7, 109, 121n21, 122n23; on redescent, 113, 126n72; on Rousseau, 137, 140–41, 161nn13–14

Boitani, Pietro, 11, 24n34, 24n37

Bolotin, David, 79n103, 79n105

books: Rousseau on, 135; and U.S. government, 2–3. *See also* writing

Borges, Jorge Luis, 5

Bork, Robert, 3

Bowra, C. M., 78n91

Brann, Eva, 96

Brennan, William, 21n6

Brint, Michael, 124n46
Bronner, S. E., 8, 206n41
Brunet, Etienne, 164n44
Burgelin, Pierre, 132, 154
Burger, Warren, 2
Burke, Edmund, 7

Calypso episode, 13, 41–45, 57–58
canon: definitions of, 4–6, 22n13;
   reinterpretation of, 5; Vico on, 169
canon debate, 2–4, 21n9, 213; Homer
   and, 8–10
capitalism, Horkheimer and Adorno on,
   170, 188
Cavafy, C. P., 27, 226
cave imagery, 100–101, 113; Horkheimer
   and Adorno on, 191
censorship, Plato and, 89–91, 93, 98
Chiron training Achilles, 139, 245
choice, 15, 212; Achilles on, 57; in
   Calypso episode, 41–45; gods on, 63;
   and government, 2; in Hades episode,
   44; Homer and, 27–31; Horkheimer
   and Adorno on, 31; of limits, 16;
   MacIntyre on, 28; Nussbaum on, 216;
   of Odysseus' soul, 106–11; in Odyssey,
   15–16; of philosopher, 112–19; Plato
   on, 103–4, 109–11; Vico on, 176
Circe episode, 14, 248; human knowledge
   in, 36–37; Rousseau on, 142, 153
citizen: versus man, education for, 133,
   140, 149, 155; of the world, 215, 219
civilization: Homer and, 30; Vico on,
   178–79, 187
class conflict: Frankfurt School on, 182–
   83; Horkheimer and Adorno on, 188,
   191
Clay, Diskin, 124n42
Clay, Jenny Strauss: on gods, 36, 69,
   73n33, 240n31; on marriage, 40; on
   wrath of Athena, 76n65, 78n97
communitarianism. See patriotism
community: in Calypso episode, 41–45;
   Horkheimer and Adorno on, 186,
   193–94, 200–201; and immortality, 58;
   Odysseus and, 14; Rousseau on, 155–

59; versus solitude, 12–13; in U.S.,
   24n37; Vico on, 203n19
competitive excellencies, 56, 77n70
Condorcet, Marie Jean de Caritat,
   marquis de, 7
Connerton, Paul, 208n57
conservative theory, 7
Constitution, U.S., 2–3, 21n6
contractarian theory, 15
cosmopolitanism, 15; critique of, 211–41;
   ideas of, 214–15, 217–18; temptations
   to, 225–32
cosmos, versus oikos, 1–25
Cranston, Maurice, 165n50
Critical Theory: limits of, 195–202; on
   Odyssey, 189–95; Vico and, 205n28
culture: Homer and, 27–31; Horkheimer
   and Adorno on, 31
culture wars. See canon debate
curiosity, 33
Cyclops episode: Aristotle on, 72n17;
   Horkheimer and Adorno on, 194;
   nature in, 32–34

Dante Alighieri, 12, 225–26
death: acceptance of, 211, 238n1;
   Achilles on, 54, 57; Frankfurt School
   on, 197; Freud on, 189–90;
   Horkheimer and Adorno on, 170,
   195–98, 237; as limit, 232–37;
   Odysseus and, 11–12; Plato on, 87–94,
   97–98, 114, 117; Rousseau on, 134–
   35, 137–38, 145–46, 148, 237; Seery
   on, 241n46
"Declaration of the Rights of Man and
   Citizen," 7
Defoe, Daniel, 144
democracy: Odyssey and, 67–70, 80n111;
   Rousseau on, 146
dependence, Rousseau on, 150
Descartes, René, 169, 176, 187
detachment: of Menelaus, 48; Rousseau
   on, 148–49, 153–54
determinism, multiculturalism and, 15
Dewey, John, 239n21
Dialectic of Enlightenment (Horkheimer

and Adorno), 30–31, 169–70, 184–89;
    critique of, 195–202; negativity of,
    210n85
Diderot, Denis, 6–7, 131, 156, 166n66
Dietrich, B. C., 59, 78n86
Diogenes the Cynic, 215, 219
diversity, 9–10, 214
divine right of kings, 70
domination, Horkheimer and Adorno on,
    192, 196
Dostoyevsky, Fyodor, 240n34

Eco, Umberto, 1
education: cosmopolitanism and, 218–19;
    Fénelon on, 143, 148–49; Horkheimer
    and Adorno on, 188; negative, 132–
    39; Odyssean, 142–49; Plato on, 87,
    93–94, 151–52; Rousseau on, 131–67;
    second, 139–42; of Sophie, 143–45,
    149–55, 166n63; of Telemachus, 35;
    Vico on, 179; Western, 13, 23n29
Edwards, Anthony T., 56, 77n68, 77n74
Ehnmark, Erland, 58, 60–61, 77n79
Einaudi, Mario, 202n3
Eliot, T. S., 5, 22n15
Elpenor episode, 233–36, 241n51
Emile et Sophie, ou Les Solitaires
    (Rousseau), 153–54
Emile, or, On Education (Rousseau), 131–
    67; illustrations of, 161n13, 244–48
endurance, Plato on, 94
Enlightenment, 6; and cosmopolitanism,
    215; Horkheimer and Adorno on, 31,
    170, 181, 184–89, 196; universalism
    of, 213
Epicureanism, 176
eros. See love
Euben, J. Peter, 97–98, 122n27
Eumaeus episode, 230–32
Eurylochus, 93

family, Rousseau on, 134, 152, 162n25,
    165nn52–53
fascism, Horkheimer and Adorno on,
    170, 188
fear, Horkheimer and Adorno on, 196–97

Feldman, Abraham, 80n111
Fénelon, François de Salignac de la
    Mothe, 163n28, 211; Télémaque, 143,
    148–49, 155
Fenik, B., 78n96
Finley, M. I., 27, 70n1
Fish, Stanley, 10
Flashar, Helmut, 119n5
Flaumenhaft, Mera, 71n14, 73n31
forgetting, 103–4
Fränkel, Hermann, 16, 58, 74n42
Frankfurt School, 169–70, 197, 204n26,
    206n41; political theory of, 201–2;
    Vico and, 205n28
Franklin, Benjamin, 240n38
Freud, Sigmund, 189–90
Friedländer, Paul, 122n27
Friedman, George, 204n26
Fromm, Erich, 208n64

Gadamer, Hans-Georg, 89, 176, 207n49
Germain, Gabriel, 74n36
Gilbert, William, 240n34
Gitlin, Todd, 7, 213–14
Glazer, Nathan, 218
gods: Achilles as, 54–55; and cosmopoli-
    tanism, 220–21; and immortality,
    77n79; and justice, 58–68; and nature,
    35–38; Orpheus and, 247; Plato on,
    86–88, 94, 103, 121n15; and poetry,
    41–42; Rousseau on, 157; social
    structure of, 67; Vico on, 172, 174;
    and violence, 63, 66
Goethe, Johann Wolfgang von, 11
good: Odysseus on, 52; Rousseau on, 155–
    59
Greene, W. C., 78n87
Greven, Michael, 206n40
Gyges, ring of: Plato on, 86; Rousseau on,
    157–58

Habermas, Jürgen, 210n85
Hades episode, 11–12, 43; and Myth of
    Er, 101; Plato on, 91
Haley, Alex, 15, 214
Hall, Dale, 116, 126n72

Hamilton, Alexander, 2
Hanson, Victor Davis, 9
happiness: Horkheimer and Adorno on,
191–93; Rousseau on, 155–59
Havelock, Eric, 60, 72nn20–21
Heath, John, 9
Hector, 55
Hegel, G. W. F., 3, 171, 204n22
Held, David, 189, 208n62
Helen, 47–49, 75n50
Hermes engraving the elements, 246
Herodotus, 62
heroes: Achilles as, 50–58; Horkheimer
on, 208n56; Menelaus as, 45–50;
Pericles as, 75n48; Plato on, 86–94; in
political life, 66
heroic code: Achilles and, 76n59, 98–99;
justice in, 62; Plato on, 96
Hesiod, 85, 87
Himmelfarb, Gertrude, 218
history: Frankfurt School on, 180–84;
Horkheimer and Adorno on, 180–81,
185–86; MacIntyre on, 29; Marx on,
181; Vico on, 171–72, 177–78
Hobbes, Thomas, 3, 152, 169, 176, 187, 197
hodon (way), 43–44, 48–49
Hollinger, David A., 8, 15, 213–16
Holocaust, Horkheimer and Adorno and,
184, 199, 201
Homer: and canon debate, 8–10, 14; and
culture, 27–31; Horkheimer and
Adorno on, 31, 185–86; importance
of, 29–30; Marx on, 181; Plato on,
83–84, 89; status of, 10; Vico on, 169–
70, 172, 175. See also Iliad; Odyssey
homophrosune (agreement), 41, 48–50
honor: and democracy, 68–70; gods and,
60; Odysseus and, 111
Horkheimer, Max, 30–31, 169–70, 182–
89, 237; critique of, 195–202, 210n85;
on Vico, 171, 180–81, 183–84,
205n27
Horowitz, Asher, 140–41, 162nn24–25
Howland, Jacob, 110, 125n61
humanity: and gods, 58–67; Horkheimer
and Adorno on, 188–89; and nature,
35–39; Nussbaum on, 215–17;

potential of, 212; and temptation, 228;
Vico on, 172
Hyland, Drew A., 238n2

identity, 213–14; in Homer, 16;
Nussbaum on, 216
identity politics, 8
Iliad (Homer): embassy episode, 51–52;
on honor, 69–70; versus Odyssey, 30,
56, 77n67; Vico on, 177
immortality, 211; Achilles on, 53, 57;
Fénelon on, 143–44; gods and, 59,
77n79; Helen and, 49, 75n50. See also
Calypso episode
independence, Rousseau on, 151
Index Librorum Prohibitorum, 5
Ingersoll, David, 167n69
invulnerability, Rousseau on, 136–37,
141–42
Ion (Plato), 85
Ithaca, political life in, 34–35, 64–65,
72n20, 79n100

Jaeger, Werner, 23n29
Jay, Martin, 209n74
Jetztzeit, 183, 206n43
Jouvenel, Bertrand de, 146
Joyce, James, 11
judgment, Vico on, 176–77
Julie (Rousseau), 134, 166n57
justice: definition of, 60–61; in Eumaeus
episode, 230–31; gods and, 58–68; and
marriage, 40; Nussbaum on, 215;
Odysseus and, 224; Plato on, 86–88,
102–3, 107–8; Vico on, 187

Kafka, Franz, 5
Kant, Immanuel, 216–17
Kellner, Douglas, 188, 206n41, 208n60
Kimball, Roger, 9
Kitto, H. D. F., 79n100
kleos (glory), 76n66; Achilles on, 53, 57
Kolakowski, Leszek, 207n51, 208n55,
210n85

language, Plato on, 83–84
Lanson, Gustav, 140–41

Lasch, Christopher, 240n42
Lattimore, Richmond, 24n36, 74n45
Left: and canon debate, 3–7; and particularism, 7–8, 213
Lenhardt, Christian, 197
Lesher, J. H., 72n23
Lethe, 103–4
Liberal-communitarian debate, 14
liberalism, 213
liberal theory, 7
Limbaugh, Rush, 9
limited transcendence, 212, 229–30
limits, 211–12, 227; choice of, 16; death as, 232–37; myths and, 1
Lincoln, Bruce, 125n59
Lloyd-Jones, Hugh, 61, 78n89
Locke, John, 3, 162n19, 197
logismos (calculation), 105
Longinus, 30, 177, 204n20
Lotus-eaters episode, Horkheimer and Adorno on, 192–93
love: Plato on, 116, 129n81; Rousseau on, 140–42, 151–52
Lucian, 227, 240n37
Luther, Martin, 4

MacIntyre, Alasdair, 28–30, 42, 74n41, 203n19
Maier, Joseph, 205n28
Maistre, Joseph de, 7
Mali, Joseph, 203n8, 203n16
man versus citizen, education for, 133, 140, 149, 155
Mann, Thomas, 81
Mansfield, Harvey, 218
Mara, Gerald M., 241n52
Marcuse, Herbert, 199–200, 204n26, 206n41, 209n68
marriage, 39–40
Marx, Karl, 3, 29, 171, 181, 183; Vico and, 126n45
Marxism, Frankfurt School on, 182–84, 206n41
Masters, Roger D., 167n75
Matthews, Rick, 167n69
McConnell, Michael, 218
McWilliams, Wilson Carey, 238n1

Melzer, Arthur M., 167n74
memory, and politics, 33
Menelaus, 45–50
Meyer, Paul, 162n24
minding one's own business, Plato on, 107–9
moly episode, 36, 220–21
morality: gods and, 58–60; Horkheimer and Adorno on, 188; Vico on, 172, 187
motherhood, Rousseau on, 134–37, 150–51
Moyer, Paul, 141
multiculturalism, 2, 213; and determinism, 15; and Homer, 9–10, 27–28
myth: Horkheimer and Adorno on, 170, 184–89, 196, 198–99, 201; Kolakowski on, 207n51; Marx on, 29; and origins, 1–2; Plato on, 169; Vico on, 172, 178–79, 187–88, 201
Myth of Er, 100–112

Nagy, Gregory, 76n66
nationalism. See patriotism
nature: Achilles and, 54, 76nn61–62; and artifice, 38–41; Homer on, 14; Horkheimer and Adorno on, 185, 194; knowledge of, 35–38, 223; in Odyssey, 32–35; Rousseau on, 139–42
need, Rousseau on, 158–59
Nelson, Cary, 23n32
Nichols, Mary, 115, 137
Nietzsche, Friedrich, 182, 209n68
Nisbet, Robert, 204n22
Noble Lie, 102–3
Norton, Anne, 218
nostalgia, 218–25
nostos, 45–46; Achilles on, 53, 57; and community, 13; definition of, 10–11; of Menelaus, 45–50; Odysseus' ambivalence about, 224. See also community
nous (mind), 51; Plato on, 91
Nussbaum, Martha C., 8, 227–29, 238n15, 239n19; on cosmopolitanism, 215–16; on Plato, 122n27

obedience, Plato on, 97
objectivity, MacIntyre on, 42

obligations, Nussbaum on, 216–17
Odysseus: anger of, 65–66; and canon
    debate, 10; character of, 10–11, 237;
    and Eumaeus, 231–32; fate of, 81;
    happiness in later life, 226–27; and
    Helen, 49–50; Horkheimer and
    Adorno on, 192; journeys to Hades,
    127n77; Nussbaum on, 228–29;
    passions of, 112; in peaceful commu-
    nity, 79nn104–105; Plato on, 94–112;
    Rousseau on, 131
Odyssey (Homer): Achilles in, 55–57; and
    canon debate, 10; choice in, 15–16;
    and cosmopolitanism, 218–25; death
    in, 233–35; Horkheimer and Adorno
    on, 186, 188–95; versus Iliad, 30, 56,
    77n67; Nussbaum on, 227–28; Plato
    on, 81–129, 237; as political theory,
    27–80; political theory of, 10–21;
    Rousseau on, 131–67. See also specific
    episode
oikos, versus cosmos, 1–25
Okin, Susan Moller, 151, 155, 165n54,
    166n63
origins, 1–6
Orpheus teaching religion, 247

Page, Denys, 43, 77n67, 234, 241n48
pampering, Rousseau on, 134
Parry, Milman, 27
participation, Horkheimer and Adorno
    on, 200, 210n75
particularism, 6, 212–13; Left and, 7–8,
    213; limits and, 229–30; Nussbaum
    on, 216; Odysseus and, 13–14; Right
    and, 7
passions: Franklin on, 240n38; of
    Odysseus, 112; Rousseau on, 137, 142–
    43, 145. See also anger; love
patriotism: versus cosmopolitanism, 218;
    in Odyssey, 219
Pericles, 75n48
persuasion, 65–66
Phaedrus (Plato), 82–84
philosopher: choice of, 112–19; Marx on,
    183; Odysseus as, 81–82; Plato on, 84,
    93, 111; Rousseau on, 158; true versus
    tyrannical, 116

philosophy: Horkheimer and Adorno on,
    191; Plato on, 81–129; versus poetry,
    6–8
phronesis (prudence), Plato on, 104–6
physical training, Rousseau on, 139
Pinsky, Robert, 219
Piovani, Pietro, 179
Plato, 3, 81–129, 169, 237; Rousseau on,
    151–52, 158, 162n25; Vico on, 175
pluralism, 2; versus cosmopolitanism, 214;
    Nussbaum on, 216
Plutarch, 151
poetry: Adorno on, 199, 201; in canon,
    23n32; gods and, 41–42; Marx on,
    181; versus philosophy, 6–8, 81–129;
    Plato on, 81–129, 119n5, 120n11;
    Vico on, 172, 174–75, 179
polis, Homer and, 9
political education, Rousseau on, 145–46
political life: Arendt on, 71n16; as blend
    of artifice and nature, 38–41; Cyclops
    episode on, 33–34; Horkheimer and
    Adorno on, 193–94, 199–200; in
    Ithaca, 34–35, 64–65, 72n20, 79n100;
    marriage and, 40; Menelaus on, 48;
    Nussbaum on, 216–17; Plato on, 99–
    100, 107–9, 112–19; Rousseau on,
    131, 133, 147–48
political theory: of Frankfurt School,
    201–2; ideas and, 3; Odyssey as, 27–80
politician, Plato on, 84
polutropos, 11, 24n33
Pompa, Leon, 203n17
Pratt, Marie Louise, 22n13
prehistory, Horkheimer and Adorno on, 193
Principles of New Science Concerning the
    Common Nature of Nations (Vico),
    171–80; frontispiece to, 173–74, 249
private man: Plato on, 107; Rousseau on,
    131
production, Marx on, 29
progress: and cosmopolitanism, 217–18;
    Horkheimer and Adorno on, 170, 186,
    196;
Vico on, 177–78

Querelle des Anciens et des Modernes, 4,
    169

rationality: and cosmopolitanism, 217; Horkheimer and Adorno on, 201; Rousseau on, 140
Rawls, John, 109, 125n65
reading, Plato on, 82–86
redescent into Cave, 101, 126n72, 127n77; choice of, 112–19; Plato on, 90; Rousseau on, 158
religion, cosmopolitanism and, 217–18
remembrance, Arendt on, 241n45
Republic (Plato), 82; on gods, 86–88; Myth of Er, 100–112; Rousseau on, 151–52, 158, 162n25. *See also* redescent
Reveries of a Solitary Walker (Rousseau), 157
rhapsodes, Plato on, 83–85
ricorsi, Vico on, 177–78, 187
Right: and canon debate, 4–7; and particularism, 7; and universalism, 8
Robinson Crusoe (Defoe), 144
Rocco, Christopher, 208n54
Rohde, Erwin, 75n51
Rosen, Stanley, 121n19
Rousseau, Jean Jacques, 131–67, 172; Marx on, 29; and Vico, 202n3
rule, Plato on, 116, 118–19
Rüter, Klaus, 76

Schadewaldt, Wolfgang, 79n98
Schwartz, Joel, 164n48, 166n63
science: and cosmopolitanism, 217; Hermes and, 36, 220–21, 246
Scylla and Charybdis episode, 212
Second Discourse (Rousseau), 150–52, 158, 172
Seery, John Evan, 21n9, 241n46
self-consciousness: in Homer, 16; Horkheimer and Adorno on, 185
self-criticism, 4
self-preservation, Horkheimer and Adorno on, 189–91, 193
self-renunciation, Horkheimer and Adorno on, 189
self-repression, Horkheimer and Adorno on, 193
Seneca, 137
sensus communis: definition of, 203n16; Vico on, 176–77, 187

sentiment, Rousseau on, 140, 144–45
Shapiro, Michael, 188
Shklar, Judith, 134, 152
Sirens episode, 13, 42–43, 74n36, 221–23; and cosmopolitanism, 211–41; Horkheimer and Adorno on, 190–92
situatedness, 15
skepticism, Vico and, 178–79
Smith, Barbara Herrnstein, 9–10, 27–28
Snell, Bruno, 16, 59
Social Contract (Rousseau), 145–47, 153
society: Nussbaum on, 216–17; Rousseau on, 133–35, 139–42, 145
Socrates: versus Achilles, 96–98, 124n42; and redescent, 114–15. *See also* Plato
solitude: Achilles on, 54–55; versus community, 12–13; in Cyclops episode, 33; Horkheimer and Adorno on, 200–201; Rousseau on, 155–59; in U.S., 24n37
Sophie: character of, 166n61; education of, 143–45, 149–55, 166n63
Sophocles, 232
soul, Plato on, 104
Spinoza, Baruch, 169, 187
Stanford University, 2, 21n3
Stanford, W. B., 24n34, 123n33
Steiner, George, 210n85
Stoicism, and cosmopolitanism, 215
Strauss, Leo, 7, 89, 99, 126n72
student protest movements, Horkheimer and Adorno and, 199–200
suitors, Plato on, 90
Sullivan, Arthur, 240n34

Taylor, A. E., 120n7
Taylor, Charles H., 222
technology: and cosmopolitanism, 217; Marx on, 29, 181
Teiresias. *See* Hades episode
Telemachus: and door episode, 16; and politics, 35, 71n20; reception by Menelaus and Helen, 47–50
Télémaque (Fénelon), 143, 148–49, 155
temptation, 74n36, 225–32; Horkheimer and Adorno on, 192–93; MacIntyre on, 42; Rousseau on, 153. *See also* Sirens episode

Thetis dipping Achilles in the River, 135, 137, 244
thirst, Plato on, 104, 125n59
Thucydides, 97
Tithonus, 44
transcendence: and cosmopolitanism, 220–21; limited, 212, 229–30; Nussbaum on, 227–29; temptation to, 227–28
Trent, Lucia, 23n32
Tudor, Henry, 202n6
tutor, in Emile, 132, 142–43, 149

underworld, Plato on, 89–91
universalism, 6, 212–13; versus cosmopolitanism, 214–15, 217; of Enlightenment, 213; Odysseus and, 13; Right and, 8

Van Nortwick, Thomas, 54–55, 76n62
veil of ignorance, 109–10, 125n65, 126n67
vengeance: chain of, 62–63, 66; gods and, 60

Vernant, Jean–Pierre, 32, 71n13
Vico, Giambattista, 30, 169–80, 187–88, 201, 203n19, 210n81; and Dialectic of Enlightenment, 184; and Frankfurt School, 205n28; Horkheimer on, 171, 180–81, 183–84, 205n27; and Marx, 126n45; and Rousseau, 202n3
violence, chain of, 62–63, 66
vision: and cosmopolitanism, 221–23; in Sirens episode, 42–43, 222–23
Voeglin, Eric, 89, 101, 120n11
Von Staden, Heinrich, 205n34

Walzer, Michael, 218
Weiss, Penny, 149
West, Thomas, 96–97, 126n69
Williams, Bernard, 16
Wolin, Sheldon, 6
women: Plato on, 151; Rousseau on, 149–55, 165n50, 166n59, 166n63; and Trojan War, 62
writing: Plato on, 82–86, 99. See also books

About the Author

~

Patrick J. Deneen is assistant professor of politics at Princeton University. He was the recipient of the 1995 American Political Science Association's Leo Strauss Award for best dissertation in political philosophy. He has published articles on ancient political theory, ancient tragedy, American political thought, and politics and religion. This is his first book.